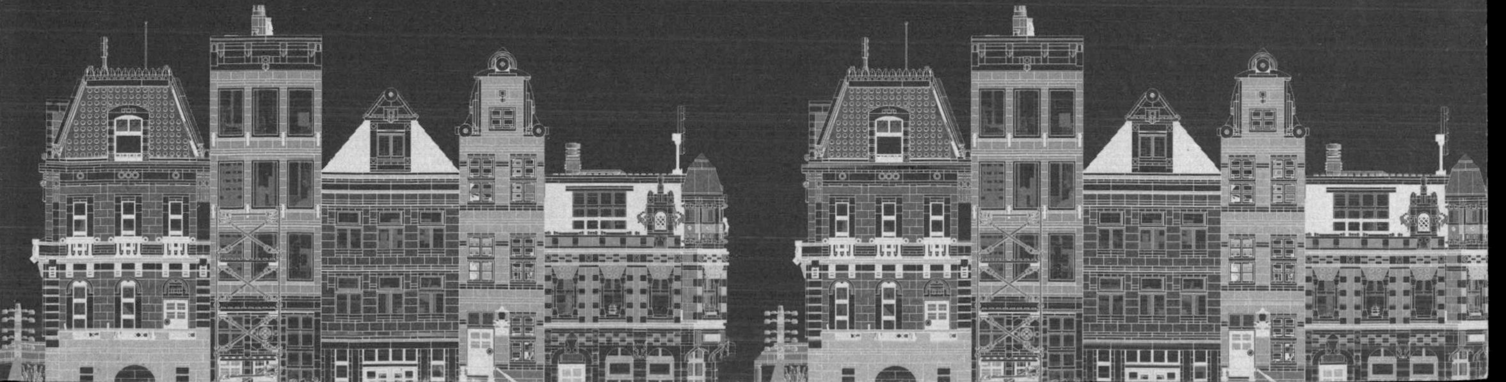

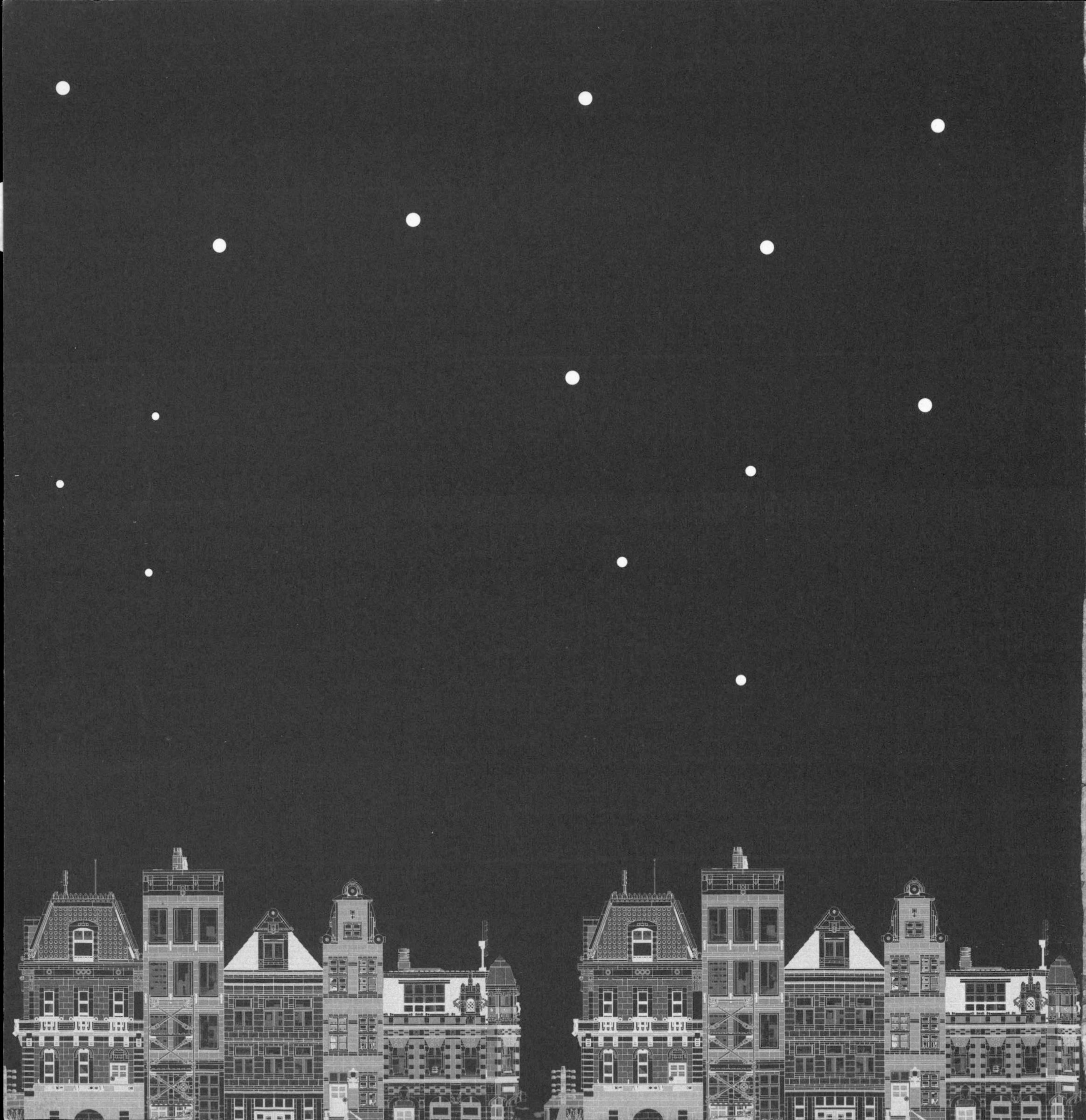

the LEGO® NEIGHBORHOOD book

BUILD YOUR OWN TOWN! BRIAN LYLES AND JASON LYLES

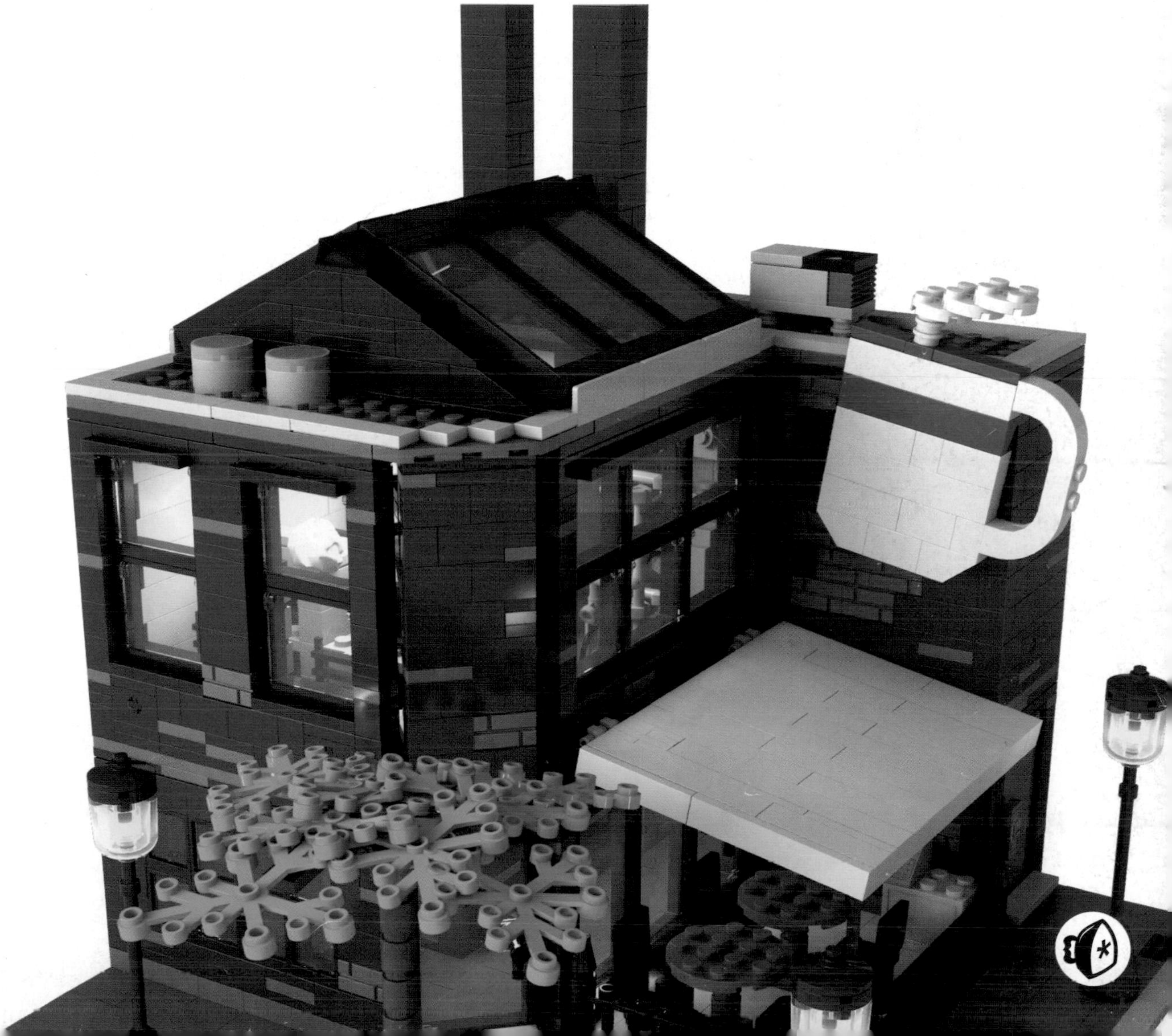

Printed in China

Second Printing

18 17 16 15 14   2 3 4 5 6 7 8 9

ISBN-10: 1-59327-571-4
ISBN-13: 978-1-59327-571-6

Publisher: William Pollock
Production Editor: Alison Law
Cover Design: Beth Middleworth
Cover Illustration and Selected 3D Renders: Mattia Zamboni
Developmental Editor: Tyler Ortman
Copyeditor: Rachel Monaghan
Compositors: Ryan Byarlay and Riley Hoffman
Proofreaders: Laurel Chun and Lisa Devoto Farrell

For information on distribution, translations, or bulk sales please contact
No Starch Press, Inc. directly:

No Starch Press, Inc.
245 8th Street, San Francisco, CA 94103
phone: 415.863.9900; info@nostarch.com; www.nostarch.com

Library of Congress Cataloging-in-Publication Data

Lyles, Brian.
The LEGO neighborhood book : build your own town! / by Brian Lyles and Jason Lyles.
pages cm
Audience: Age 10.
ISBN-10: 1-59327-571-4
ISBN-13: 978-1-59327-571-6
1. Neighborhoods--Models--Juvenile literature. 2. City planning--Juvenile literature. 3. LEGO toys--Juvenile literature. I. Lyles, Jason. II. Title.
TD160.L95 2014
688.7'25--dc23
2014022194

Production Date: 10/6/14
Plant & Location: Printed by Everbest Printing (Guangzhou, China), Co. Ltd
Job / Batch #: 43040-0 / 705058

Contents

★ = pages with building instructions

Preface

This book is dedicated to Jack, Ben, Joshua, Virginia, Ellie, and Daisy.

We loved playing with LEGO when we were kids, and like a lot of kids, we dreamed of becoming LEGO designers when we grew up. But also like most other kids, we put our LEGO bricks away in the attic when we reached our early teens.

When we came back to LEGO as adults, we marveled at the things people were building—the astounding models featured online.

What really turned our heads, though, were the amazing minifig-scale buildings that LEGO had released. There was a wonderful community of builders trying to emulate the "modular building" style and improve upon it, too. We first fell in love with the Fire Brigade (set #10197). The rest, as they say, is history.

We've built dozens of models since buying our Fire Brigade; there's just something irresistible about using little building blocks to create models that emulate architectural details, creating a miniature world. You can find building instructions for many of these models at our website, *http://www.brickcitydepot.com/*.

We wrote this book to share our passion. We hope you get lots of ideas for building your own models in these pages.

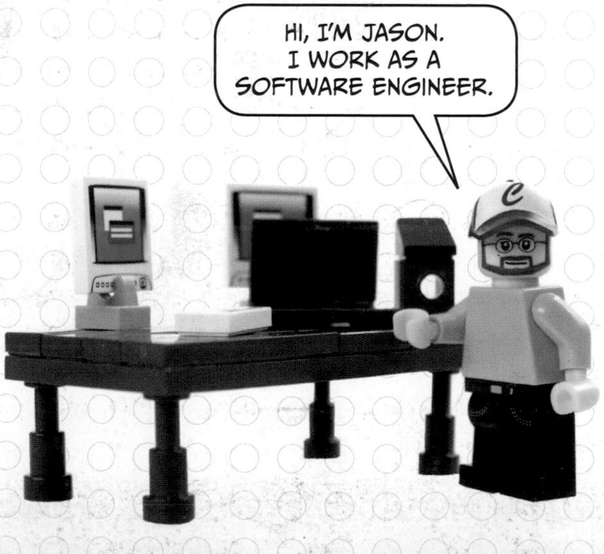
HI, I'M JASON. I WORK AS A SOFTWARE ENGINEER.

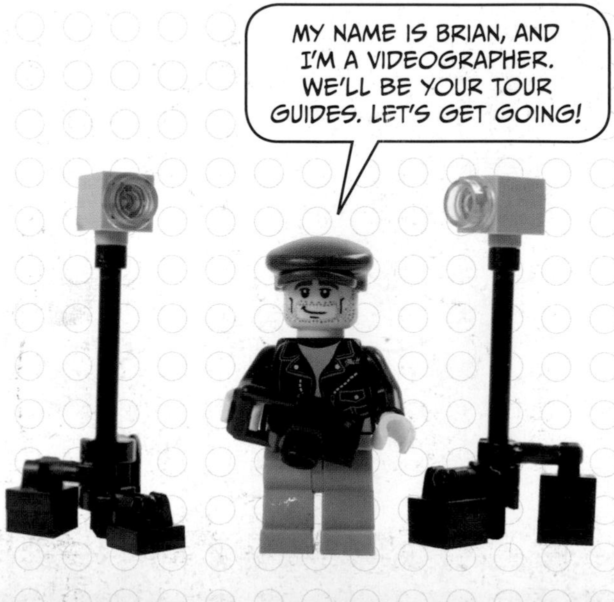
MY NAME IS BRIAN, AND I'M A VIDEOGRAPHER. WE'LL BE YOUR TOUR GUIDES. LET'S GET GOING!

Getting Started with the Café Corner Standard

1

Before you can make your own beautiful buildings, you'll need to understand the fundamentals. If you've ever built the LEGO Group's official modular building kits, then you already know the basics of how LEGO buildings can be connected to form streets, neighborhoods, and cities. If you're new to modular buildings, then you'll want to pay special attention. You'll need this knowledge to make sure that the buildings you create line up with official LEGO sets.

In October 2007, the LEGO Group released its first modular building, Café Corner (set #10182). This first building set the standard (sometimes called the *Café Corner Standard*) for how all later modular buildings would connect to one another and how the sidewalk would look. This style of building was developed by Jamie Berard, a designer at LEGO, and then embraced by a community of fans.

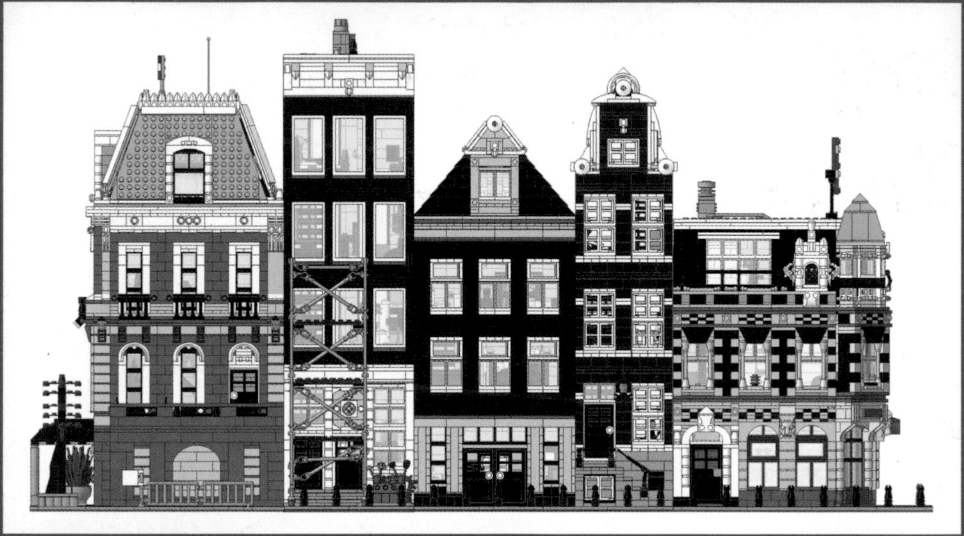

The buildings connect to form a block or row of buildings.

Base Size

All modular building sets to date use a 32×32-stud base, composed of either a single 32×32 plate or two 16×32 plates. So, to adhere to the standard, you need to build in 16-stud-wide increments too: 16×32, 32×32, 48×32, and so forth. You can, of course, create larger buildings by combining baseplates.

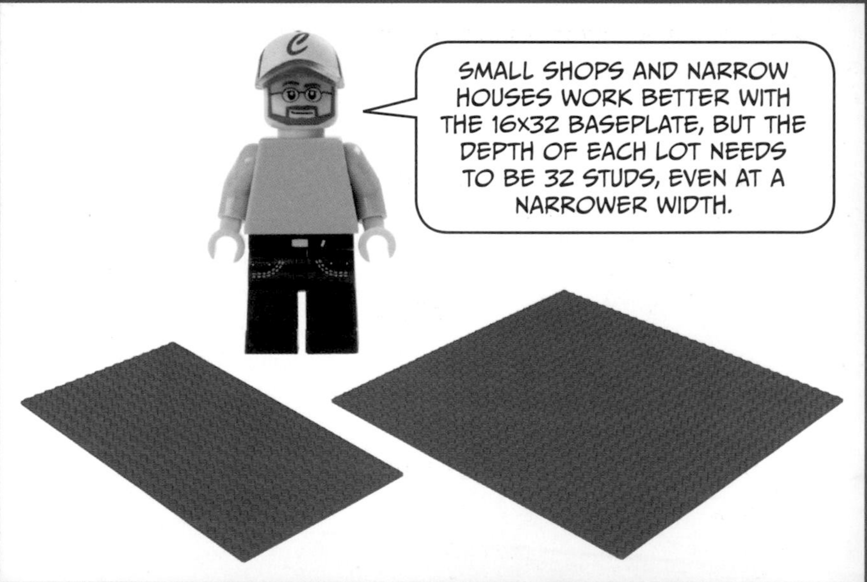
SMALL SHOPS AND NARROW HOUSES WORK BETTER WITH THE 16×32 BASEPLATE, BUT THE DEPTH OF EACH LOT NEEDS TO BE 32 STUDS, EVEN AT A NARROWER WIDTH.

A 16×32 plate versus a 32×32 square plate

Connecting the Buildings

Buildings are connected to one another at the base via LEGO Technic pins. You'll use four Technic bricks (part #3700) and two Technic pins (part #2780) for each connection.

Of course, you must space these Technic bricks consistently to match other buildings.

For a corner building, the placement of the Technic bricks remains the same: the 9-stud, 10-stud, 9-stud pattern shown at right.

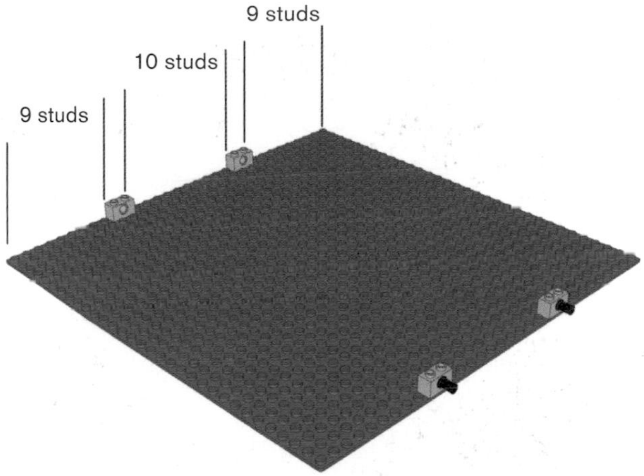

Even though you don't have a building yet, you'll want to place these Technic parts first for planning purposes.

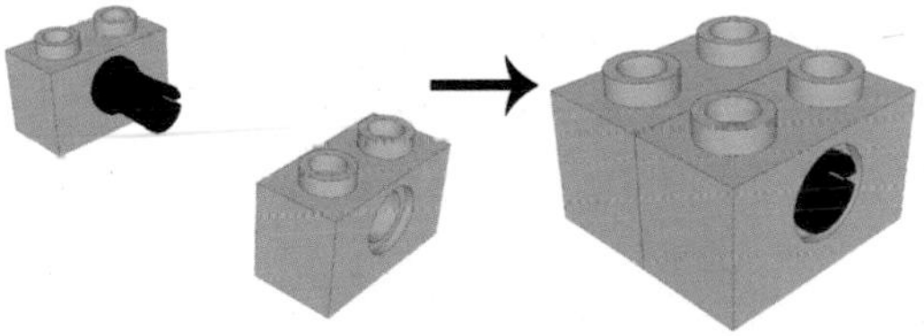

Technic pins hold your town together. They also allow you to build houses separately and connect them when you're finished.

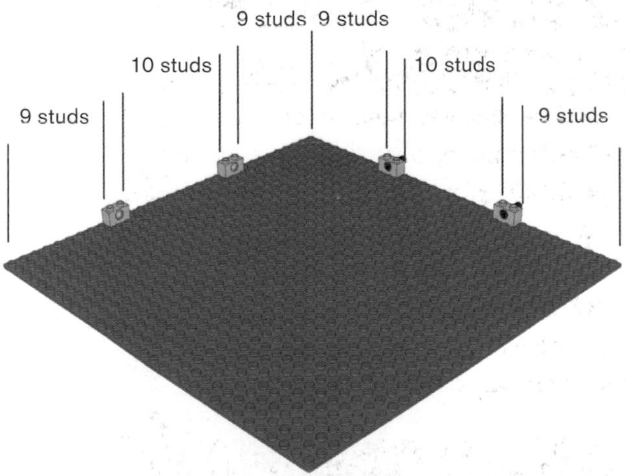

Corner buildings maintain the same connections at the same spacing, just on a different side of the plate.

The Sidewalk

The sidewalk has a standard depth as well, but it has more options for versatility. Sidewalks may have stoops, staircases, flower boxes, or other details protruding from the building.

In the image below, you can see the first row of studs has light grey tiles covering it.

The second row of sidewalk studs is primarily made up of 1 × 2 dark bluish-grey tiles. This second row of studs also has two 1 × 2 tile grills that represent sewer grates, spaced six studs away from the outside edge of the plate.

The next four rows of studs are occupied by 2 × 2 dark grey tiles running from left to right. The seventh row of the sidewalk is also made up of 1 × 2 dark grey tiles.

The eighth and last row of the sidewalk is made up of light grey tiles.

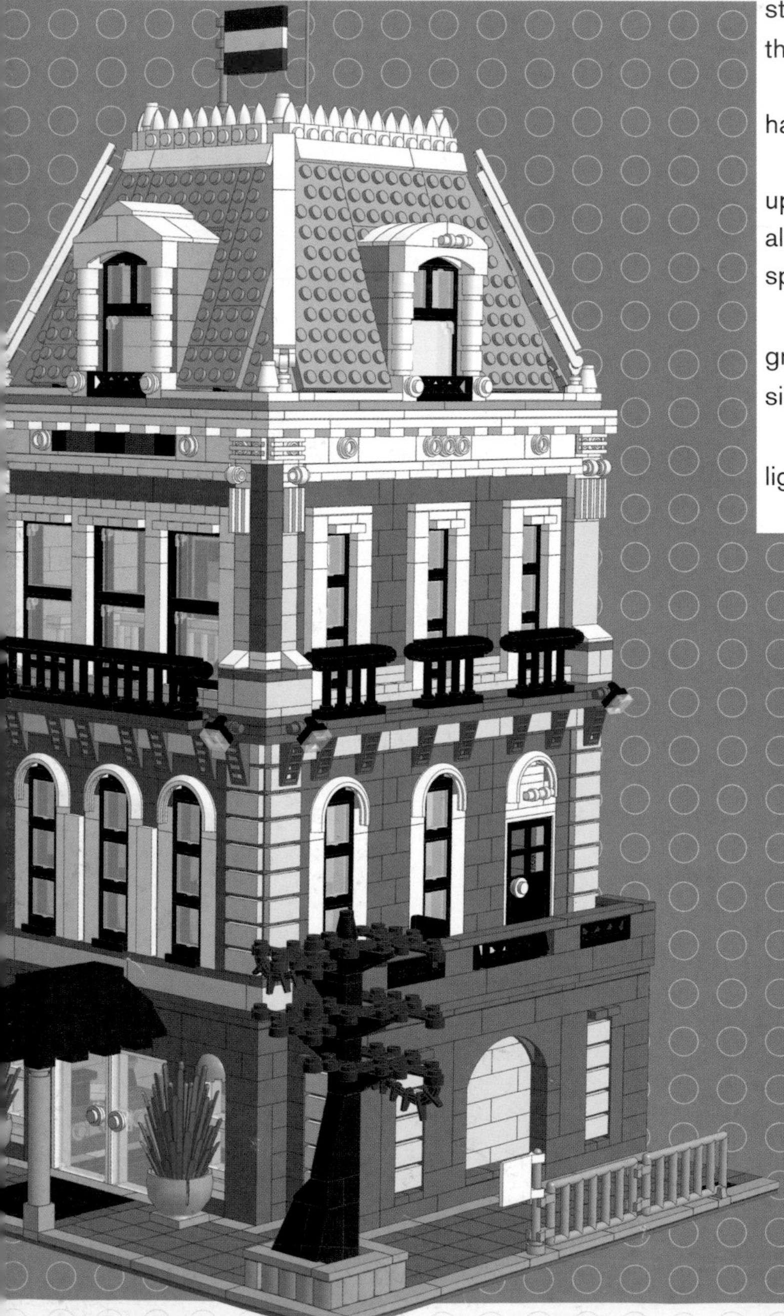

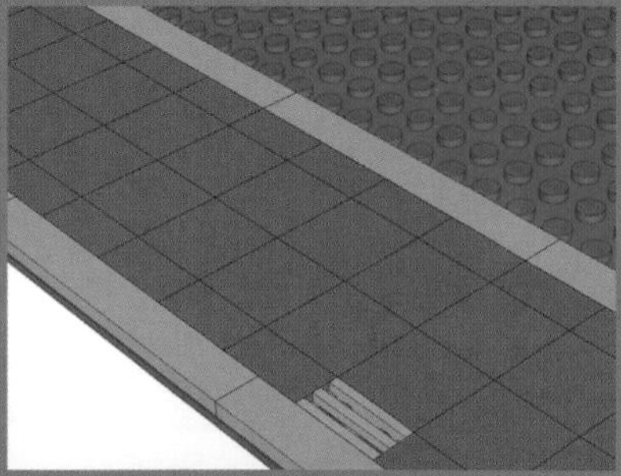

A finished sidewalk

A corner building will have a sidewalk on two edges of its baseplate, often with a design or colored pattern at the corner of the sidewalk.

All LEGO modular buildings also feature a white lamp post on the right side of the sidewalk. The exact placement is always different. You'll want to decide on the best place for lamp posts in your own models. For example, if your building has a door on the right side, you could move a lamp post to the rightmost edge. Several official LEGO buildings place the lamp post right beside another object, like a fire hydrant or a mailbox, to keep the rest of the sidewalk clear for pedestrians.

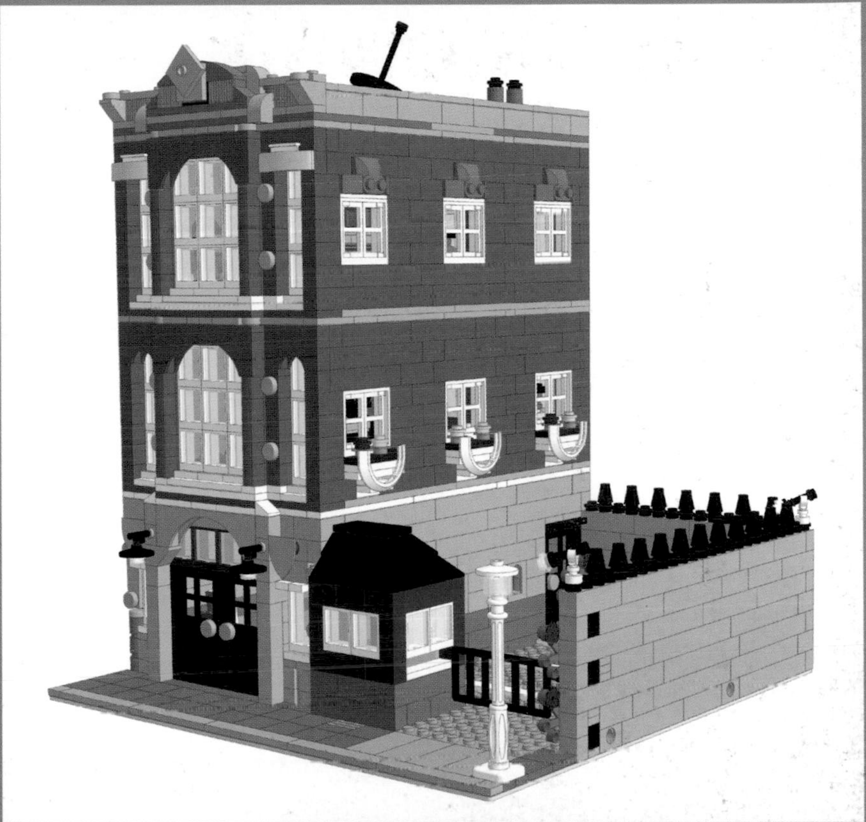

The lamp post is usually on the right side.

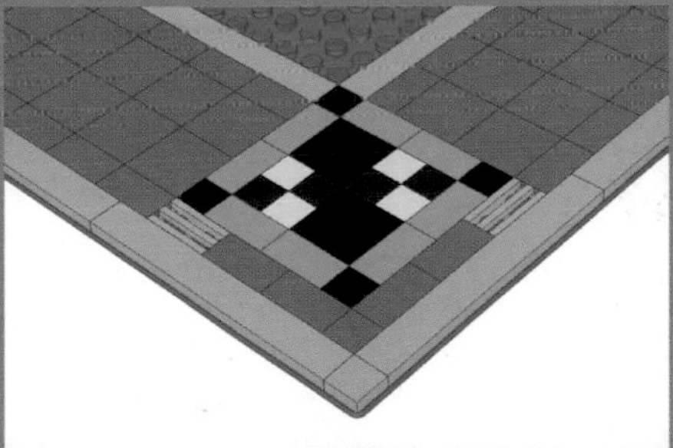

This pattern gives a pop of color to the sidewalk.

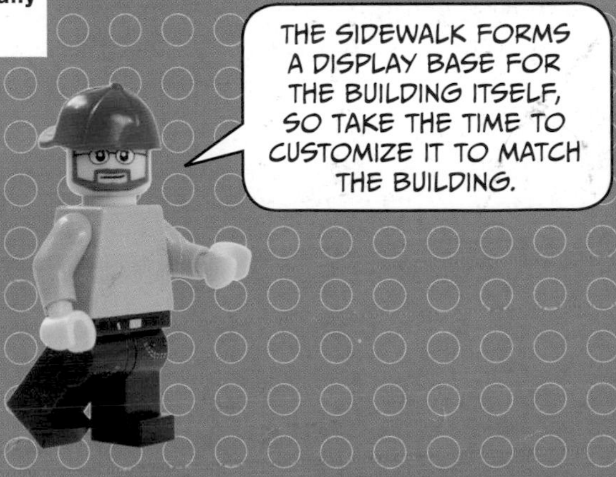
THE SIDEWALK FORMS A DISPLAY BASE FOR THE BUILDING ITSELF, SO TAKE THE TIME TO CUSTOMIZE IT TO MATCH THE BUILDING.

Building Depth and Height

With your sidewalk complete and your Technic bricks in place, you can get started with the building itself. While there's an effective minimum of 15 studs for the depth of your building (the distance between the Technic bricks, plus a single row of studs in front), there are really no other rules. The depth of the building can vary from 15 to 24 studs, and some builders choose to make it very shallow from front to back to save pieces or to give their inhabitants a backyard. If you are creating a building with a large interior, you can build all the way to the back row of studs on the plate to allow for more space inside.

The height of the building and each floor is an aesthetic and practical decision. Most builders add at least one or two bricks above a doorframe before the next level starts. Some buildings have vaulted ceilings on the first floor or a big lobby, so the first floor would need to be much taller to accommodate the interior requirements. The building's height is up to you, but remember that the sidewalls of taller buildings are visible when placed next to a shorter building. If you have a really tall building, consider adding windows (or other spots of visual interest) to the sides of the building to break up the flat, boring walls.

Creating Stackable Levels

Why are they called modular buildings, anyway? It's not just the buildings that can be connected. Each building has stackable levels that you can remove to see inside; they're composed of modules that you can build separately from the whole. Around the top of the walls there is a layer of tiles so the next level can sit on the level below without grabbing any studs.

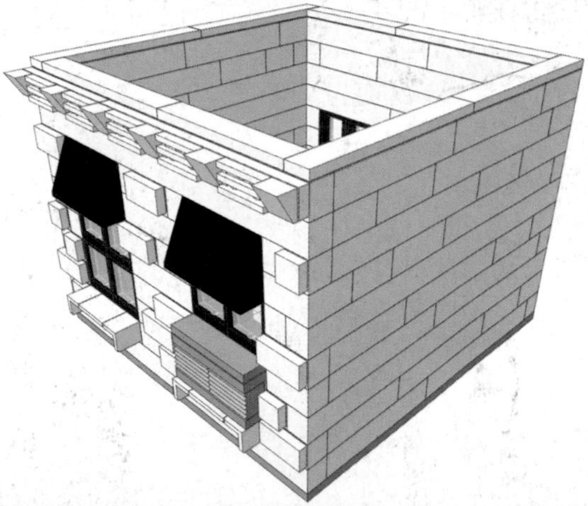

Tiles go around the top of the walls so the level above won't connect to the one below.

There are several ways of locking the levels in place. One method is to place plates around the edges on the bottom of the level, as shown in the image to the right. This keeps the level above from sliding off or moving around.

Another method is to use a few studs on the level below to grab the level above. The trick is using just enough studs to keep the level from moving but not enough to keep it locked in place. Sometimes when you use this method, the plates will lift off and stick to the level above.

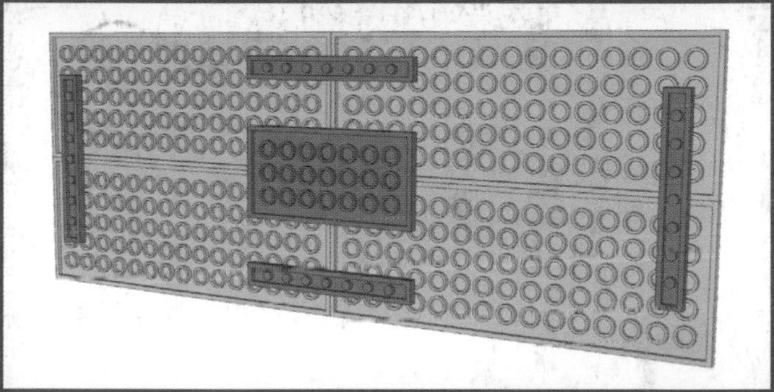

The plates placed at the edge of this structure effectively form a lip.

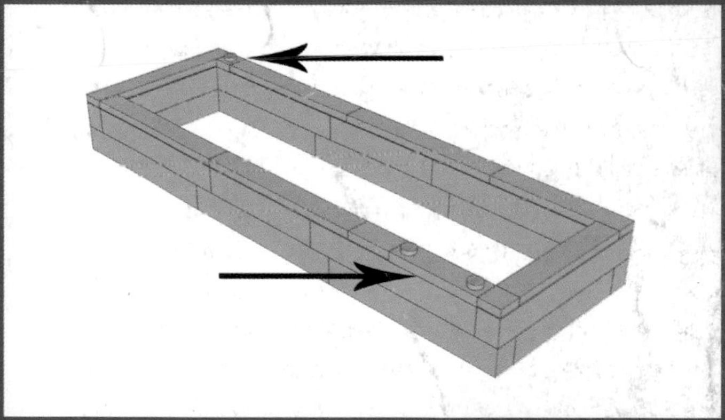

A minimum number of studs allows for a modular connection.

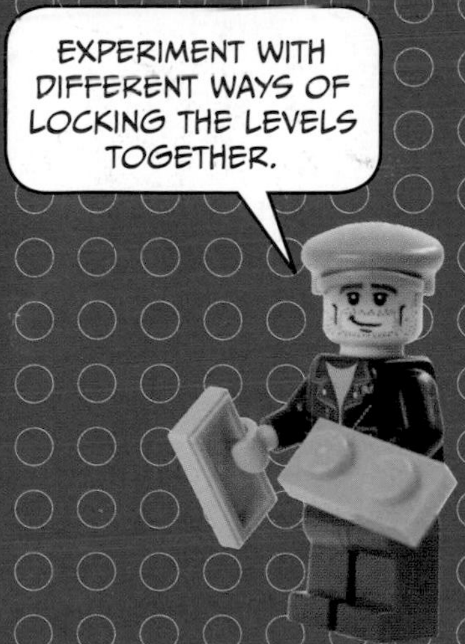
EXPERIMENT WITH DIFFERENT WAYS OF LOCKING THE LEVELS TOGETHER.

Go Your Own Way

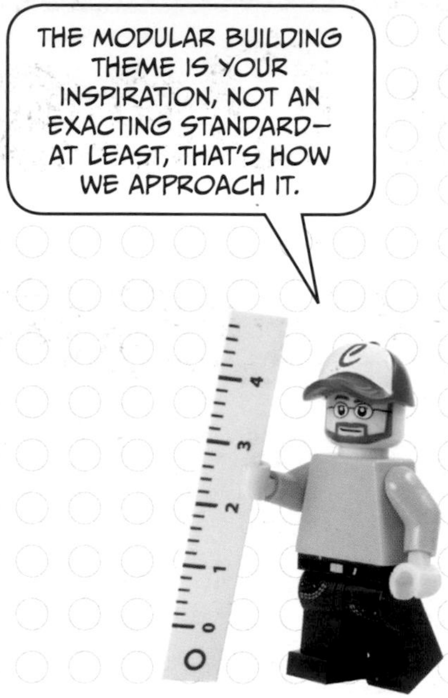
THE MODULAR BUILDING THEME IS YOUR INSPIRATION, NOT AN EXACTING STANDARD— AT LEAST, THAT'S HOW WE APPROACH IT.

Now that you know the standards, feel free to completely ignore them!

Why would we spend the time laying out the standards and then tell you to ignore them? You have to know the rules before you can know how to break them, right? Look around the city where you live, especially if there's an older part of town. There's no standard in real life; most of the cities we live in are charmingly chaotic. Buildings come in different shapes, sizes, widths, and architectural styles. Sometimes buildings have alleyways between them or large trees out front; some may be recessed from the road, while others are almost on top of it; some may be very skinny, while others are very wide; and some are two stories, or four stories, or more. Experiment!

Buying Bricks

If you don't already know about BrickLink, put down this book and go to *http://bricklink.com/* right now. BrickLink is a huge aftermarket website where thousands of sellers from all over the world sell millions of individual LEGO pieces in just about every part and color combination ever made.

The Design Process

2

The first step of any build is deciding what type of building to make. You should have a good idea of what you are going to build—whether it's a police station, a house, or a restaurant—before you actually start. Once you've decided, you have two options: you can either build something entirely from memory, or you can find real inspiration. Just like artists sketching or painting, you'll likely find reference material invaluable.

If you're at a total loss about what to build, a good way to get started is to visit areas that feature buildings you like. You'll start to notice architectural details and design. Take pictures of complete buildings or parts that you want to add to your own design.

And if you want to build something inspired from another country, just hop online. Search the Web for images, use Google Street View, fly over cities using Google Earth, or treat yourself to a 3D bird's-eye view using Bing Maps. You can "drive" down almost any street in the world today, for free. You can also search for specific buildings (like a fire station, museum, or city hall) or even a certain architectural style.

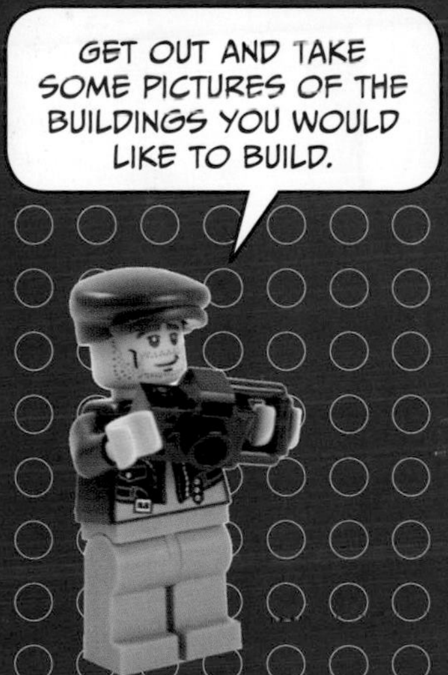
GET OUT AND TAKE SOME PICTURES OF THE BUILDINGS YOU WOULD LIKE TO BUILD.

Choosing Colors

Houses and businesses come in all shapes and colors. Adding vibrant colors to your houses can look great and bring some life into your city, but you might also want to throw in some more realistically colored houses, using dark red for brick houses, as well as white, tan, and some darker colors. Dark blue, dark green, dark orange, and dark tan all give a house some color without being over the top. The muted "sand" colors such as sand blue and sand green look great, too. On the right are some examples of modular buildings in these colors.

Using primary colors such as red and blue might not be your first pick, but when done properly, as in the Notting Hill–inspired houses on the next page, these colors can look great.

One key factor in determining the color for the house or building is the parts you have available to you. It's a good idea to check the color guide in the BrickLink catalog (*http://www.bricklink.com/catalog.asp*) to see which pieces are made in the color you want to use. Certain plate and brick lengths aren't made in every color, so this can restrict how you build certain parts of the model.

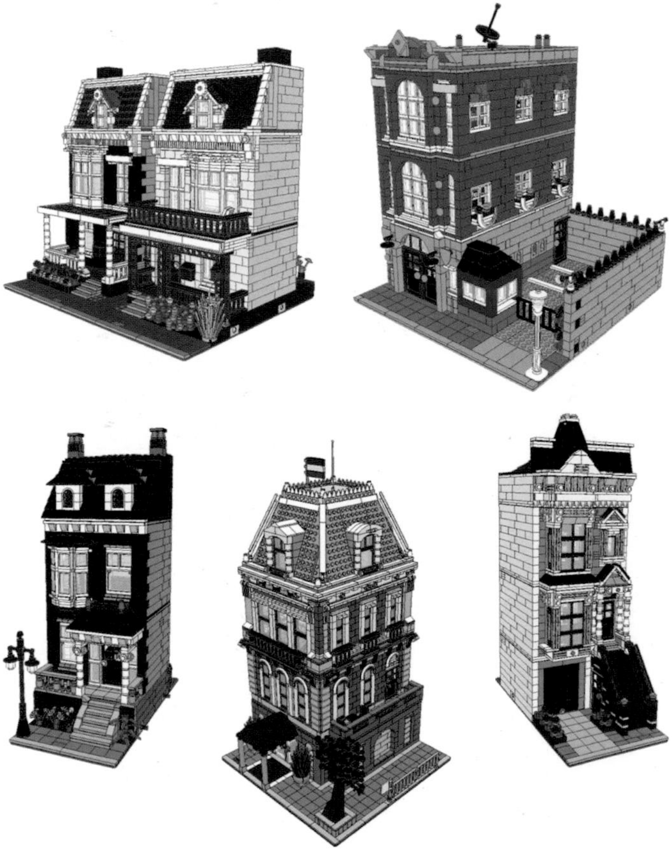

Clockwise from top left: dark blue and tan, dark orange, dark tan, sand blue, and dark red

Accent Colors

Great looking LEGO buildings have one thing in common: they use color thoughtfully. Having a main color and accent colors can really help your model look cohesive and realistic.

When inventing your own color combinations, you can use the color wheel to help you determine what colors would look good together. Opposites (that is, colors across from each other on a color wheel) attract. The Internet is also full of tools for real-life homeowners planning to paint their houses' exteriors. Different architectural styles often have common color schemes. Take advantage of any resource available to you while planning.

Let's see how you can use accent colors to help bring the model alive.

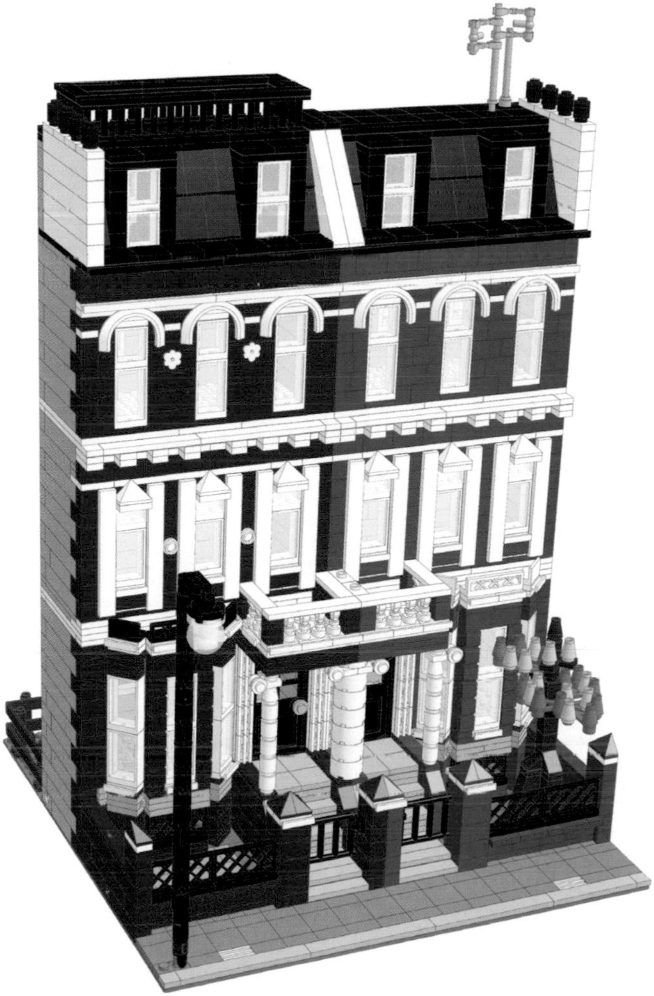

This build was inspired by two houses in Notting Hill, London.

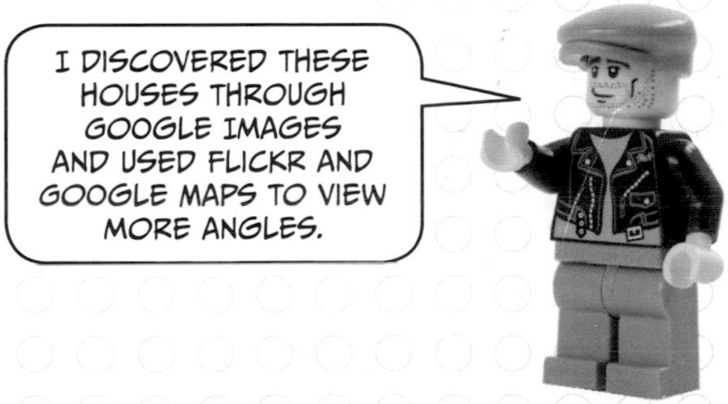
I DISCOVERED THESE HOUSES THROUGH GOOGLE IMAGES AND USED FLICKR AND GOOGLE MAPS TO VIEW MORE ANGLES.

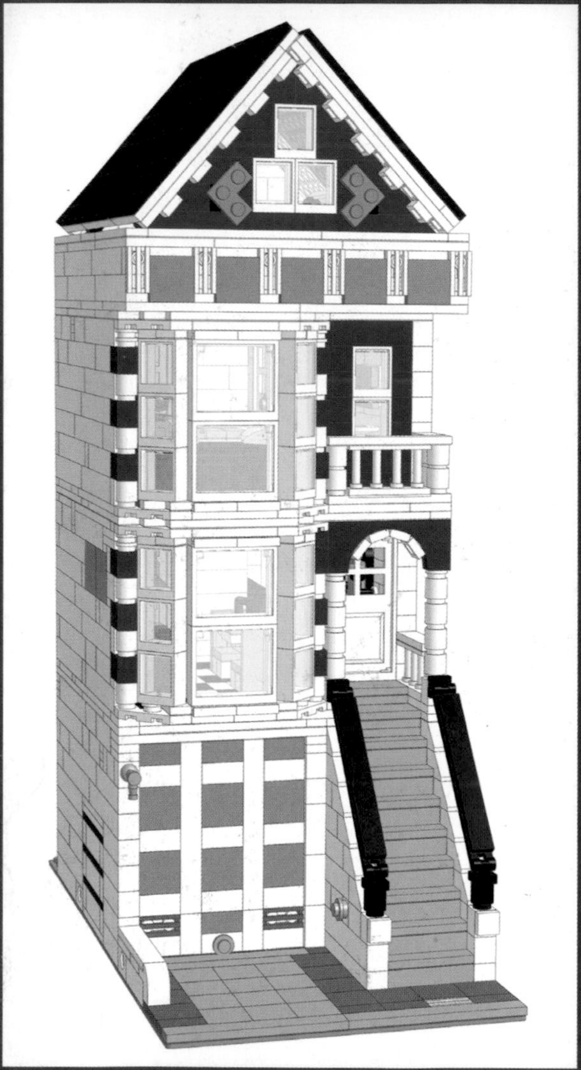

This row house uses dark tan for the garage door and roof area to help break up the dark green and white.

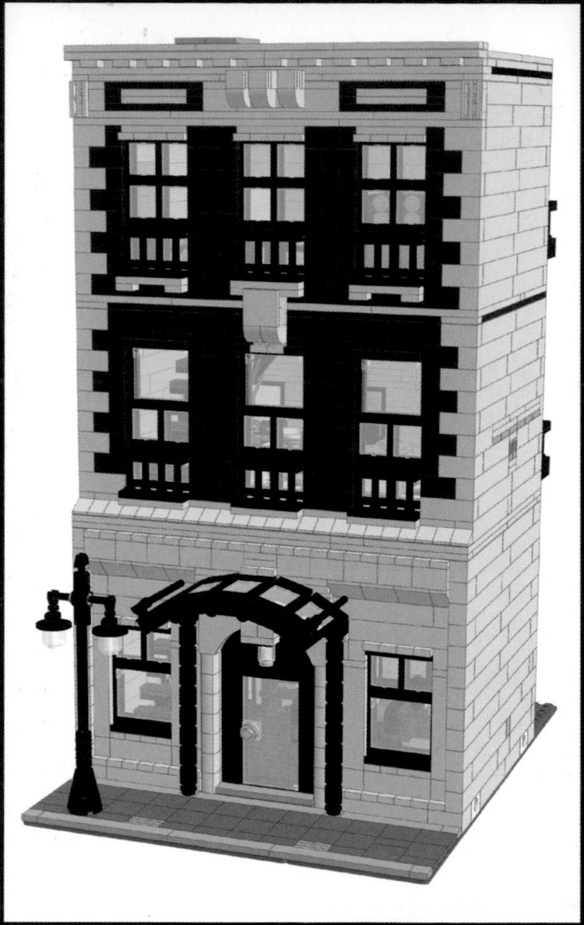

On this brownstone house, the main colors are tan and brown. The accent color is black, which you can see in the street lamp, awning, windows, and railings.

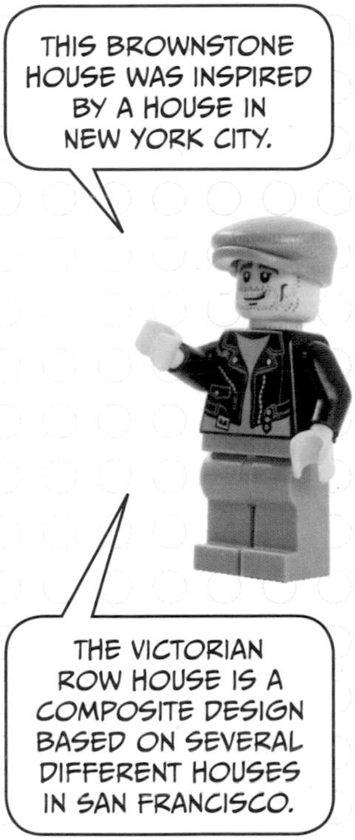
THIS BROWNSTONE HOUSE WAS INSPIRED BY A HOUSE IN NEW YORK CITY.
THE VICTORIAN ROW HOUSE IS A COMPOSITE DESIGN BASED ON SEVERAL DIFFERENT HOUSES IN SAN FRANCISCO.

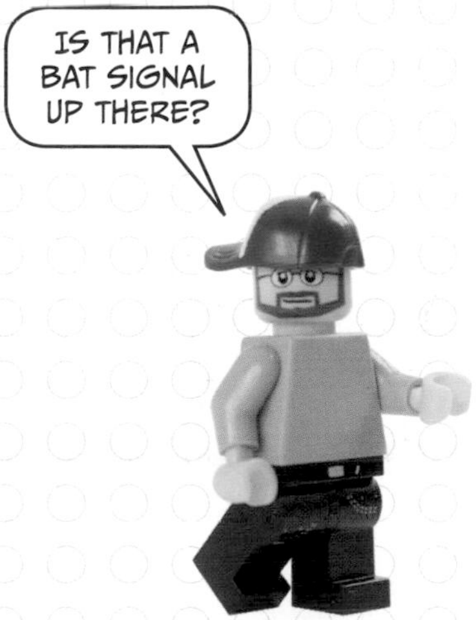
IS THAT A BAT SIGNAL UP THERE?

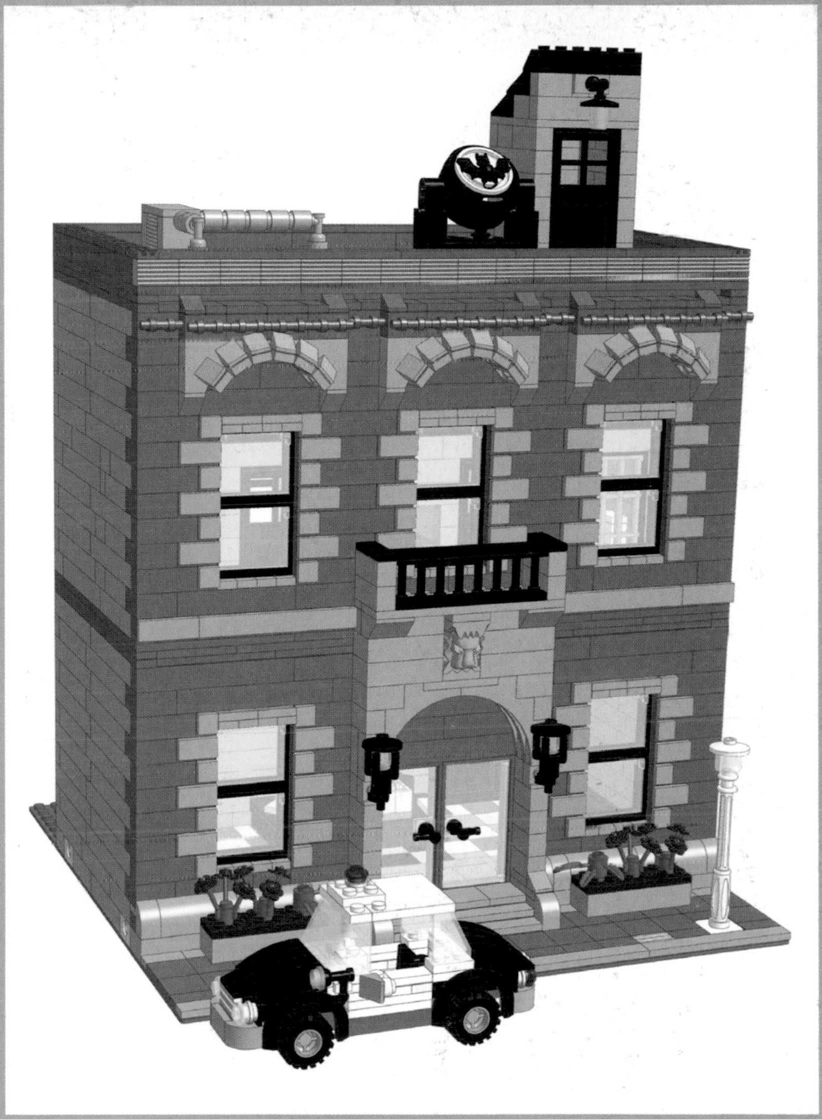

In this police station, black was used for the railing, windows, and light fixtures, while light bluish-grey was used in conjunction with dark bluish-grey to mimic stone.

Trim Color

One natural place to use an accent color is the trim of a building. While the real-world use of fancy trim and molding has definitely decreased over the years, it can still give your building some pizzazz. Choose a contrasting color, just like any other kind of accent color. White or wood-color is common.

Different styles of architecture take very different approaches to trim size and color.

Symmetry

Symmetry is important when it comes to architecture. On the facing page are some examples that illustrate symmetry in a building's design.

Keeping the length of the bricks uniform on the front of the building can showcase a commitment to symmetry and enhance the look of the model.

You can apply the same rule of symmetry to tiles and plates. Taking the time to make a flawless, symmetrical facade goes a long way toward making your model look professional and complete.

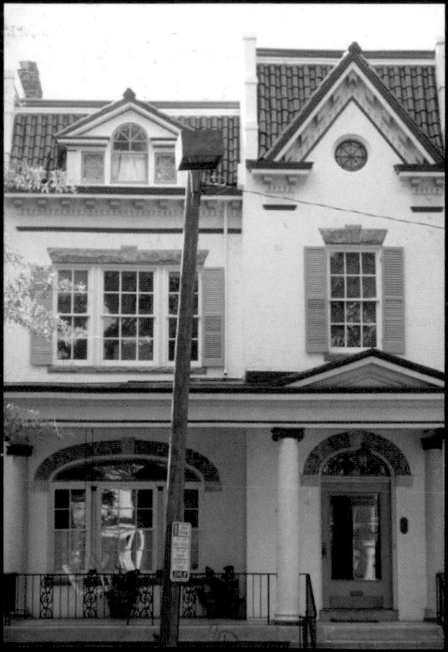

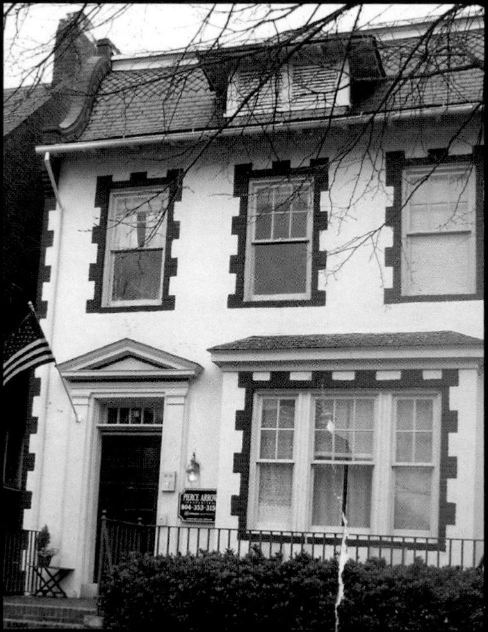

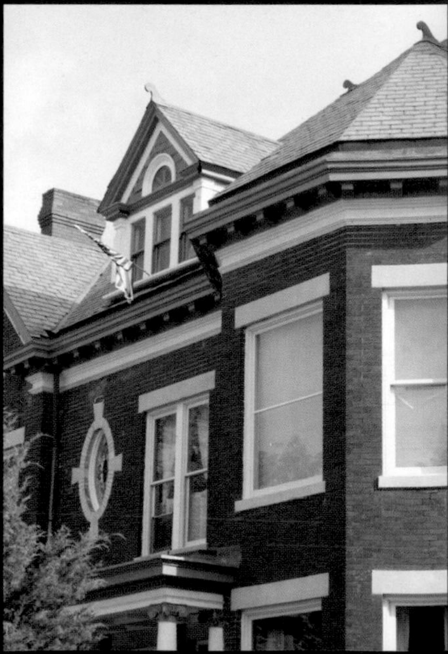

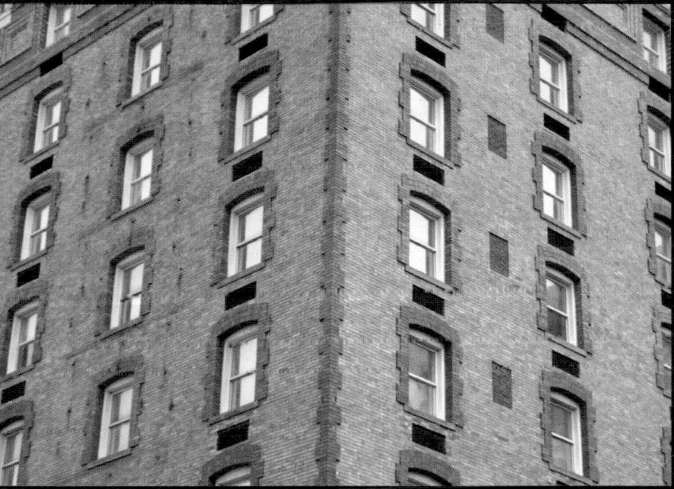

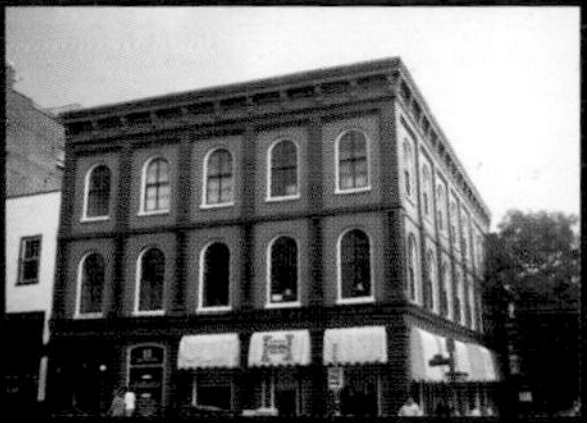

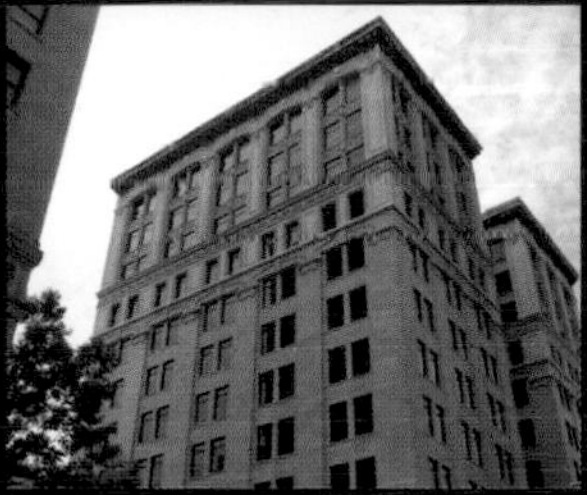

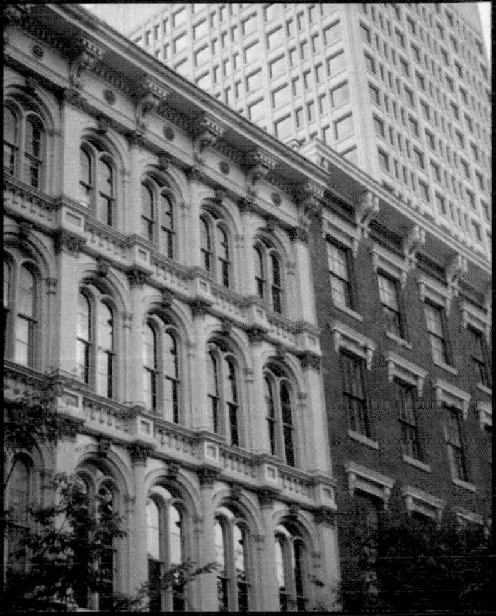

Different kinds of buildings will have different kinds of symmetries.

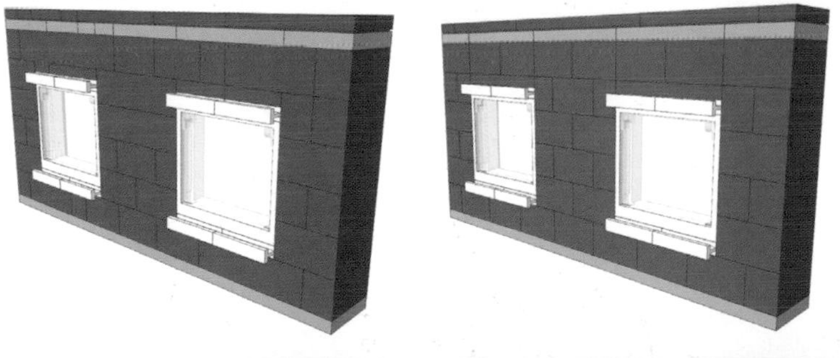

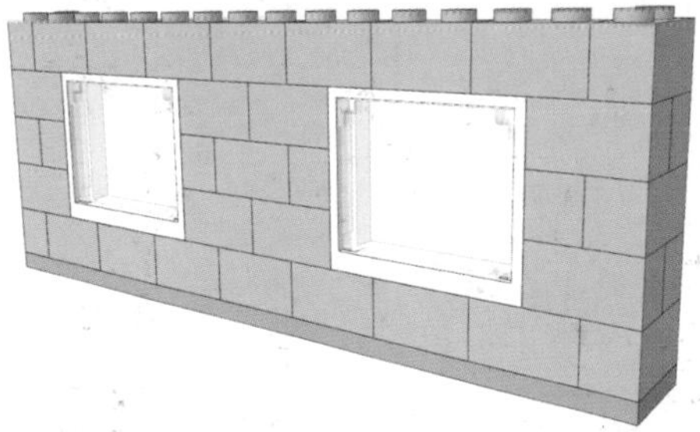

On the left, you can see a model that uses different pieces on its left and right sides. The example on the right shows a more pleasing, symmetrical facade.

Uniform bricks mimic the regular appearance of real masonry.

Get Started!

Just start building. You're going to make mistakes along the way. You'll make designs that look terrible and nothing like what you imagined or nothing like what you're trying to copy. Don't get discouraged. For every building we make that we like enough to use for instructional purposes, there's another building we made that turned out horribly. Don't forget about stepping away from the problem, too. We currently have 10 buildings set aside because there's some aspect of each building that we haven't figured out how to fix yet.

Sometimes when we get stuck with a part of a building, we will make that part of the model easily detachable. That way, we can build multiple versions of a section of the building and pop them on and off to see which version looks the best.

Probably the most important time-saving tip we can offer for the design process is to spend your time refining the facade until you're happy with it. The facade is what faces the street, so it's what gets seen first. If your building is sandwiched between other buildings in a display, the facade may be the only part of the building that shows. We've spent a lot of time building interiors, sidewalls, and rear walls on buildings that we ultimately abandoned because we couldn't make the facade look like we wanted it to.

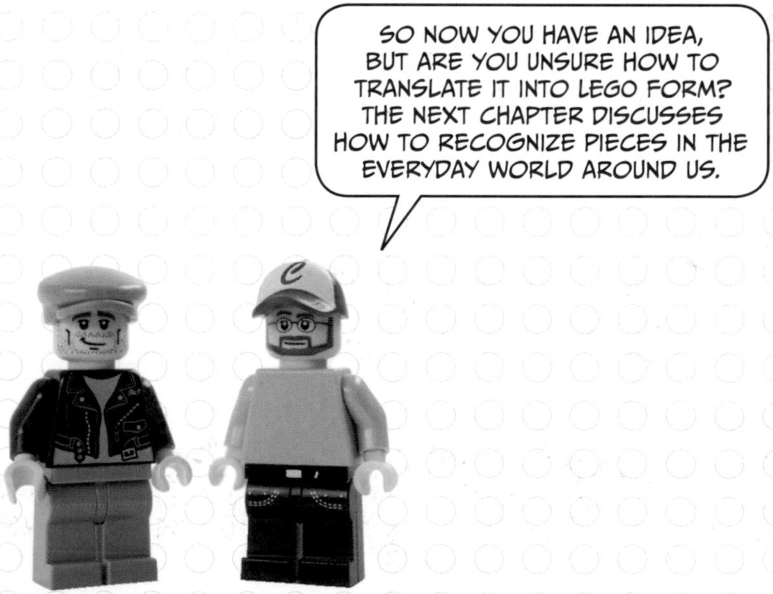
SO NOW YOU HAVE AN IDEA, BUT ARE YOU UNSURE HOW TO TRANSLATE IT INTO LEGO FORM? THE NEXT CHAPTER DISCUSSES HOW TO RECOGNIZE PIECES IN THE EVERYDAY WORLD AROUND US.

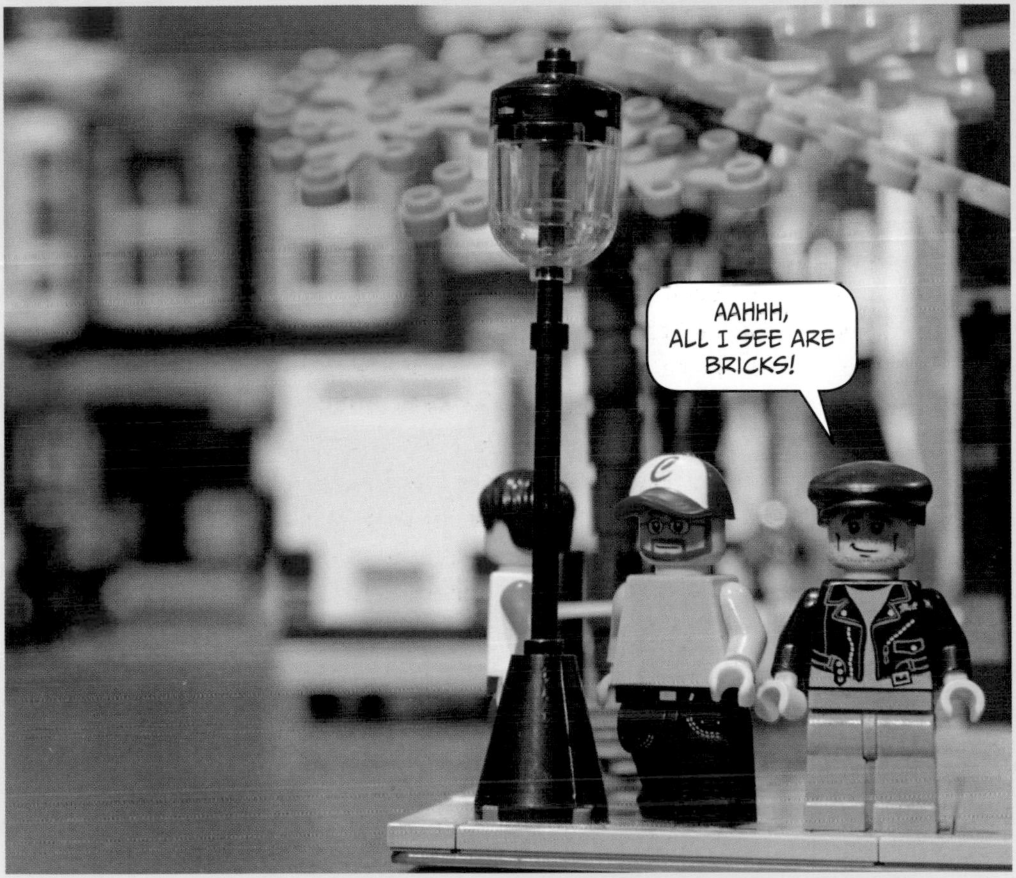

3

Bricks Everywhere

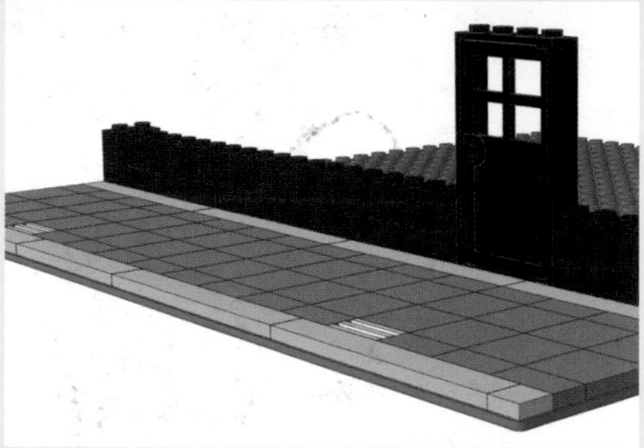

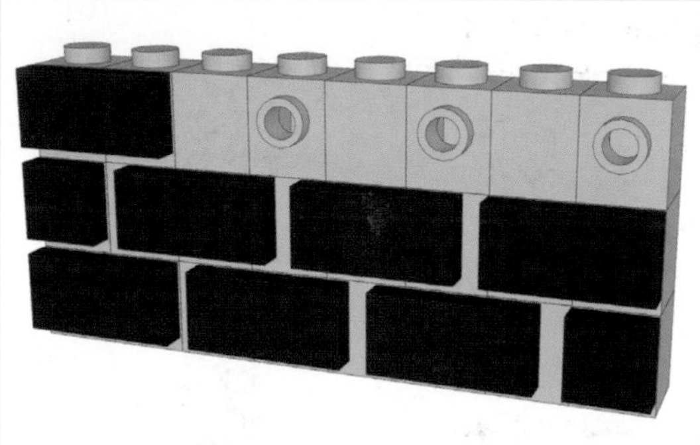

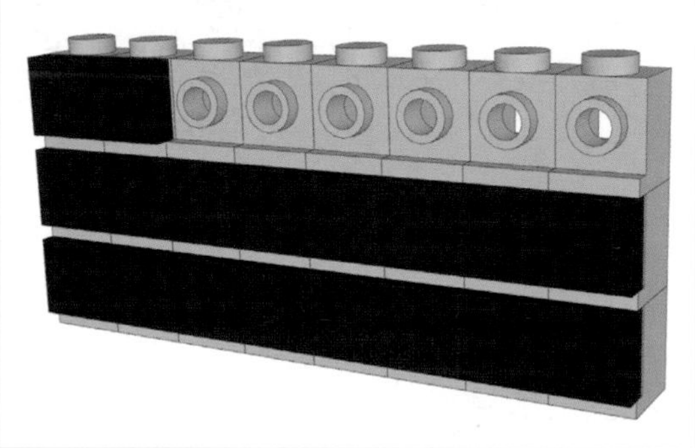

As you're building, try to imagine the real-life reference building as a giant LEGO model. As crazy as that might sound, it will help you identify which architectural details actually look like individual LEGO pieces already. And on some projects, you will find a piece you just *have* to use, and this will help determine the scale of the model, too.

If the building is made of cement blocks, stones, or bricks, you might consider using 1×2 bricks or only plates to give it a look that mimics real masonry. Above is an example of using 1×2 bricks to model a brick wall.

There are other ways to create a simple brick wall, too. Check out the examples on the right.

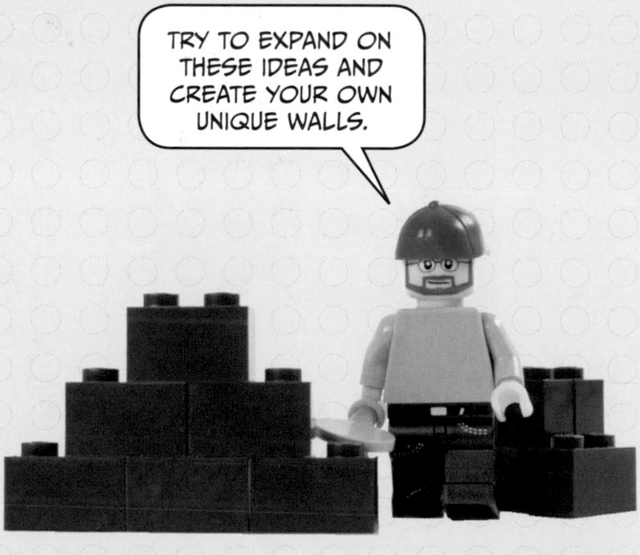
TRY TO EXPAND ON THESE IDEAS AND CREATE YOUR OWN UNIQUE WALLS.

In the picture to the right, you can see a window with an interesting frame. How many pieces can you see right away? You can imagine those slopes and the grills at first glance. Of course, after you choose the pieces necessary to create an object, you'll need to determine how to actually attach those pieces to a building.

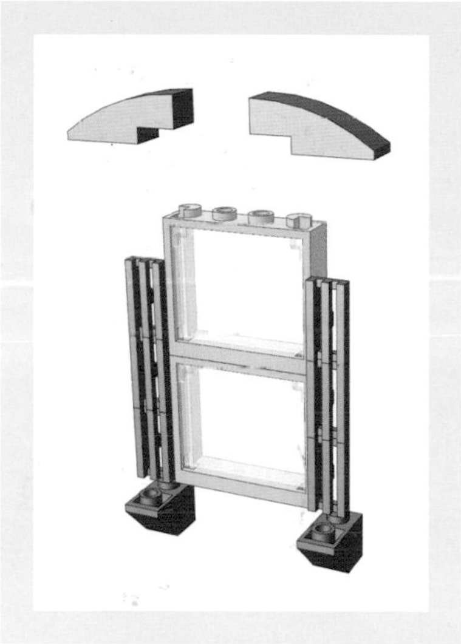

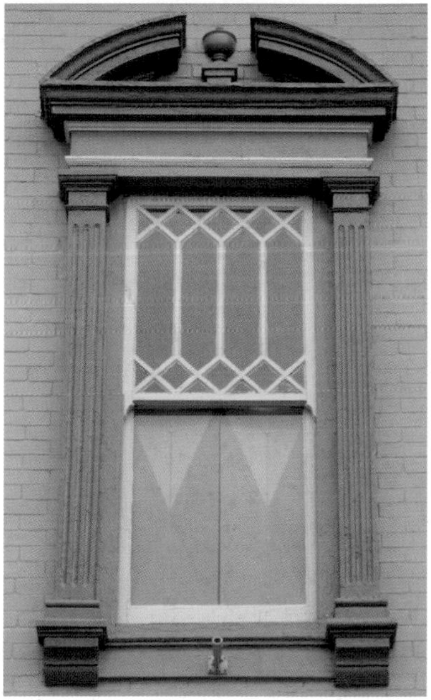

On the side of this building, there are rows of bricks that have vertical grooves. The brick on the right immediately comes to mind.

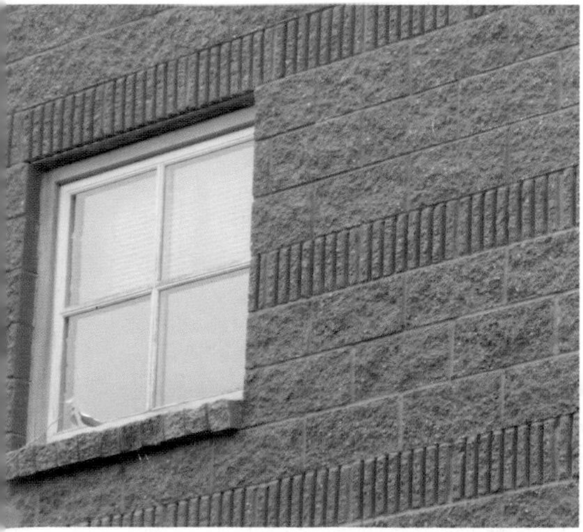

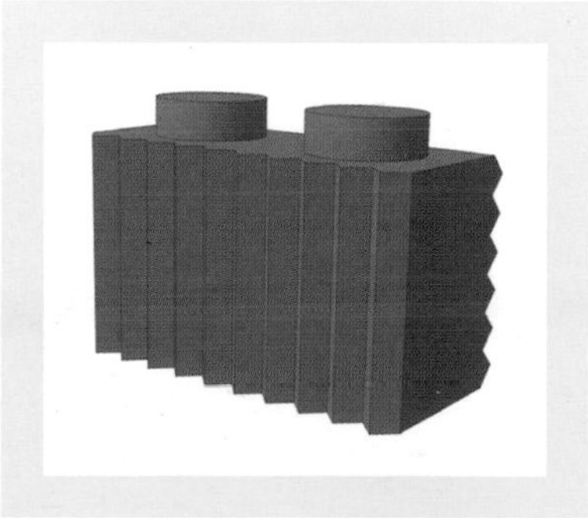

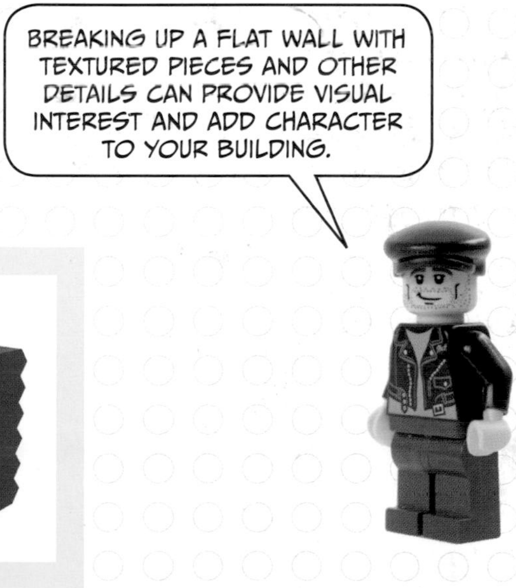
BREAKING UP A FLAT WALL WITH TEXTURED PIECES AND OTHER DETAILS CAN PROVIDE VISUAL INTEREST AND ADD CHARACTER TO YOUR BUILDING.

The slope and cone at right nicely mimic the trim on this yellow house.

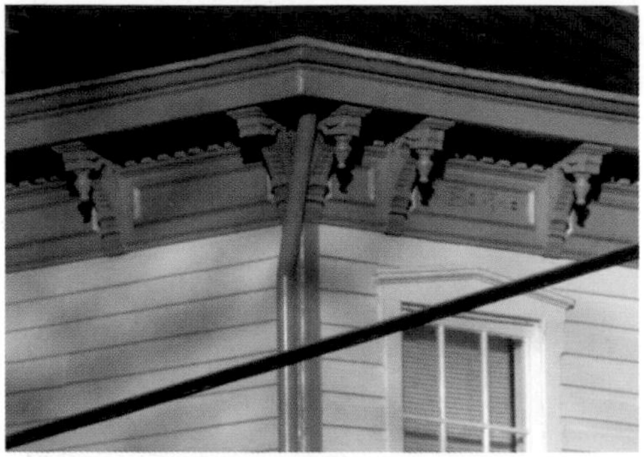

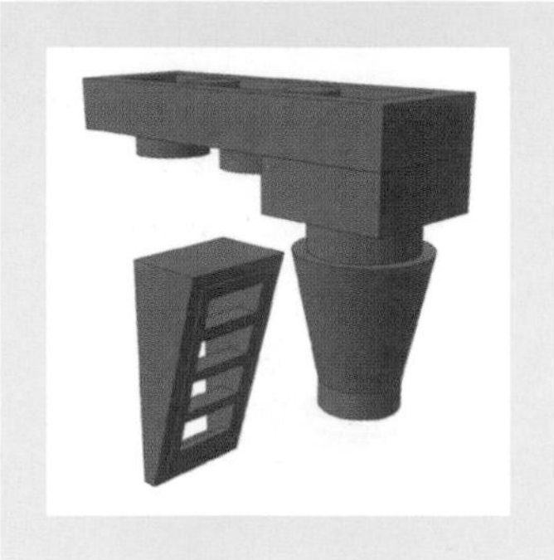

Some patterns might not be obvious at first. Check out the pattern on the right side of this wall. A similar look could be built with 2/3 slopes as shown.

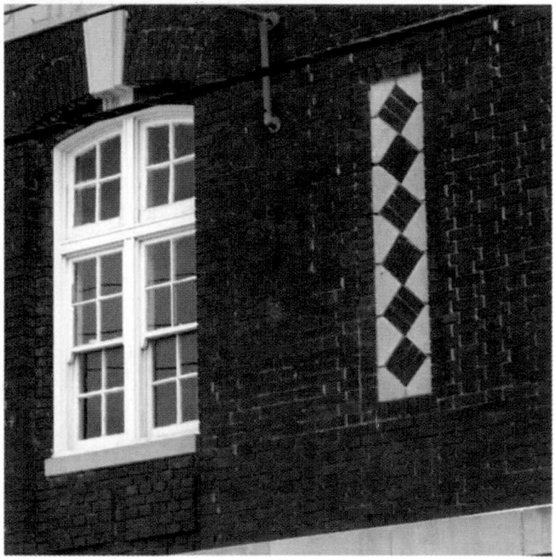

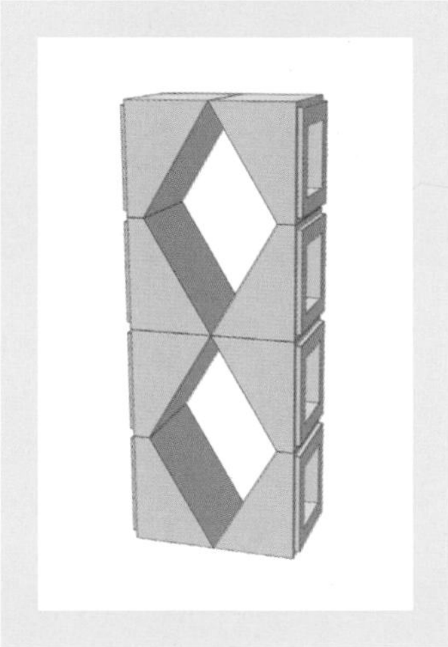

The green awning below has a curved shape. In the picture on the right, you can see the curved bricks that would match that shape.

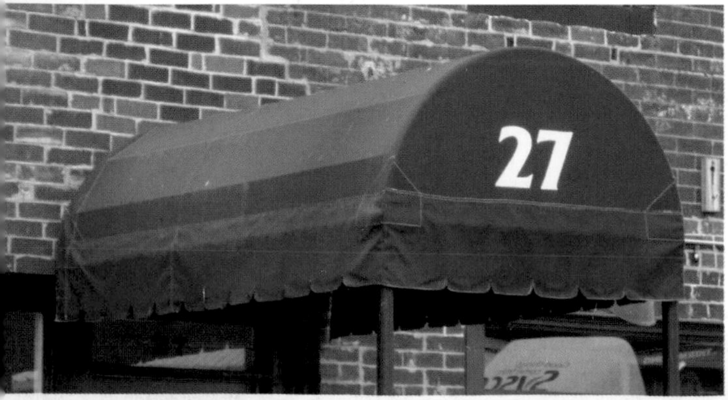
27

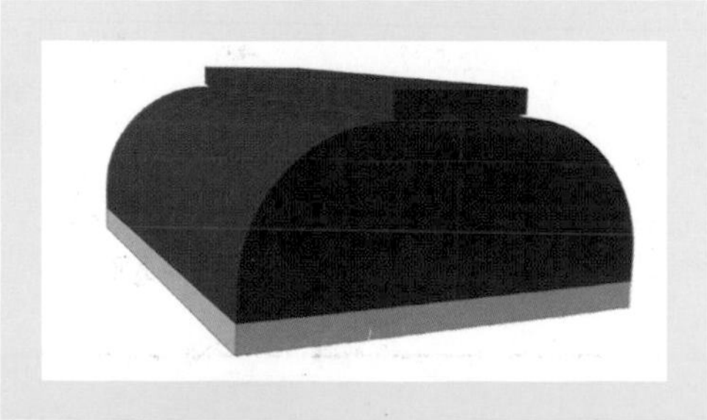

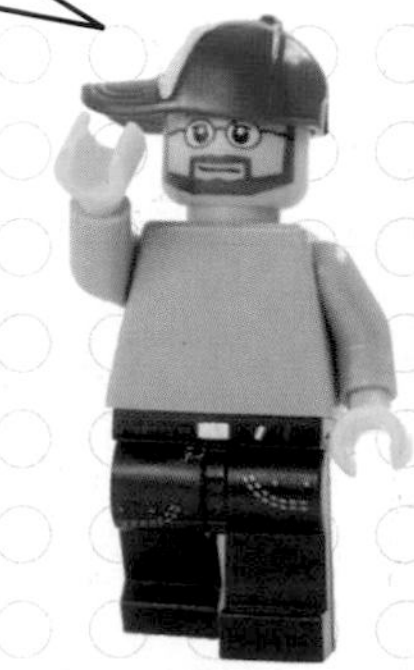
A STICKER ON THE FRONT OF THAT AWNING WOULD REALLY HELP COMPLETE THE LOOK.

Several parts of this building immediately stand out, such as the white arch above the door and the door itself. The black grills could be used on a brick-built door, and this white arch matches up nicely.

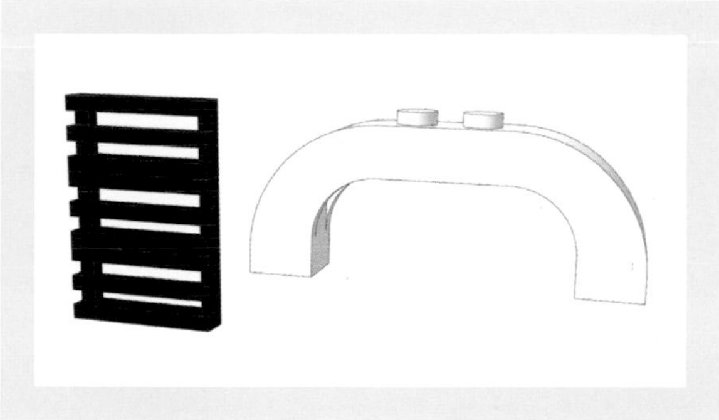

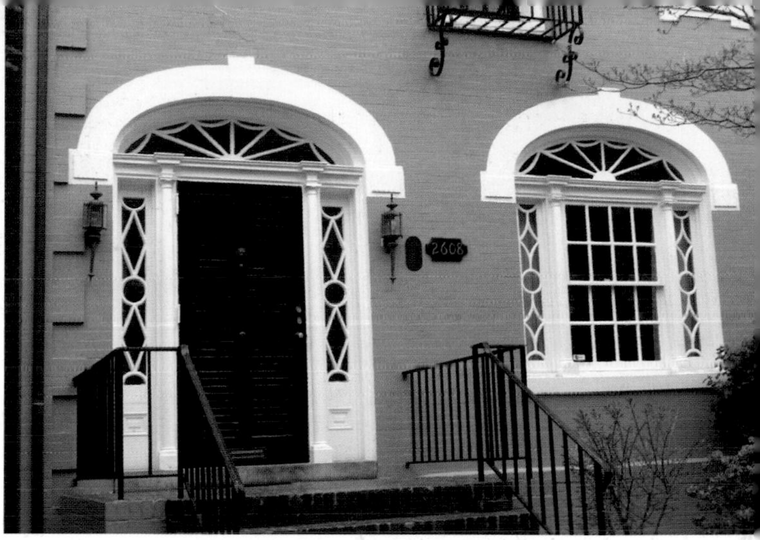

The real-world house above was the inspiration for the model below.

This molding features shapes that look like flowers. This big flower is a good match.

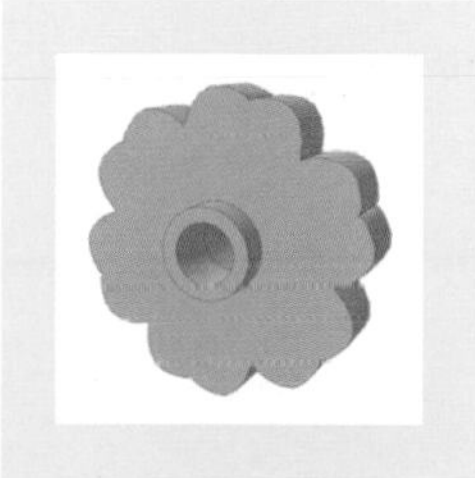

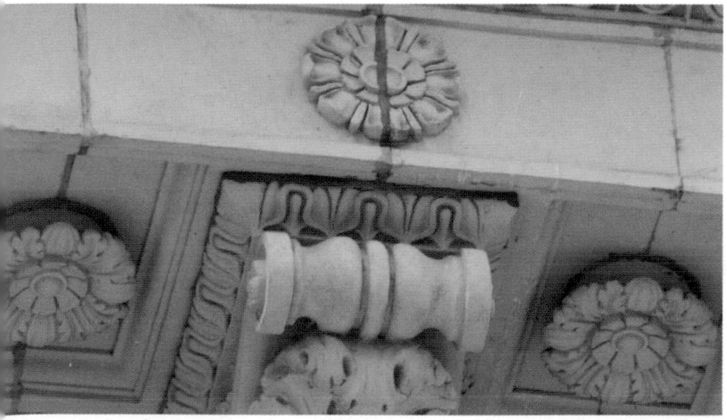

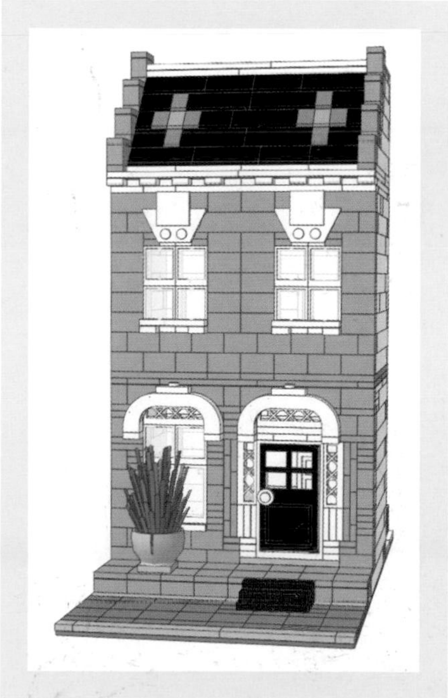

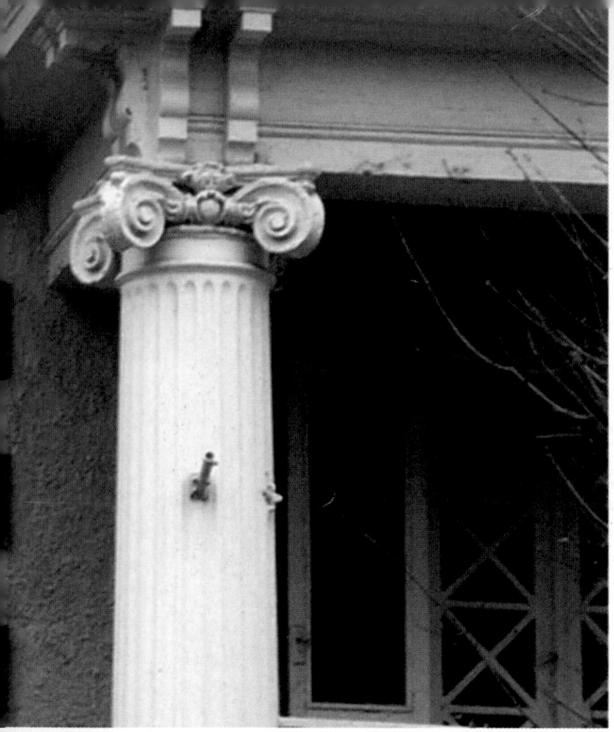

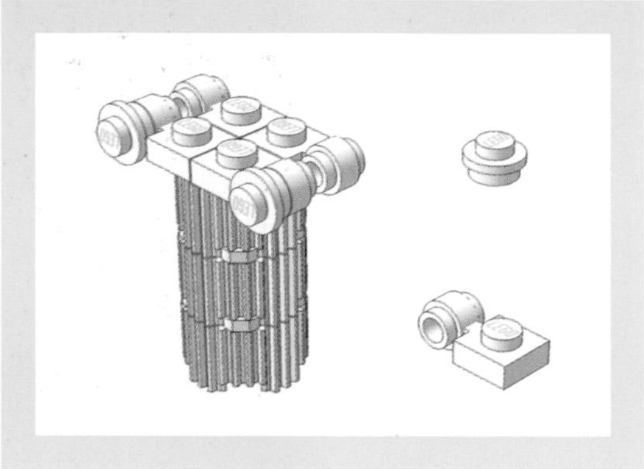

The top of this classic Ionic column has decorative corners, which you can emulate with two parts.

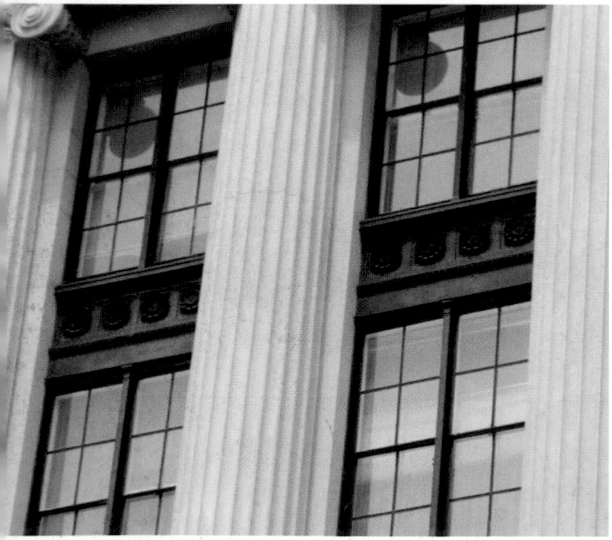

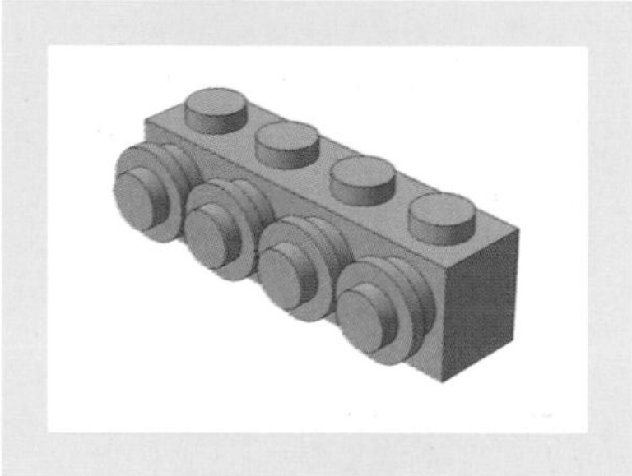

Between these windows is a decorative element that looks like a row of round plates.

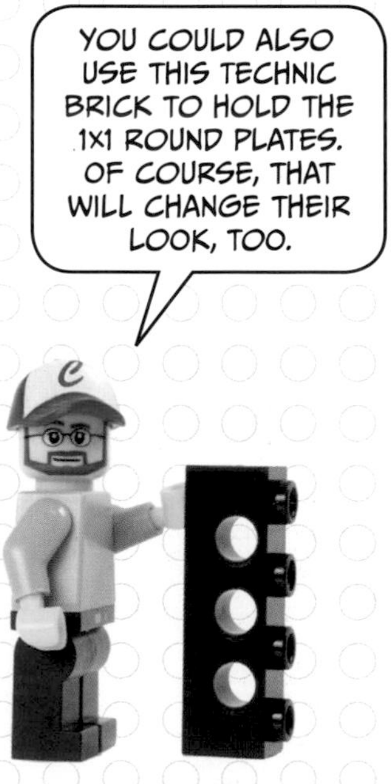
YOU COULD ALSO USE THIS TECHNIC BRICK TO HOLD THE 1X1 ROUND PLATES. OF COURSE, THAT WILL CHANGE THEIR LOOK, TOO.

The arch over the curved windows shown here is an easy build: use a 1×4 arch over a window with a round top. The white door rails at the bottom represent the window ledge.

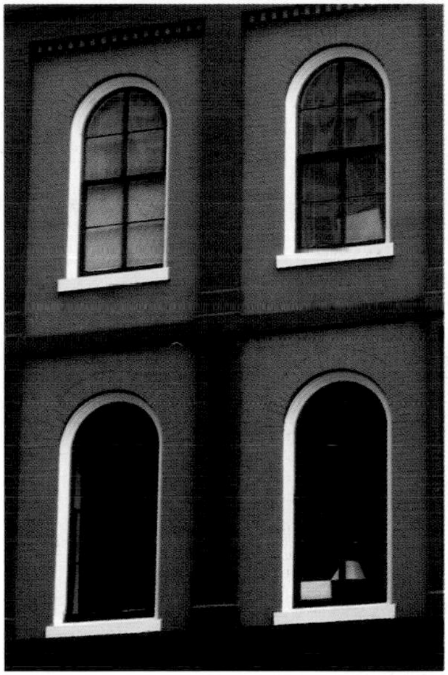

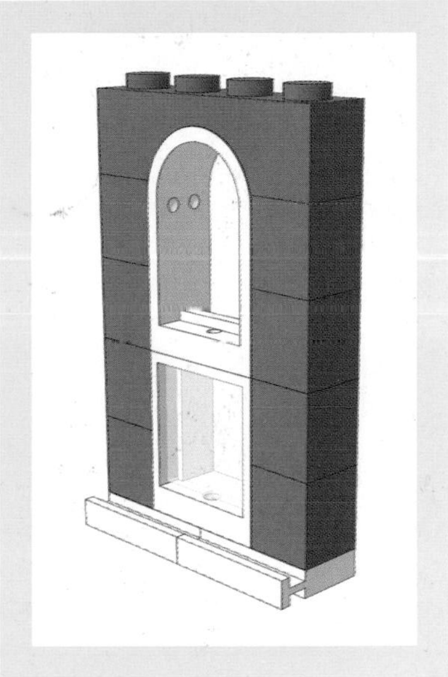

Think creatively and look at your pieces from all angles. The square part between the top and bottom columns on this building looks like a 1×1 brick or plate turned on its side.

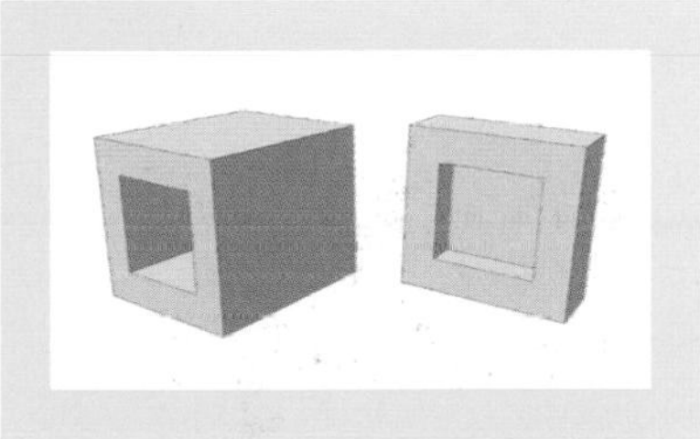

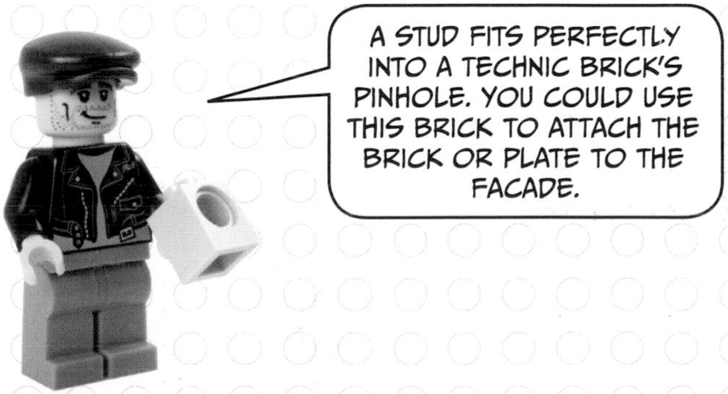
A STUD FITS PERFECTLY INTO A TECHNIC BRICK'S PINHOLE. YOU COULD USE THIS BRICK TO ATTACH THE BRICK OR PLATE TO THE FACADE.

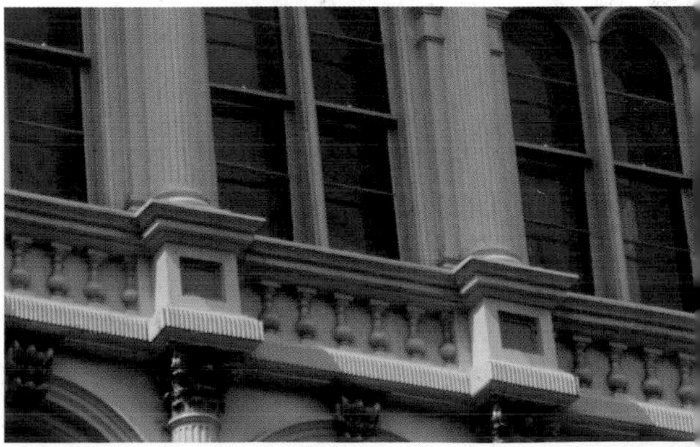

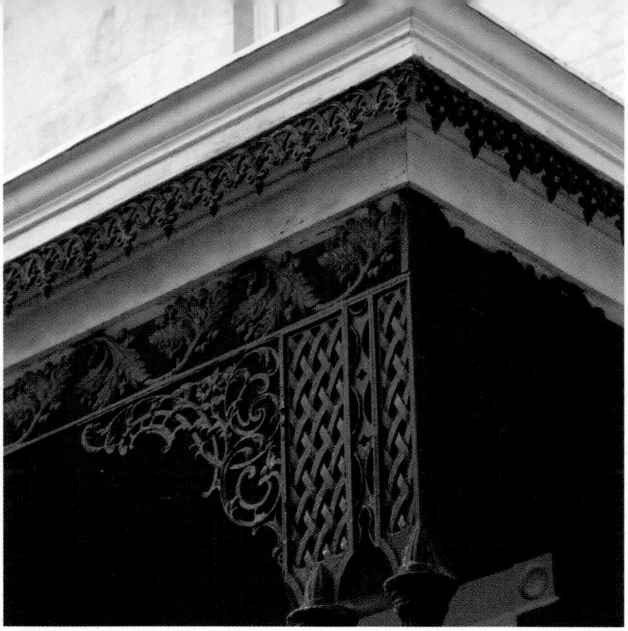

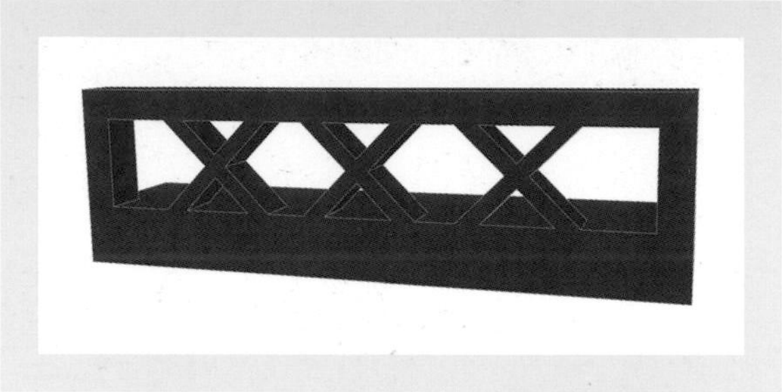

You can simulate the black wrought iron work shown on the left using this 1×4 fence lattice piece.

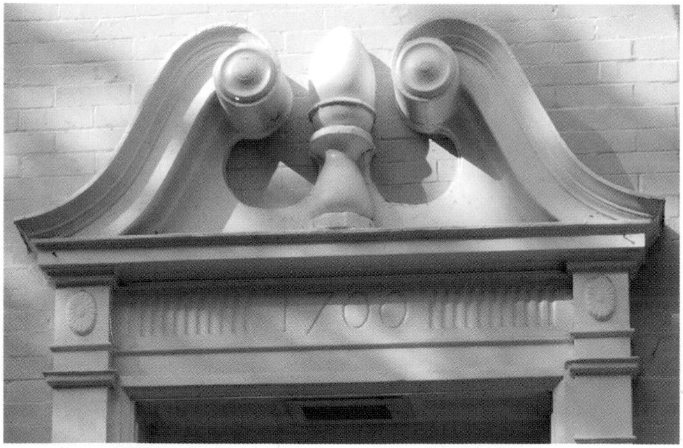

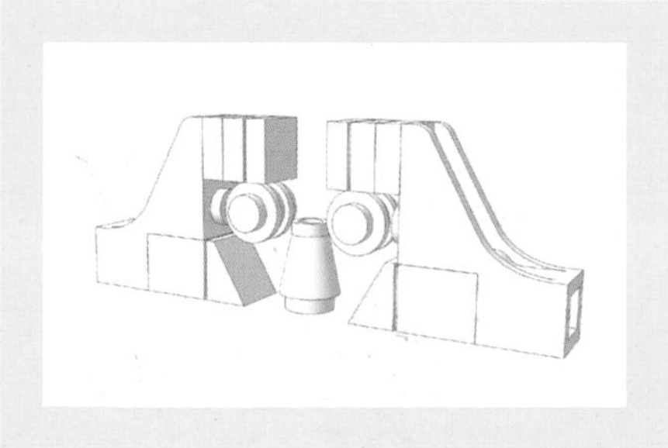

This detail work above this doorway looks complicated at first, but with the right pieces you can approximate the look.

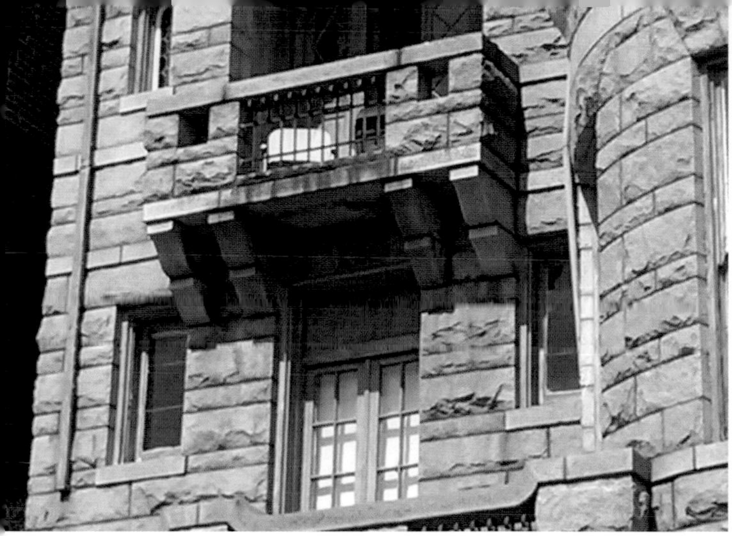

The supports for this balcony look almost exactly like the 1×2, 45-degree inverted slope.

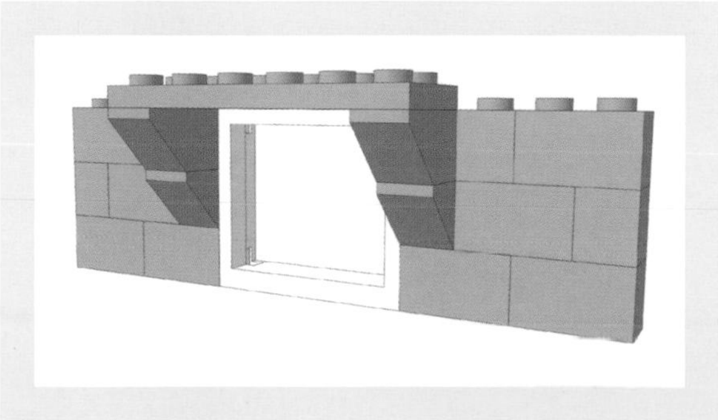

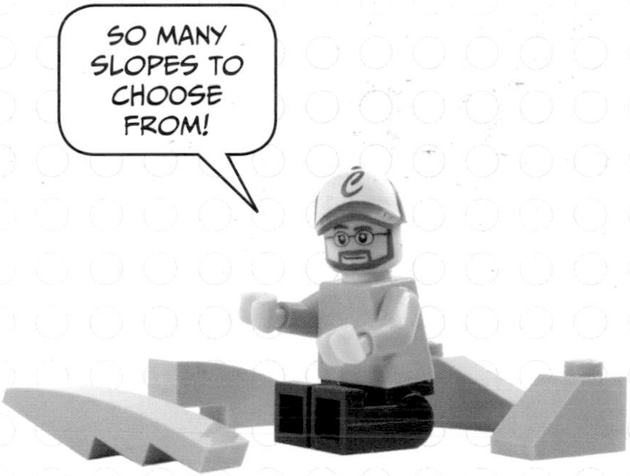
SO MANY SLOPES TO CHOOSE FROM!

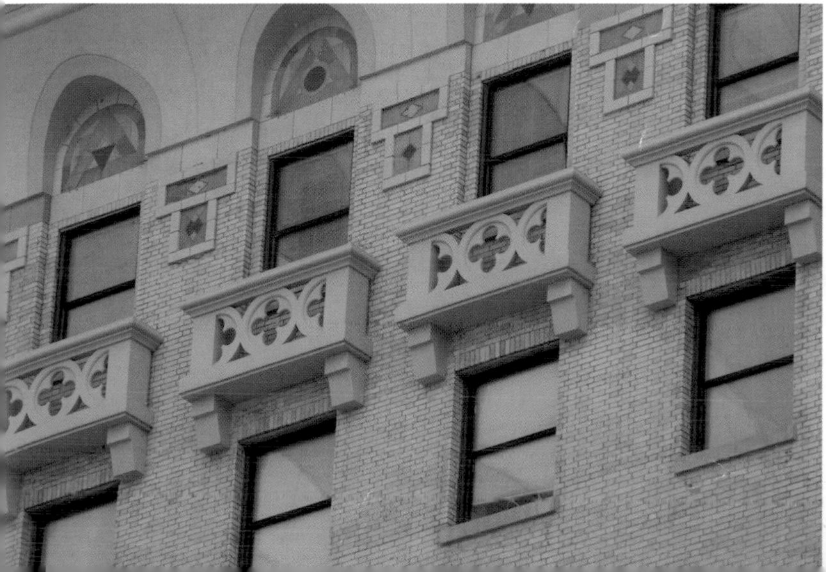

The supports under this window ledge feature slopes as well, but perhaps a studs not on top (SNOT) technique would look better here.

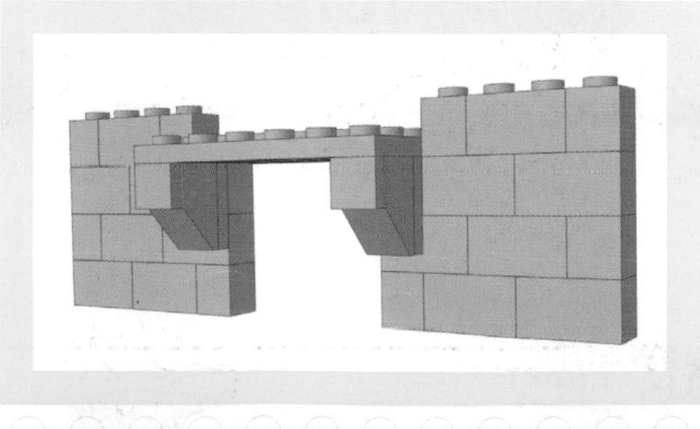

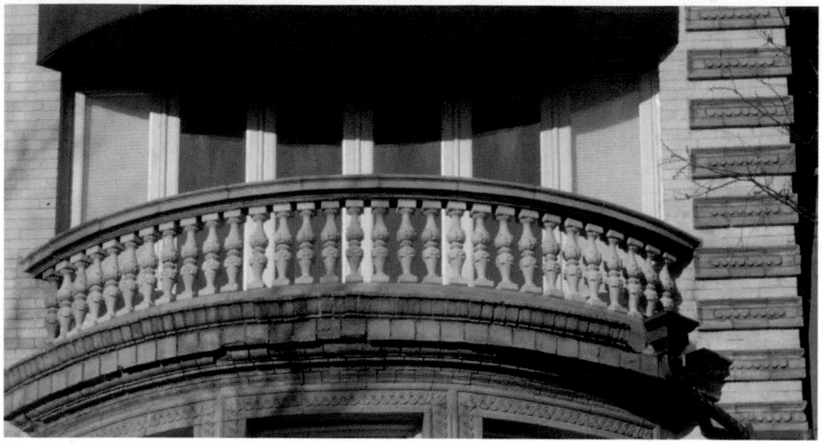

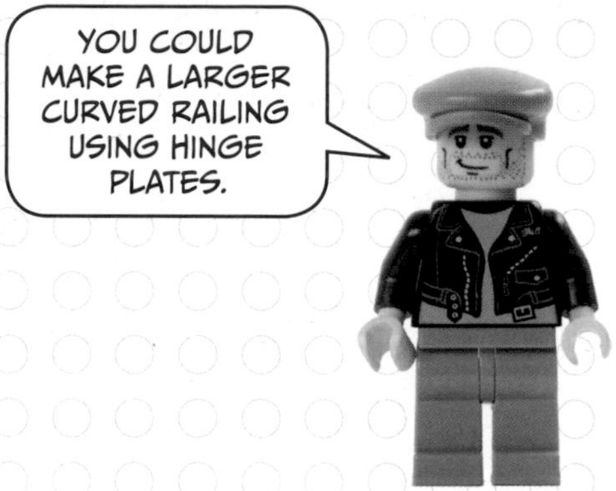
YOU COULD MAKE A LARGER CURVED RAILING USING HINGE PLATES.

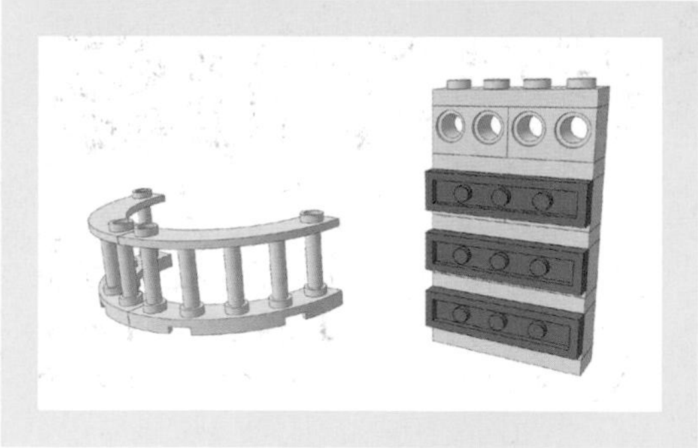

The railing in this example is obvious, but on the right side of the building you can see trim that looks like a LEGO plate turned on its side, facing outward.

This corner brick pattern looks like tiles attached to the side of the building. You could also achieve this look using only bricks.

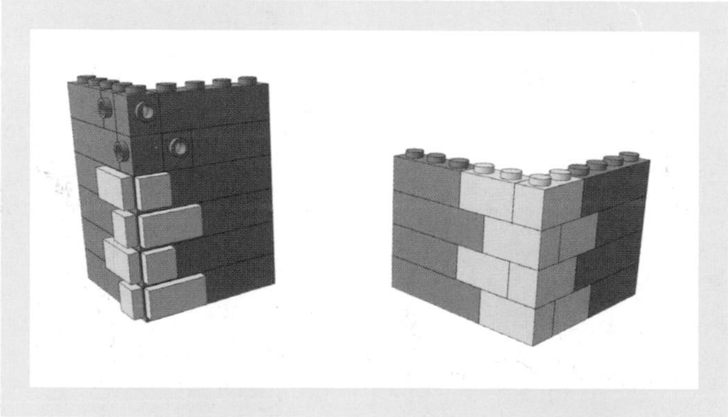

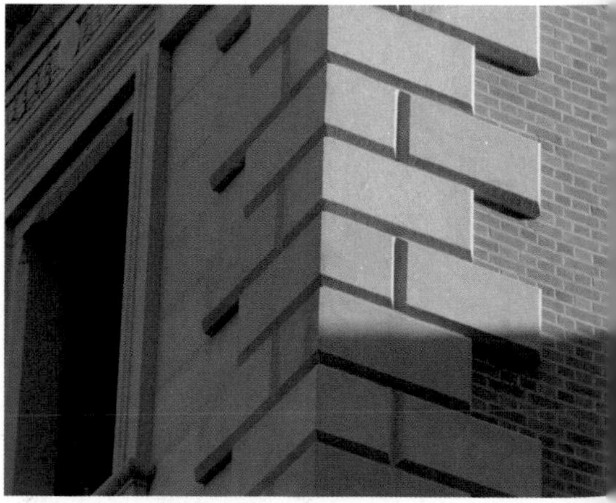

4

The Details

Details are key to making your building unique. The way you make the windows, the trim, the colors, the lights, and all the decorations in between is what sets each model apart. In this chapter, we'll explore the details of building exteriors.

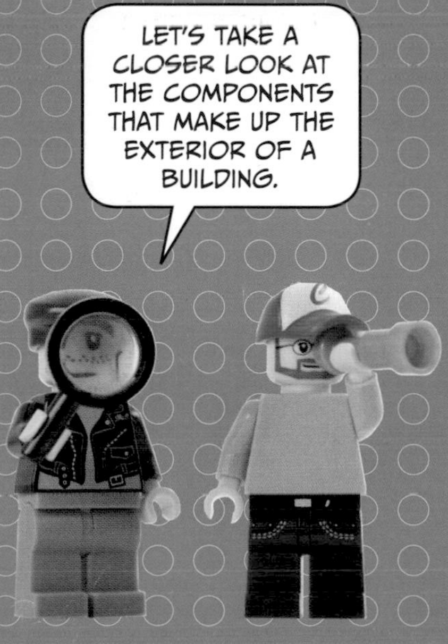
LET'S TAKE A CLOSER LOOK AT THE COMPONENTS THAT MAKE UP THE EXTERIOR OF A BUILDING.

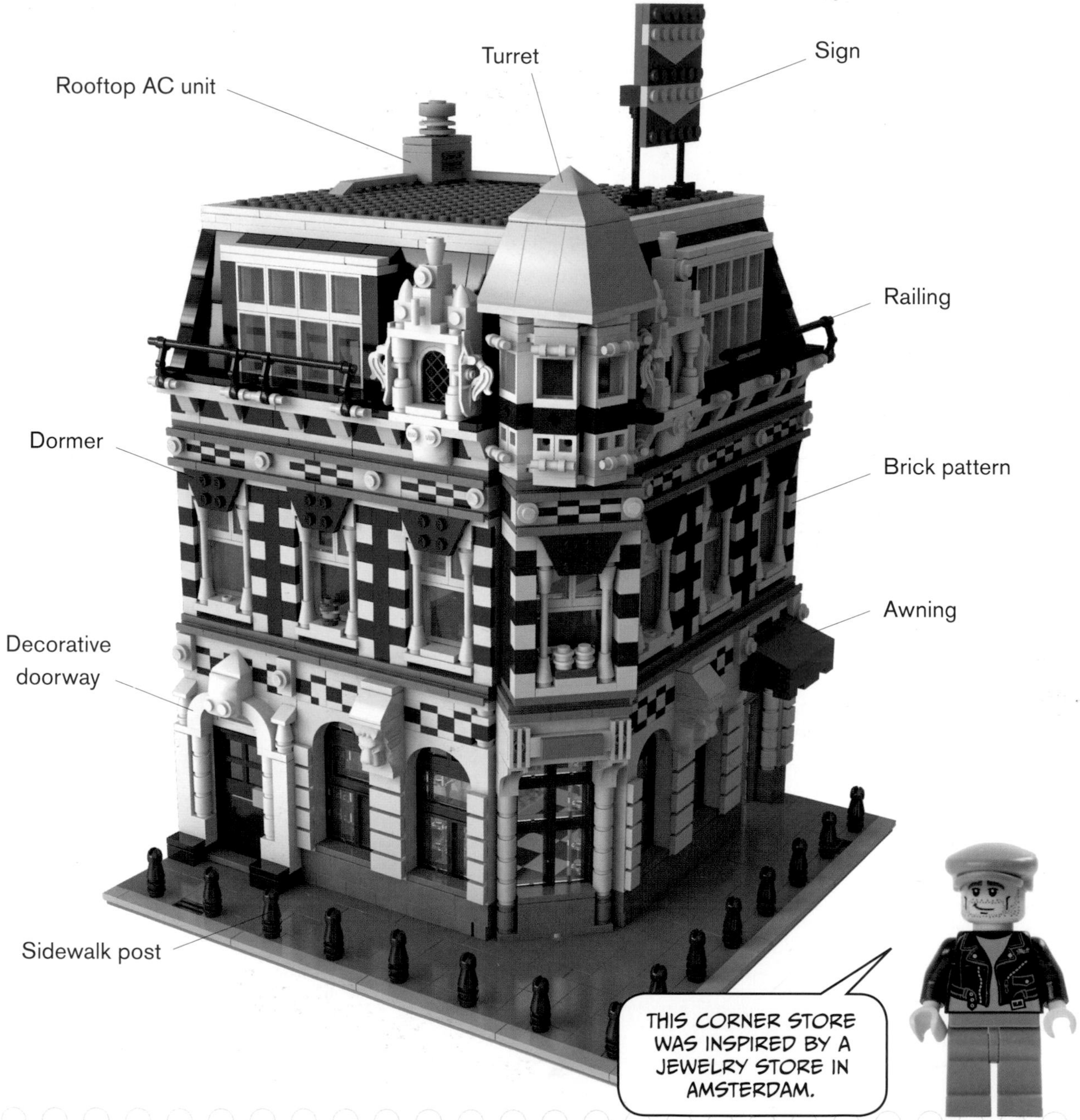
Rooftop AC unit
Turret
Sign
Railing
Dormer
Brick pattern
Awning
Decorative doorway
Sidewalk post
THIS CORNER STORE WAS INSPIRED BY A JEWELRY STORE IN AMSTERDAM.

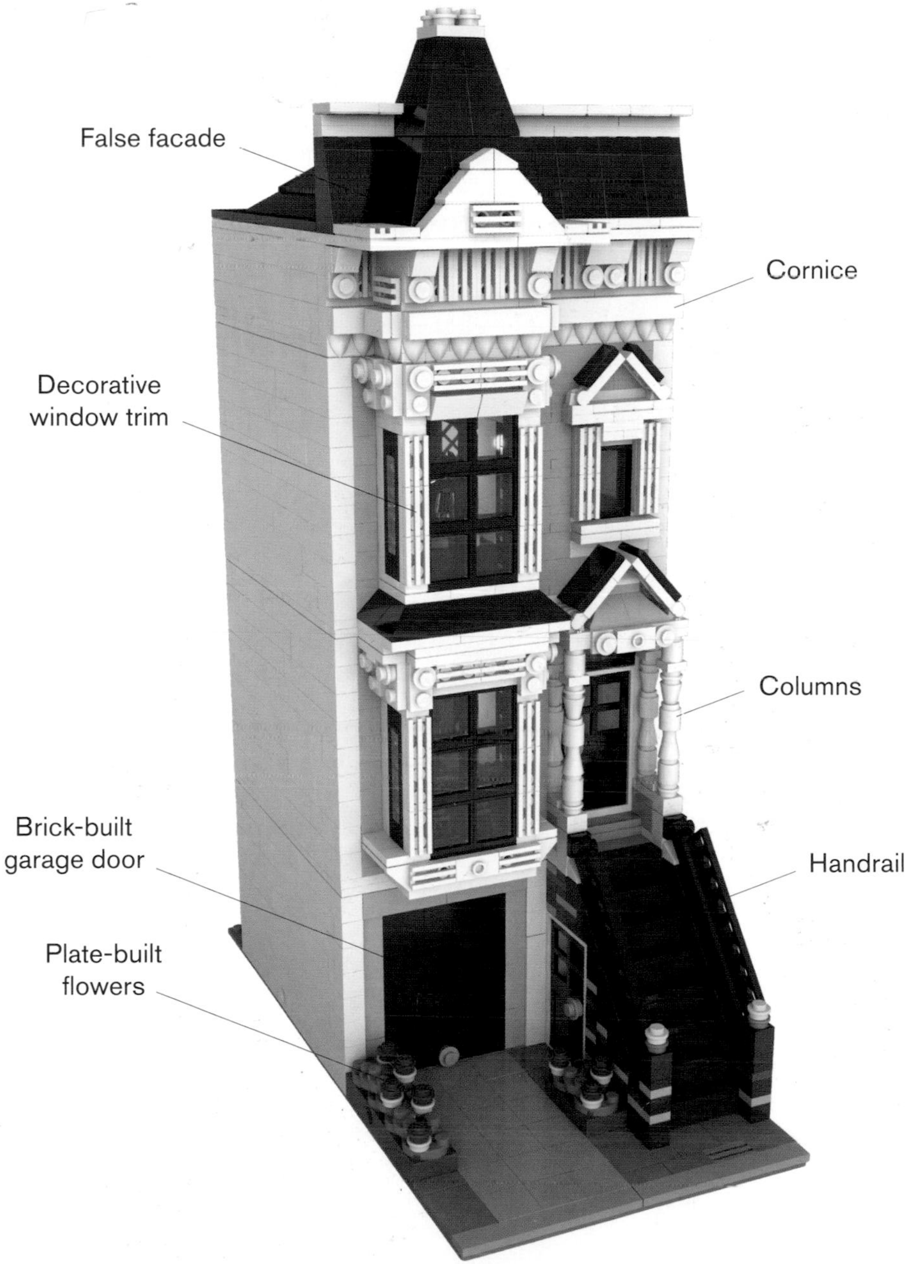
False facade
Cornice
Decorative window trim
Columns
Brick-built garage door
Handrail
Plate-built flowers

Roof Moldings and Cornices

Here are a few examples of real-world trim molding along rooflines. Which pieces could be used to replicate these looks?

With so many different LEGO parts, there are bound to be several combinations you can use to get the look you want. Check out these examples of trim, which use a variety of methods for similar effects.

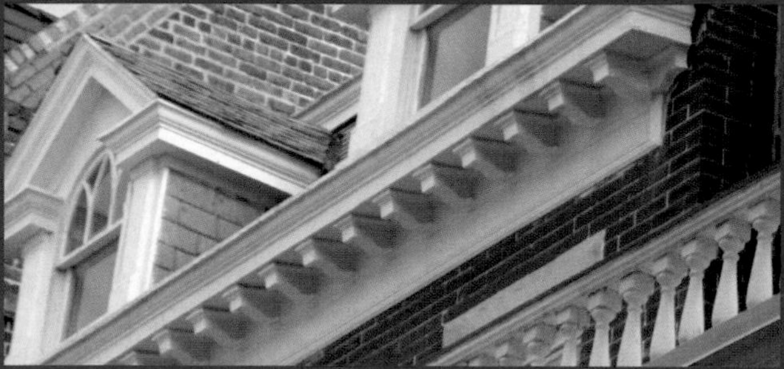

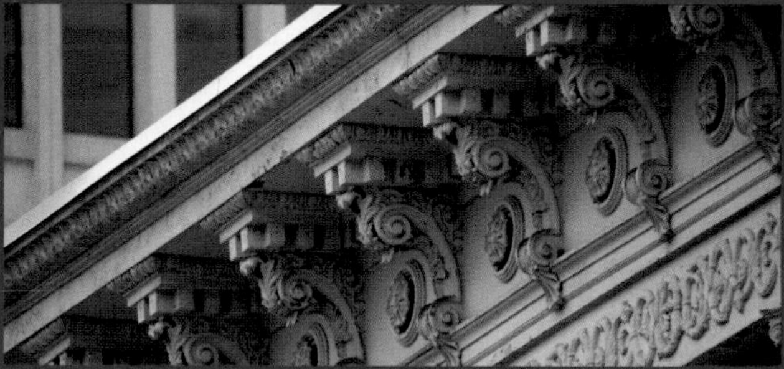

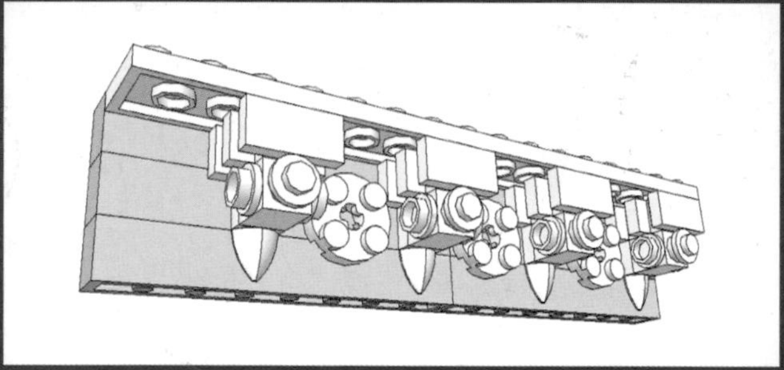

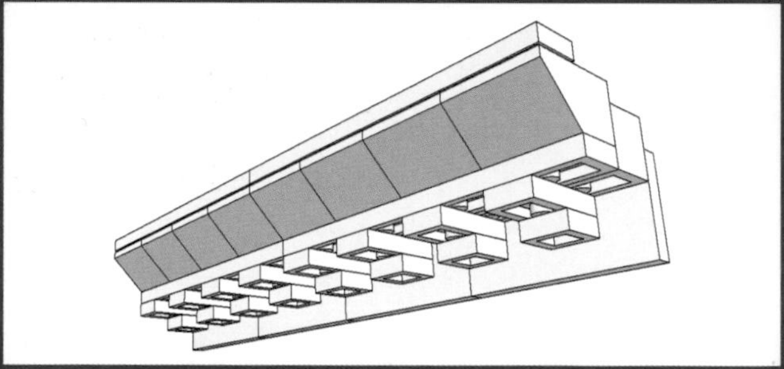

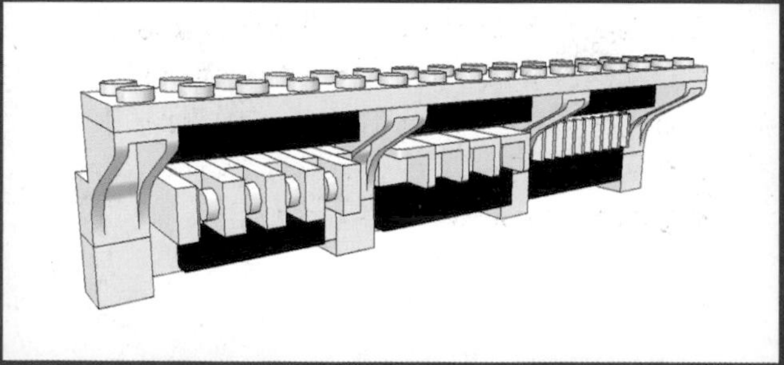

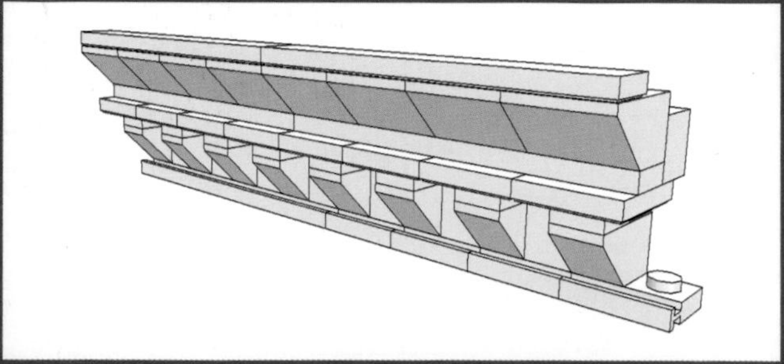

Lights

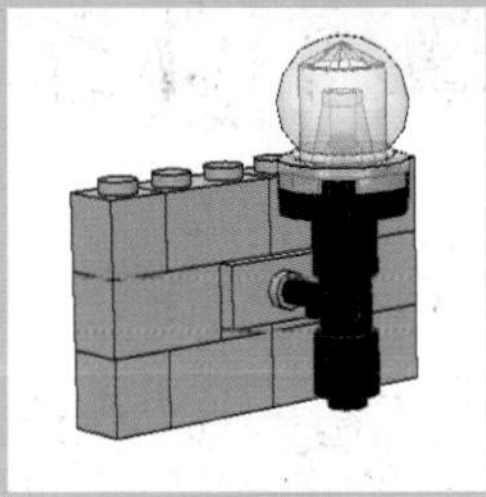

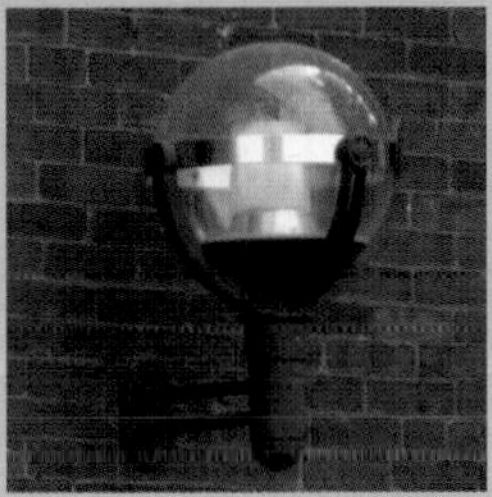

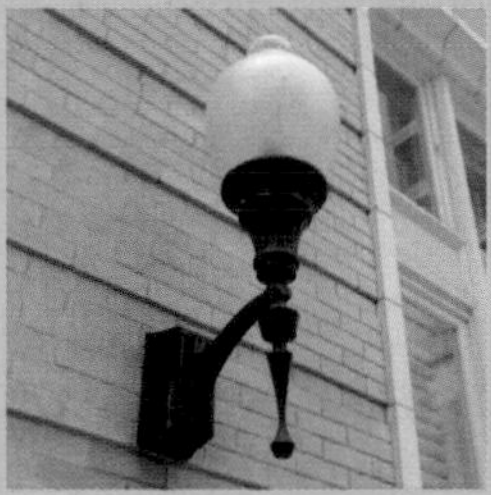

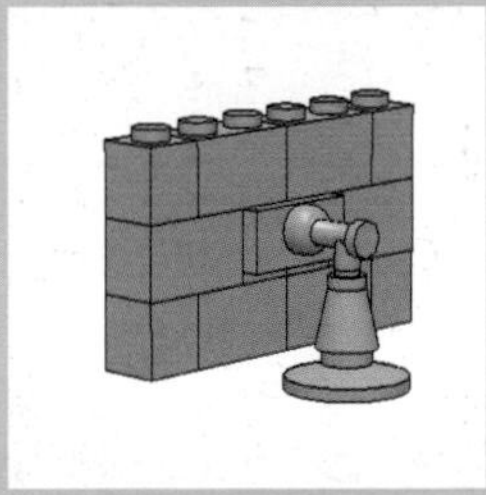

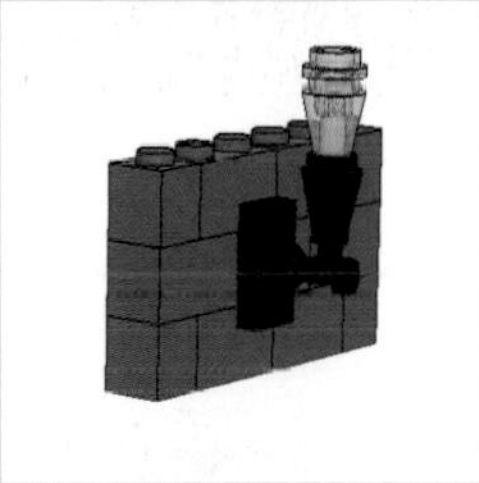

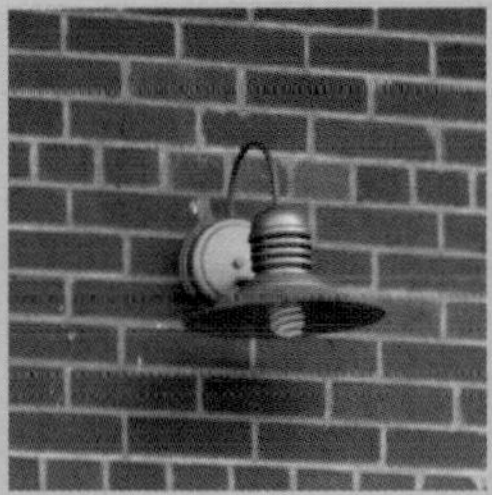

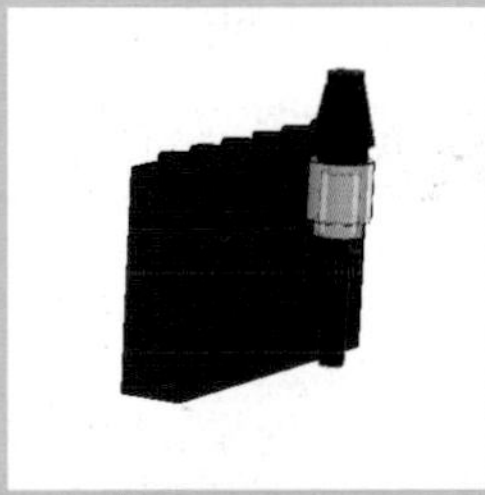

One way to help break up a flat wall is to add a light. You can add one or two beside a door or space them out evenly to light the whole sidewalk. Check out these samples to get an idea of different designs.

Columns and Railings

Look over these pictures and try to imagine which LEGO pieces you would use.

You can make columns any number of ways, from simple to complex (often using SNOT techniques).

Railings and fences can be very simple, or you can use more ornate pieces to create a balustrade.

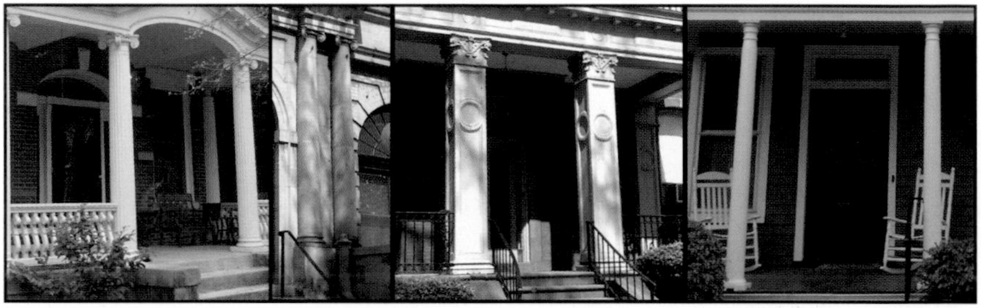

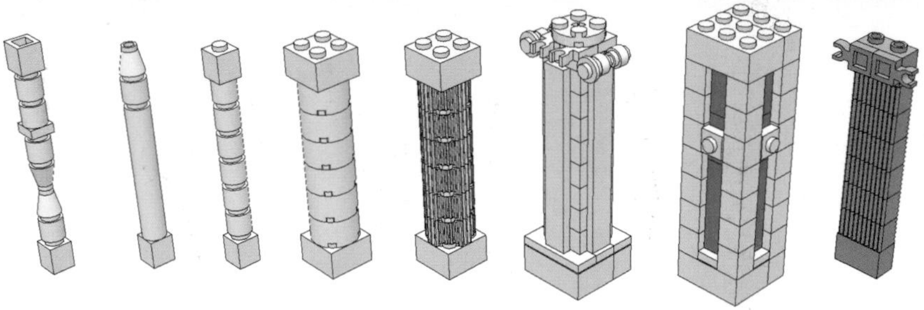

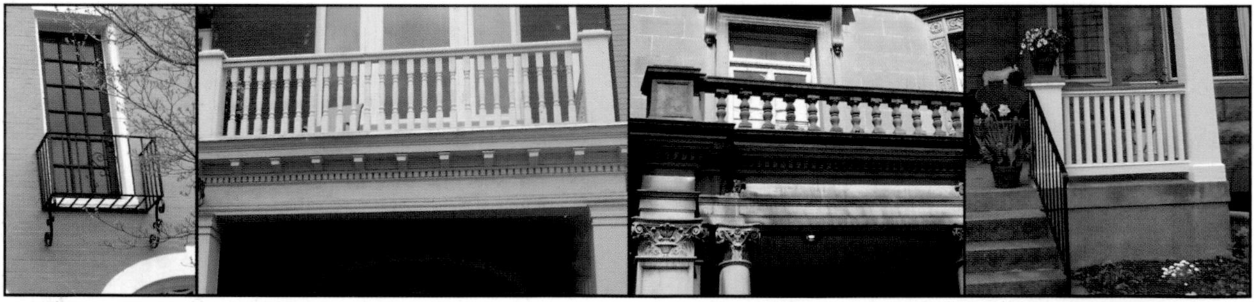

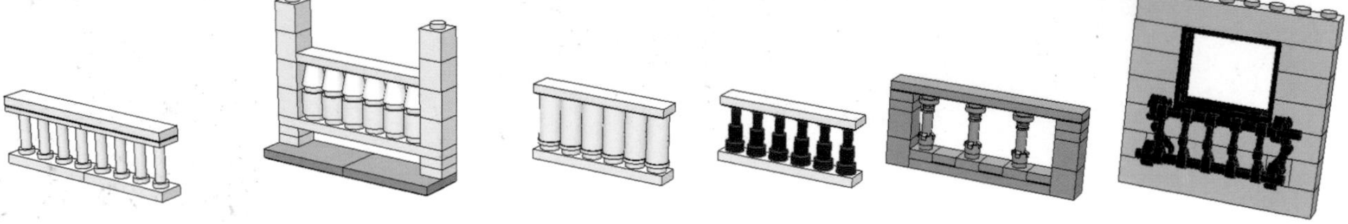

Windows and Shutters

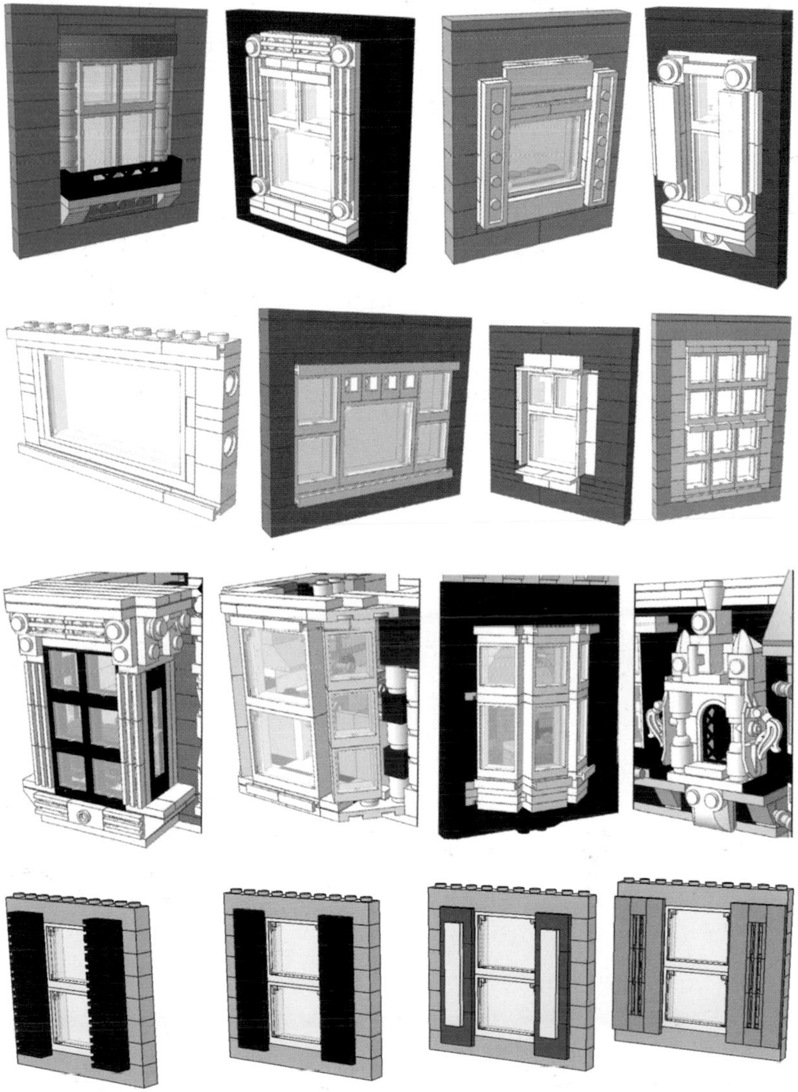

Windows are so important to a building's look that architects sometimes call them "the eyes" of a structure. Check out these examples of how to create vastly different looks by using various pieces in and around the windows.

For a long time, LEGO made windows that had shutter tabs that could hold shutter pieces. More recent window pieces don't have those built in, but you can still make shutters using other elements.

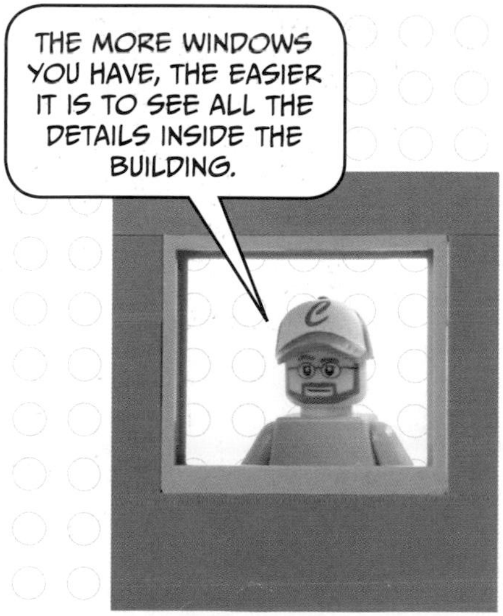
THE MORE WINDOWS YOU HAVE, THE EASIER IT IS TO SEE ALL THE DETAILS INSIDE THE BUILDING.

Plant Life

Bring your building to life with some plants and trees. Check out these examples of trees, bushes, ivy, and even a greenhouse.

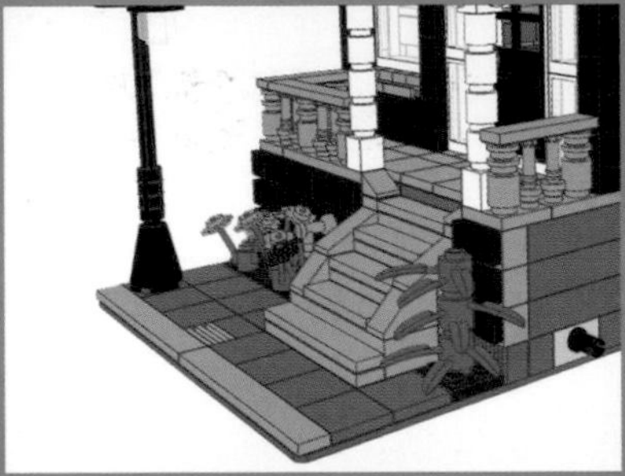

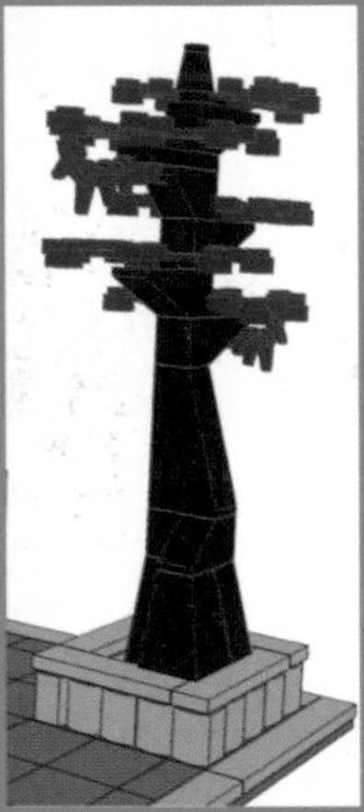

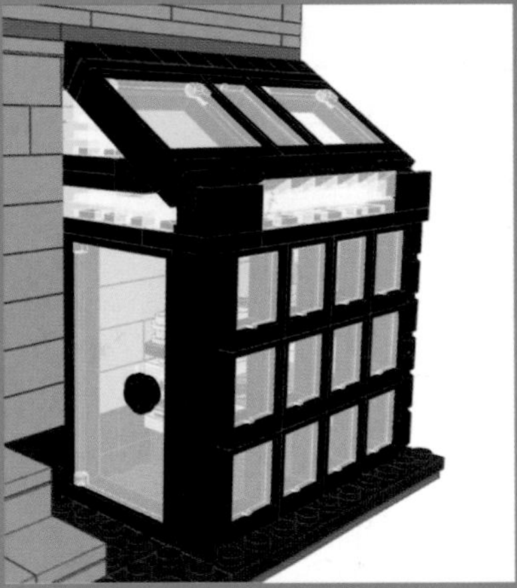

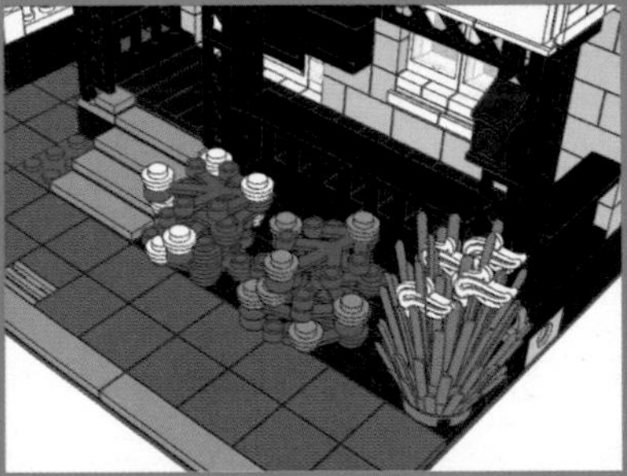

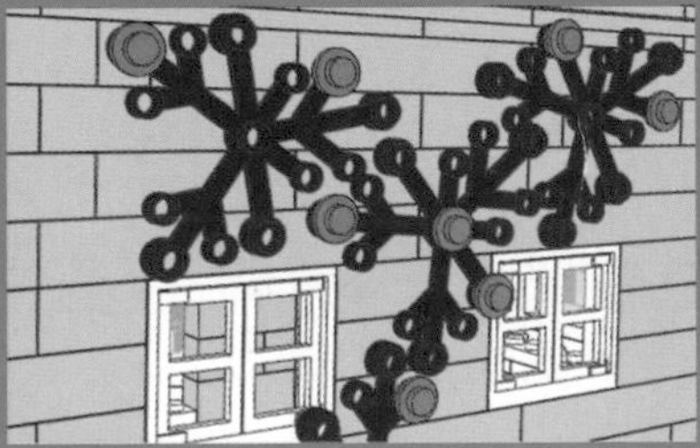

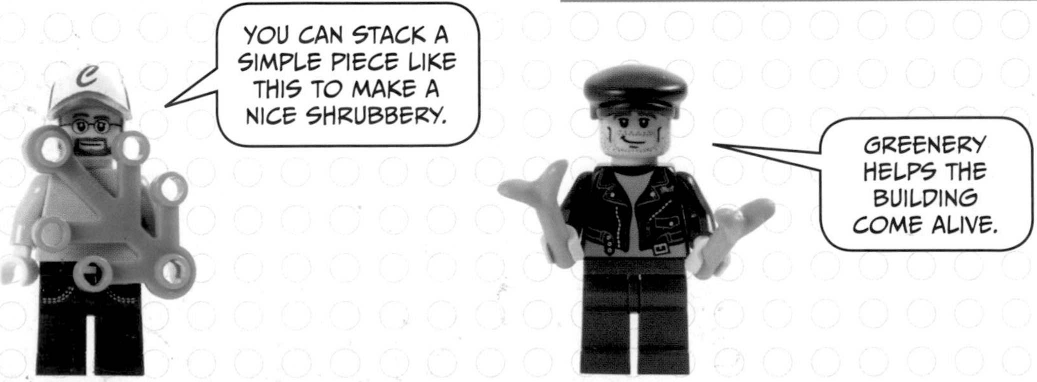
YOU CAN STACK A SIMPLE PIECE LIKE THIS TO MAKE A NICE SHRUBBERY.
GREENERY HELPS THE BUILDING COME ALIVE.

Newspaper Racks

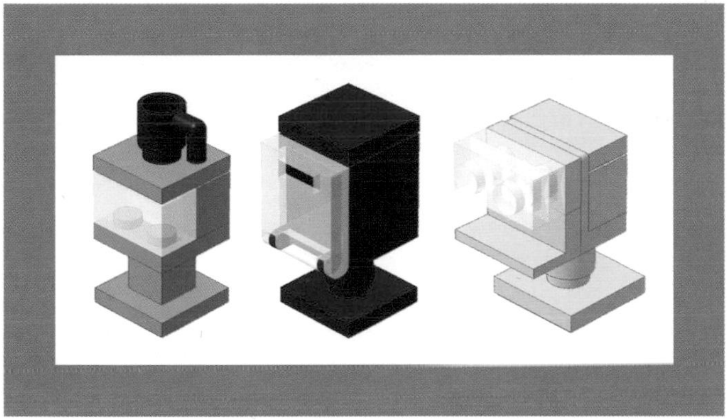

Take a walk down a typical sidewalk, and you'll see there is a lot more than just flat, grey cement. Adding real-world details can give your building even more flair.

Usually you see these newspaper or magazine dispensers grouped together on street corners.

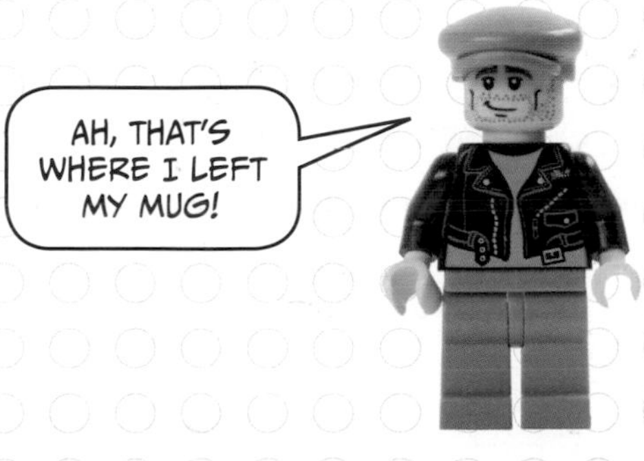
AH, THAT'S WHERE I LEFT MY MUG!

Fire Hydrants

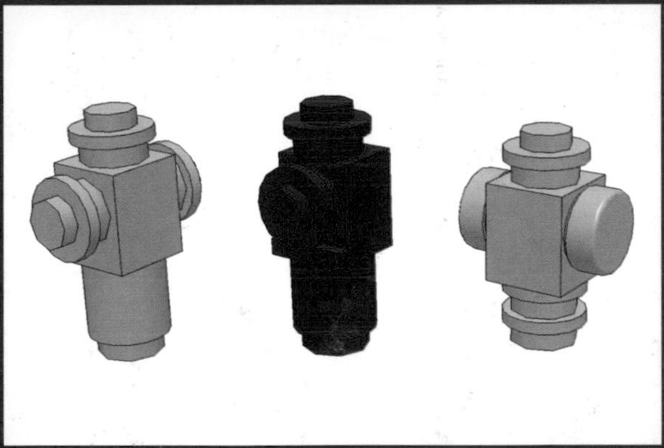

Here are a few examples of how to make a fire hydrant. You can mix up the colors to match a certain city that you are trying to copy.

Parking Meters

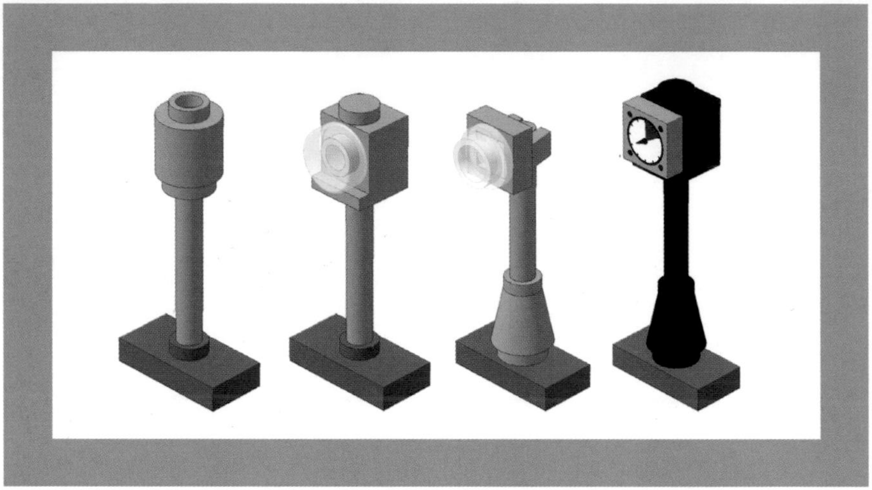

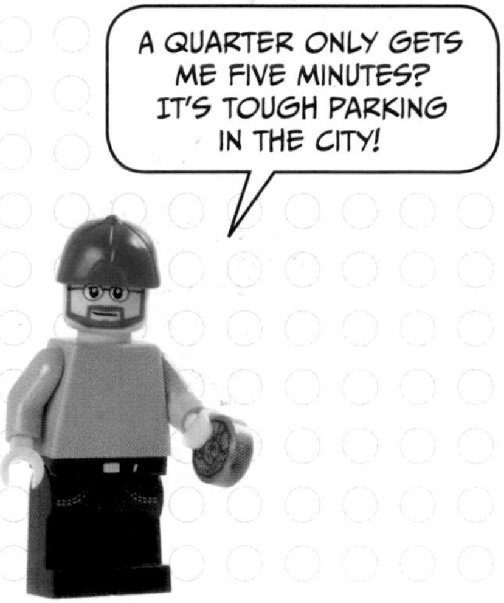
A QUARTER ONLY GETS ME FIVE MINUTES? IT'S TOUGH PARKING IN THE CITY!

Want some parking meters to line the streets of your LEGO city? Here are a few ways to make some.

Benches

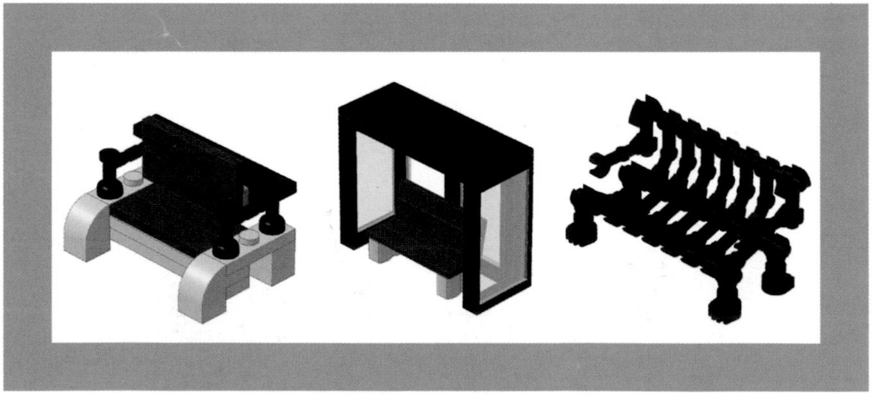

Here are a few examples of different benches and a bus shelter.

Park Bench

1
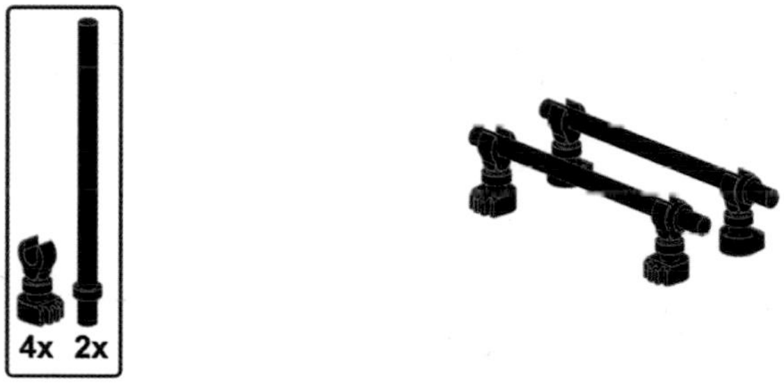
4x 2x

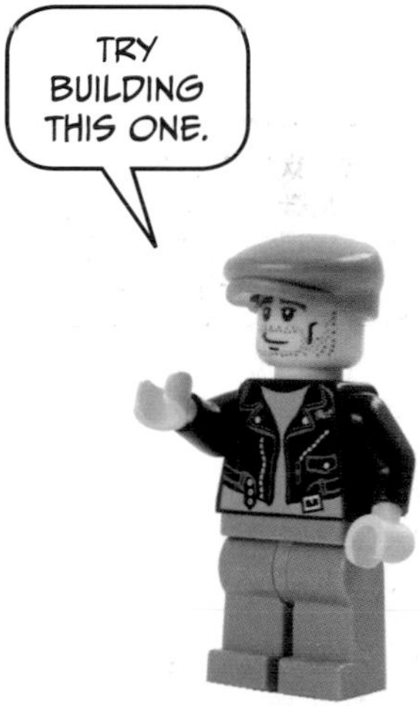
TRY
BUILDING
THIS ONE.

2
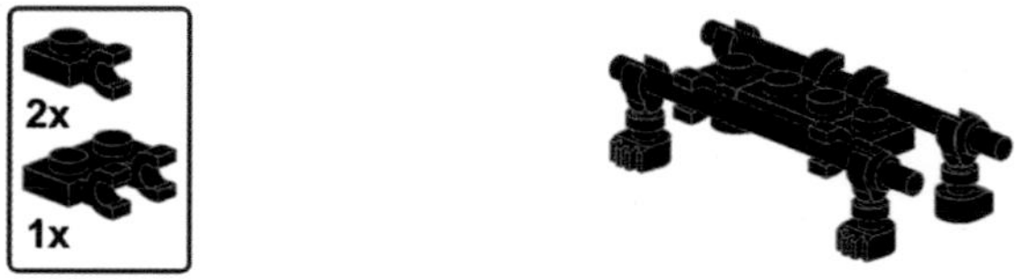
2x
1x

3
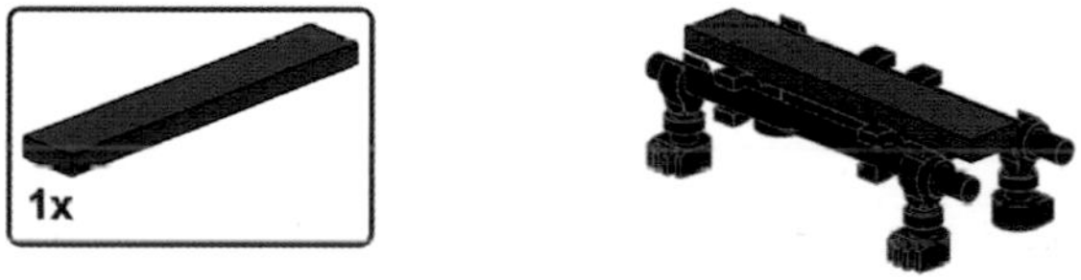
1x

4
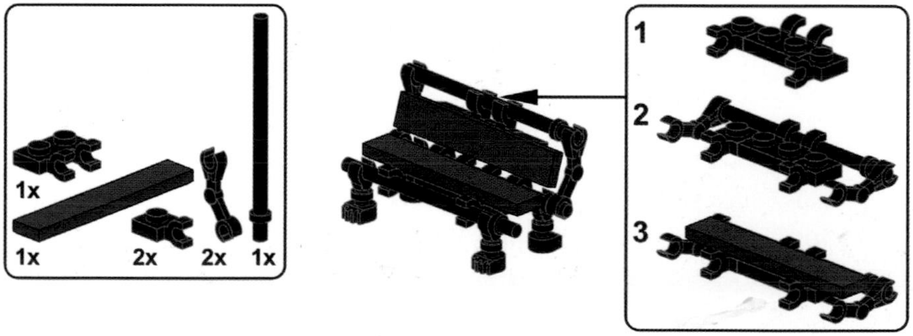
1x
1x
2x
2x
1x
1
2
3

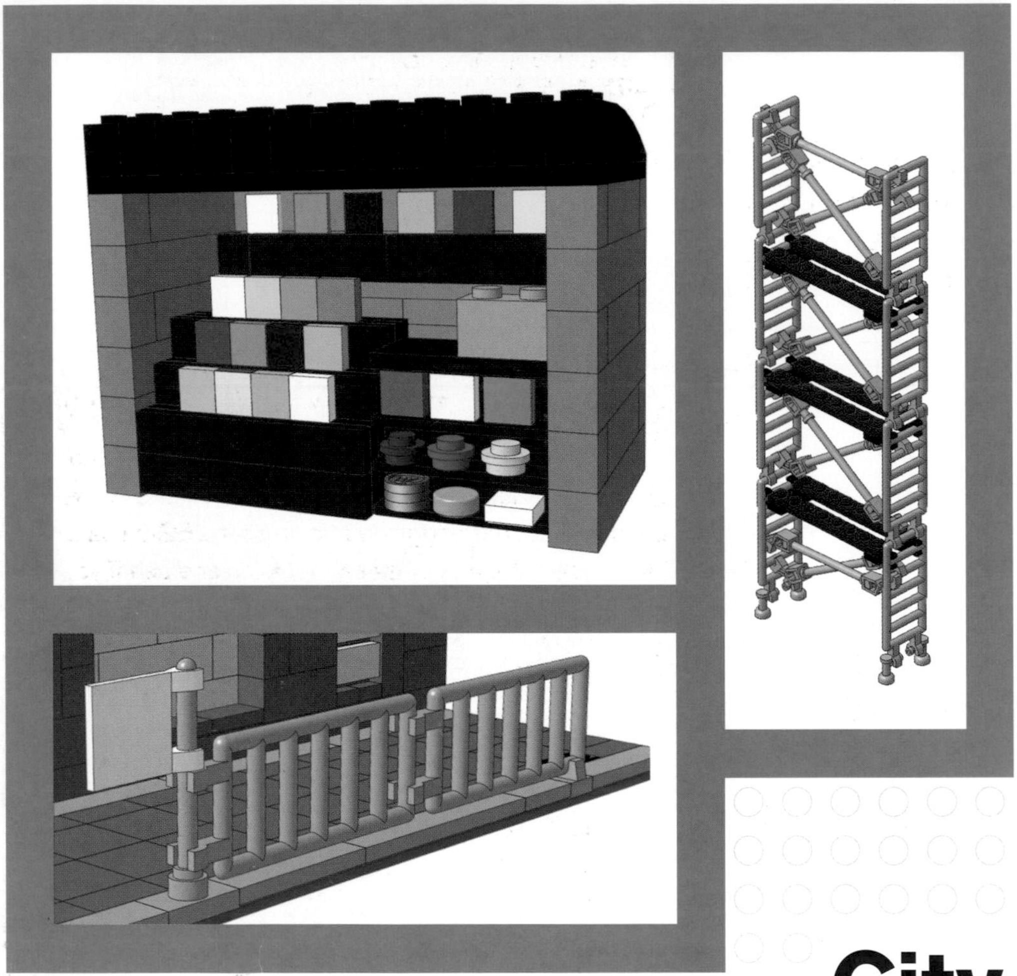

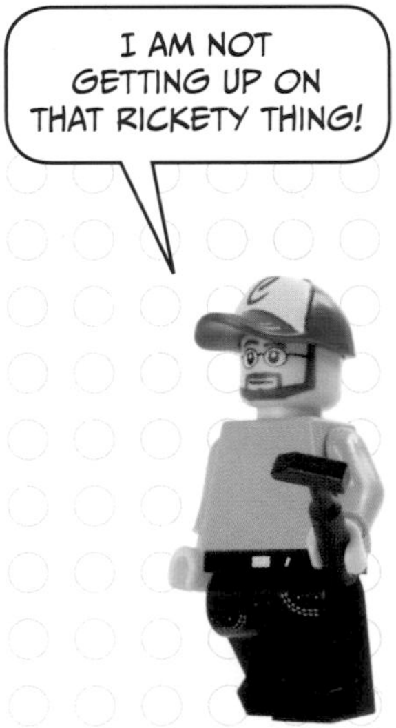
I AM NOT GETTING UP ON THAT RICKETY THING!

City Living

Give your street some visual interest with a bike rack, newsstand, or some scaffolding. Perhaps some workers could be repainting or fixing up a house.

Your city needs stoplights to help control the flow of traffic. You can build a simple light on the side of the street or go more elaborate and have one that hangs over the street.

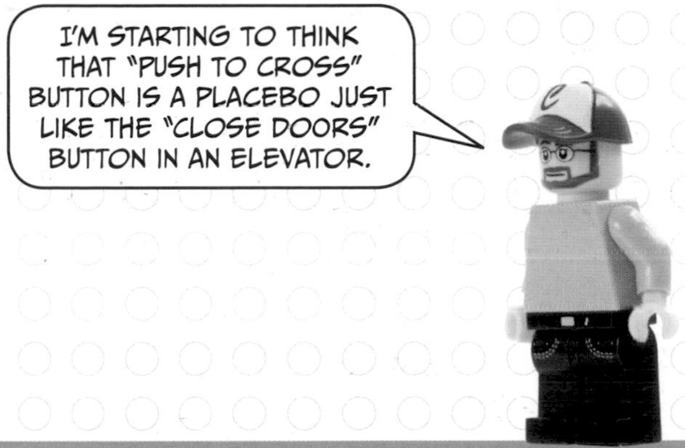
I'M STARTING TO THINK THAT "PUSH TO CROSS" BUTTON IS A PLACEBO JUST LIKE THE "CLOSE DOORS" BUTTON IN AN ELEVATOR.

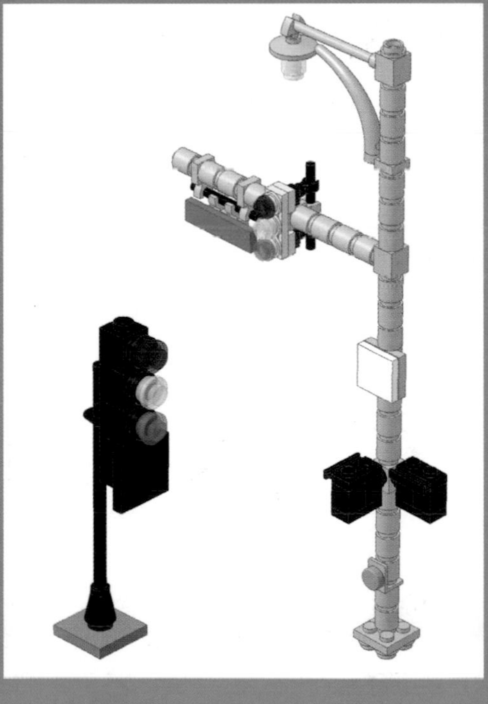

You aren't limited to the simple lamp post that LEGO provides; there are many unique lamp posts out there that are begging to be made in LEGO scale. Take a look at some of these examples and see if you can figure out how they were made.

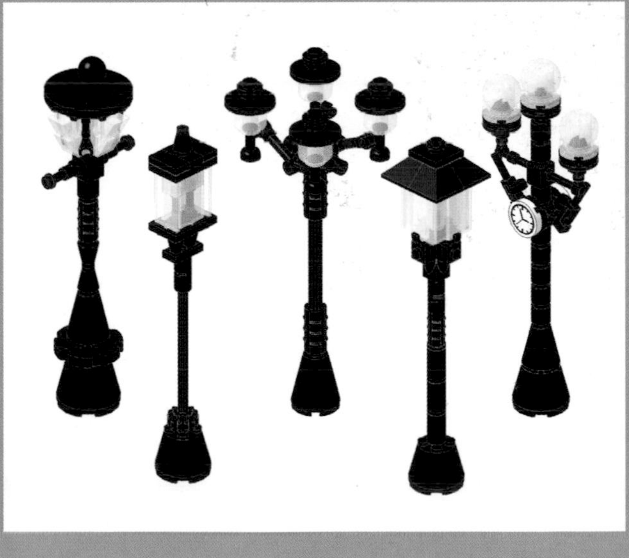

Traffic Light

1

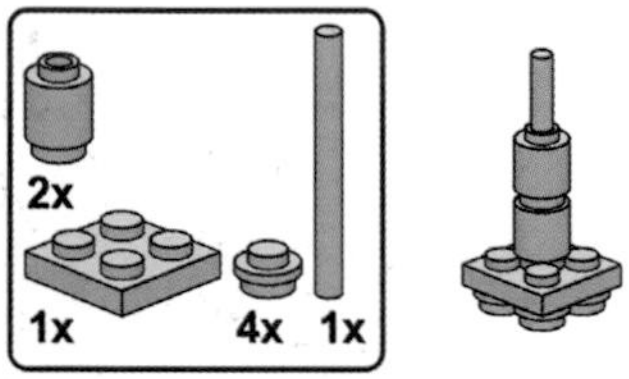
2x
1x
4x
1x

2

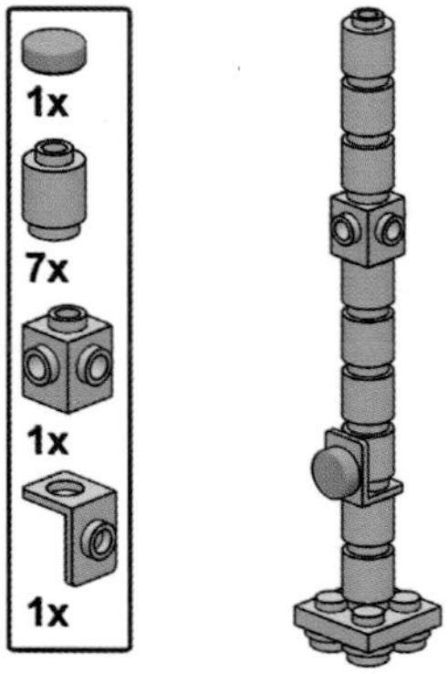
1x
7x
1x
1x

3

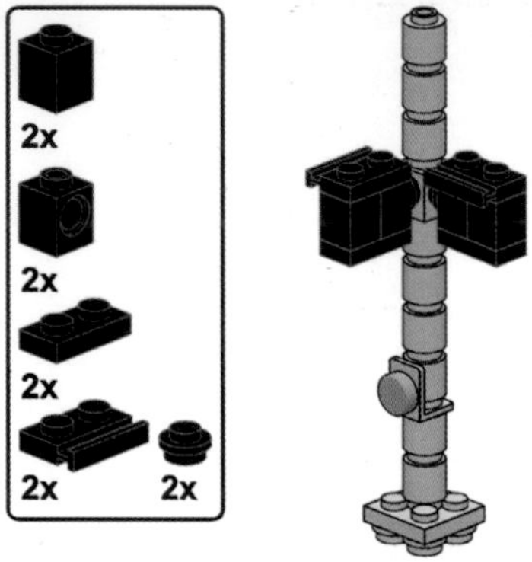
2x
2x
2x
2x
2x

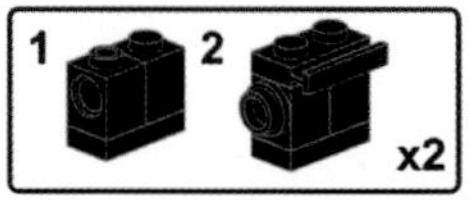
1
2
x2

4

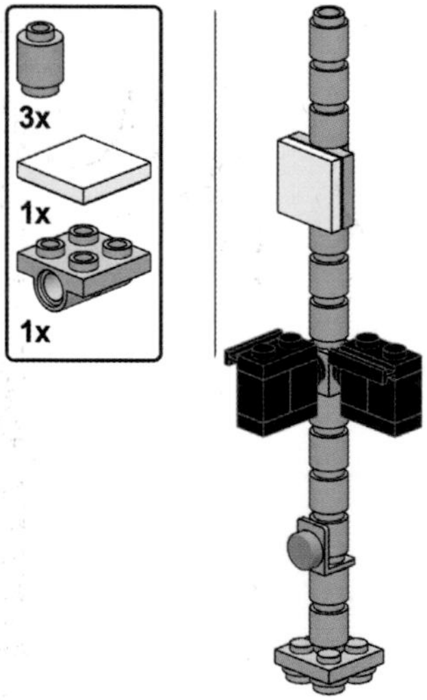
3x
1x
1x

5

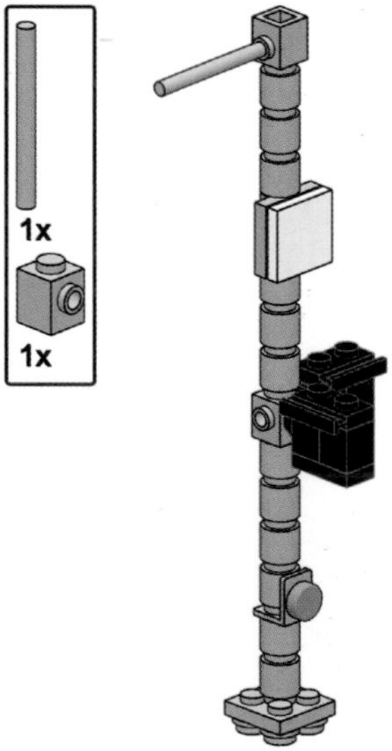
1x
1x

6

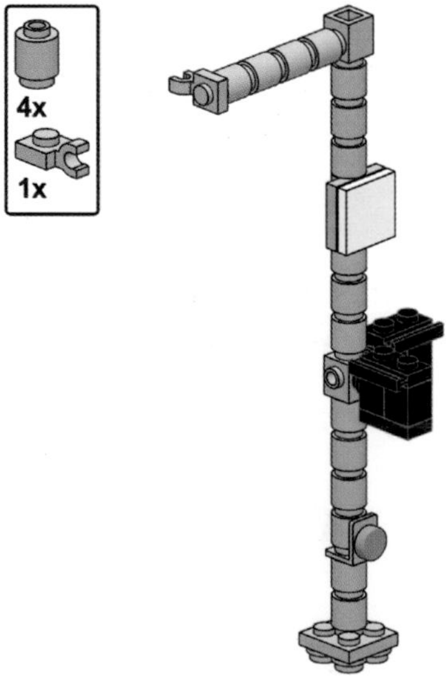
4x
1x

7

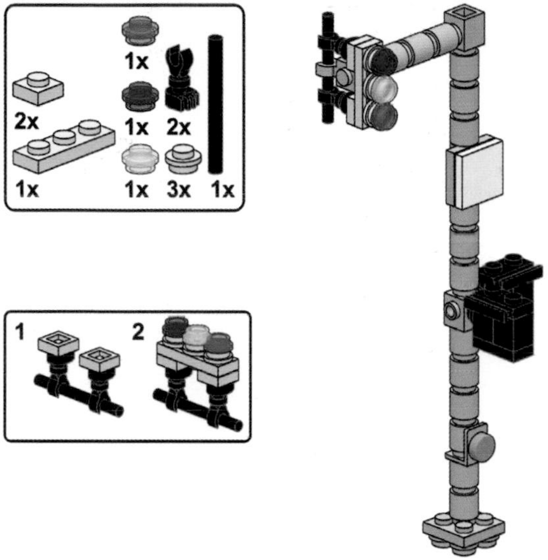
1x
2x
1x 2x
1x 1x 3x 1x
1
2

8

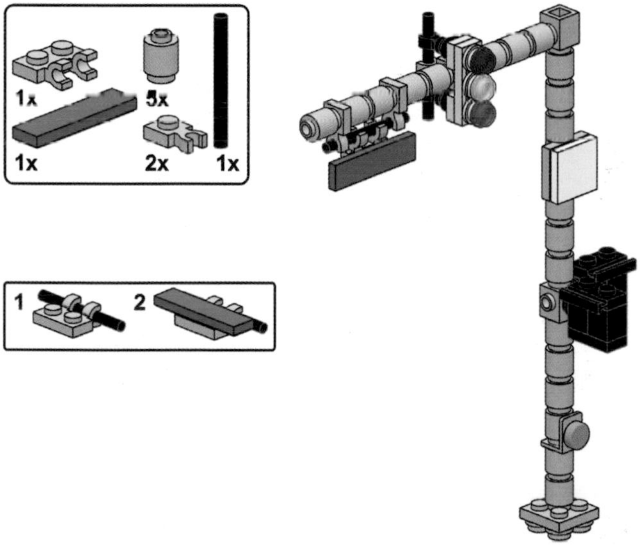
1x 5x
1x 2x 1x
1
2

9

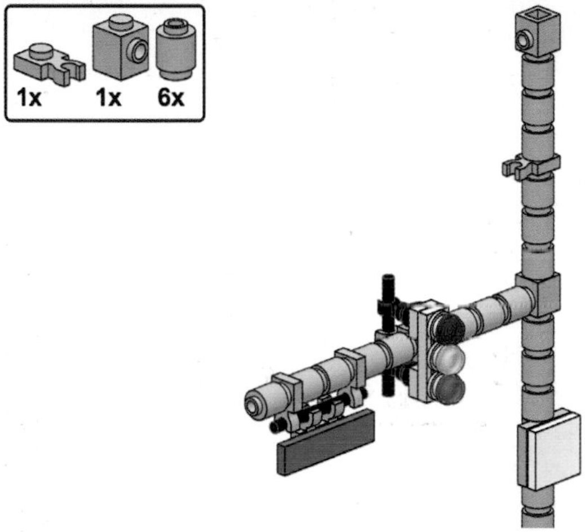
1x 1x 6x

10

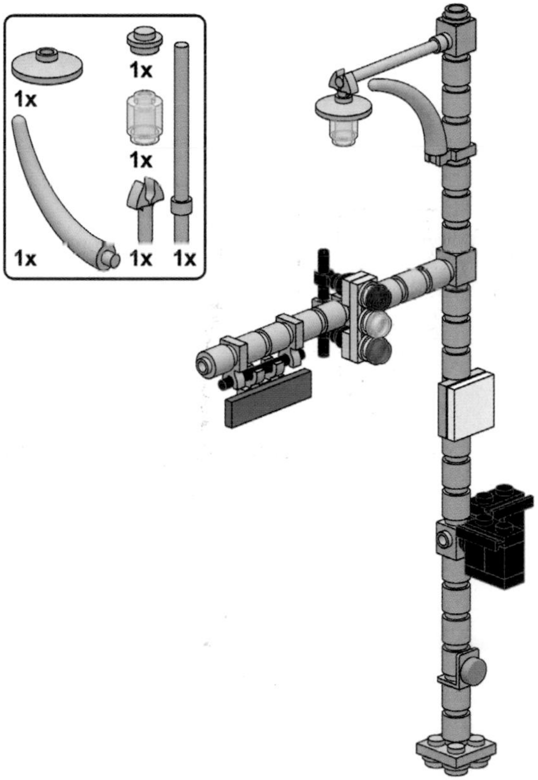
1x
1x
1x
1x 1x 1x

Street Light

1

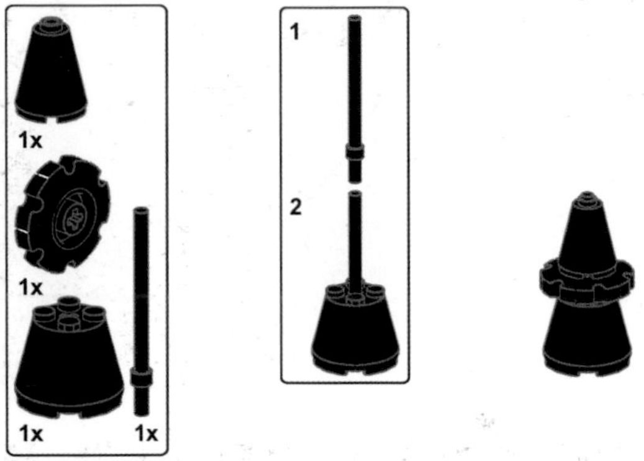
1x
1x
1x
1x
1
2

2

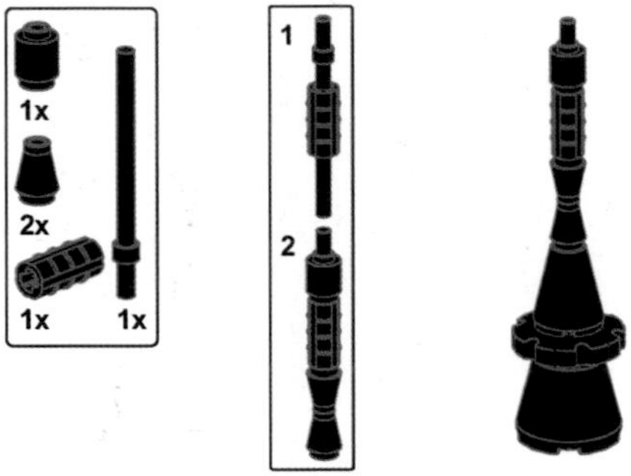
1x
2x
1x
1x
1
2

3

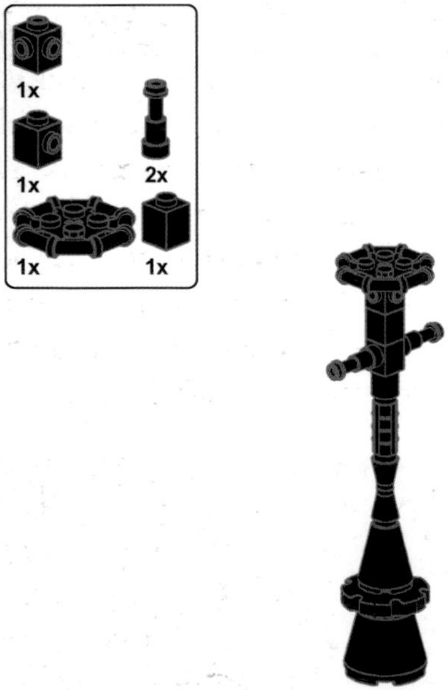
1x
1x
2x
1x
1x

4

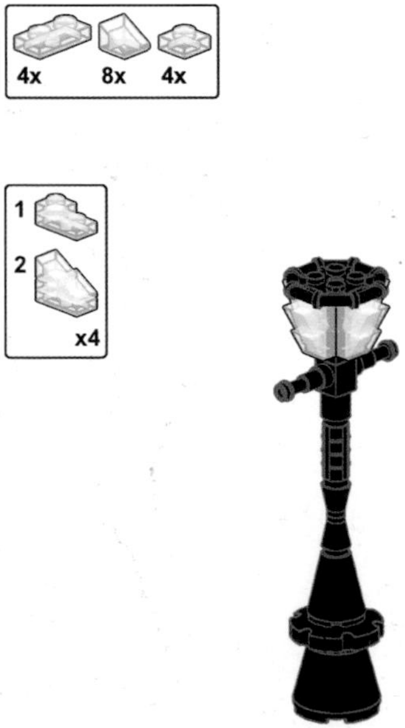
4x
8x
4x
1
2
x4

5

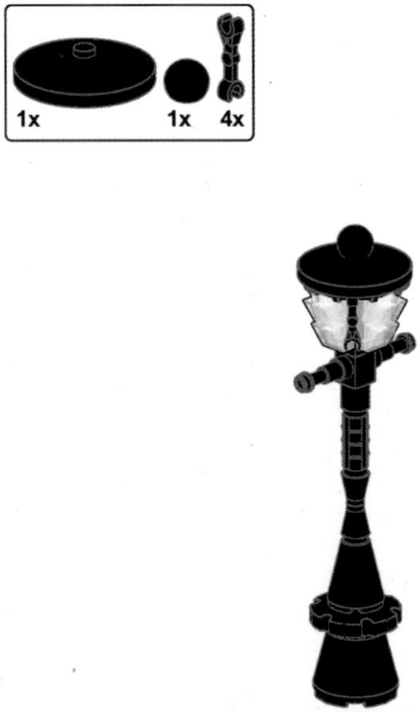
1x
1x
4x

5

The Interior

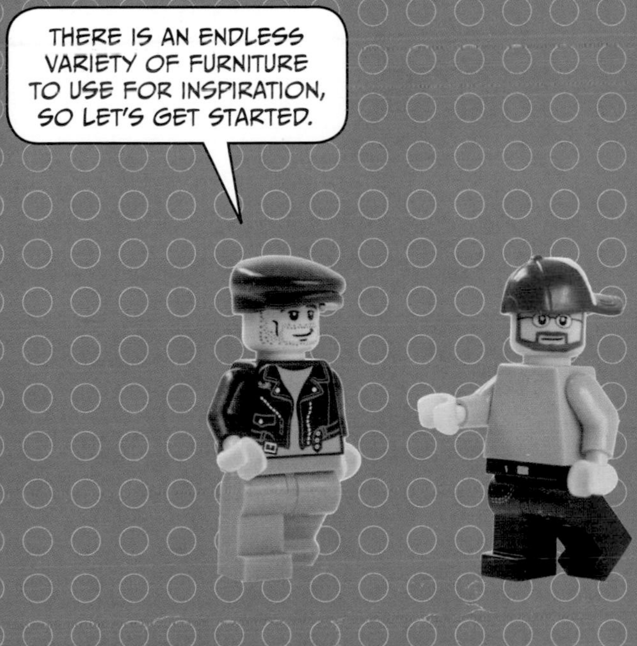
THERE IS AN ENDLESS VARIETY OF FURNITURE TO USE FOR INSPIRATION, SO LET'S GET STARTED.

Furnishing the inside of your building can really help complete the overall look of your creation. In this chapter, we will go through each room of a house and show some furniture examples to help you get started. We hope these designs will inspire you to tinker and create your own versions for your building.

Living Room

Let's start with the living room. Try copying the furniture in your own house as a jumping-off point.

The console table shown here features some nice fringed table lamps for a retro look.

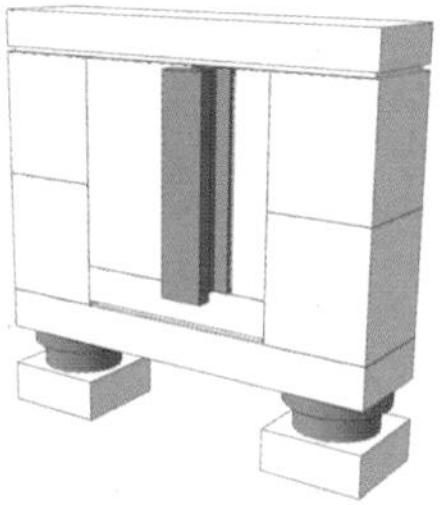

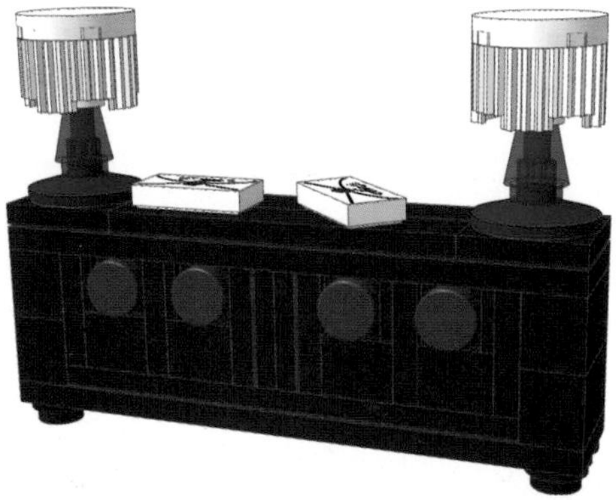

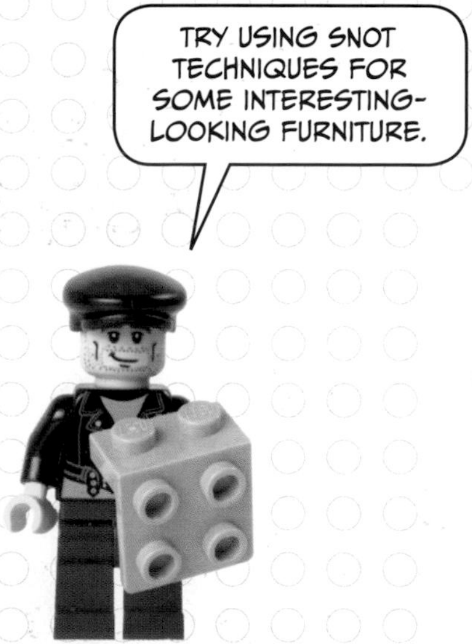
TRY USING SNOT TECHNIQUES FOR SOME INTERESTING-LOOKING FURNITURE.

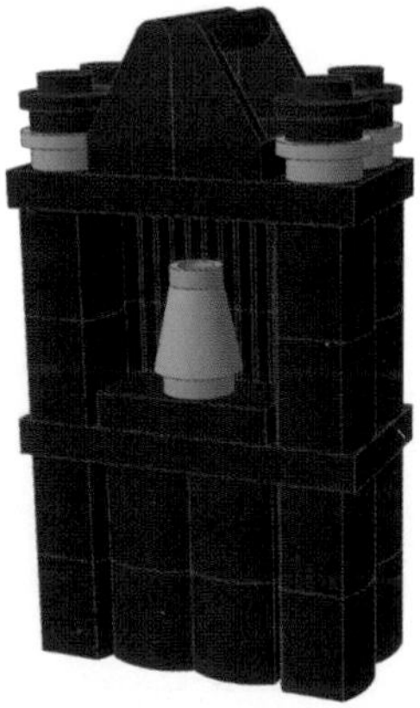

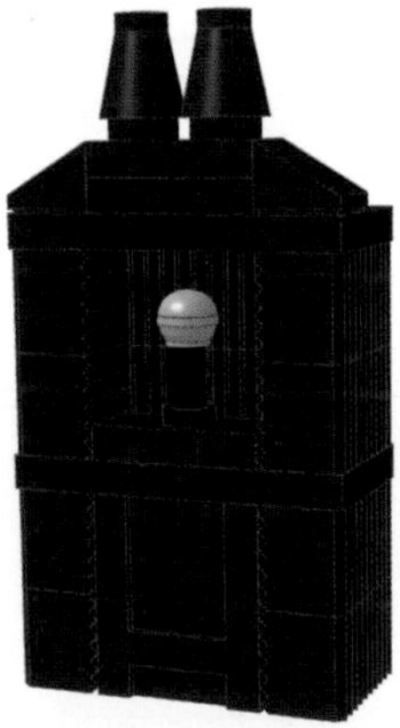

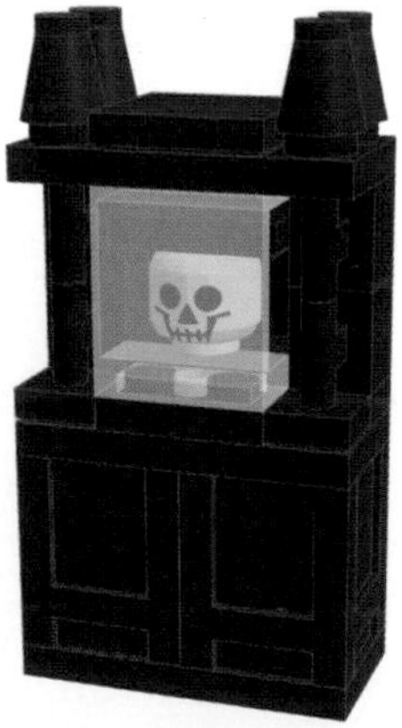

Console Table

1

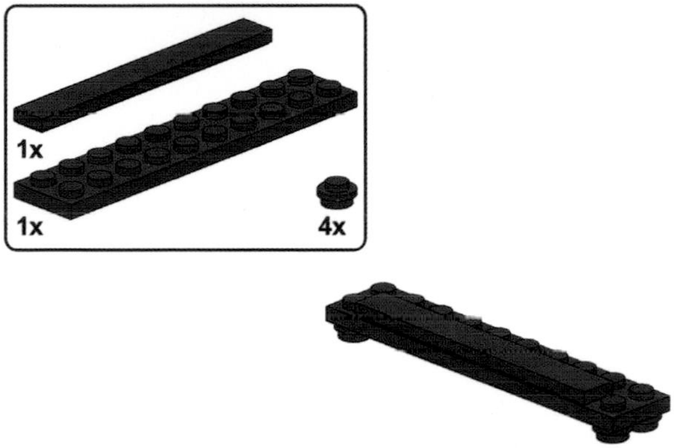
1x
1x
4x

2

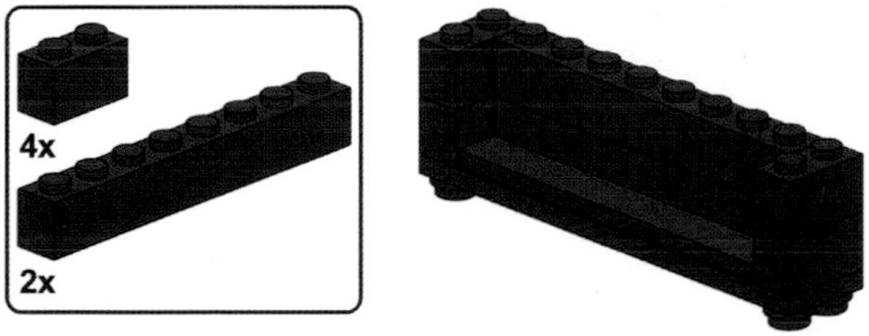
4x
2x

3

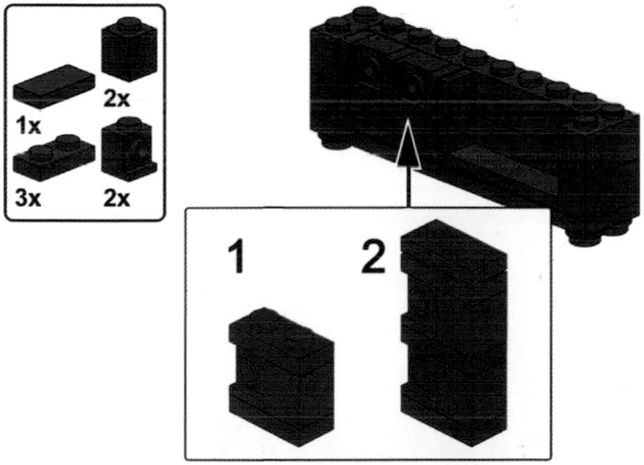
2x
1x
3x
2x
1
2

4

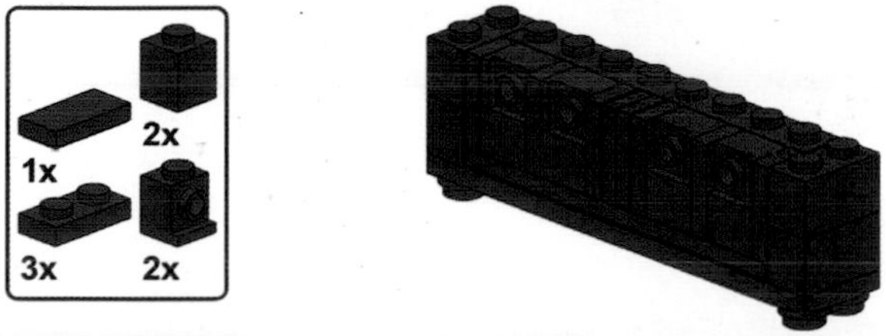
2x
1x
3x
2x

5

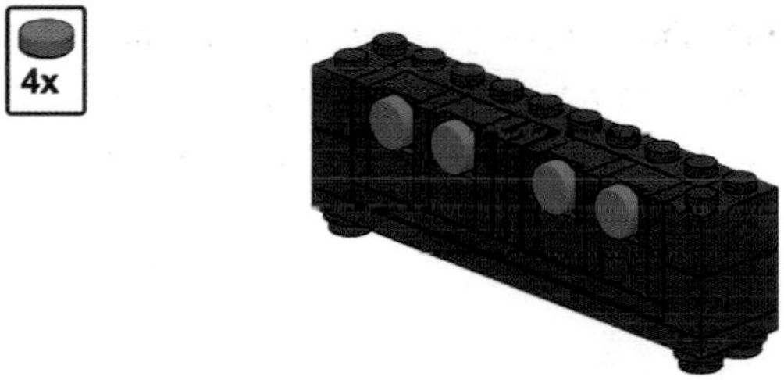
4x

6

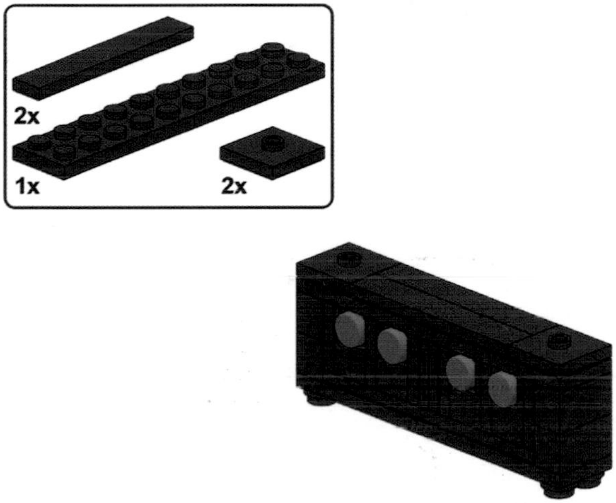
2x
1x
2x

7

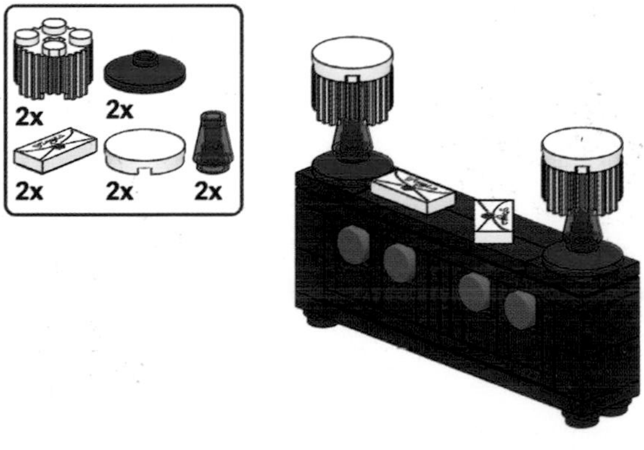
2x
2x
2x
2x
2x

Shelving

Stand-alone shelves or shelves attached to the wall can hold personal items and accessories to give a house character.

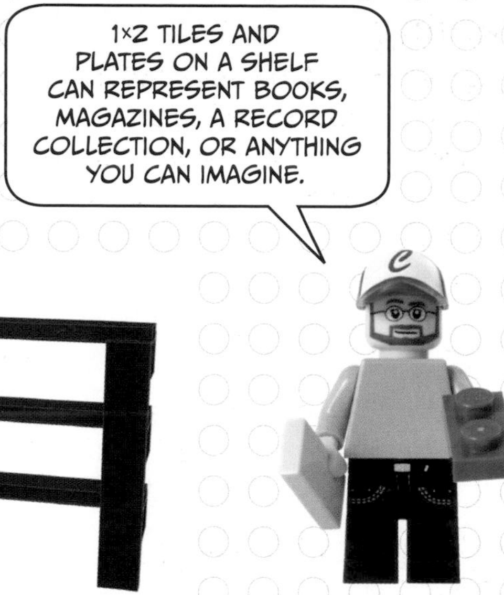
1×2 TILES AND PLATES ON A SHELF CAN REPRESENT BOOKS, MAGAZINES, A RECORD COLLECTION, OR ANYTHING YOU CAN IMAGINE.

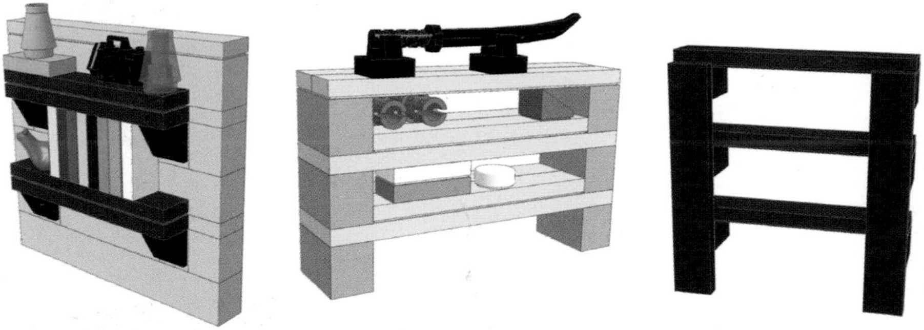

TVs

Your minifigs need entertainment, right? Give them a TV appropriate to the time period of your city.

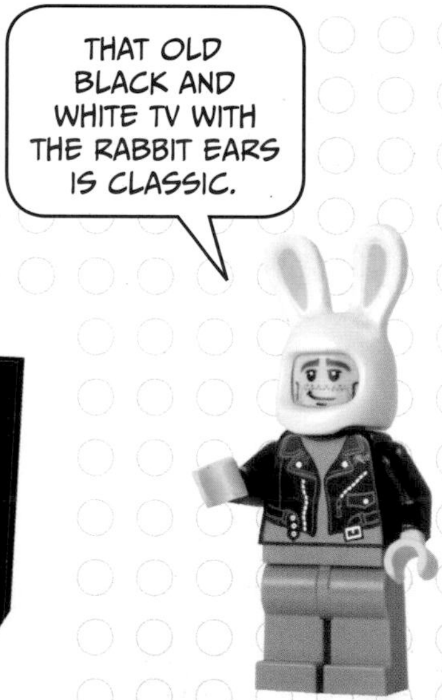
THAT OLD BLACK AND WHITE TV WITH THE RABBIT EARS IS CLASSIC.

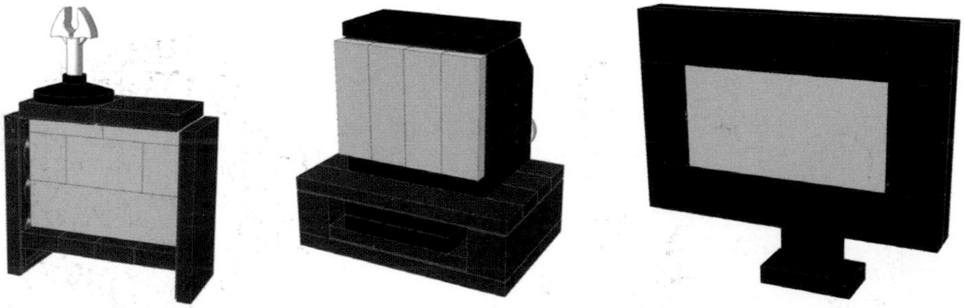

Seating

Using the same color for sofas and chairs creates the look of a matching set.

There are so many ways to make chairs that each house could have something unique.

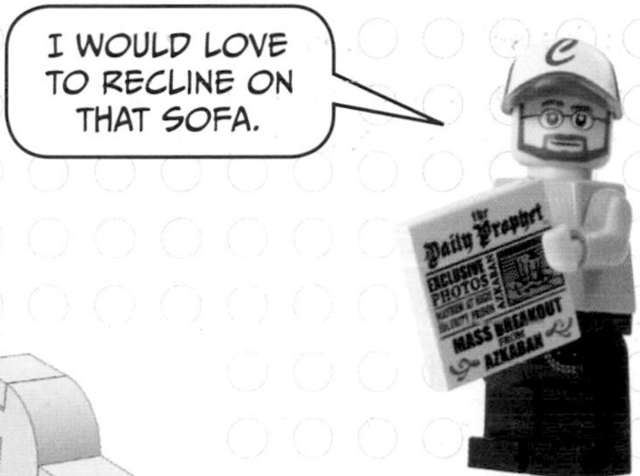

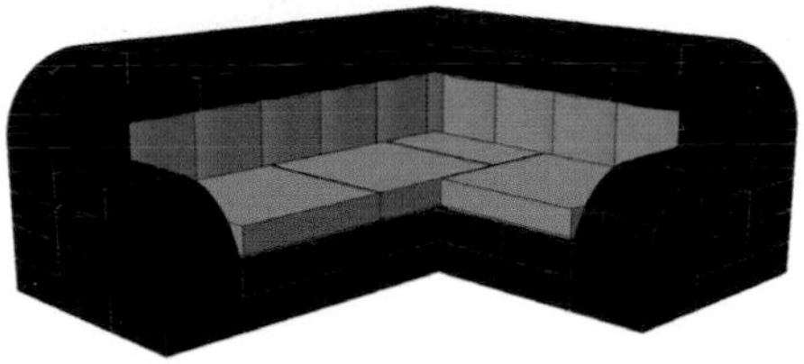

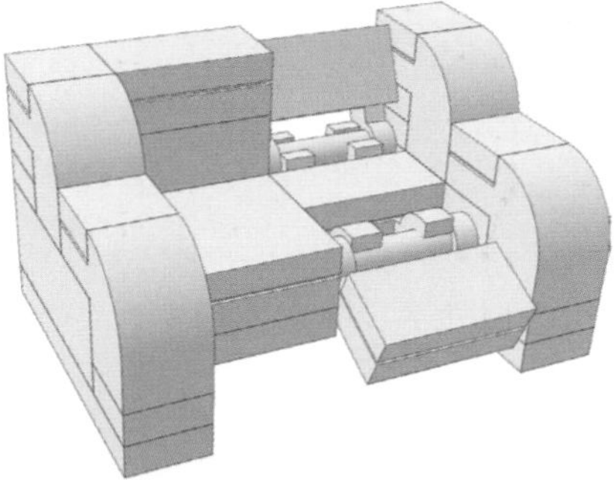

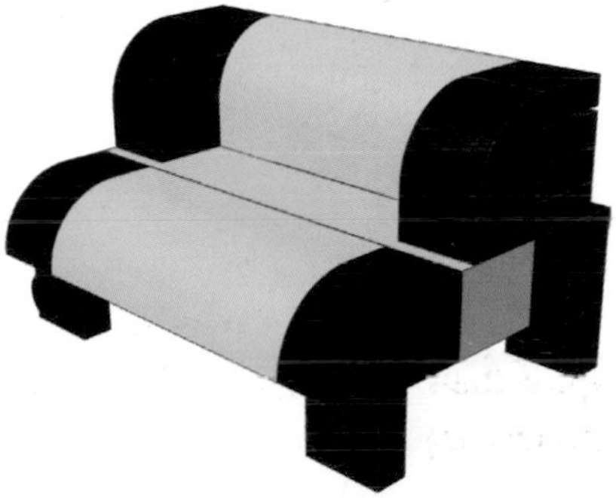

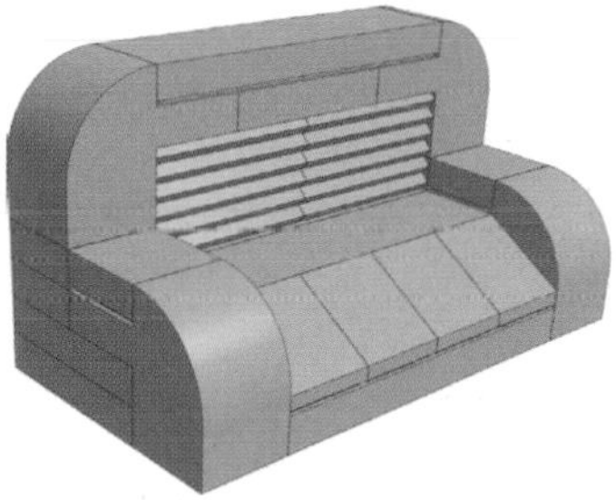

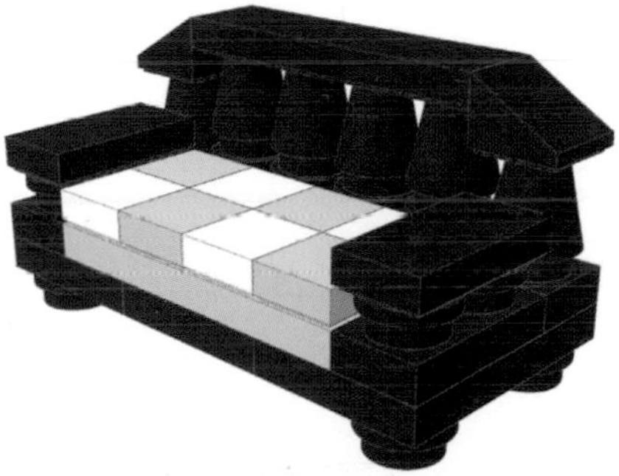

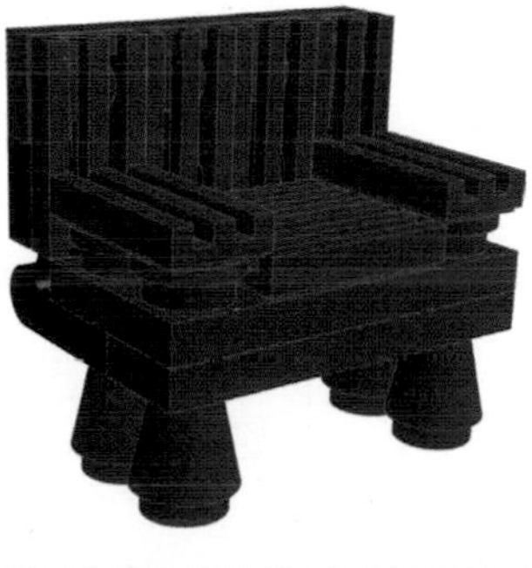

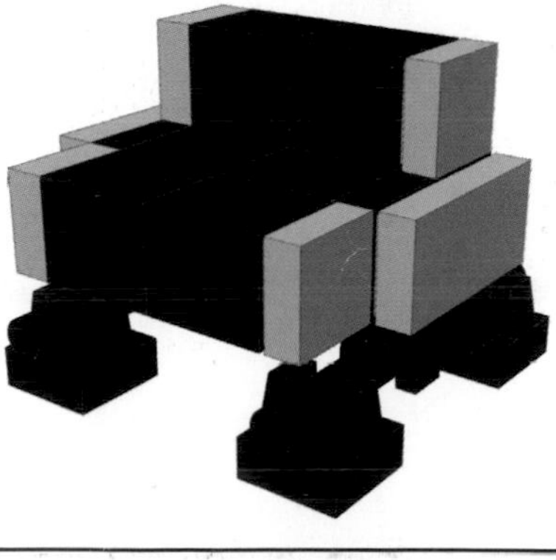

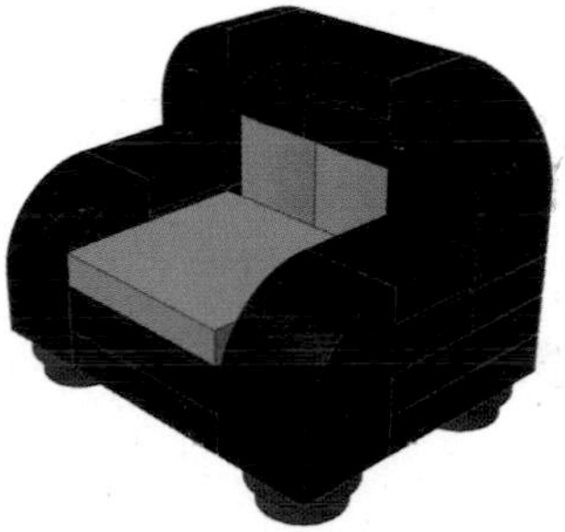

Recliner

1
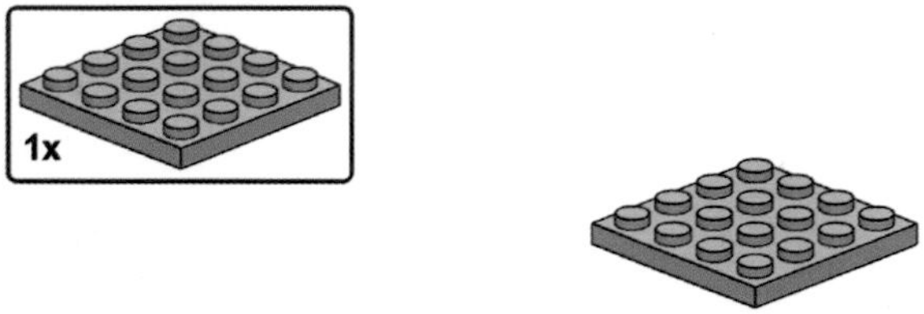
1x

2
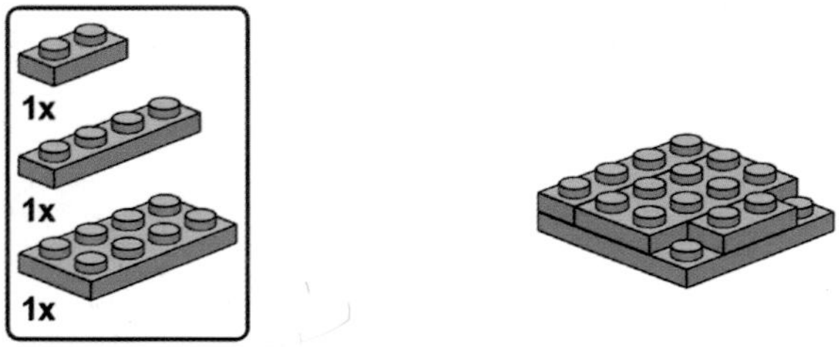
1x
1x
1x

3
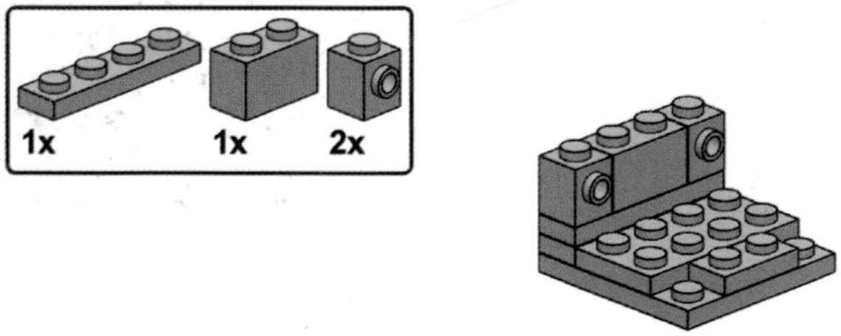
1x
1x
2x

4
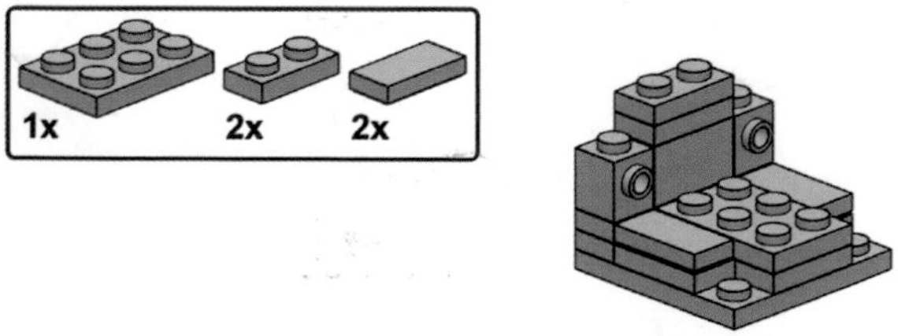
1x
2x
2x

5
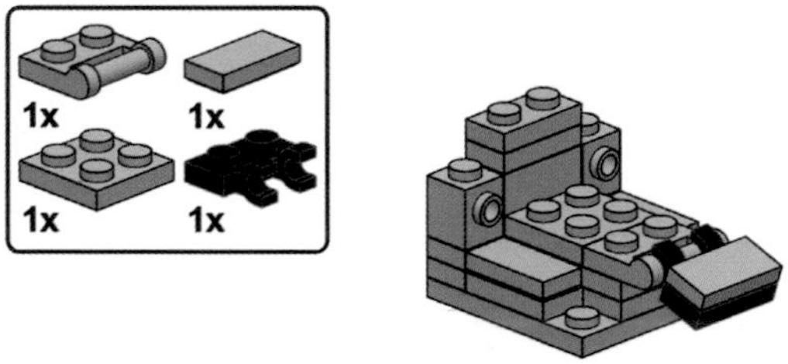
1x
1x
1x
1x

6
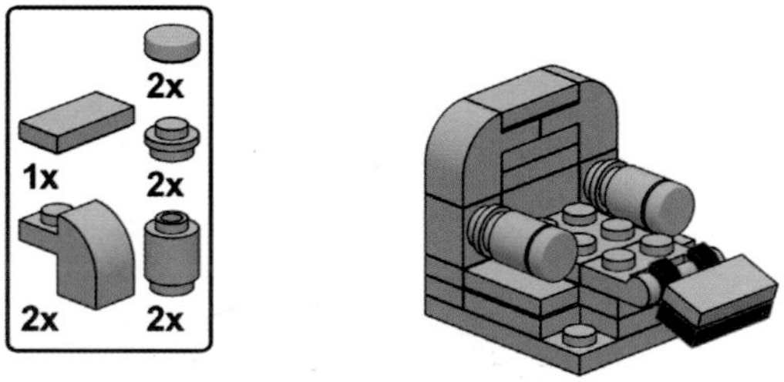
2x
1x
2x
2x
2x

7
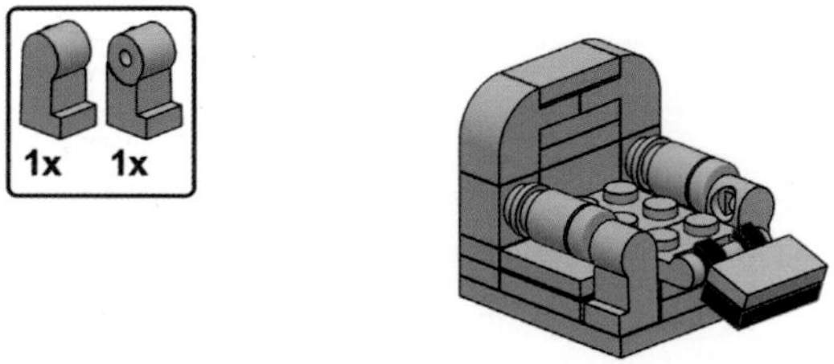
1x
1x

Lighting

There are countless ways to add lights to the living space. You could create table and floor lamps as well as sconces or ceiling lights.

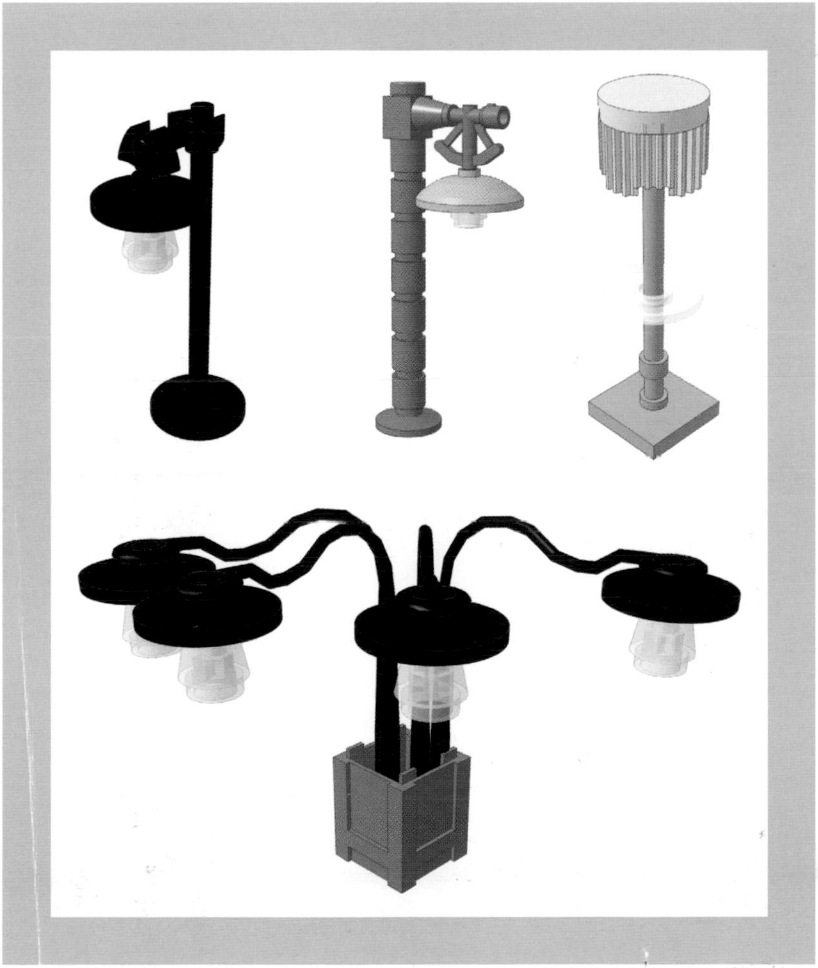

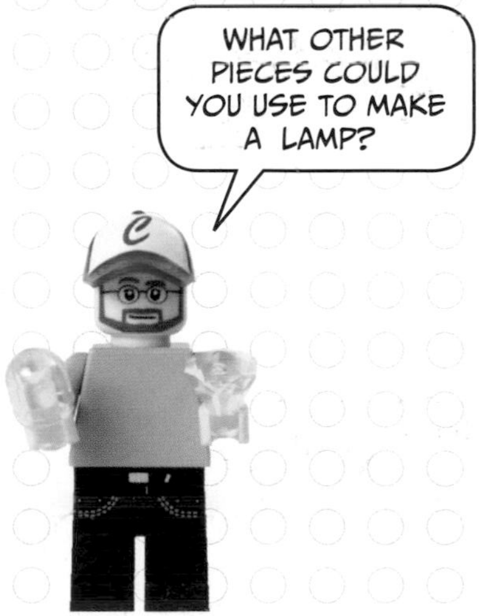
WHAT OTHER PIECES COULD YOU USE TO MAKE A LAMP?

Plants

Including some plants inside the house can make your interiors more colorful.

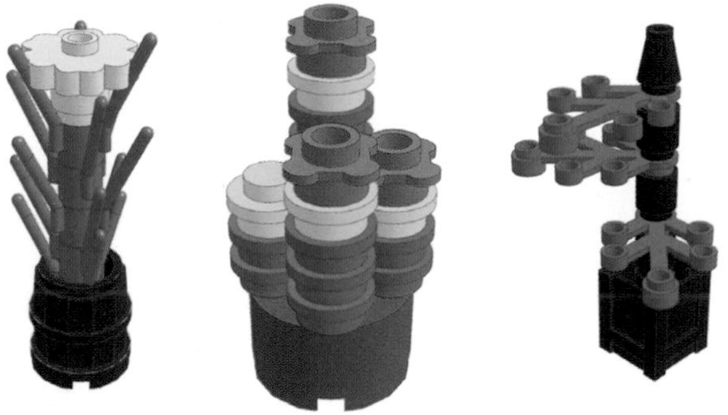

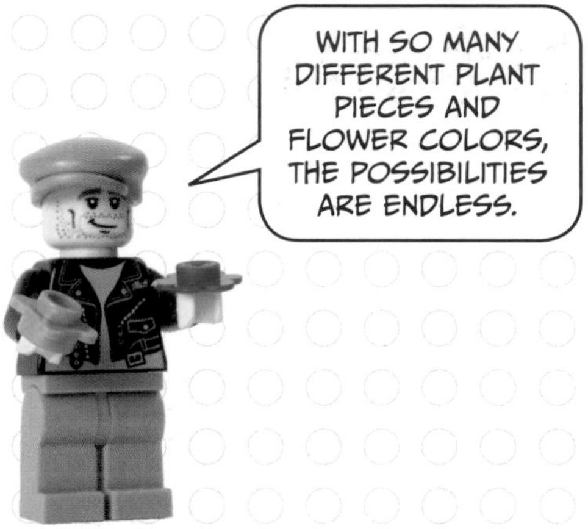
WITH SO MANY DIFFERENT PLANT PIECES AND FLOWER COLORS, THE POSSIBILITIES ARE ENDLESS.

Art

Artwork can really help bring some life into your room.

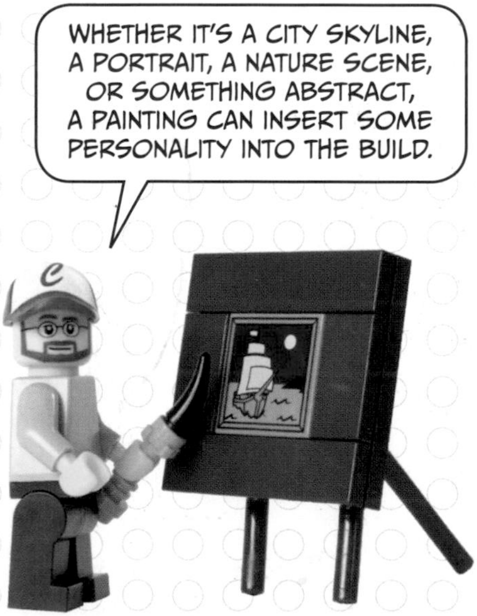
WHETHER IT'S A CITY SKYLINE, A PORTRAIT, A NATURE SCENE, OR SOMETHING ABSTRACT, A PAINTING CAN INSERT SOME PERSONALITY INTO THE BUILD.

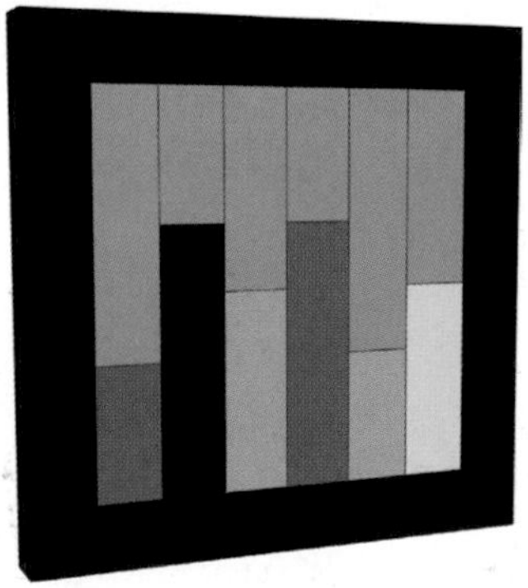

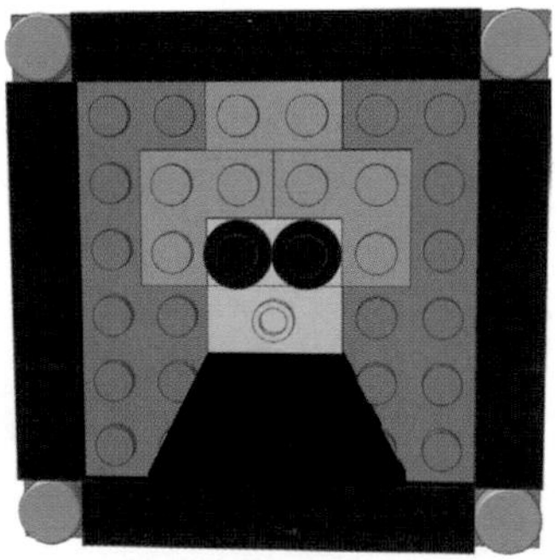

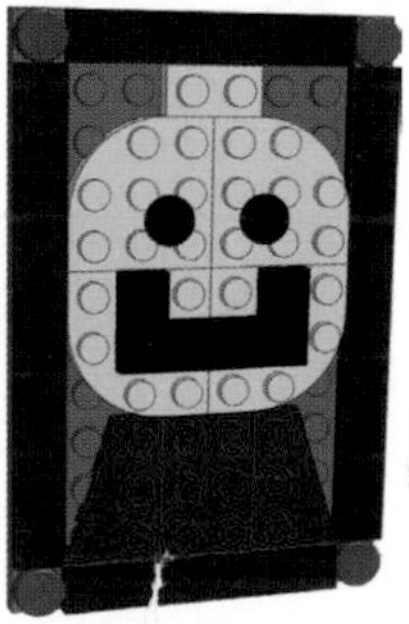

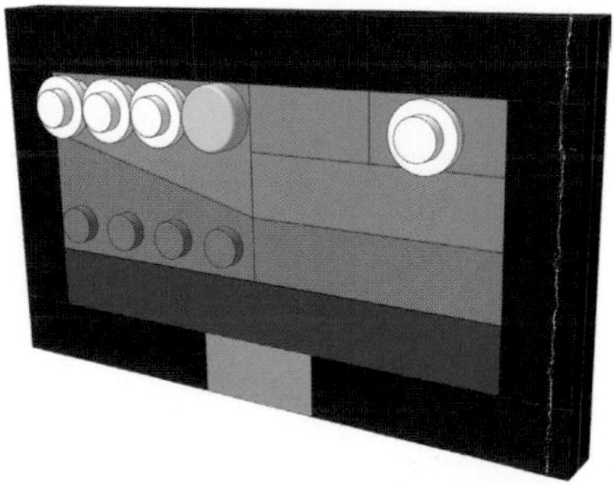

Kitchen

Let's step into the kitchen and see what's cooking.

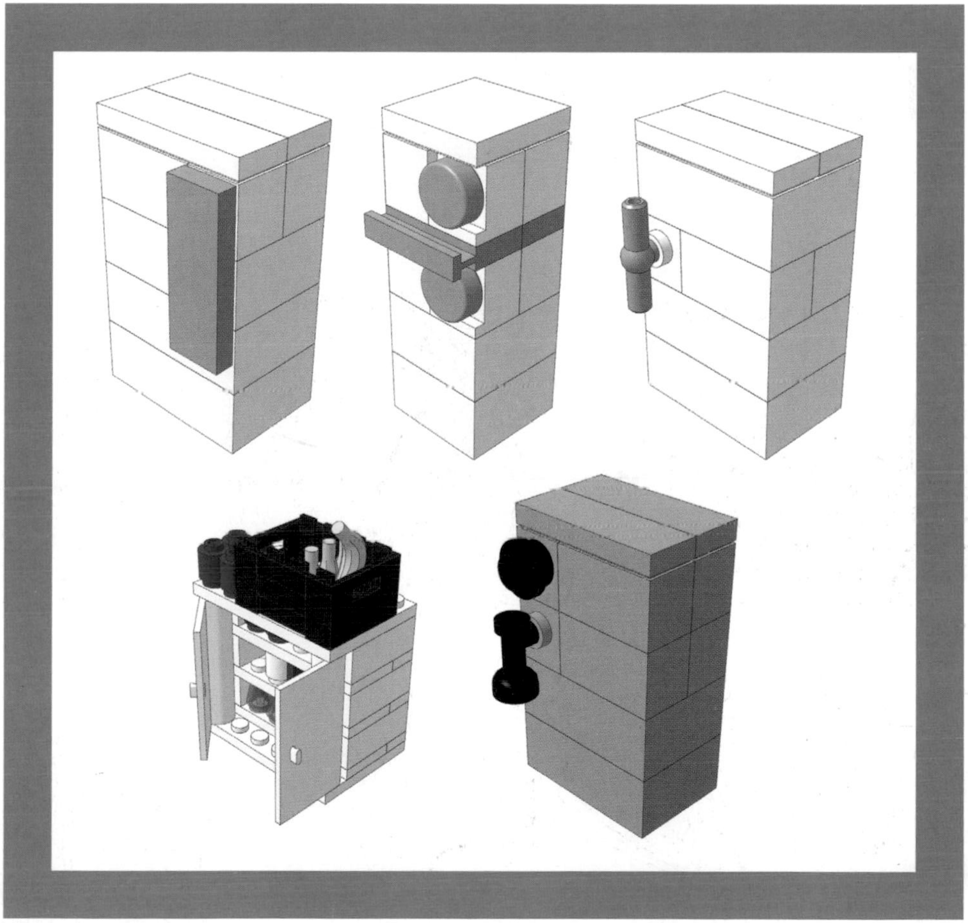

Appliances

These ovens vary only slightly in style, but you can customize the stove by making one of the burners red-hot or putting a pan on top.

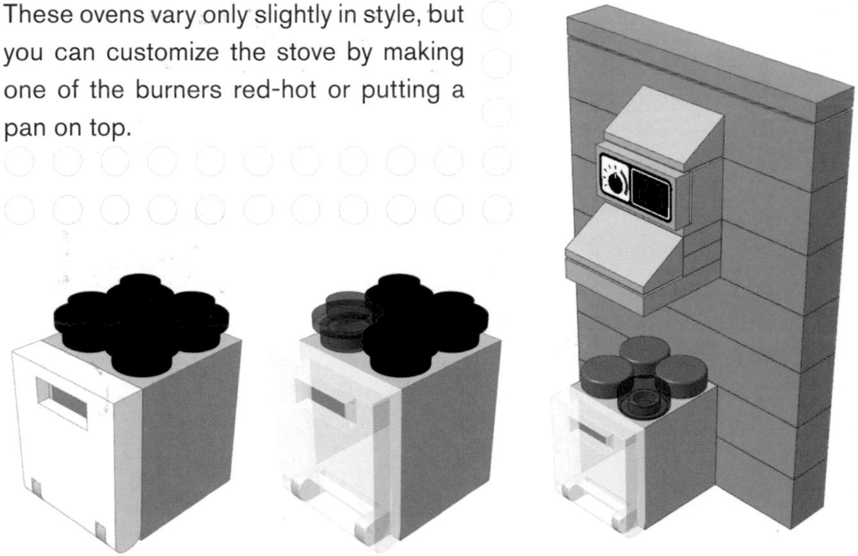

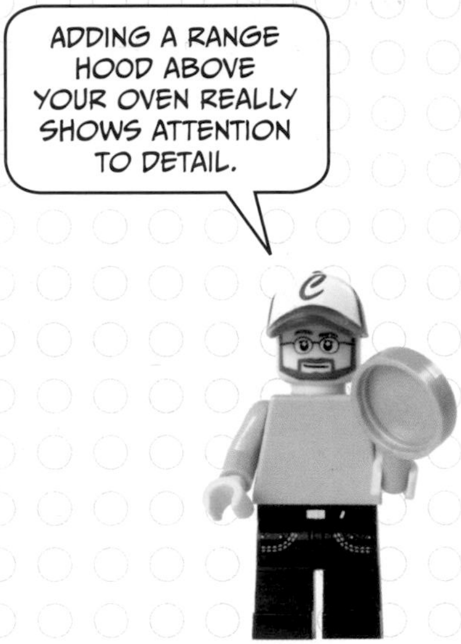
ADDING A RANGE HOOD ABOVE YOUR OVEN REALLY SHOWS ATTENTION TO DETAIL.

Try creating some items similar to these for your kitchen. A dishwasher, coffeemaker, microwave, island, and toaster are just some of the items that make up the overall look of the kitchen.

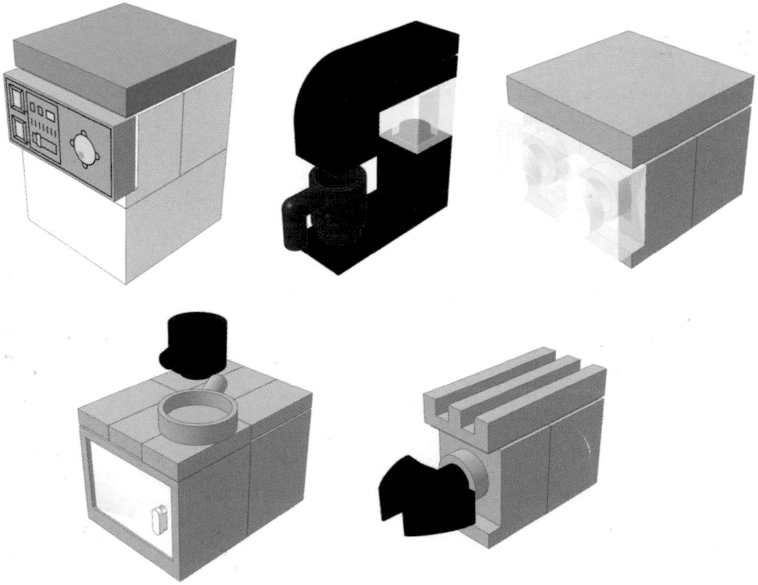

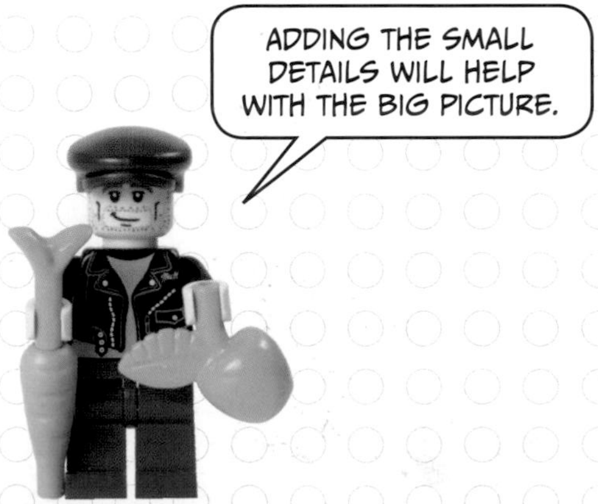
ADDING THE SMALL DETAILS WILL HELP WITH THE BIG PICTURE.

Cabinets

Cabinets can be set into the wall to conserve space, or they can hang directly on it.

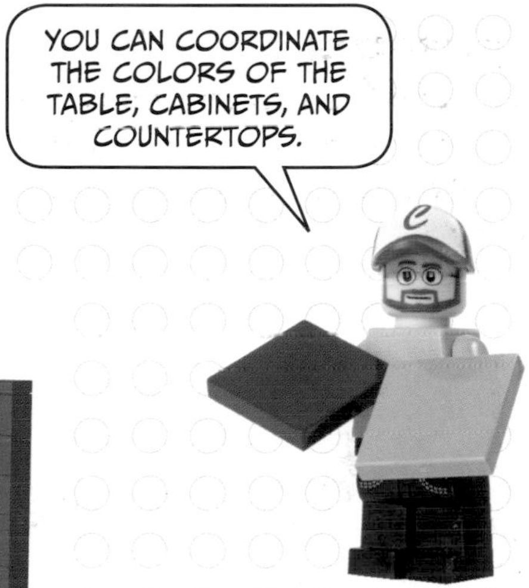
YOU CAN COORDINATE THE COLORS OF THE TABLE, CABINETS, AND COUNTERTOPS.

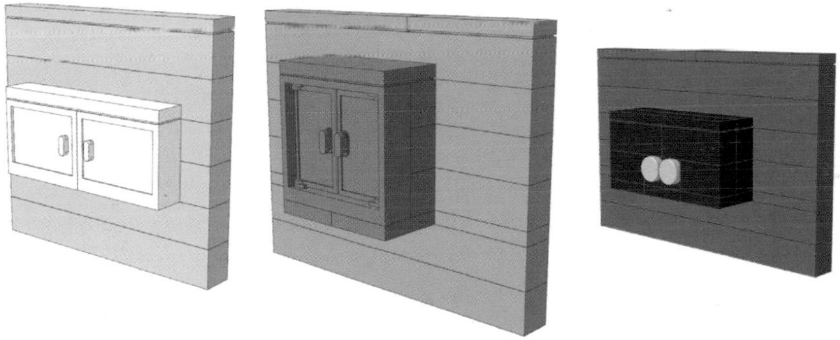

Sinks

Sinks come in different colors, sometimes to match the appliances.

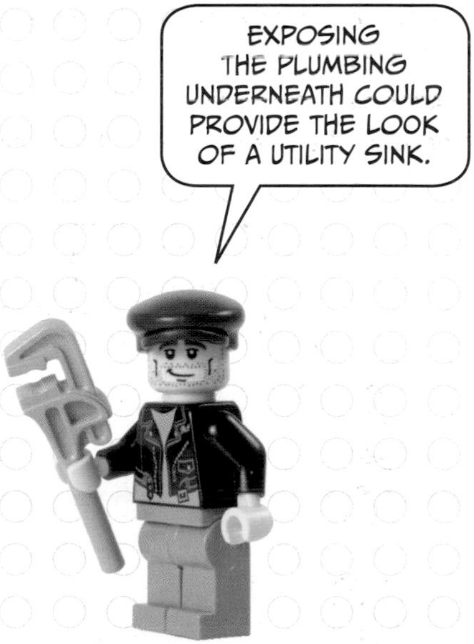
EXPOSING THE PLUMBING UNDERNEATH COULD PROVIDE THE LOOK OF A UTILITY SINK.

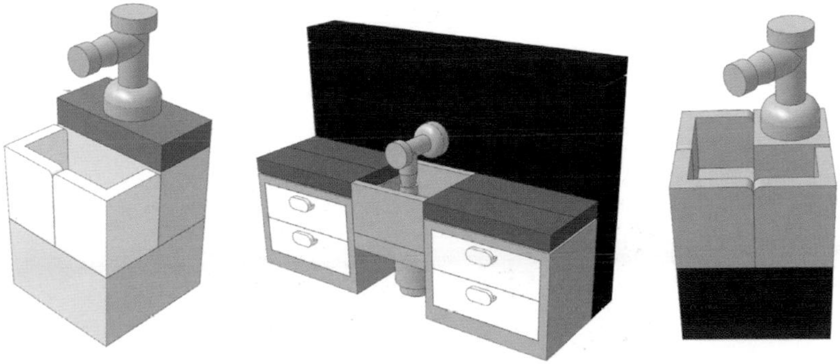

Dining Room

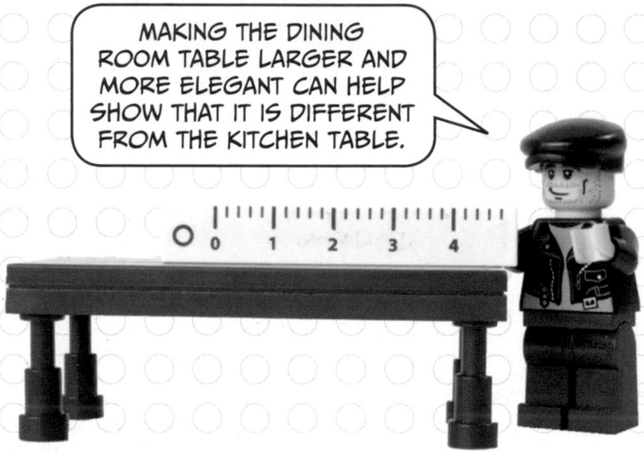
MAKING THE DINING ROOM TABLE LARGER AND MORE ELEGANT CAN HELP SHOW THAT IT IS DIFFERENT FROM THE KITCHEN TABLE.

Let's take a quick look in the dining room to see some fancier tables and chairs.

Try making a matching table and chairs or maybe some barstools for a counter.

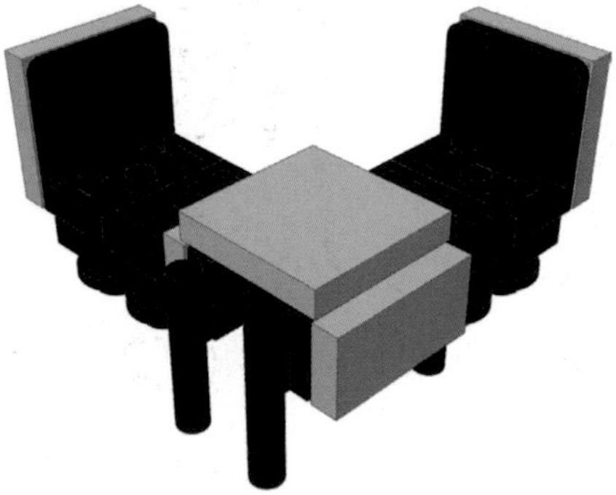

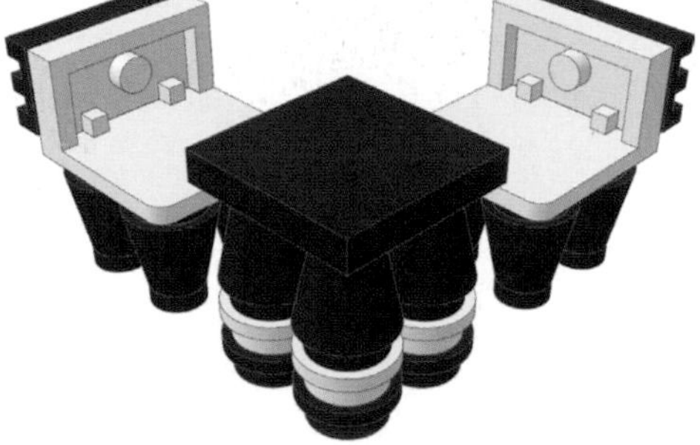

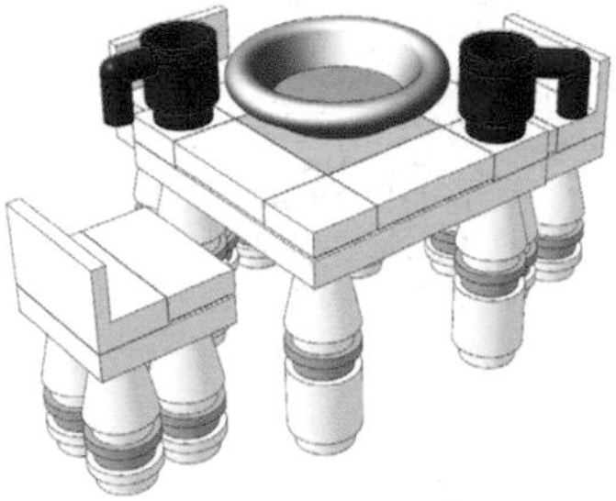

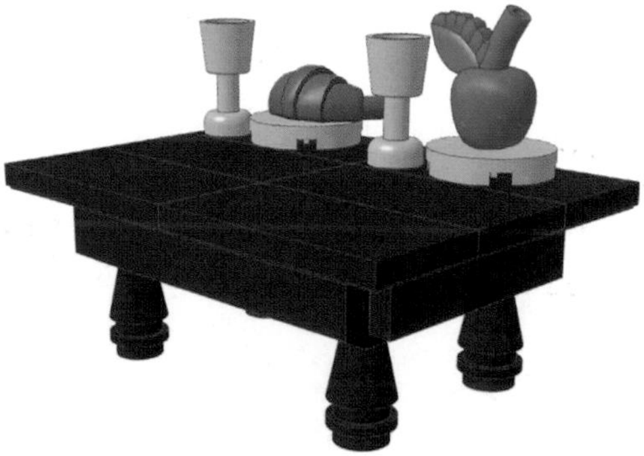

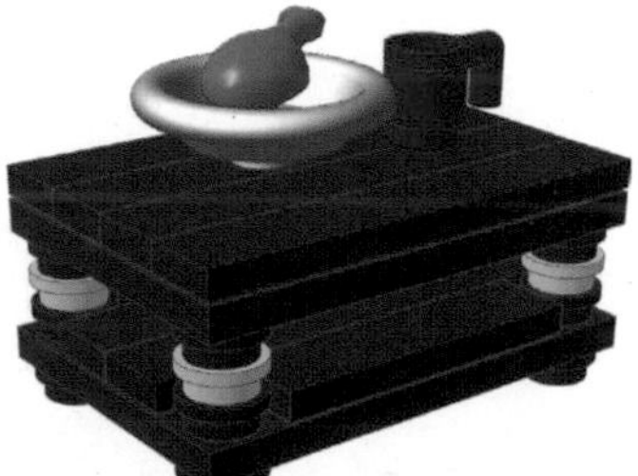

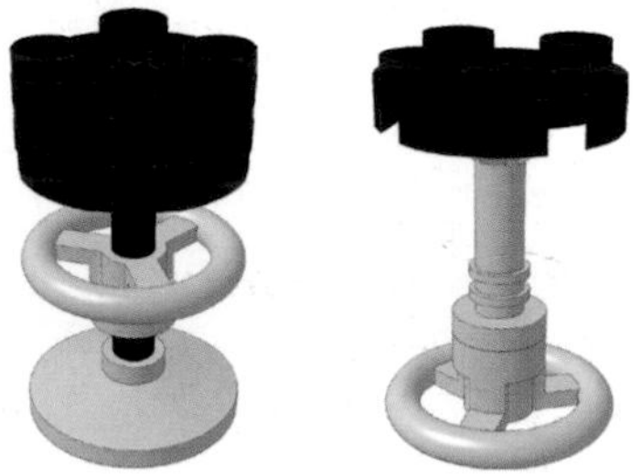

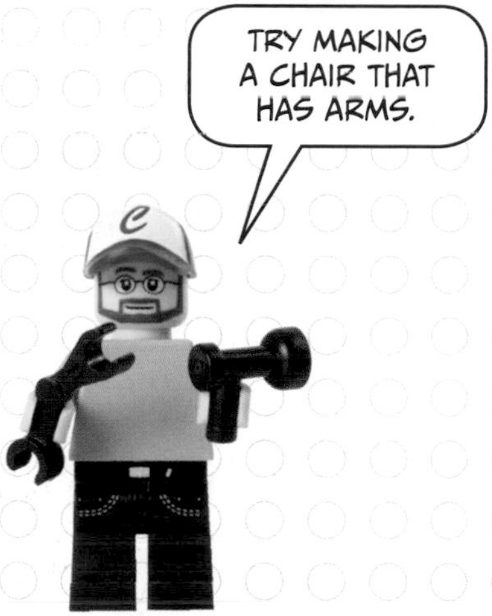
TRY MAKING A CHAIR THAT HAS ARMS.

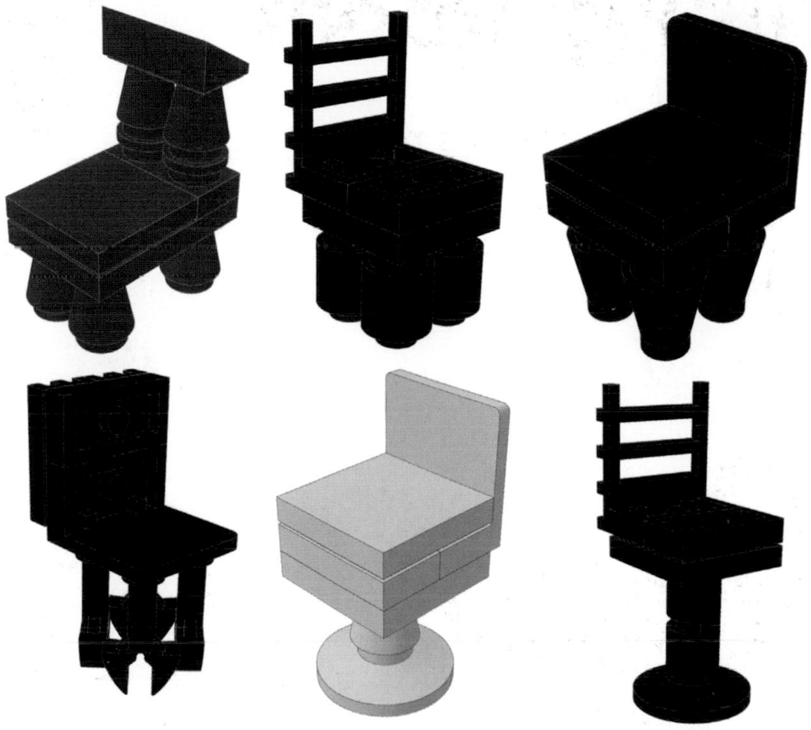

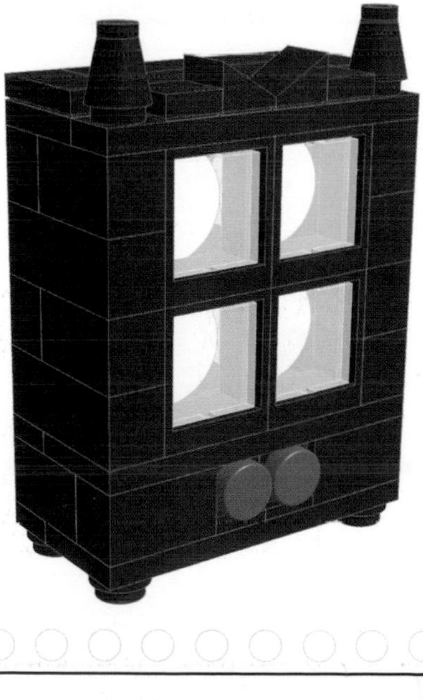

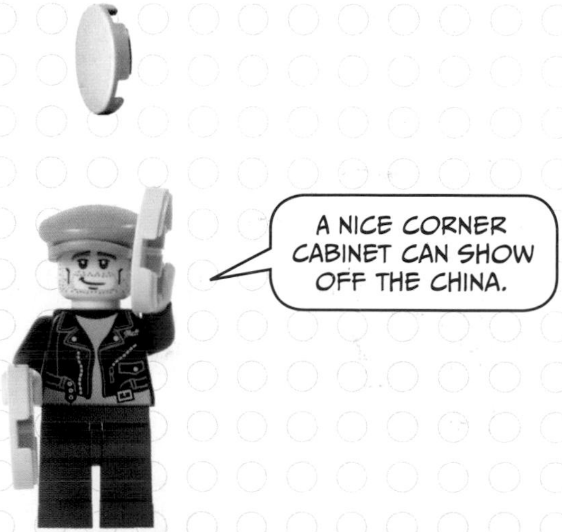
A NICE CORNER CABINET CAN SHOW OFF THE CHINA.

Bedroom

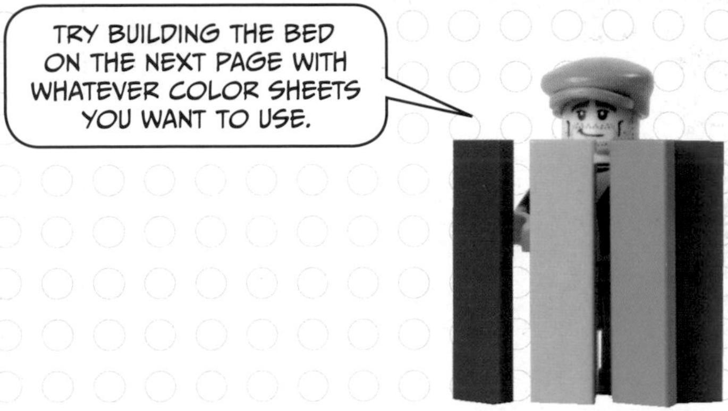
TRY BUILDING THE BED ON THE NEXT PAGE WITH WHATEVER COLOR SHEETS YOU WANT TO USE.

Beds come in all shapes and sizes. Whether it be a canopy, a bunk bed, a twin, a king, or one that has a mattress sliding off the frame, a good bed can be the centerpiece of the room.

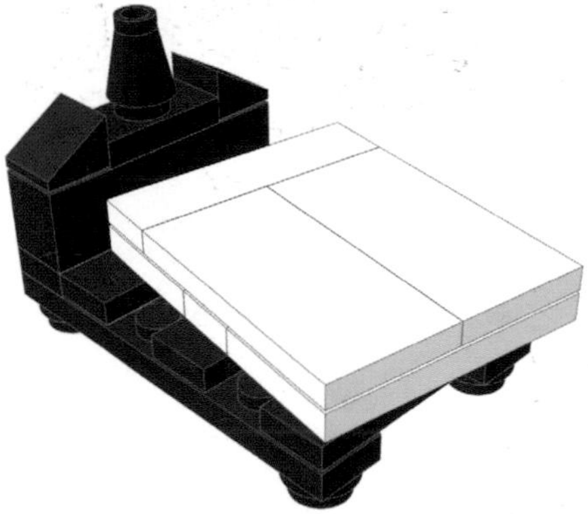
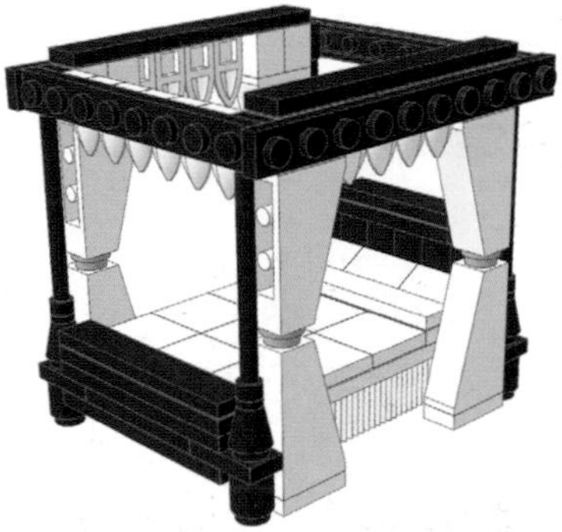
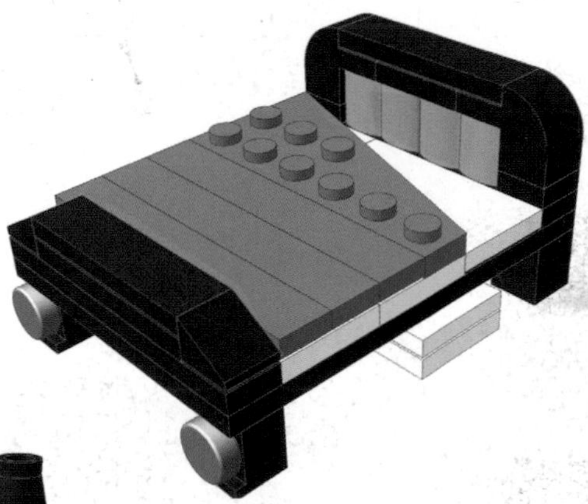
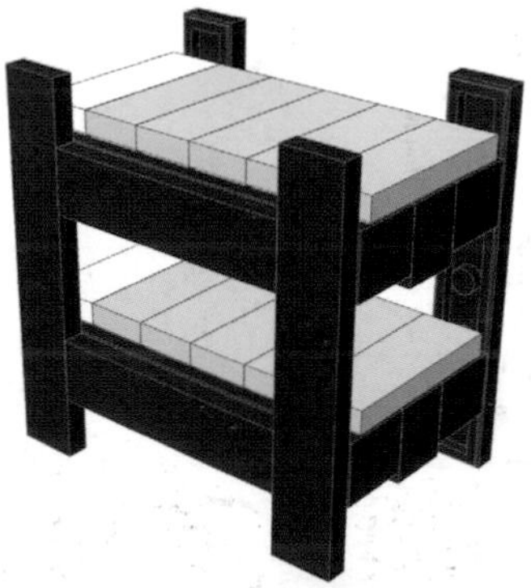
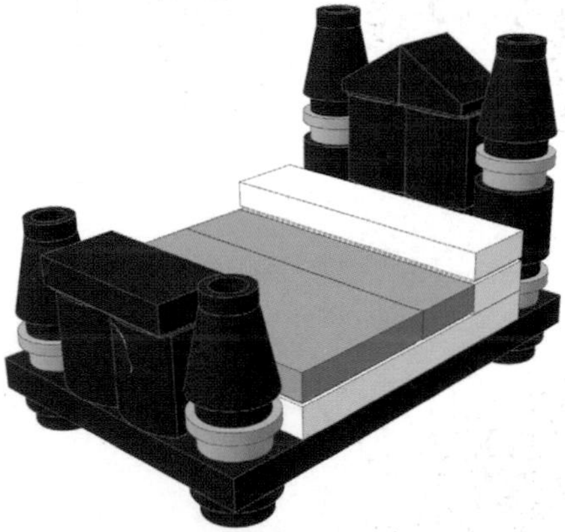
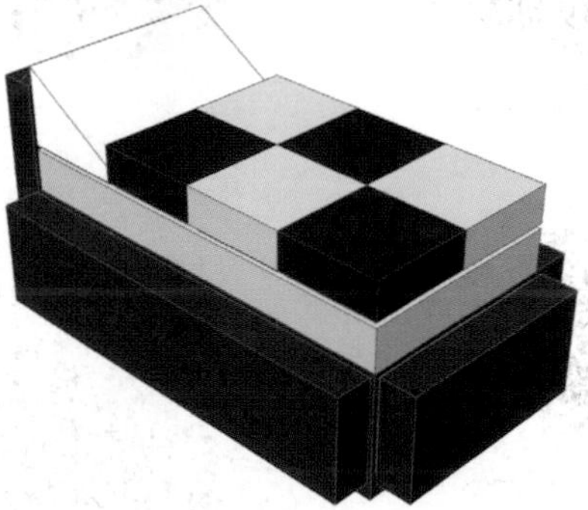

King Bed

1

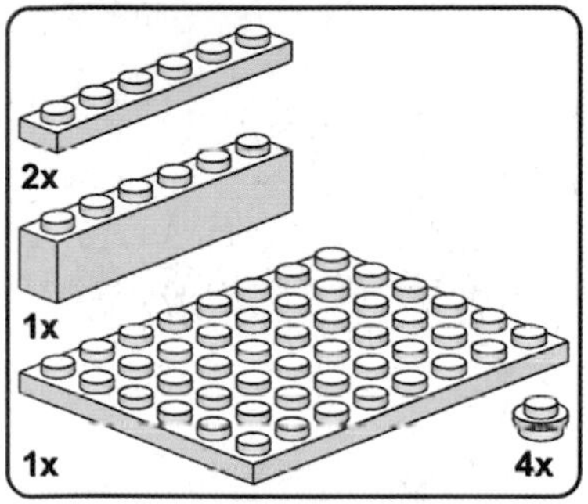
2x
1x
1x
4x

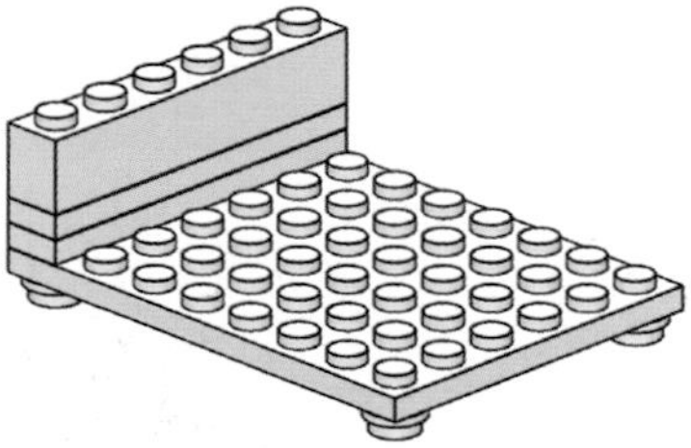

2

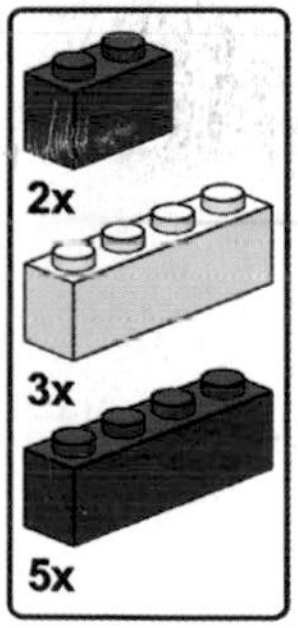
2x
3x
5x

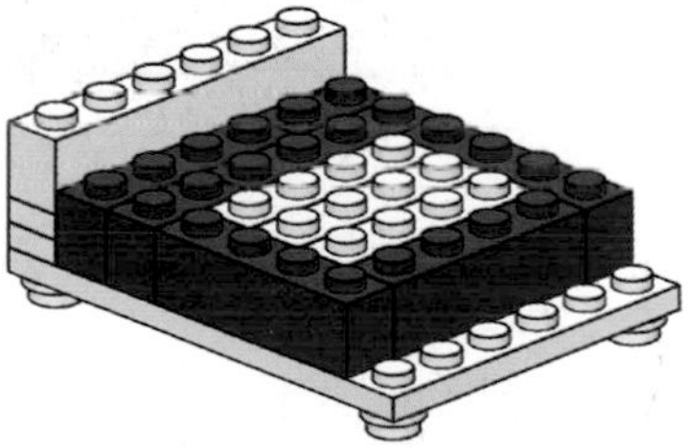

3

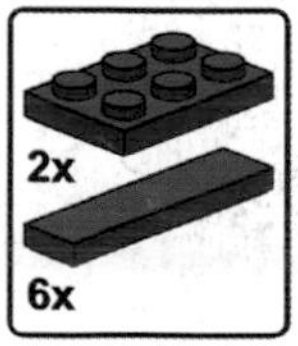
2x
6x

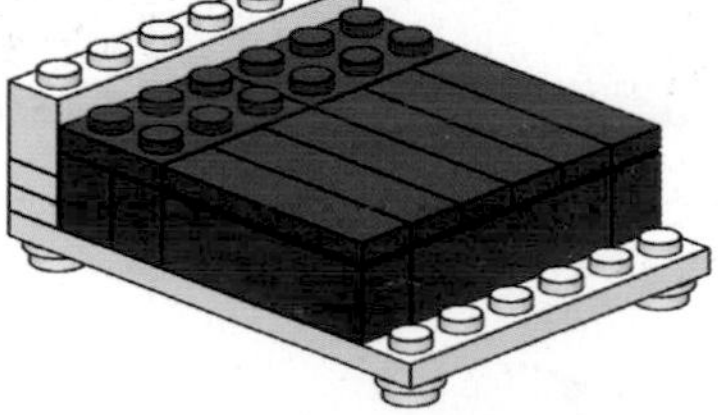

4

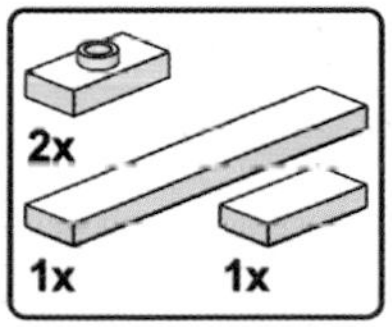
2x
1x
1x

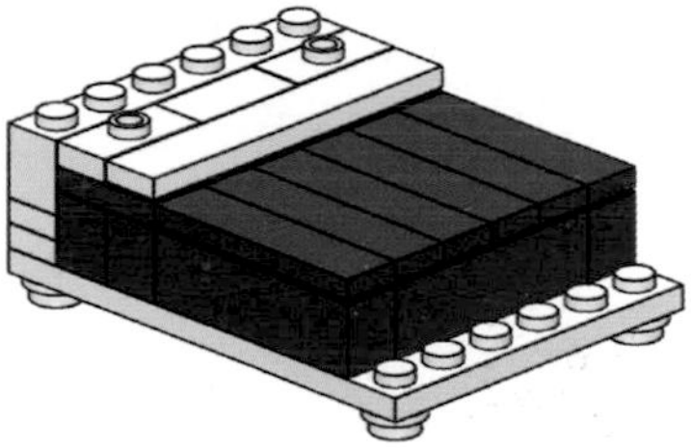

5

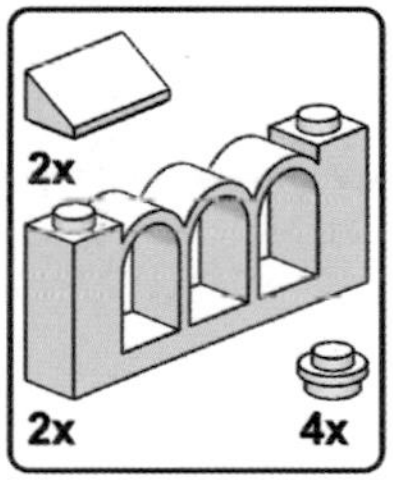
2x
2x
4x

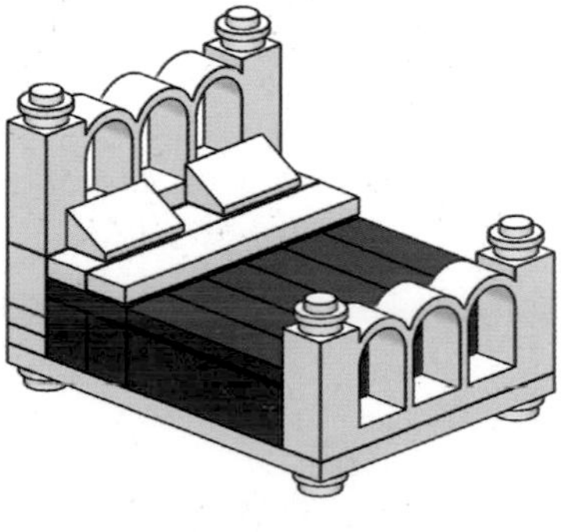

Dresssers and Nightstands

Let's look at a few examples of dressers and nightstands. Nightstands are like bookends for the bed. To add detail, place objects on them such as alarm clocks, lamps, or books.

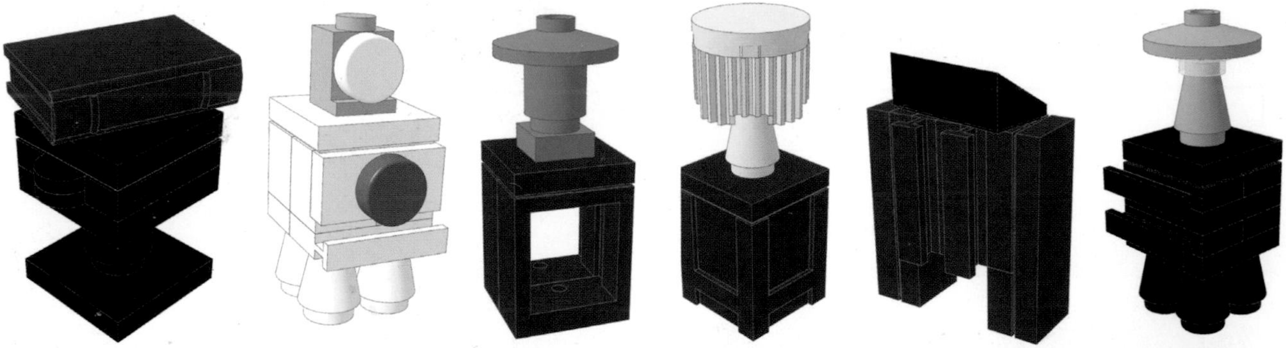

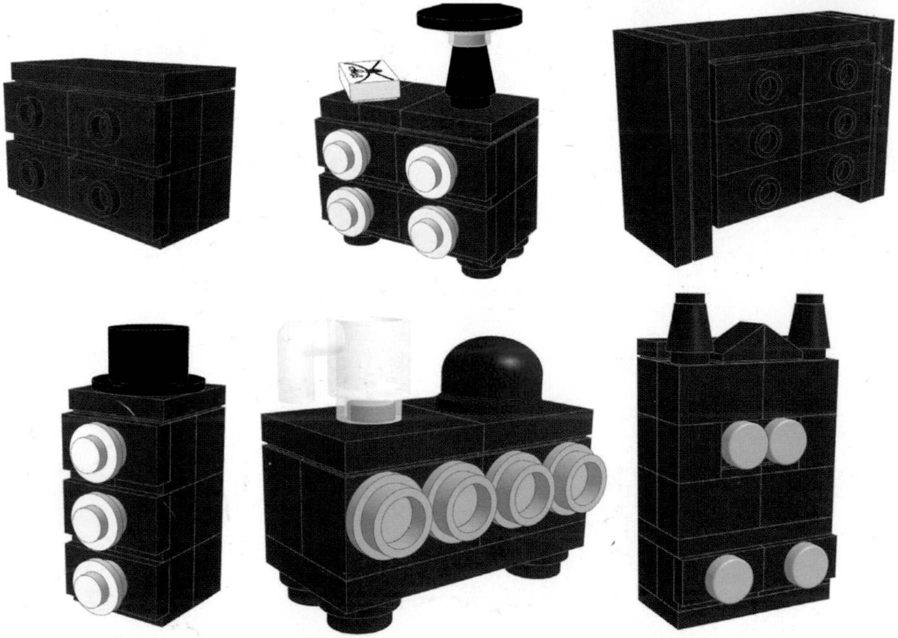

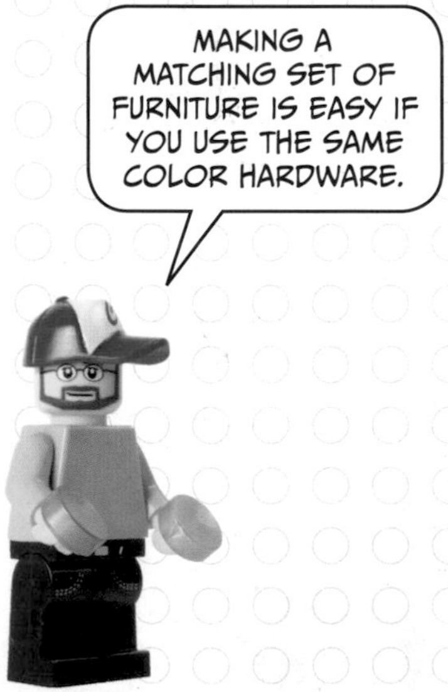
MAKING A MATCHING SET OF FURNITURE IS EASY IF YOU USE THE SAME COLOR HARDWARE.

Kids' Rooms

A child's bedroom typically looks really different from an adult's bedroom and should have furniture and knickknacks to reflect that.

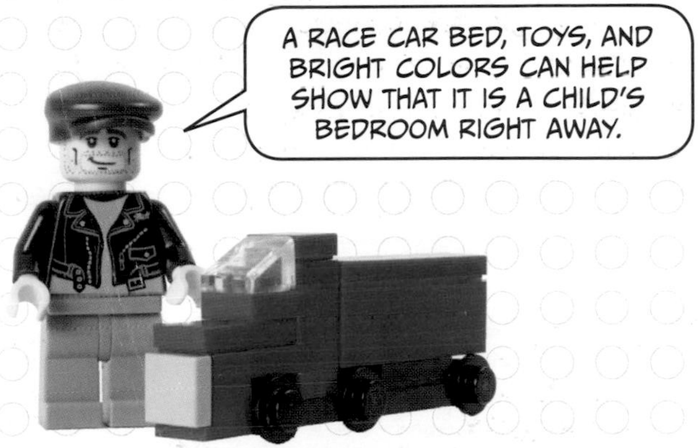
A RACE CAR BED, TOYS, AND BRIGHT COLORS CAN HELP SHOW THAT IT IS A CHILD'S BEDROOM RIGHT AWAY.

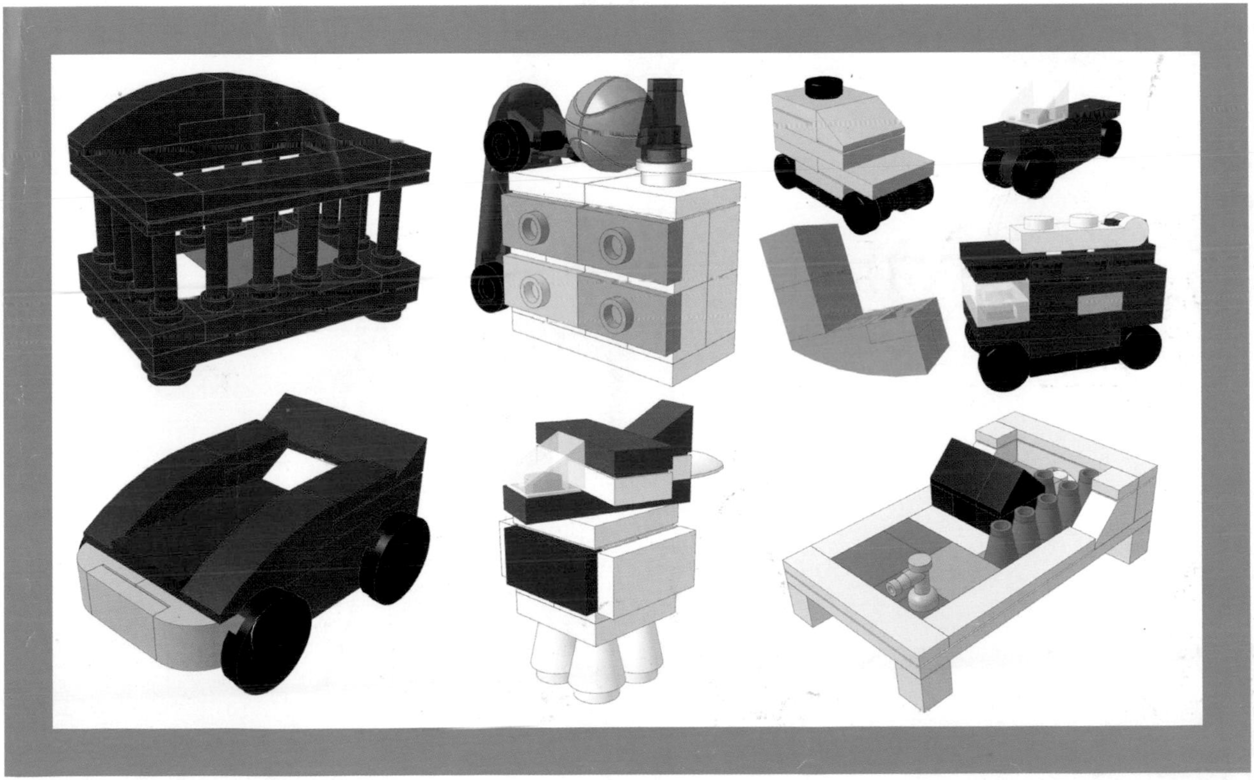

Kid's Race Car Bed

1

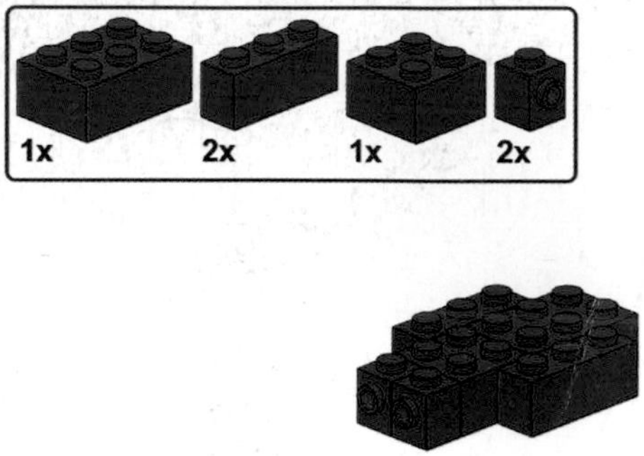
1x
2x
1x
2x

2

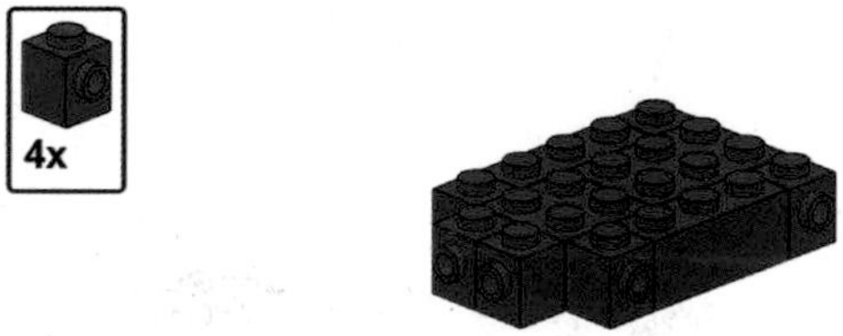
4x

3

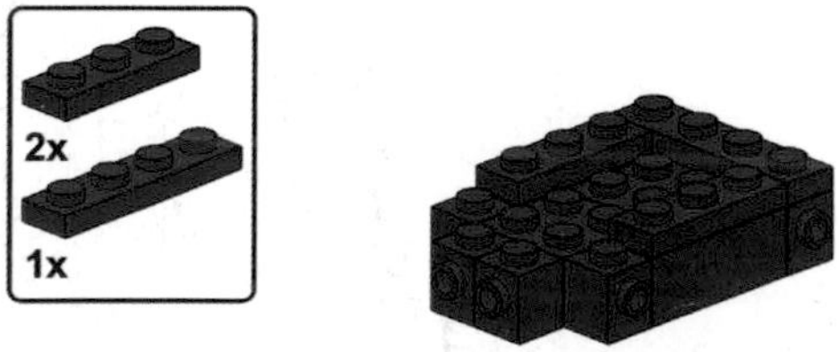
2x
1x

4

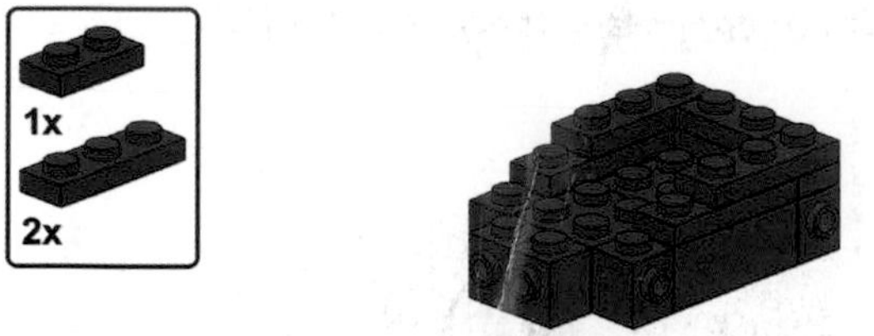
1x
2x

5

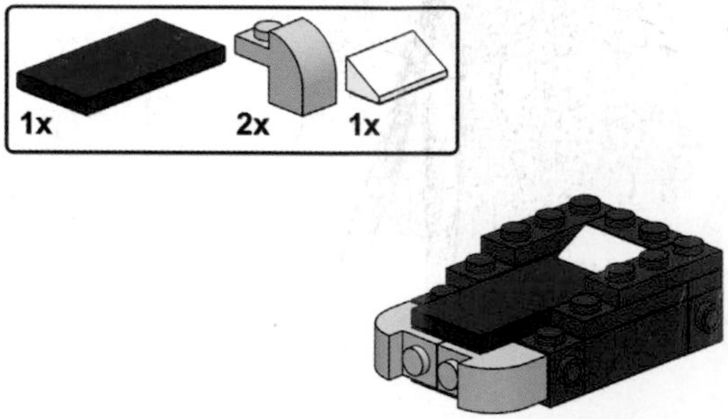
1x
2x
1x

6

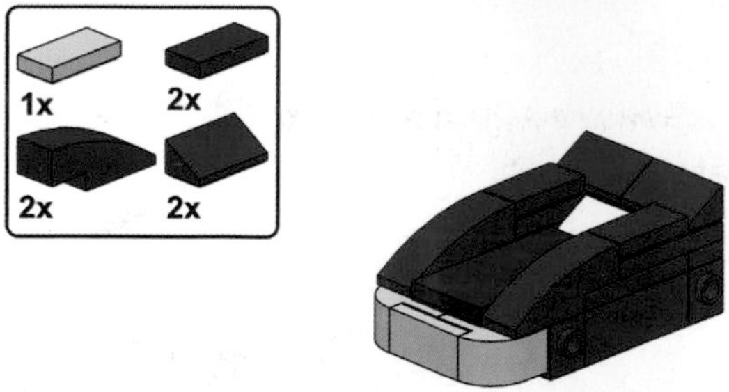
1x
2x
2x
2x

7

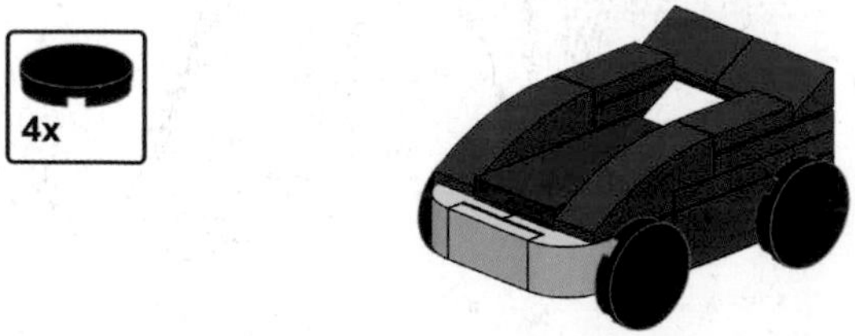
4x

Bathroom

Let's stop by the bathroom to see some of its components made in LEGO.

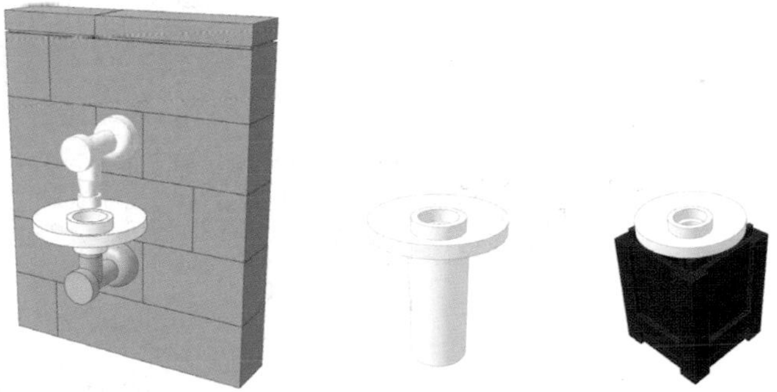

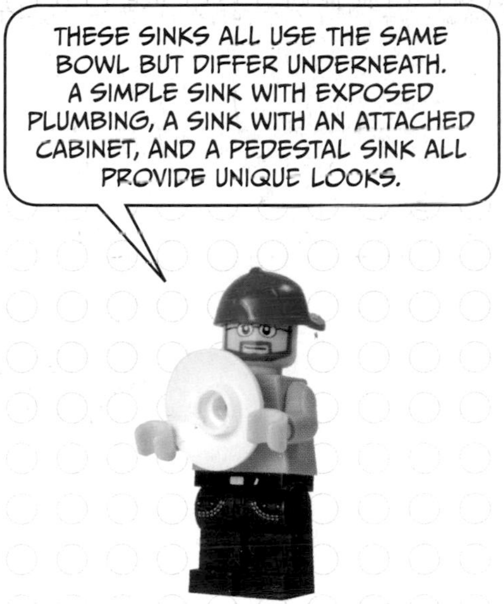
THESE SINKS ALL USE THE SAME BOWL BUT DIFFER UNDERNEATH. A SIMPLE SINK WITH EXPOSED PLUMBING, A SINK WITH AN ATTACHED CABINET, AND A PEDESTAL SINK ALL PROVIDE UNIQUE LOOKS.

Mount a mirror on the wall above your sink.

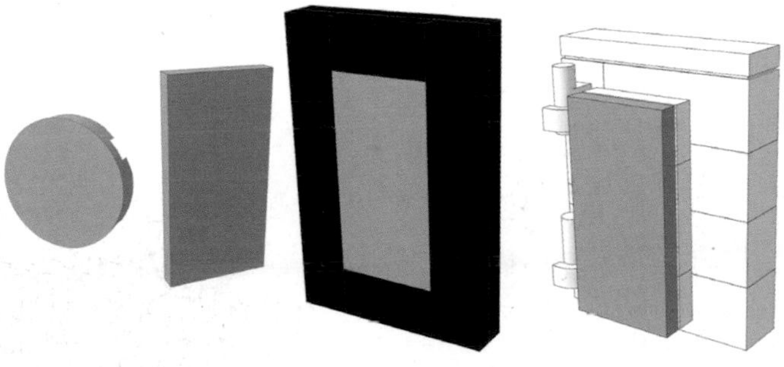

Rounding out the bathroom is the toilet.

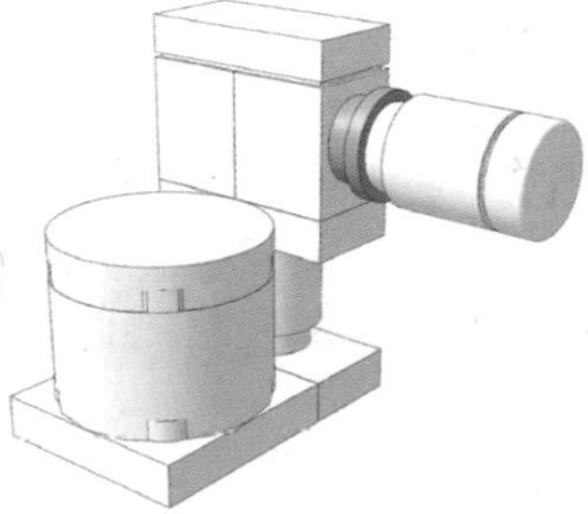

Bathtub

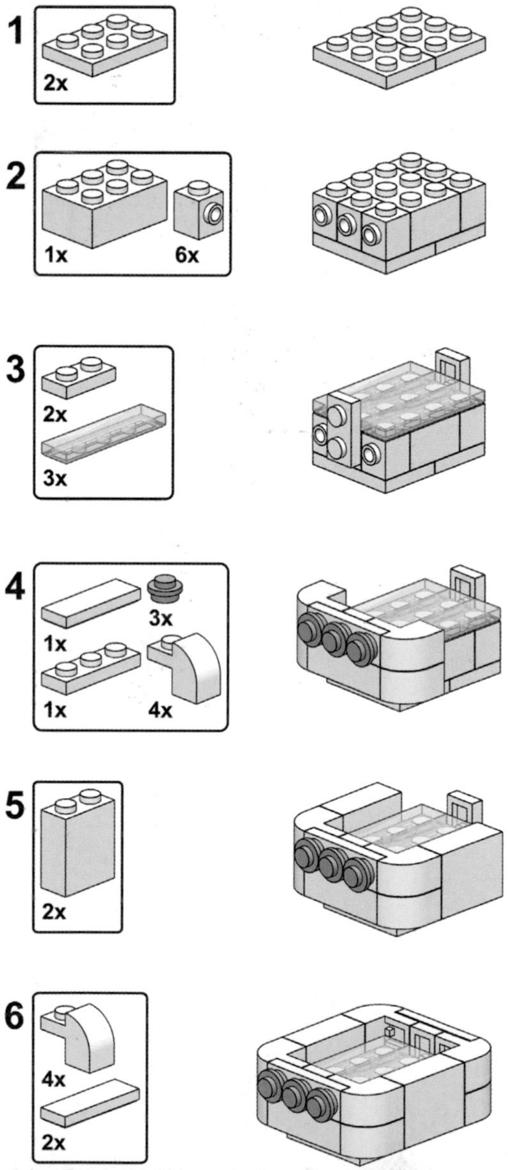

1
2x
2
1x
6x
3
2x
3x
4
3x
1x
1x
4x
5
2x
6
4x
2x

These stand-alone tubs are great for larger bathrooms.

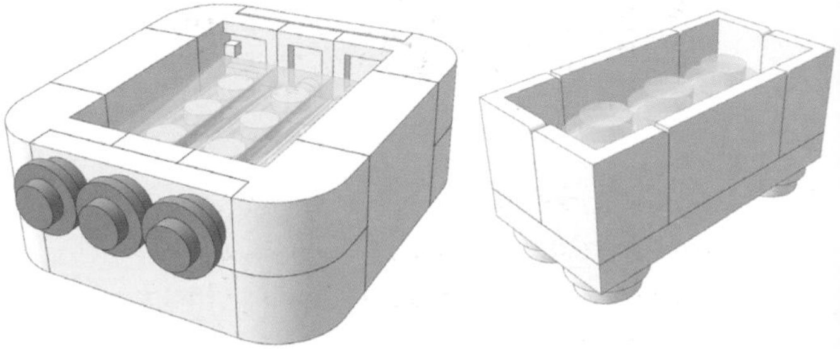

You can choose between this tub with a shower or a stall shower depending on the size of the bathroom.

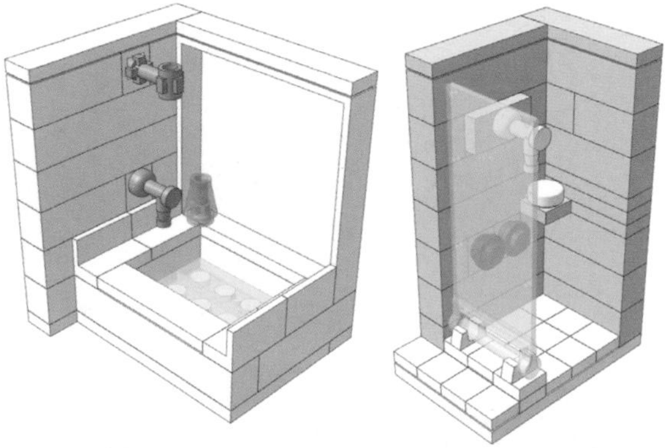

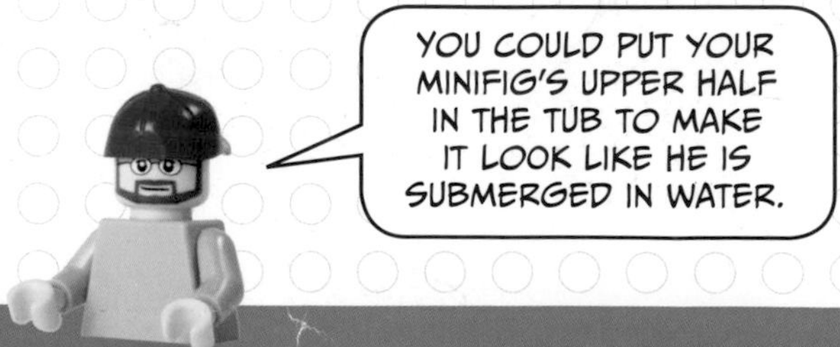

YOU COULD PUT YOUR MINIFIG'S UPPER HALF IN THE TUB TO MAKE IT LOOK LIKE HE IS SUBMERGED IN WATER.

Commercial Buildings

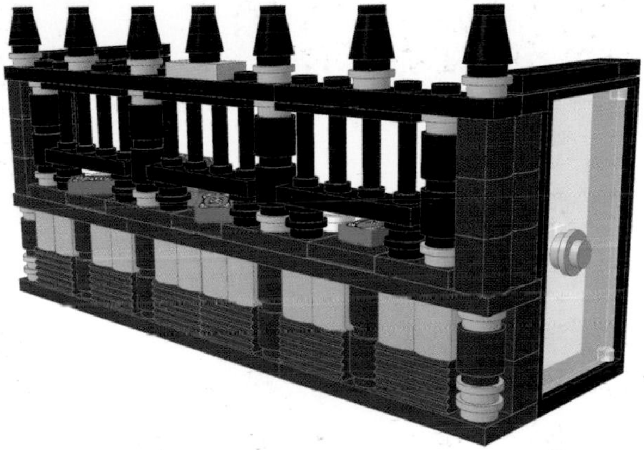

Homes are certainly not the only style of modular building. Here are some examples of furniture from different commercial buildings.

Bank

This group of office furniture was used in our National Bank model.

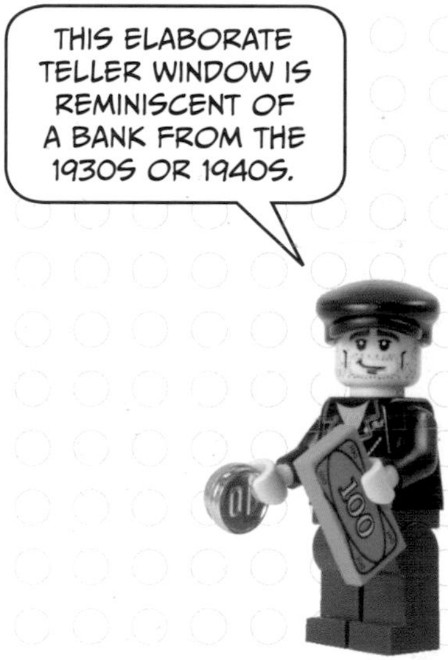
THIS ELABORATE TELLER WINDOW IS REMINISCENT OF A BANK FROM THE 1930S OR 1940S.

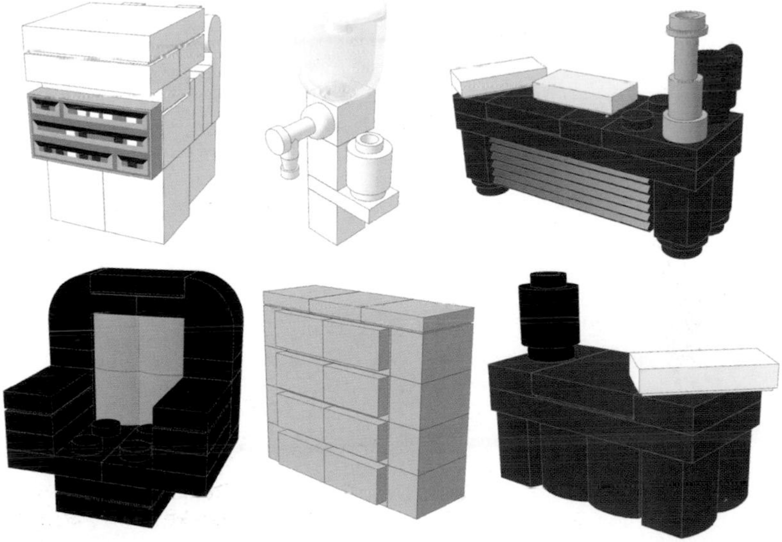

Restaurant

Here are some examples of items found in a restaurant kitchen. A larger sink, a prep table, and shelves of ingredients help fill up the kitchen fast.

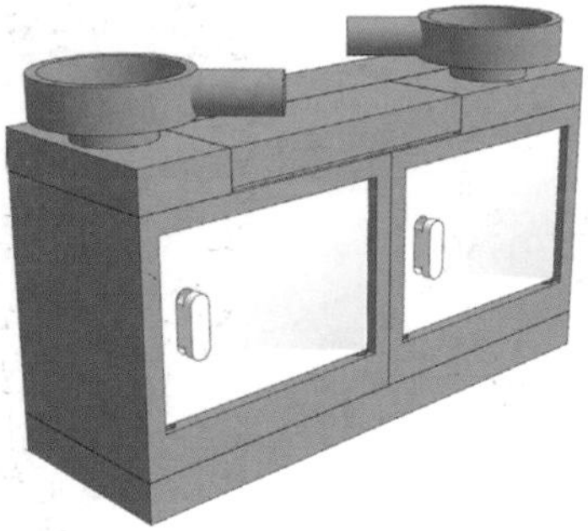
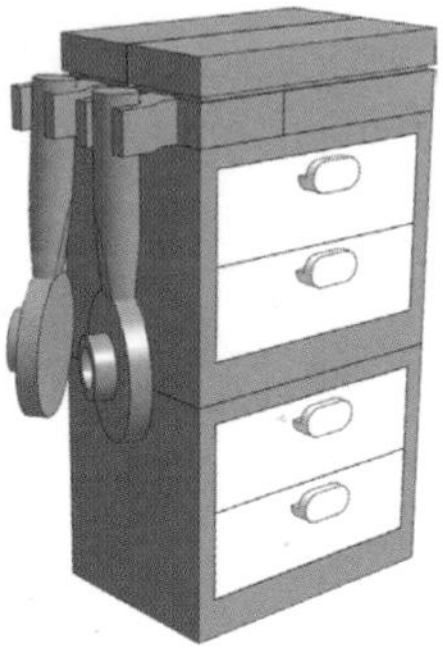
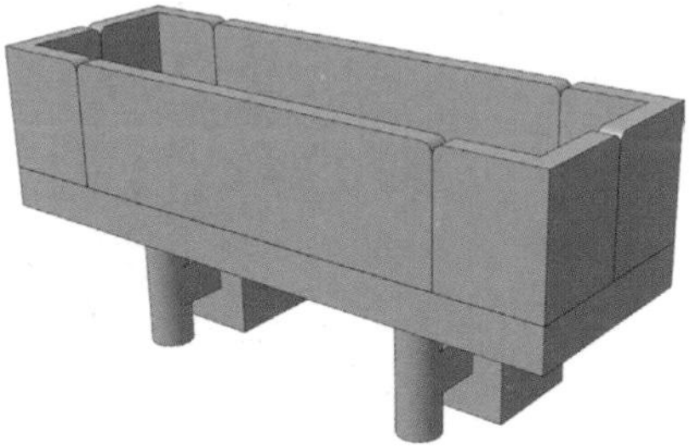
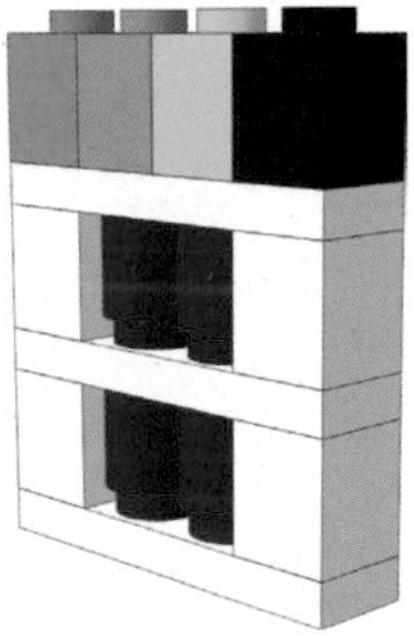

The dining area of the restaurant usually has booths, tables, chairs, a bar, and some decorative elements like plants or pictures on the walls.

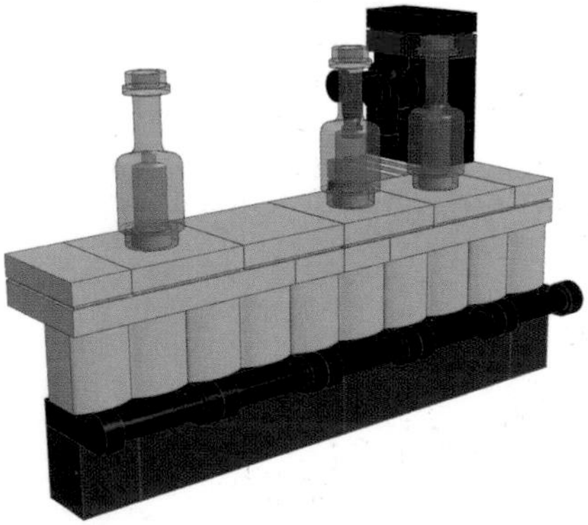
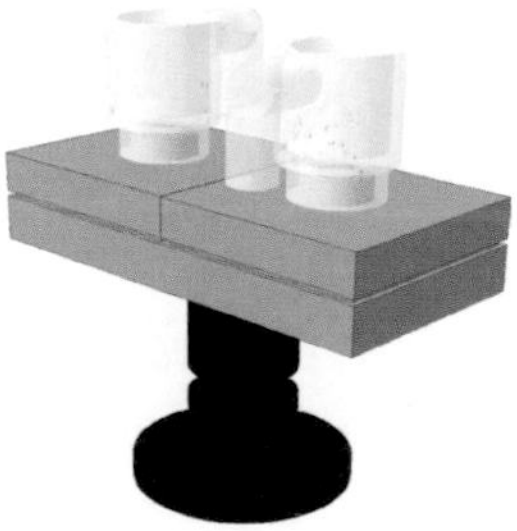
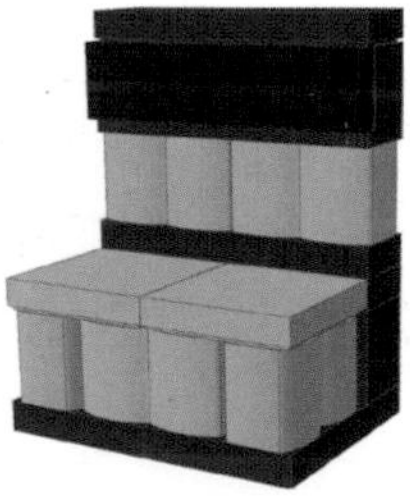

Hotel

Check out these examples of furniture that you would find in a hotel room.

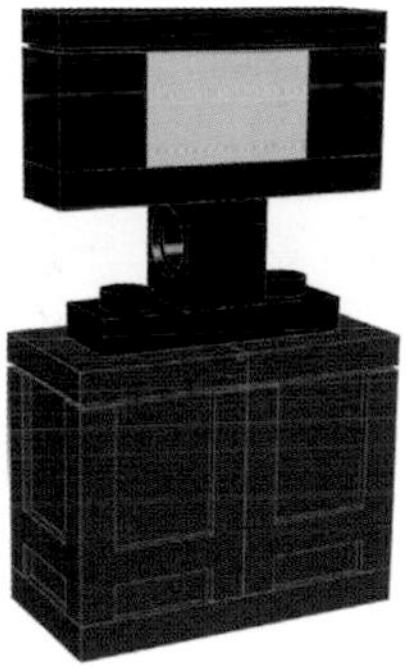

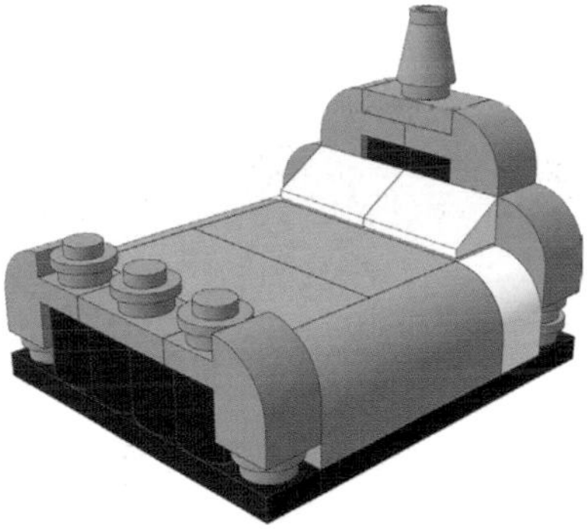

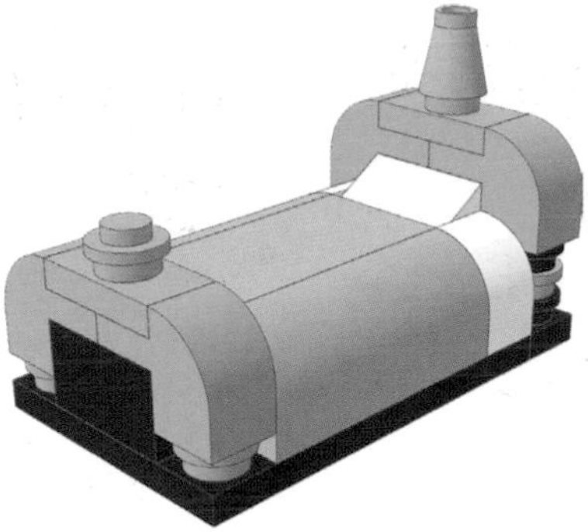

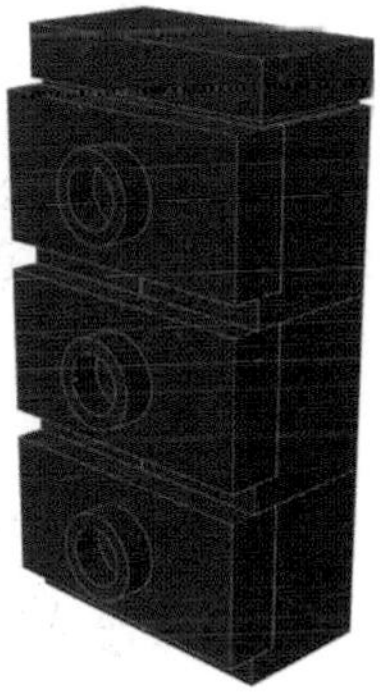

The mailbox, flower pedestal, key machine, and front desk could be found in the lobby area.

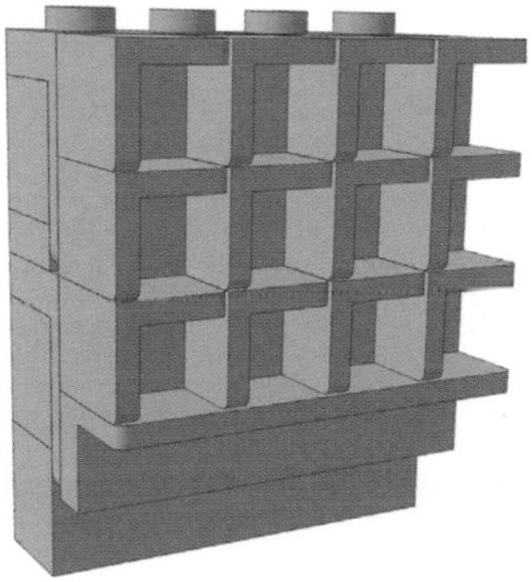

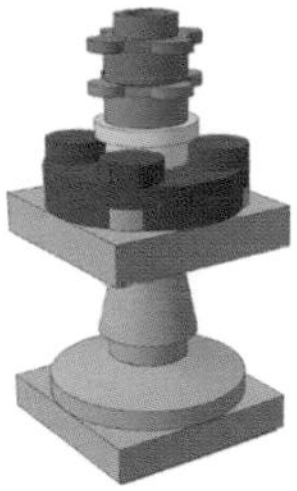

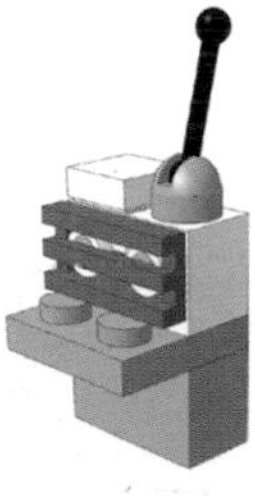

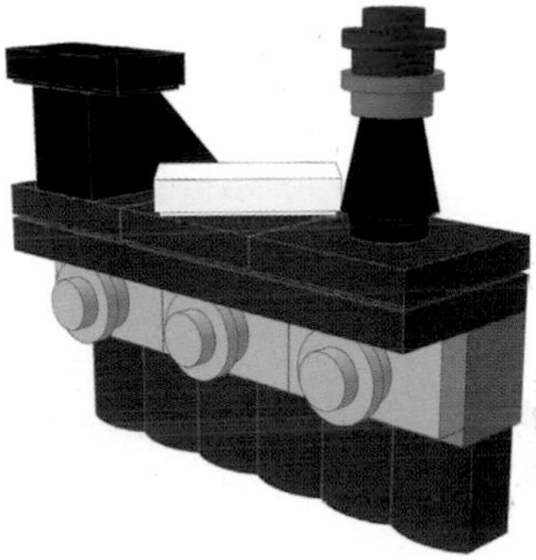

Jewelry Store

These display cabinets would look great in a jewelry or antique store.

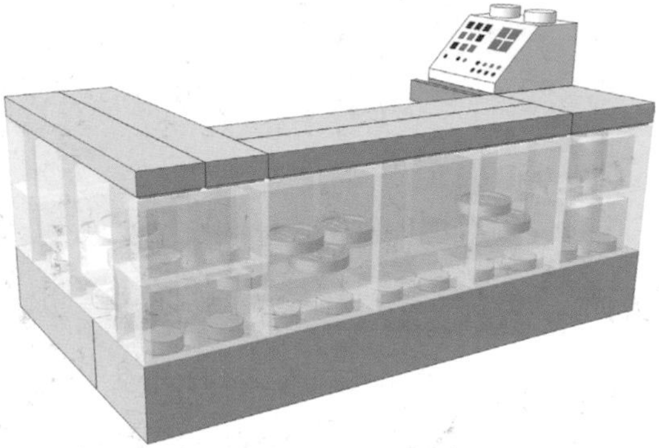

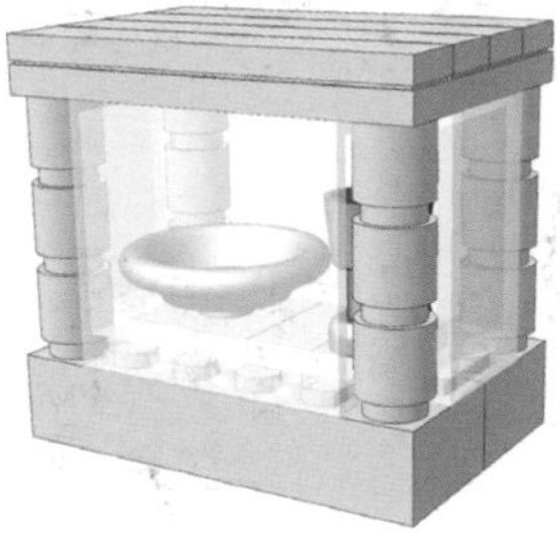

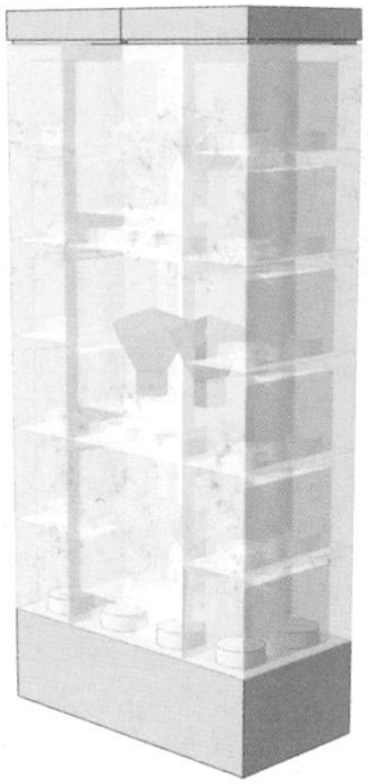

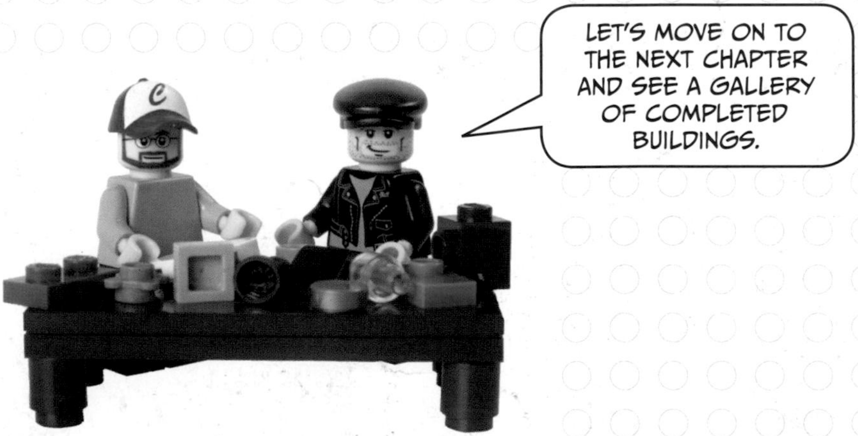
LET'S MOVE ON TO THE NEXT CHAPTER AND SEE A GALLERY OF COMPLETED BUILDINGS.

6

Modular Building Gallery

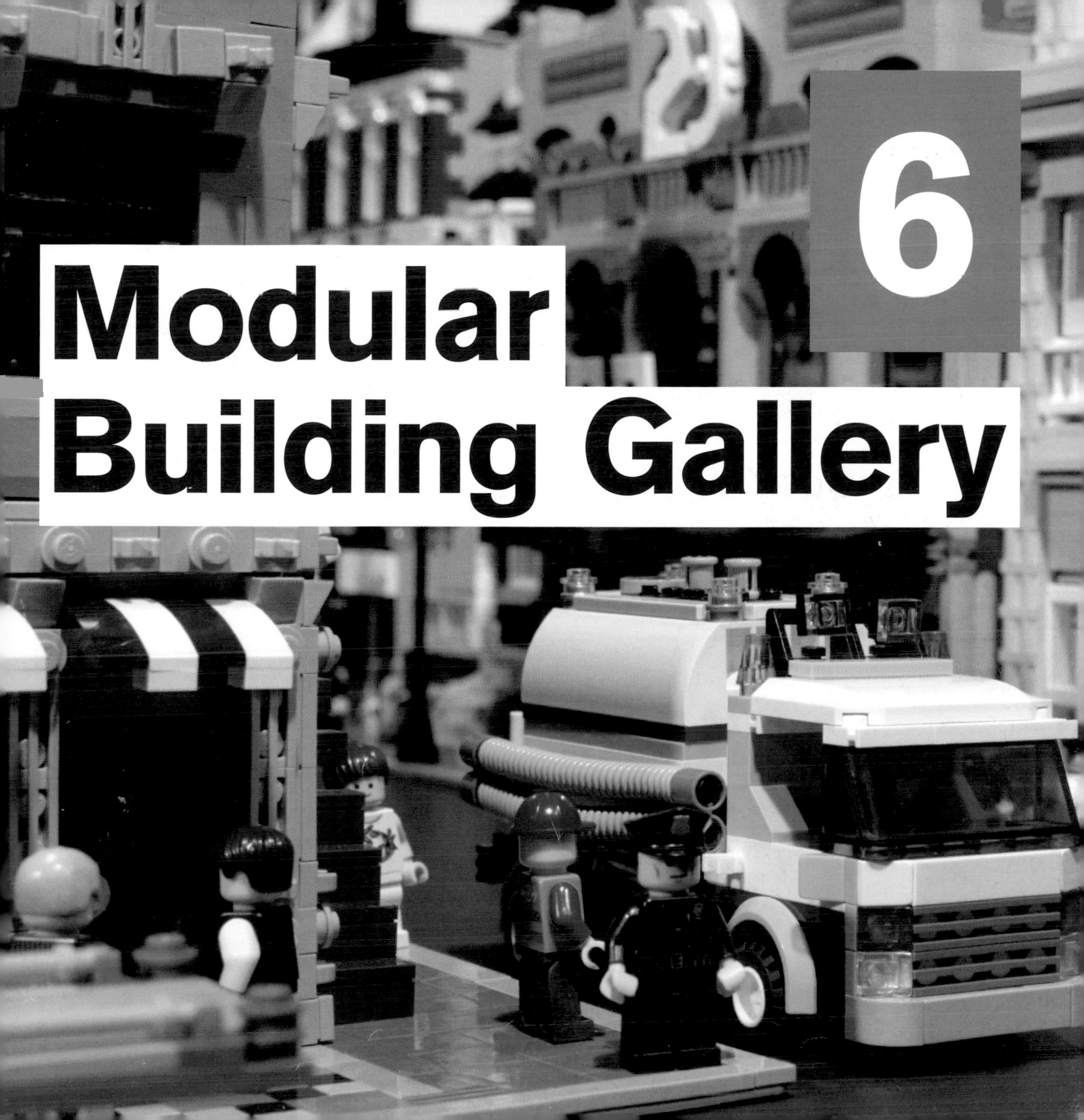

Have a look at some of the modular buildings that we've created. If you haven't yet created an original LEGO build, we encourage you to give it a try. Get inspired by the models in this chapter, as well as those created by the LEGO Group.

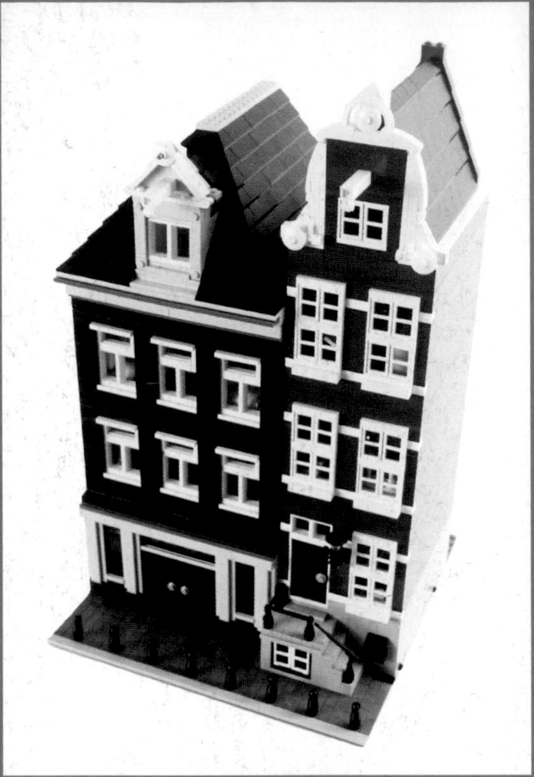

These houses represent two of the many styles that line the canals in Amsterdam. The skinny apartment building with steeply sloped roofs and the posts next to the canal make this scene unmistakably Dutch.

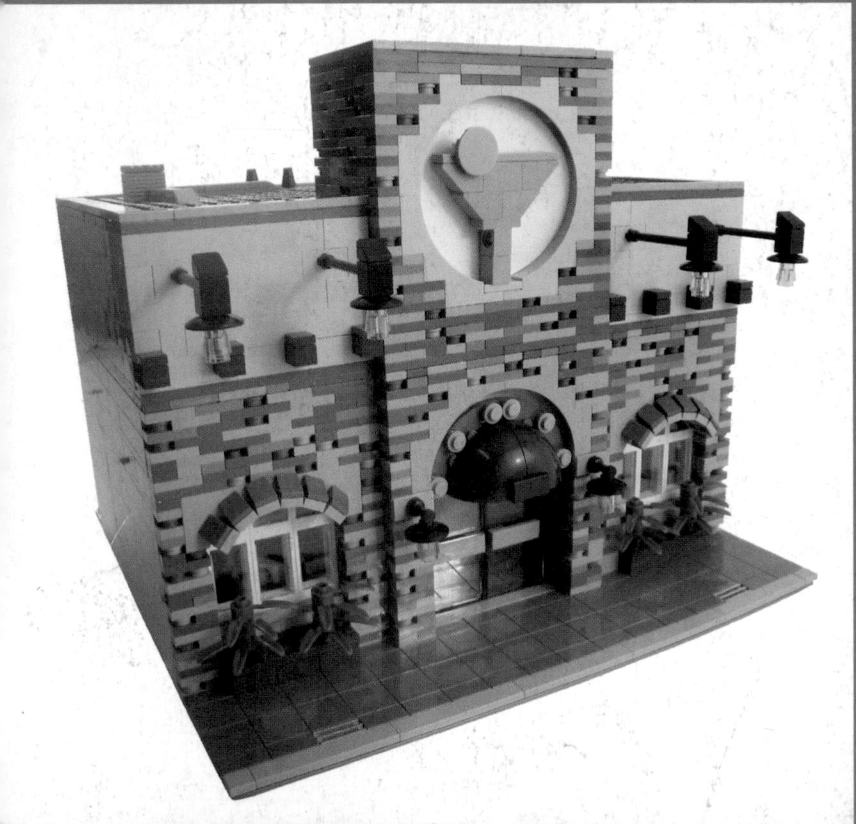

***City Restaurant* has a great sign, as well as a facade with some creative stonework. It has a full kitchen in the back.**

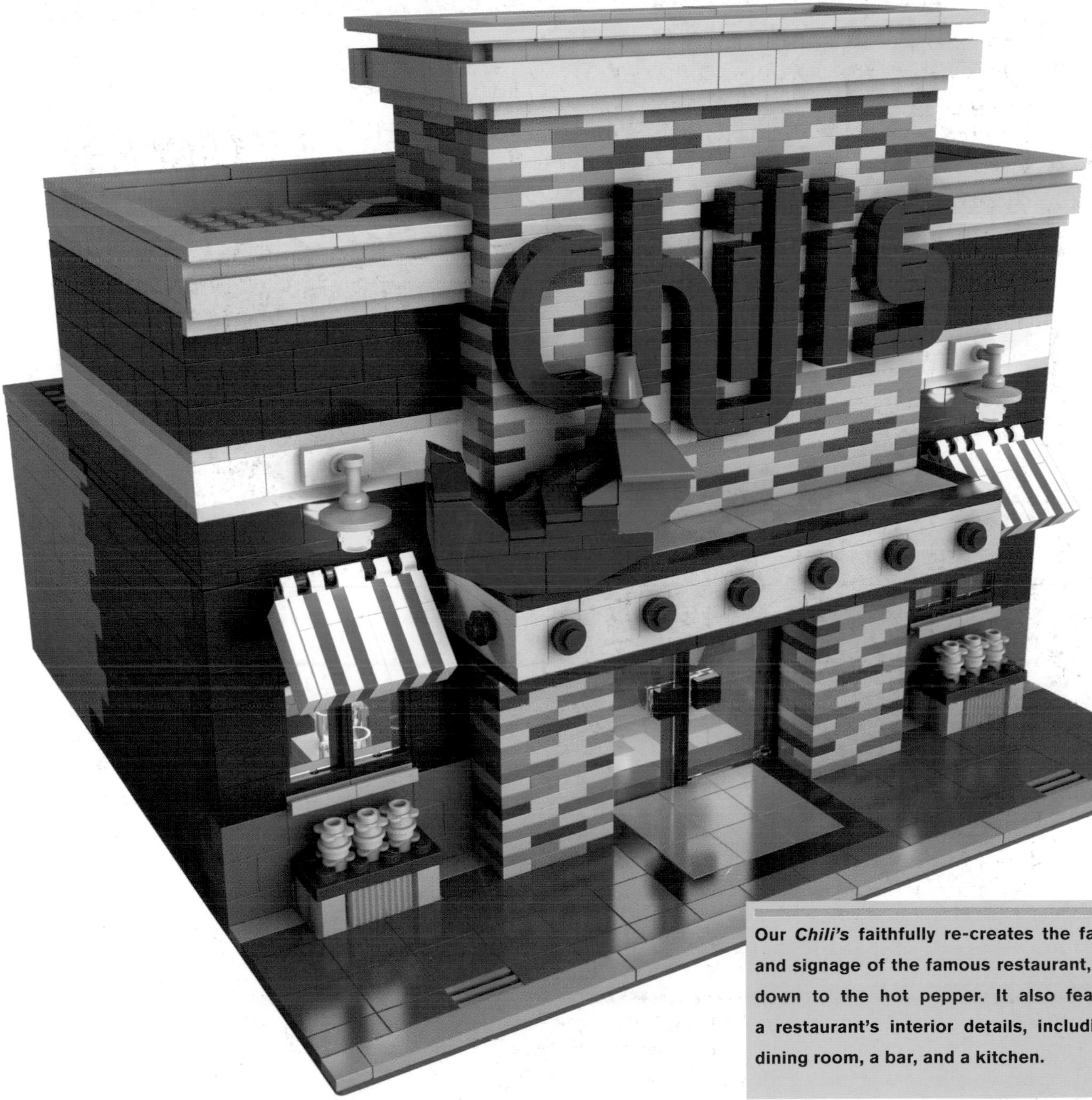

Our *Chili's* faithfully re-creates the facade and signage of the famous restaurant, right down to the hot pepper. It also features a restaurant's interior details, including a dining room, a bar, and a kitchen.

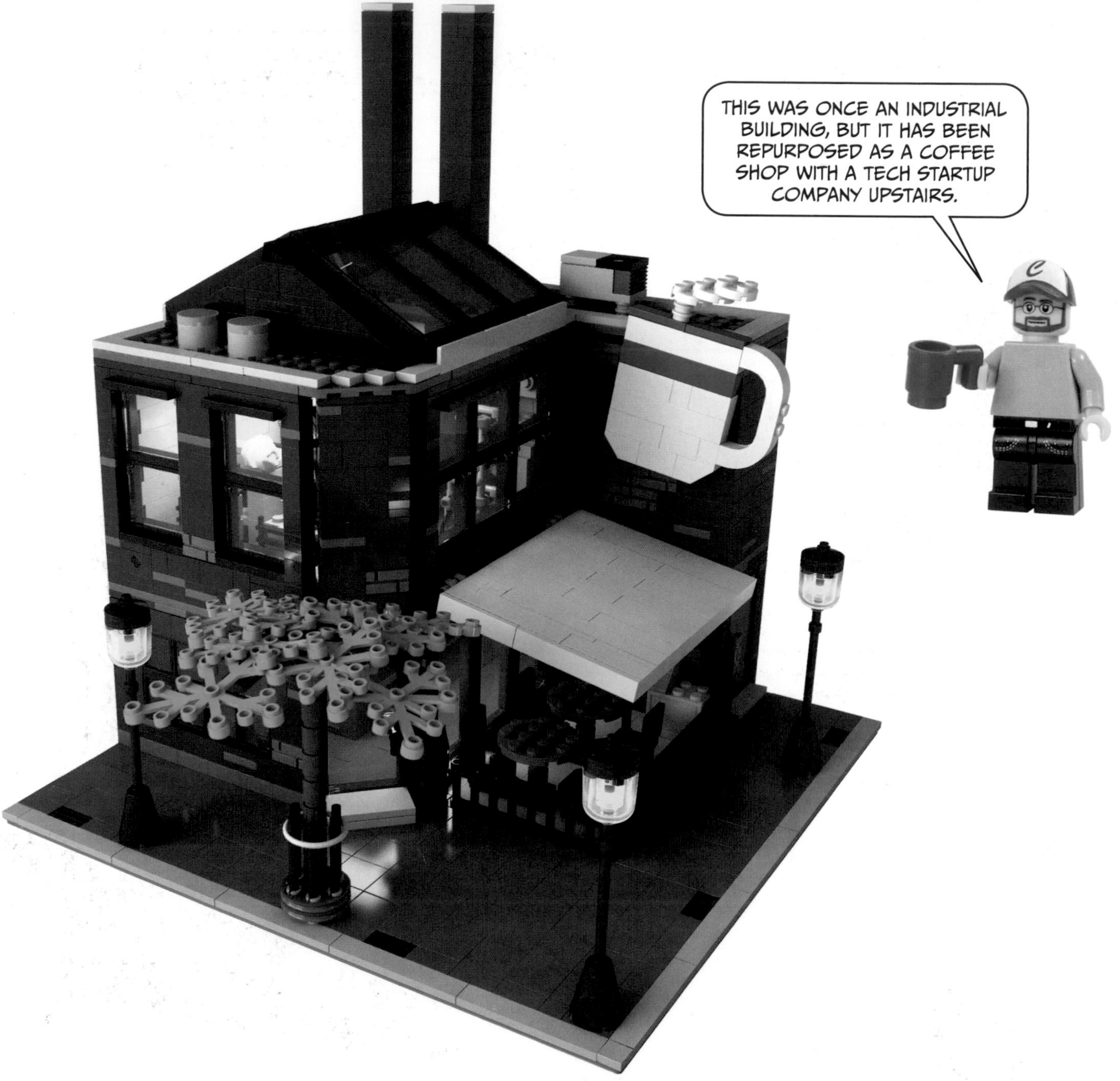
THIS WAS ONCE AN INDUSTRIAL BUILDING, BUT IT HAS BEEN REPURPOSED AS A COFFEE SHOP WITH A TECH STARTUP COMPANY UPSTAIRS.

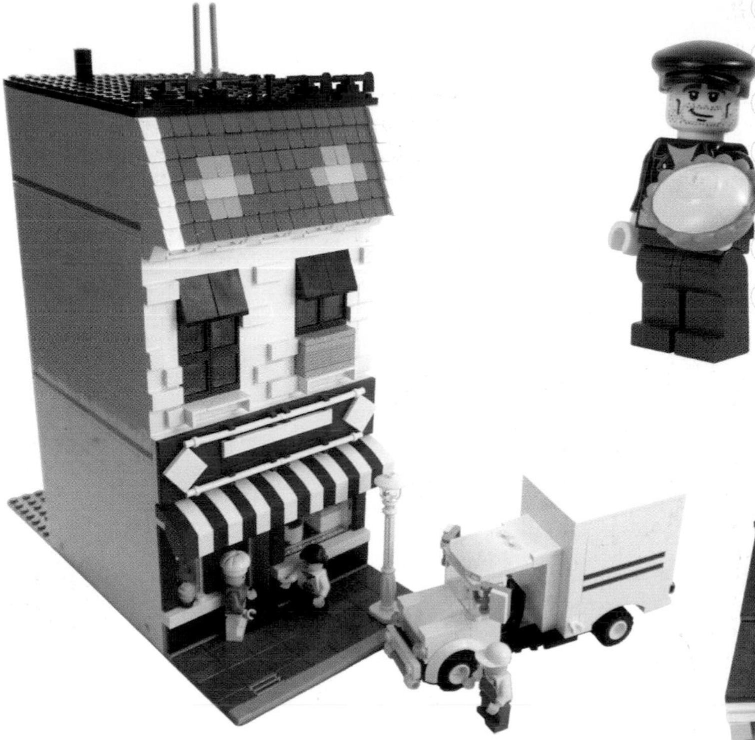
THIS BAKERY WAS INSPIRED BY A CAKE SHOP IN NEW JERSEY. IT HAS AN APARTMENT ON THE SECOND FLOOR.

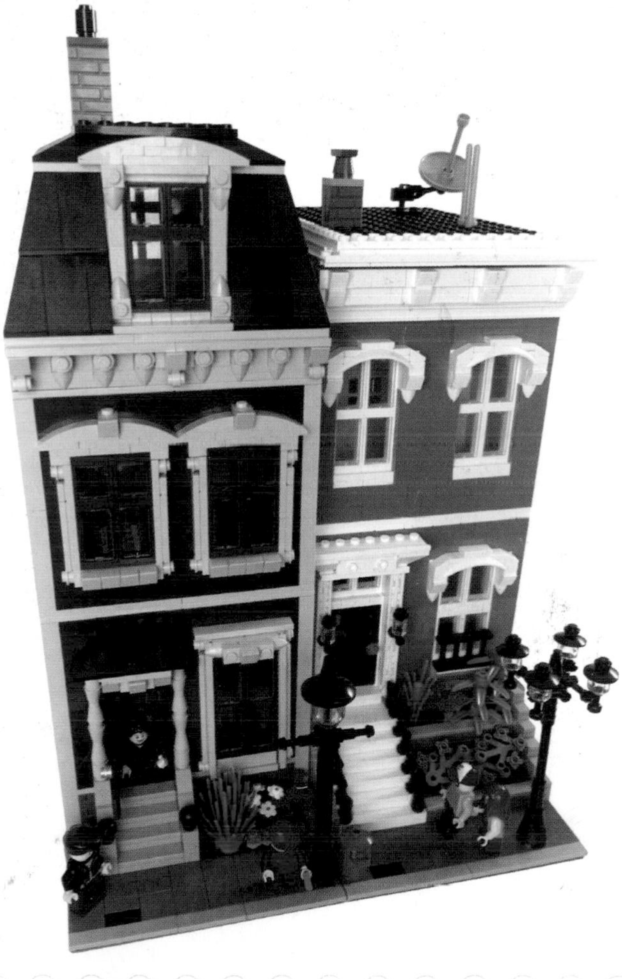

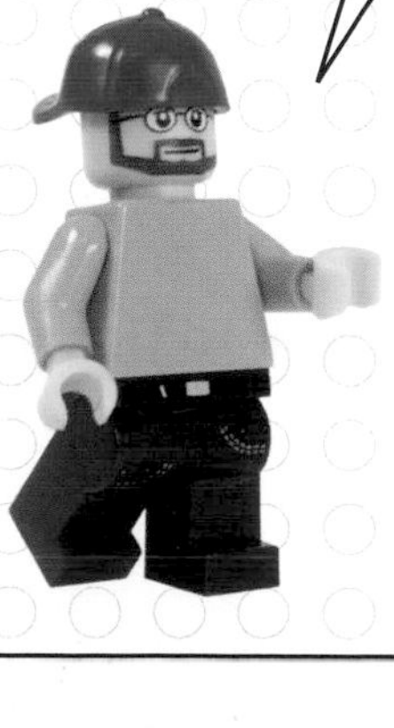
THE SAND-BLUE HOUSE ON THE RIGHT WAS COPIED FROM A HOUSE IN THE GEORGETOWN NEIGHBORHOOD OF WASHINGTON, DC.

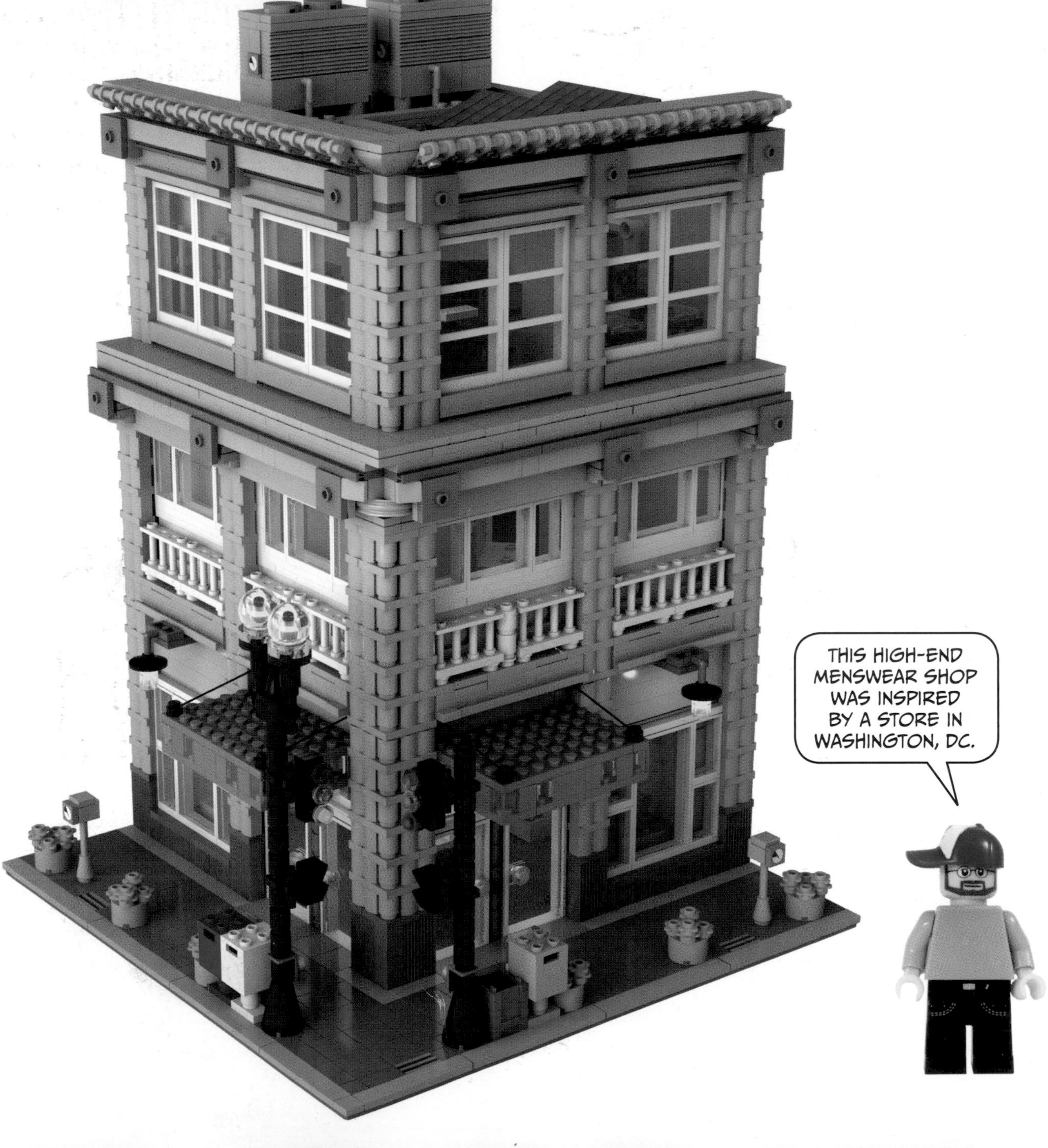
THIS HIGH-END MENSWEAR SHOP WAS INSPIRED BY A STORE IN WASHINGTON, DC.

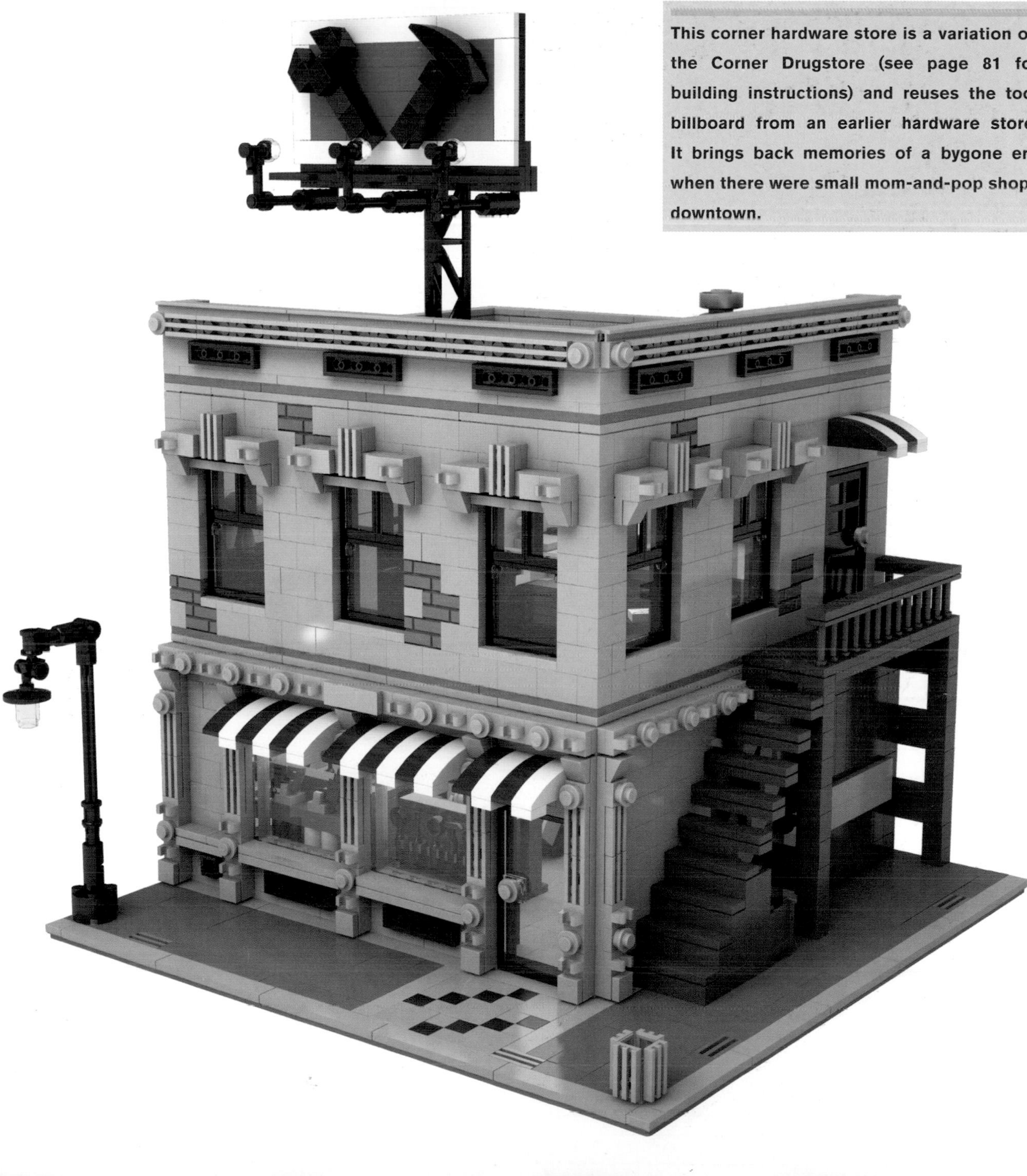

This corner hardware store is a variation on the Corner Drugstore (see page 81 for building instructions) and reuses the tool billboard from an earlier hardware store. It brings back memories of a bygone era when there were small mom-and-pop shops downtown.

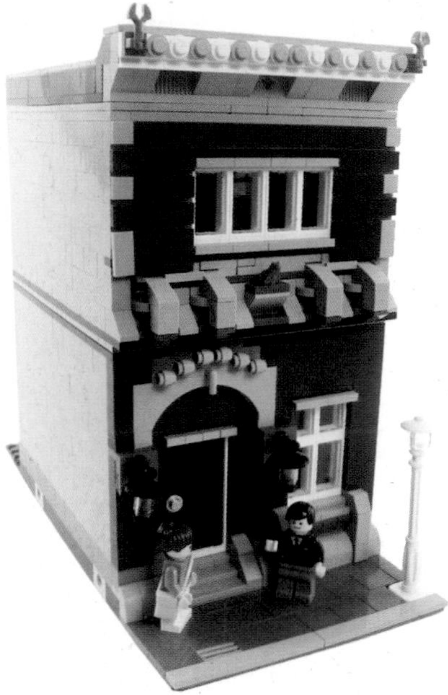

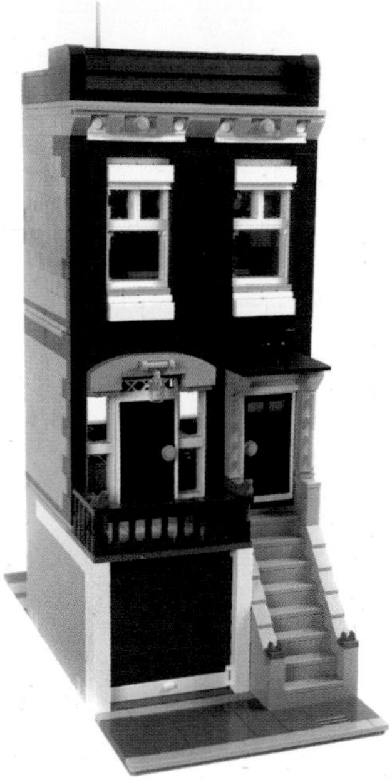

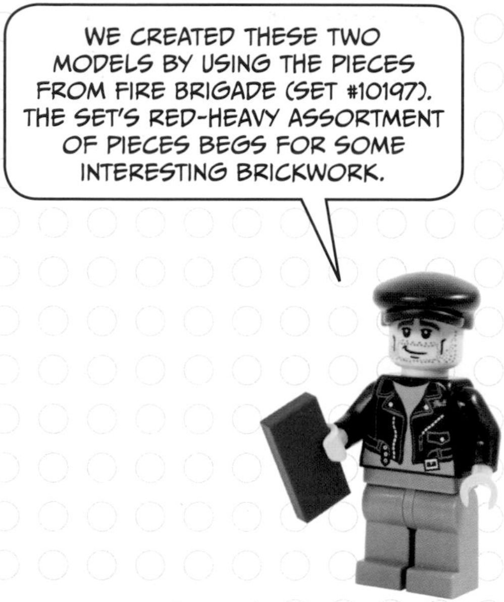
WE CREATED THESE TWO MODELS BY USING THE PIECES FROM FIRE BRIGADE (SET #10197). THE SET'S RED-HEAVY ASSORTMENT OF PIECES BEGS FOR SOME INTERESTING BRICKWORK.

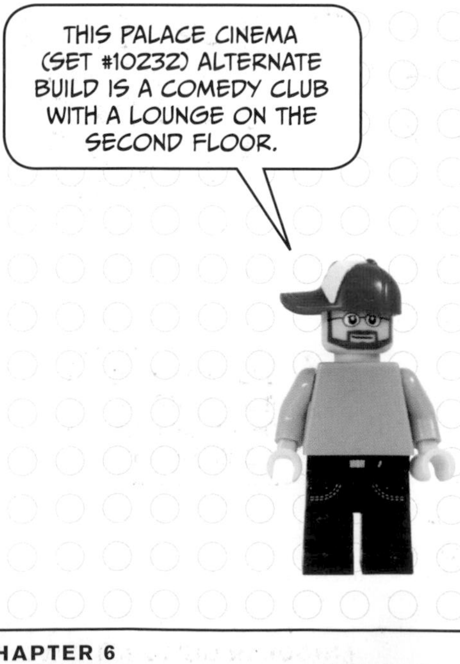
THIS PALACE CINEMA (SET #10232) ALTERNATE BUILD IS A COMEDY CLUB WITH A LOUNGE ON THE SECOND FLOOR.

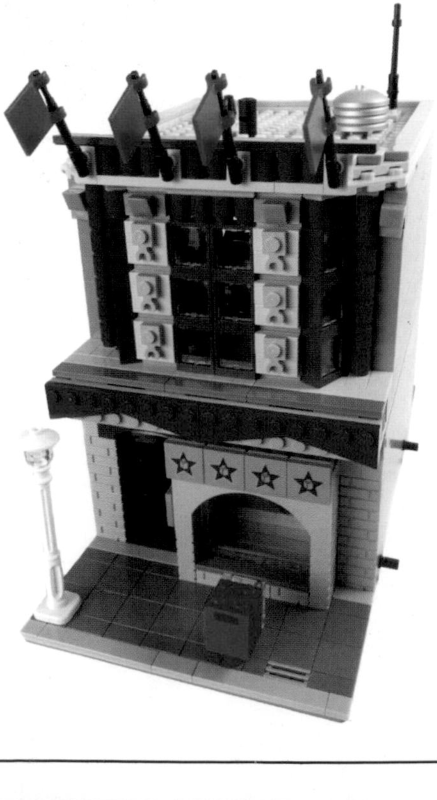

Club 23 is a speakeasy that is accessed through the phone booth outside and has a false storefront.

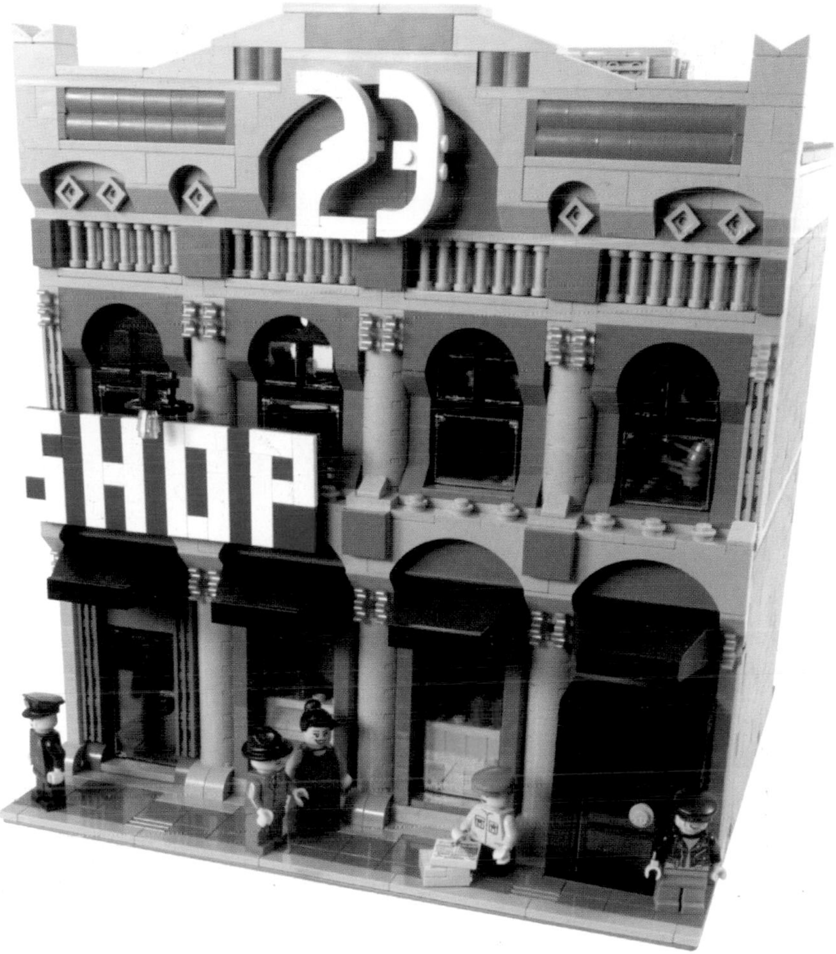
23

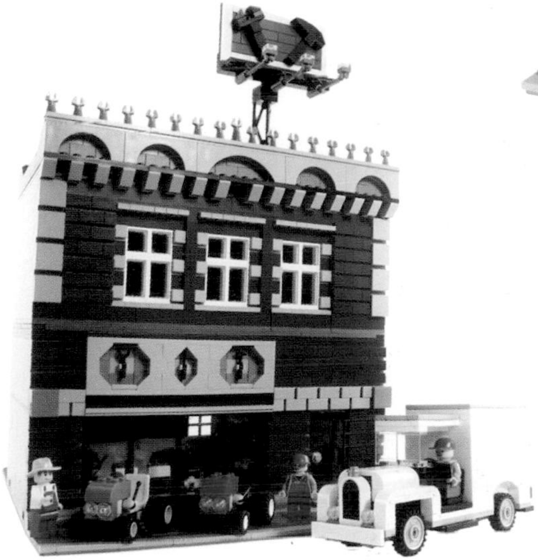

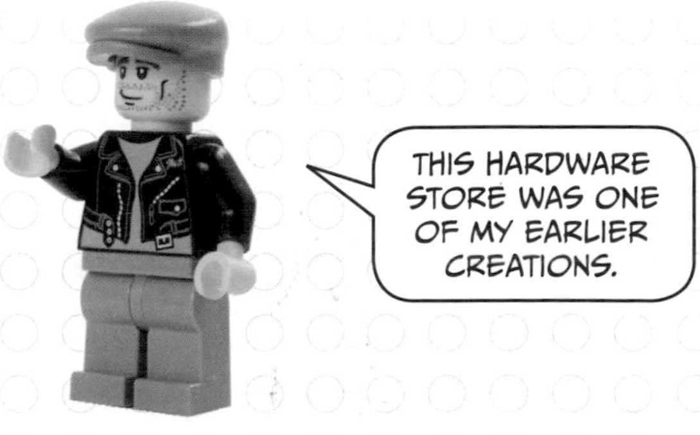
THIS HARDWARE STORE WAS ONE OF MY EARLIER CREATIONS.

This architecture firm has an open lobby on the first floor that extends up to the third floor. The top floor features a commanding view of the city that surrounds it.

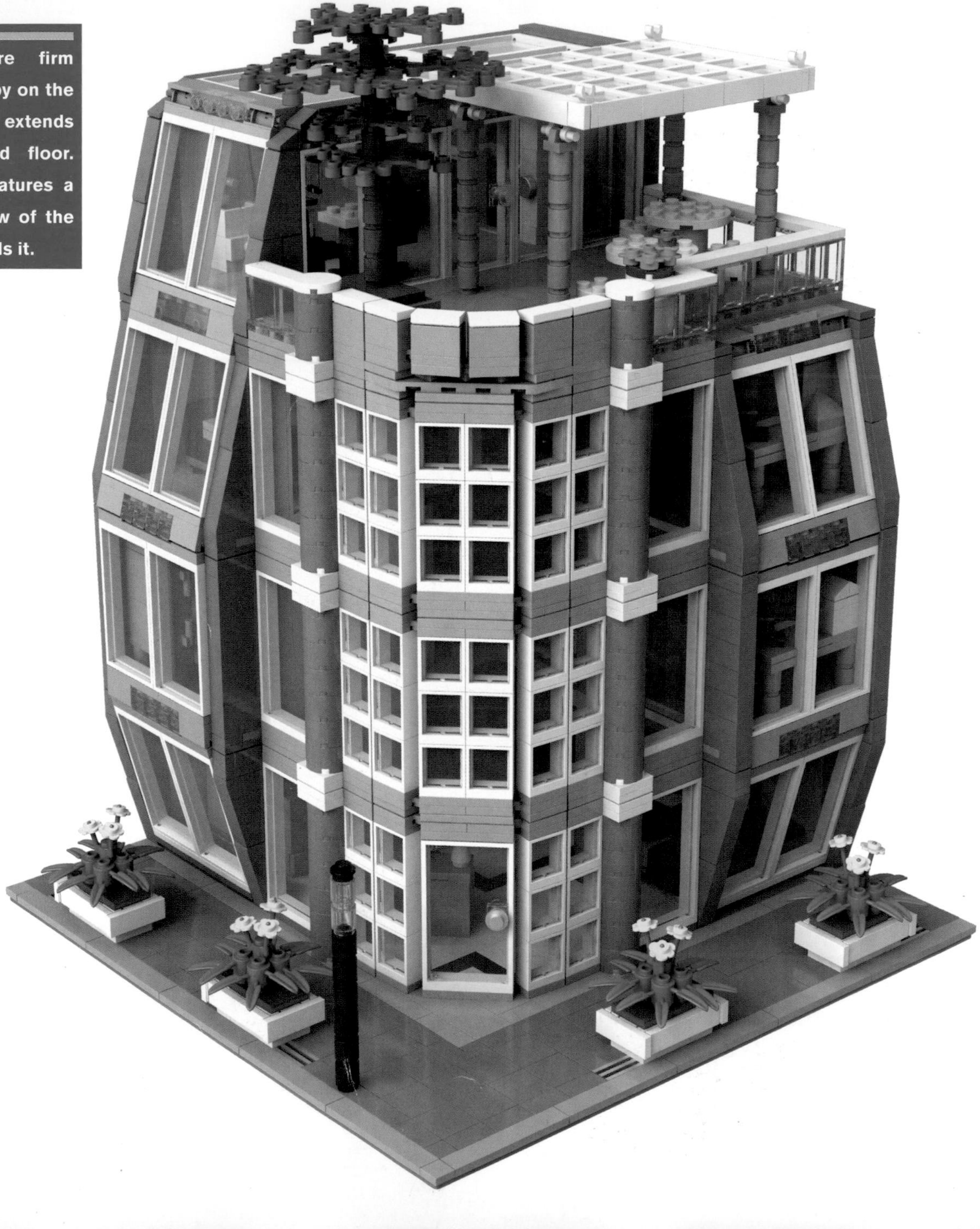

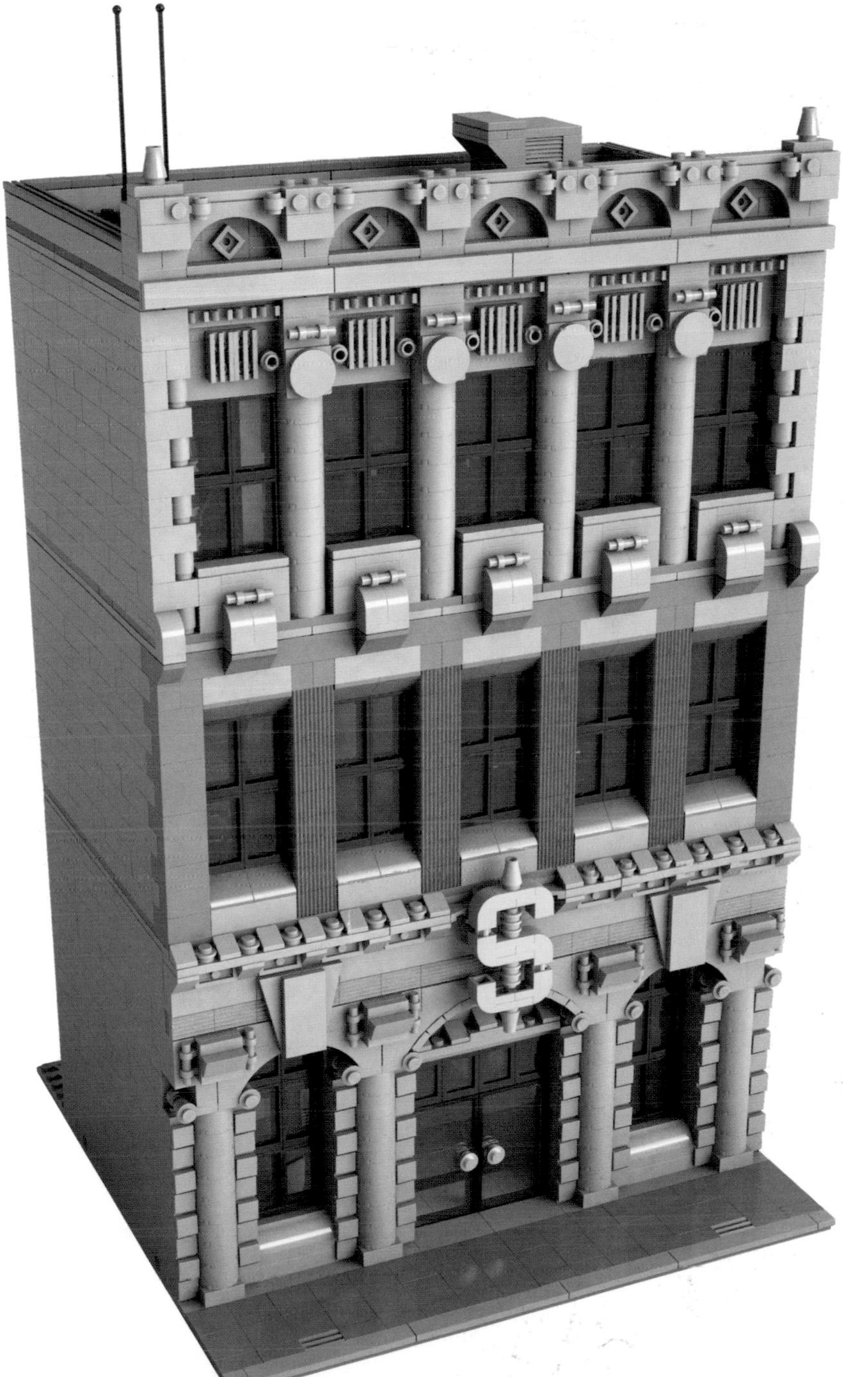

The *National Bank* was inspired by a bank in Richmond, Virginia, and features neoclassical architecture.

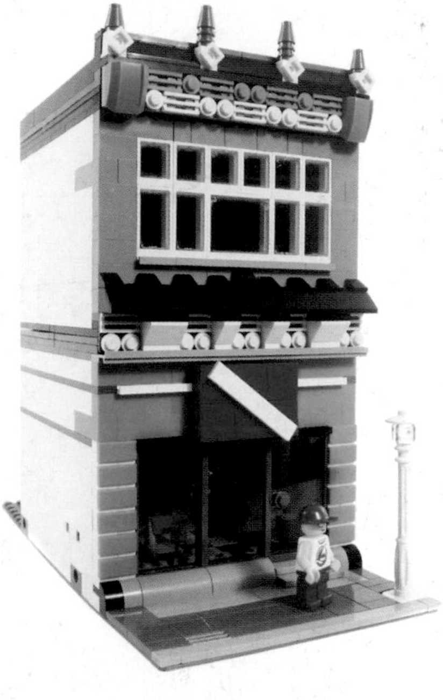

A dive shop

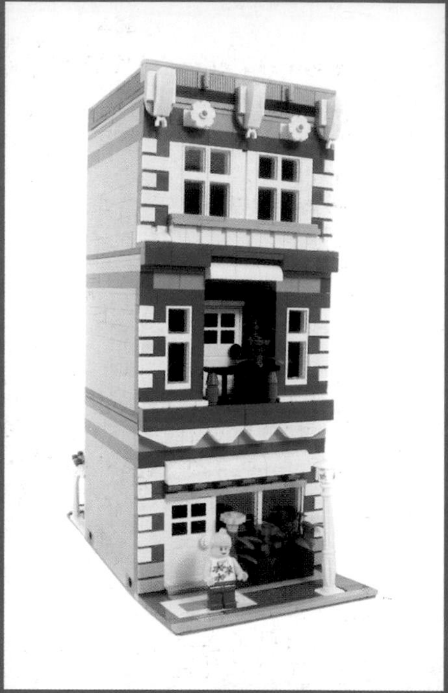

This three-story flower shop has two shades of blue on the facade.

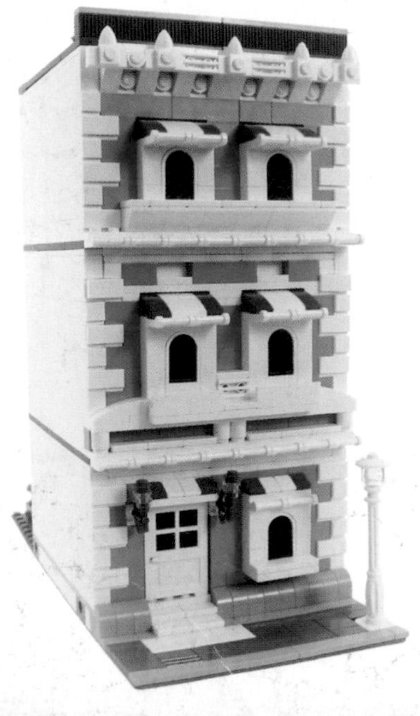

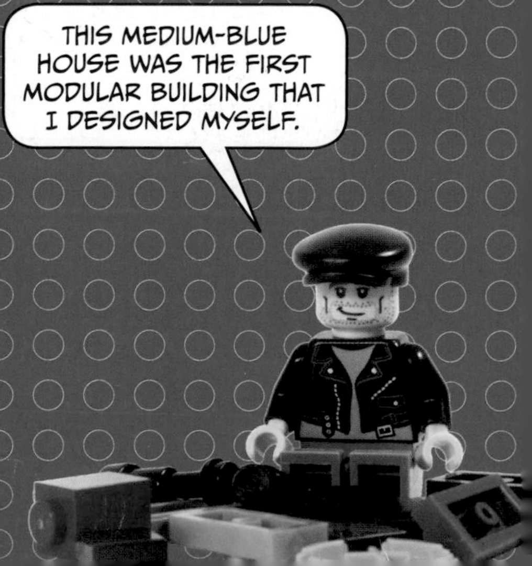
THIS MEDIUM-BLUE HOUSE WAS THE FIRST MODULAR BUILDING THAT I DESIGNED MYSELF.

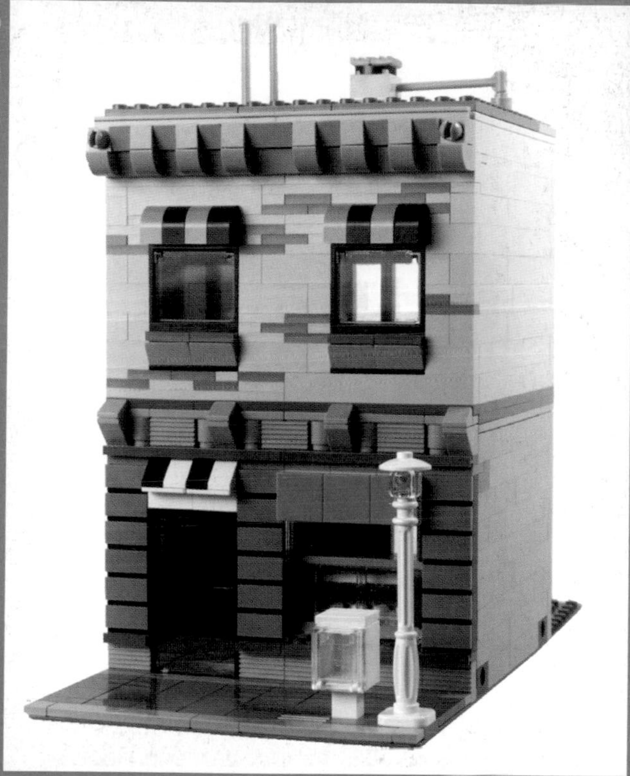

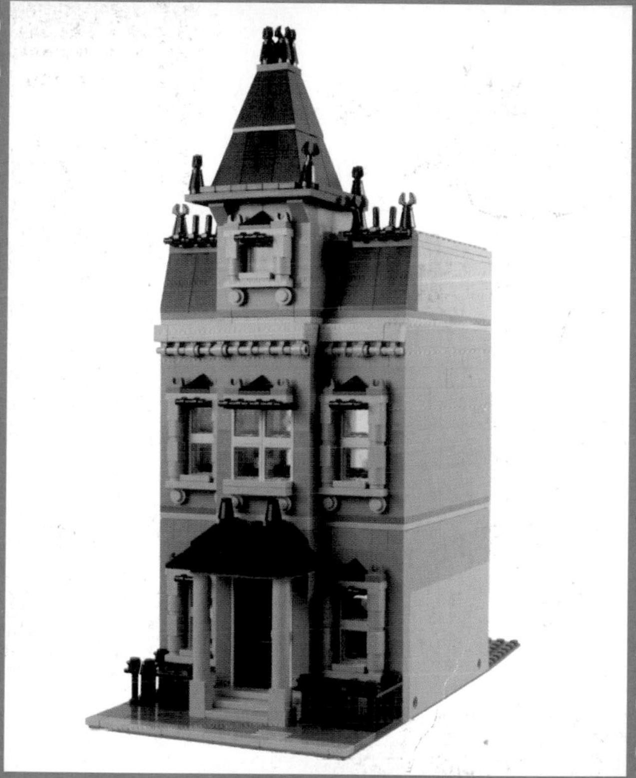

This store was made with the pieces from Grand Emporium (set #10211).

The *Mansard Row House* was created with the pieces from Haunted House (set #10228) and a baseplate. Don't feel like you have to use a LEGO modula building as your initial inspiration!

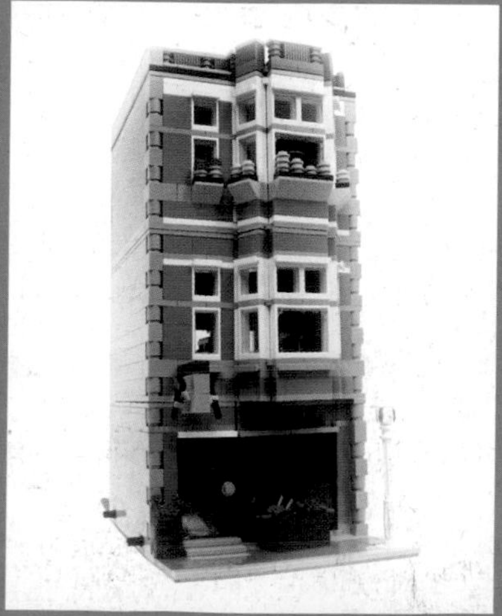

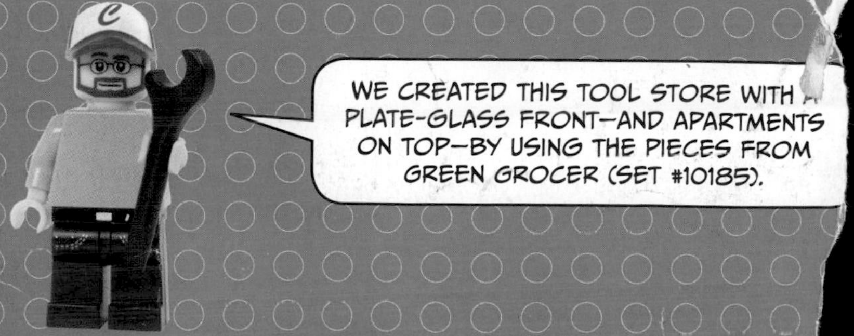
WE CREATED THIS TOOL STORE WITH A
PLATE-GLASS FRONT—AND APARTMENTS
ON TOP—BY USING THE PIECES FROM
GREEN GROCER (SET #10185).

Mini Modulars

These are smaller-scale versions of some of our models. The size for these builds is 8×8, rather than 32×32. Building small is a great creative challenge!

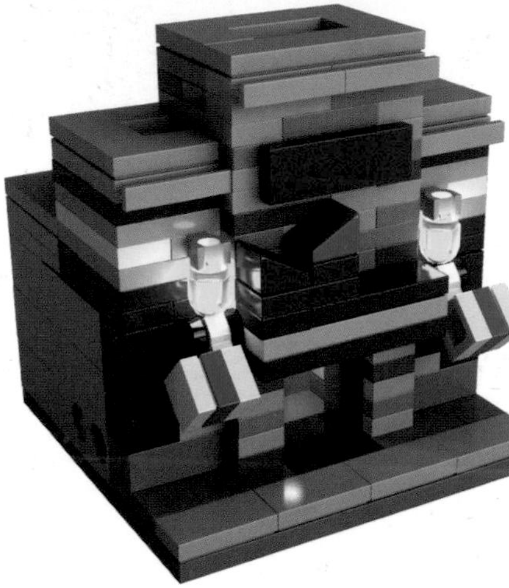

Chili's Restaurant

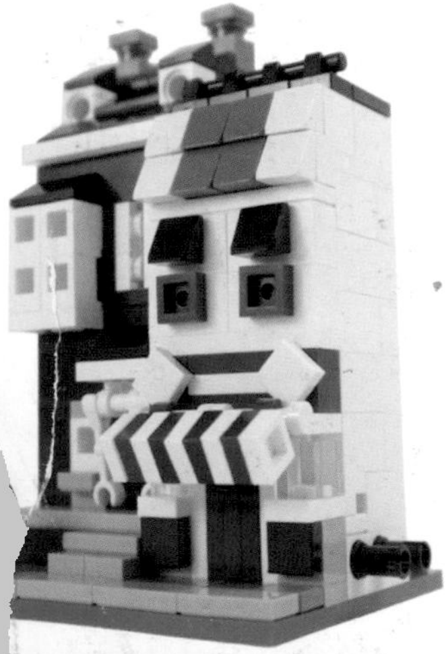

ial Revival House & Bakery

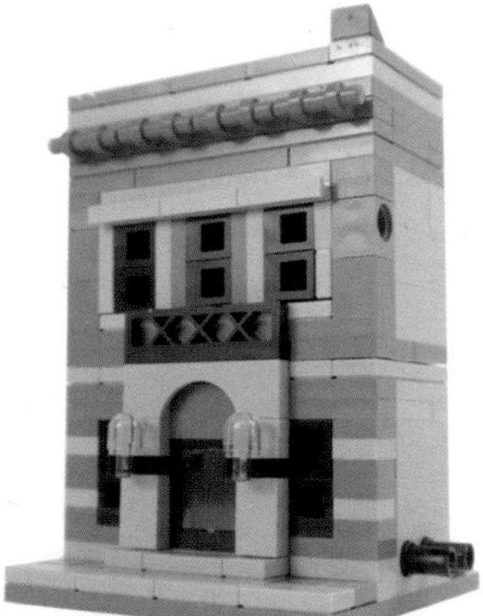

Police Station

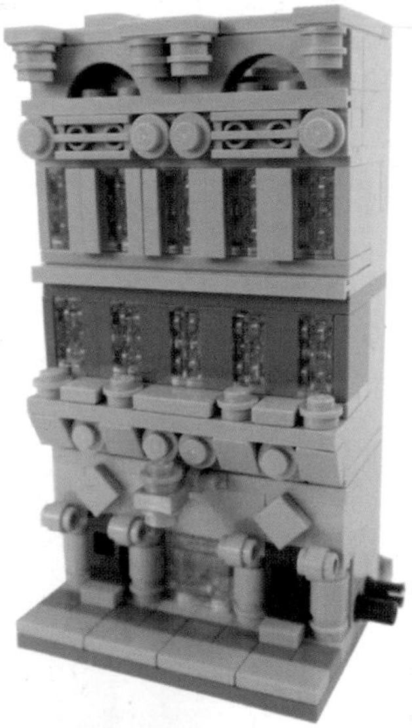

National Bank

Corner Drugstore

The corner drugstore re-creates an icon of classic Americana. You can almost see the soda jerk behind the counter. The drugstore has a small shop area as well as a back room for deliveries. Stairs lead to the second floor apartment, which has a fully furnished interior for the owner of the store. An apothecary's mortar-and-pestle sign, as well as the "SODA" billboard on the roof, make the building instantly identifiable even before you look inside.

We encourage you to experiment and customize our creations. We'll give you some ideas as you build!

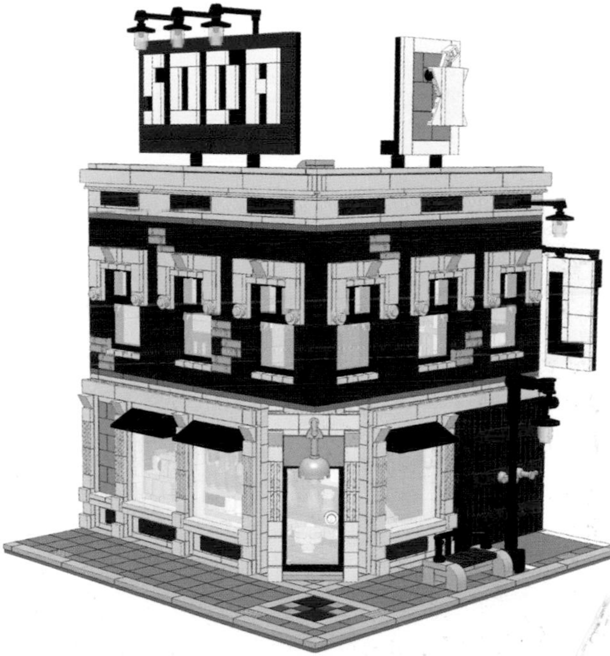

Bill of Materials

For a parts list you can download, visit *http://nostarch.com/legoneighborhood/*.

While you're there, you can also find building instructions for a delivery truck that fits perfectly in the stockroom.

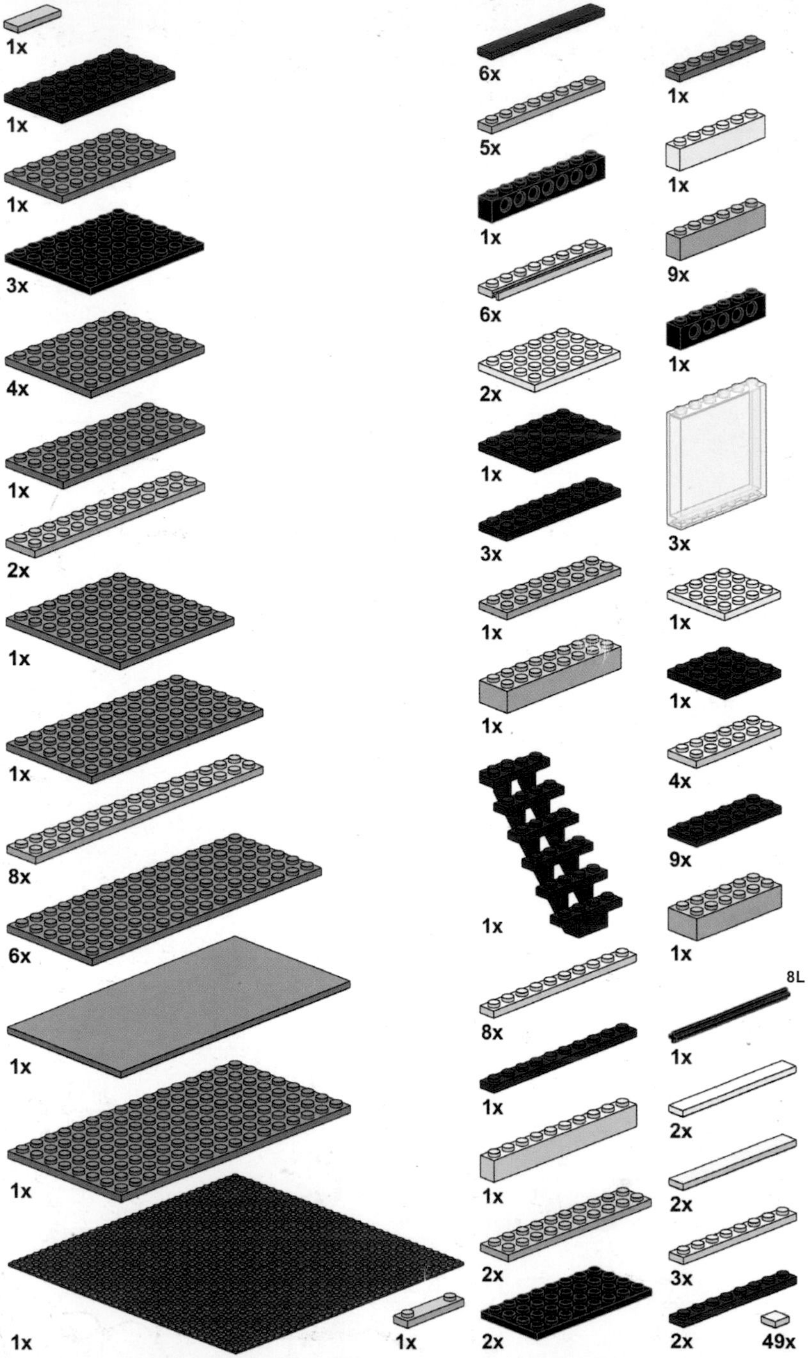

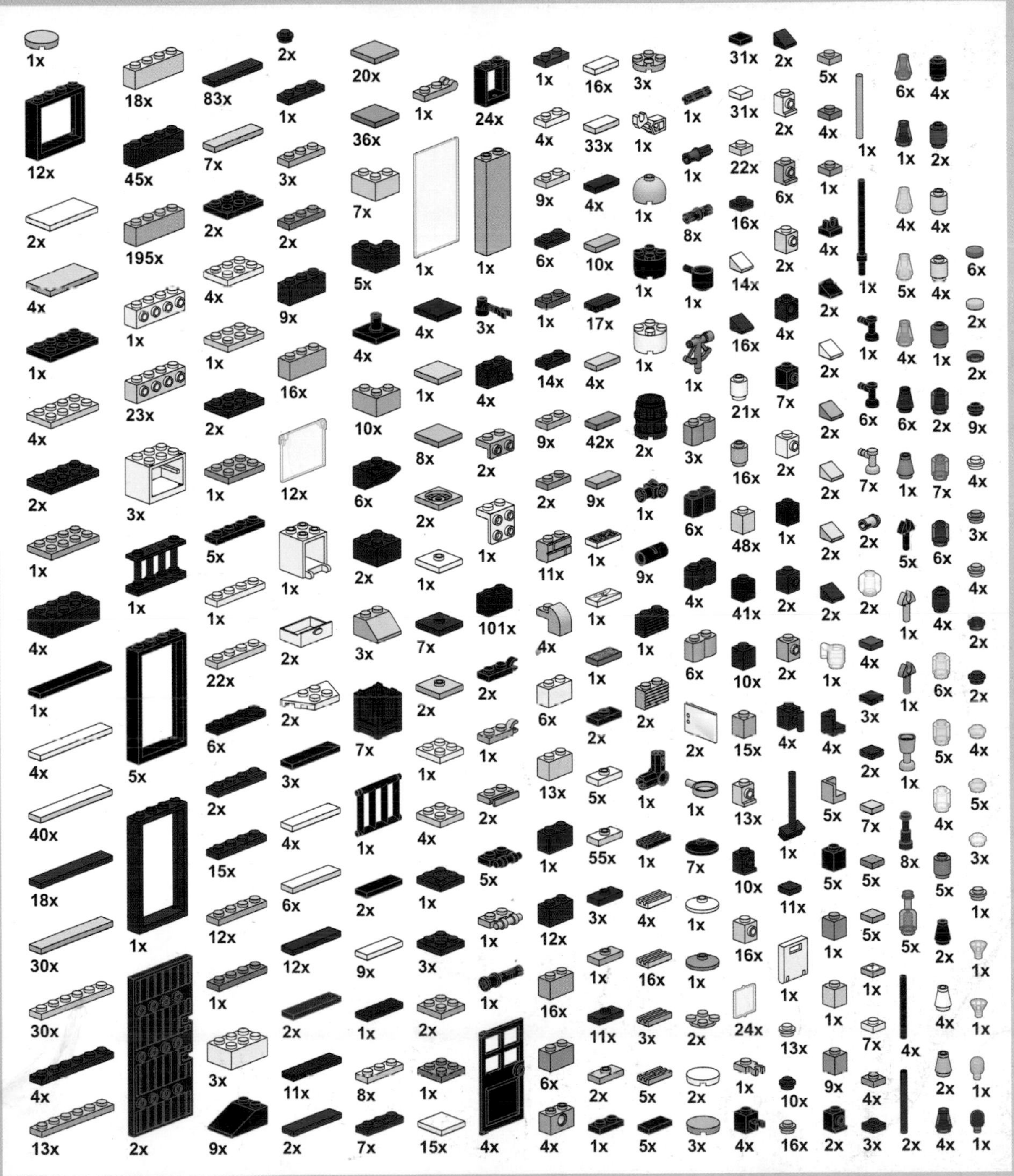

1x
12x
2x
4x
1x
4x
2x
1x
4x
1x
4x
40x
18x
30x
30x
4x
13x
18x
45x
195x
1x
23x
3x
1x
5x
1x
2x
83x
7x
2x
4x
1x
2x
1x
5x
1x
22x
6x
2x
15x
12x
1x
3x
9x
2x
1x
3x
2x
9x
16x
12x
1x
2x
2x
3x
4x
6x
12x
2x
11x
2x
20x
36x
7x
5x
4x
10x
6x
2x
3x
7x
1x
2x
9x
1x
8x
7x
1x
1x
4x
1x
8x
2x
1x
7x
2x
1x
4x
1x
3x
2x
1x
15x
24x
1x
3x
4x
2x
1x
101x
2x
1x
2x
5x
1x
1x
4x
1x
4x
9x
6x
1x
14x
9x
2x
11x
4x
6x
13x
1x
12x
16x
6x
4x
16x
33x
4x
10x
17x
4x
42x
9x
1x
1x
1x
2x
5x
55x
3x
1x
11x
2x
1x
3x
1x
1x
1x
1x
2x
1x
9x
1x
2x
1x
1x
4x
16x
3x
5x
5x
1x
1x
8x
1x
1x
3x
6x
4x
6x
2x
1x
7x
1x
1x
2x
2x
3x
31x
31x
22x
16x
14x
16x
21x
16x
48x
41x
10x
15x
13x
10x
16x
24x
1x
4x
2x
2x
6x
2x
4x
7x
2x
1x
2x
2x
4x
1x
11x
1x
13x
10x
16x
5x
4x
1x
4x
2x
2x
2x
2x
2x
2x
1x
4x
5x
5x
1x
1x
9x
2x
1x
1x
1x
6x
7x
2x
2x
4x
3x
2x
7x
5x
5x
1x
7x
4x
3x
6x
1x
4x
5x
4x
6x
1x
5x
1x
1x
1x
8x
5x
4x
2x
4x
2x
4x
4x
1x
2x
7x
6x
4x
6x
5x
4x
5x
2x
4x
2x
4x
6x
2x
2x
9x
4x
3x
4x
2x
2x
4x
5x
3x
1x
1x
1x
1x
1x

First Floor

1

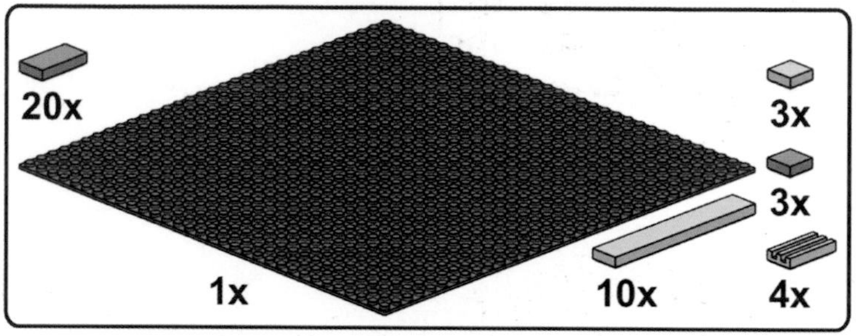
20x
3x
3x
1x
10x
4x

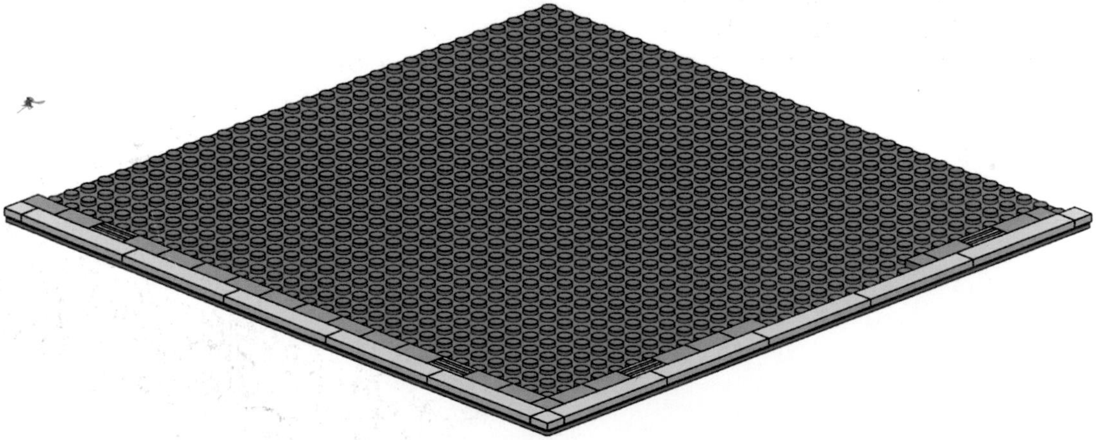

2

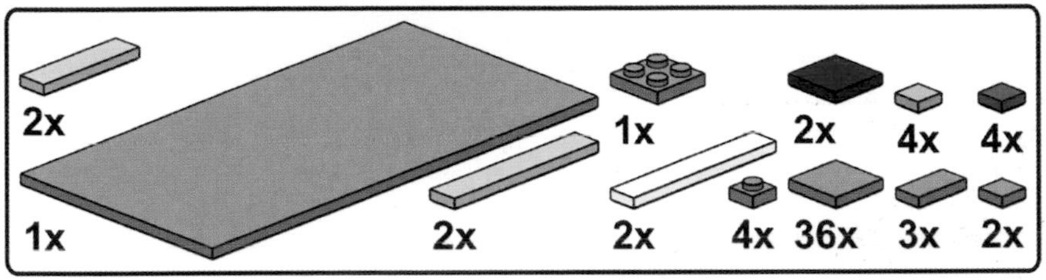

2x
1x
2x
1x
2x
2x
4x
4x
2x
4x
36x
3x
2x

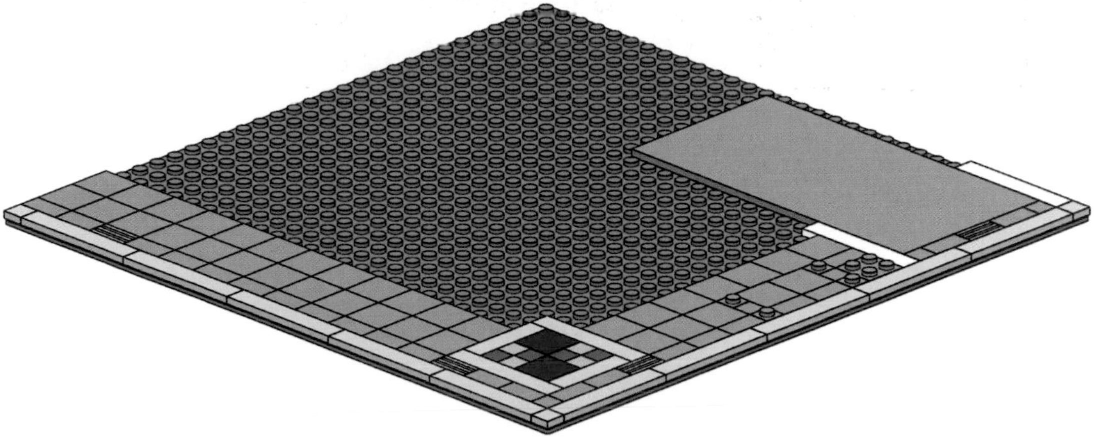

3

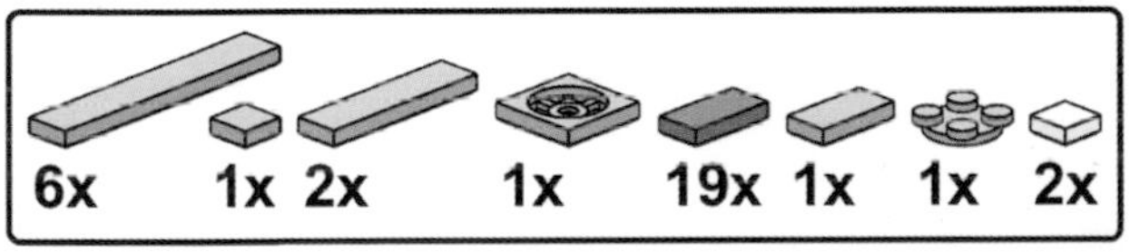

6x
1x
2x
1x
19x
1x
1x
2x

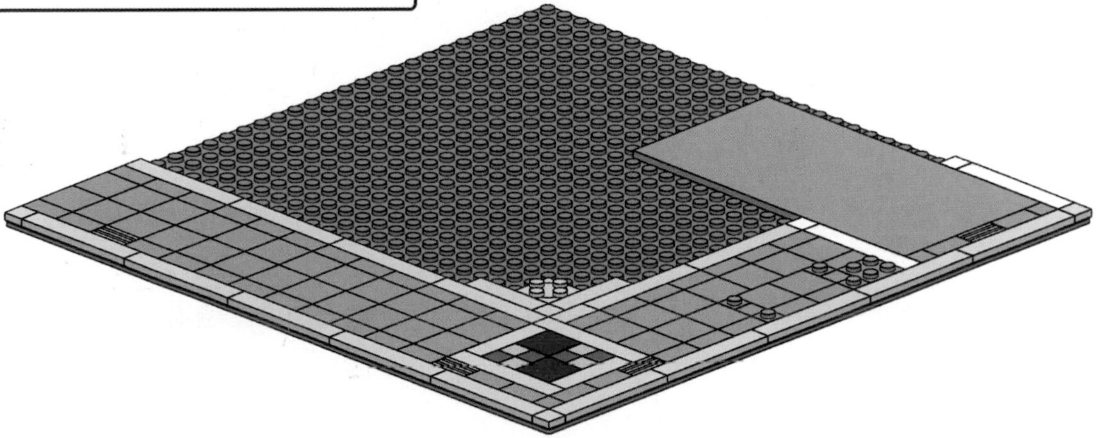

4

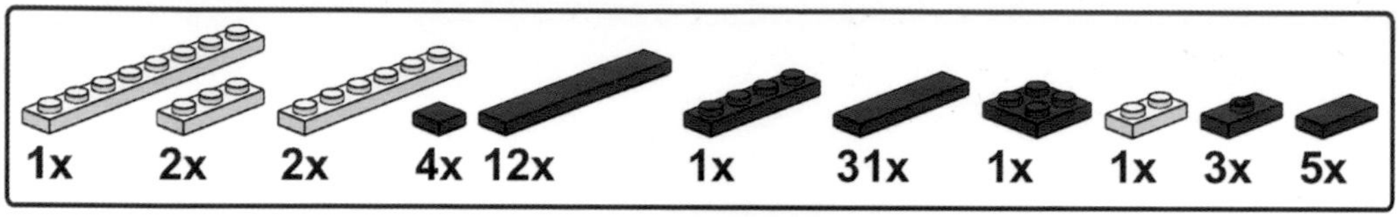
1x
2x
2x
4x
12x
1x
31x
1x
1x
3x
5x

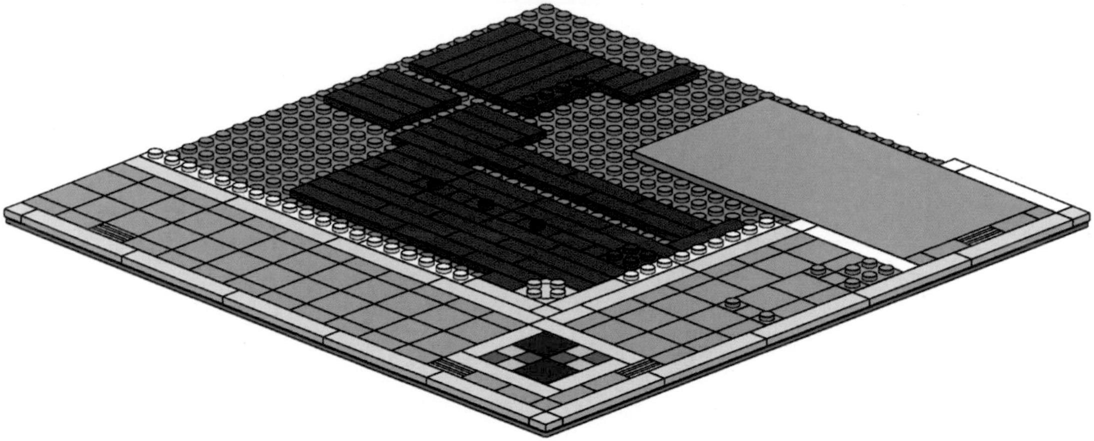

5

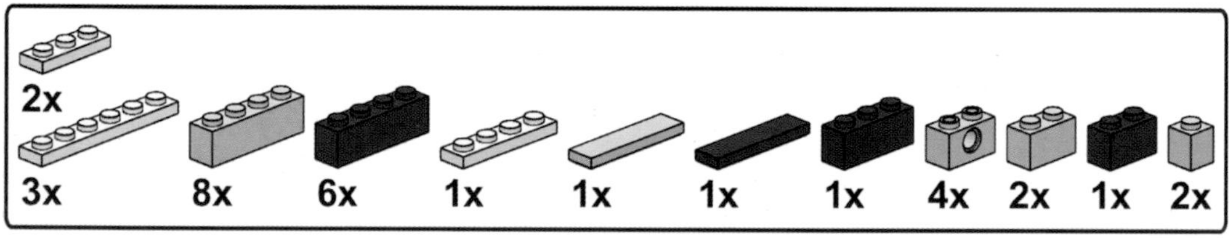
2x
3x
8x
6x
1x
1x
1x
1x
4x
2x
1x
2x

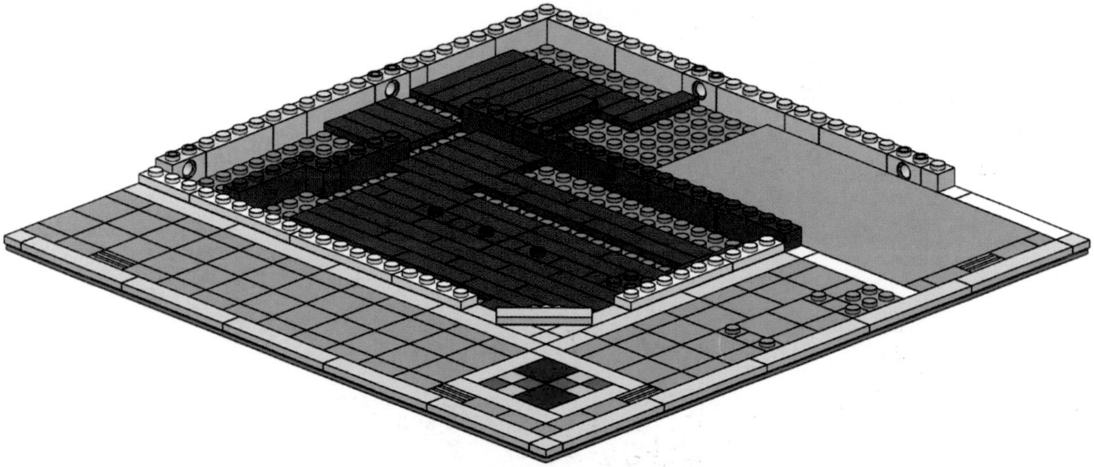

6

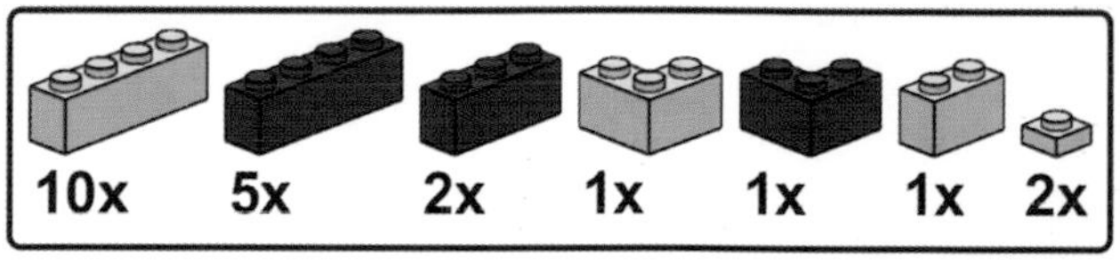
10x
5x
2x
1x
1x
1x
2x

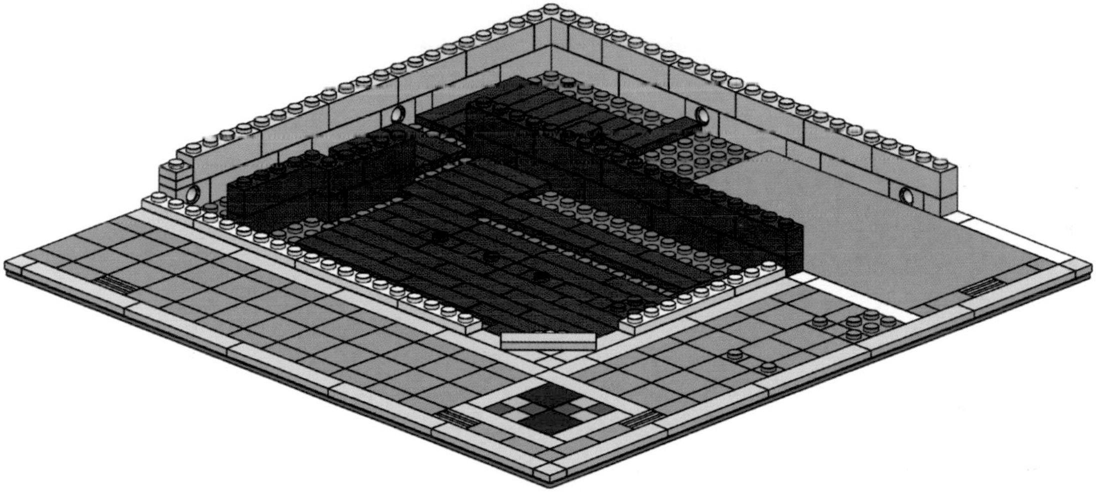

7

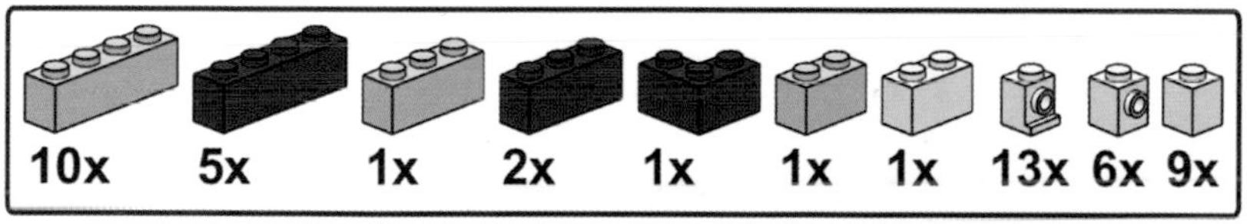
10x
5x
1x
2x
1x
1x
1x
13x
6x
9x

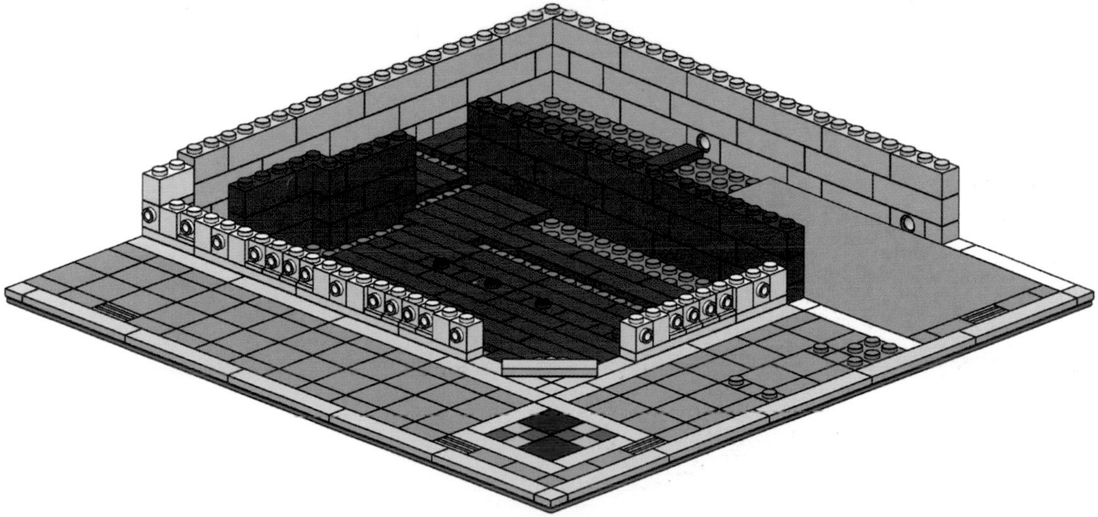

8

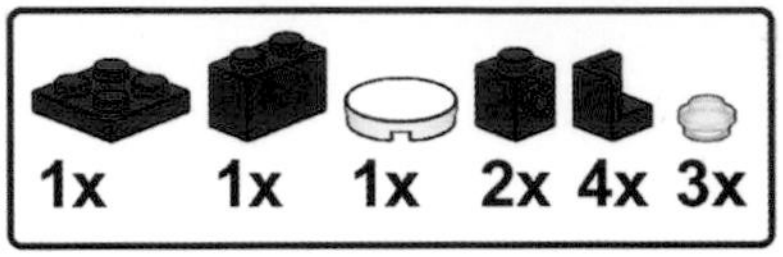

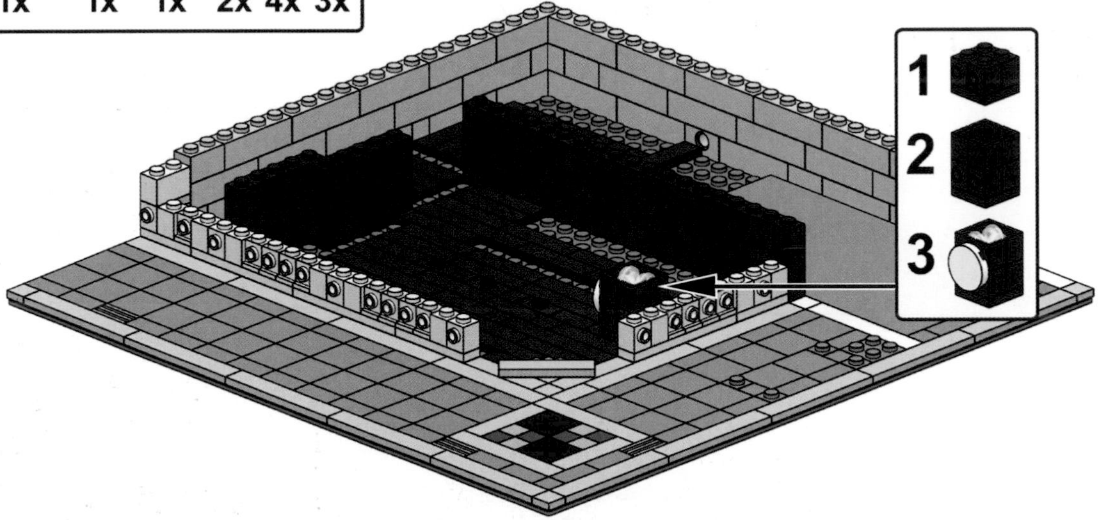

9

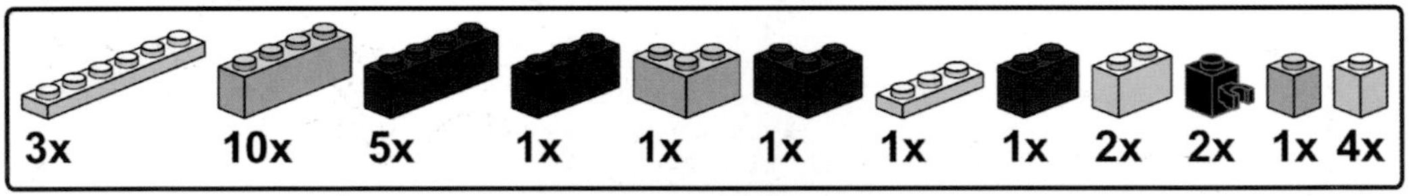

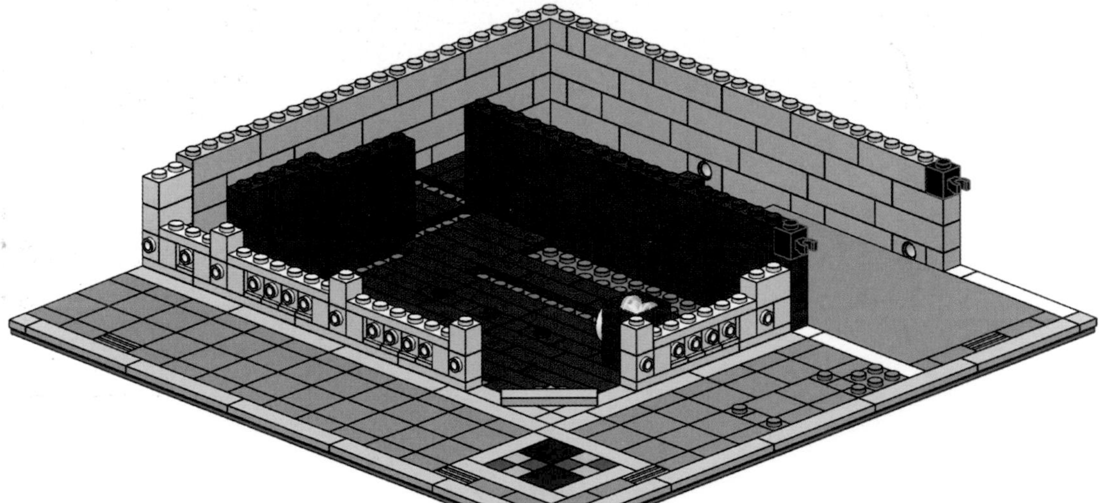

10

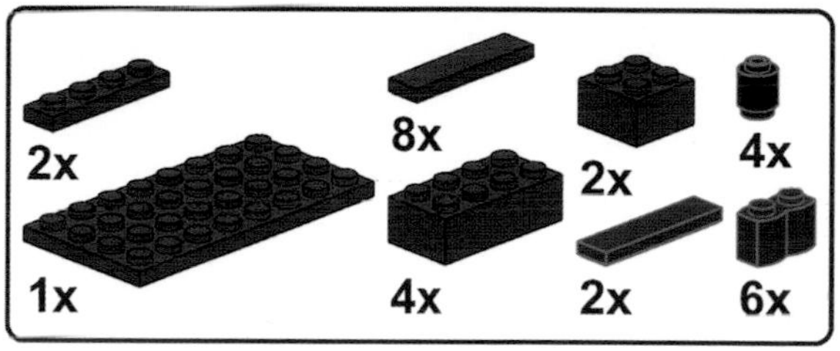
2x
1x
8x
4x
2x
2x
4x
6x

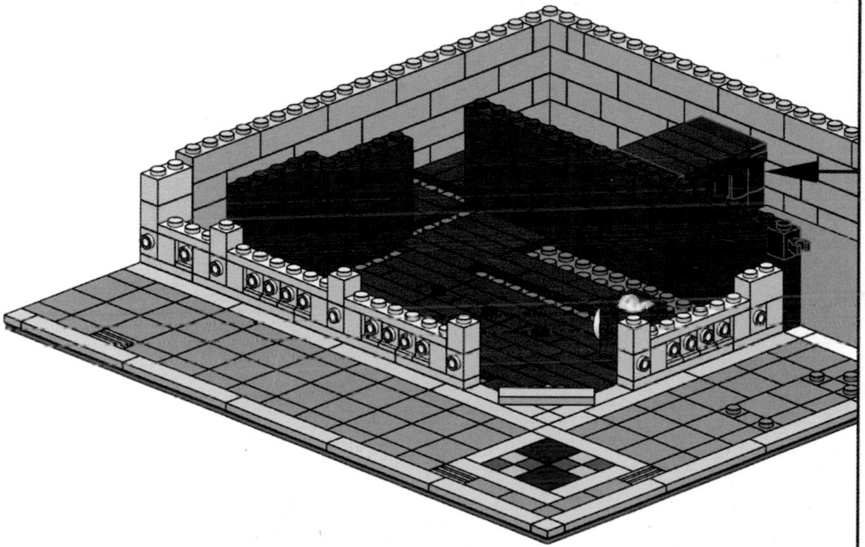

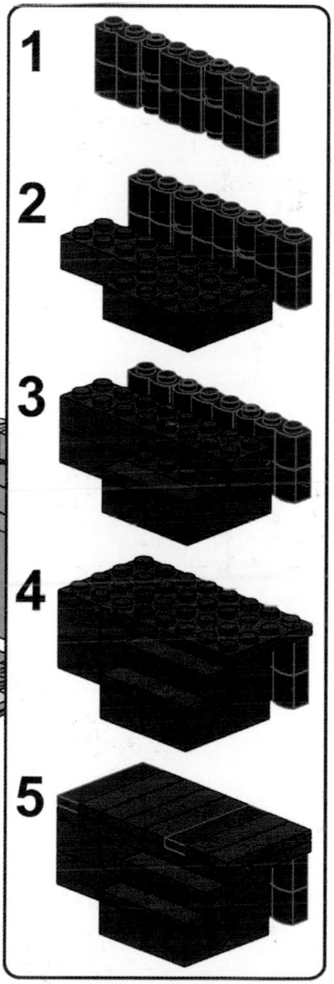
1
2
3
4
5

11

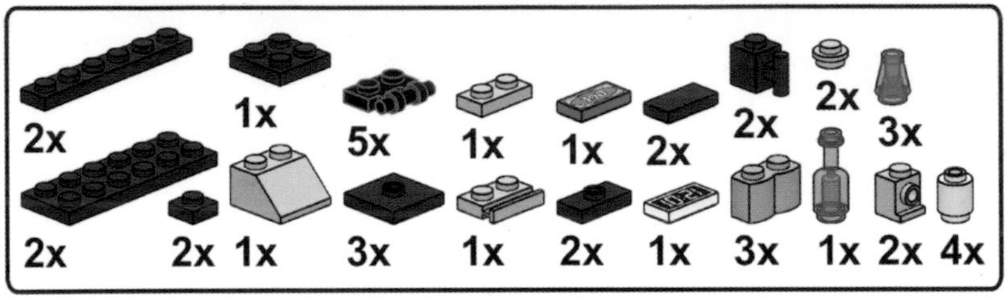

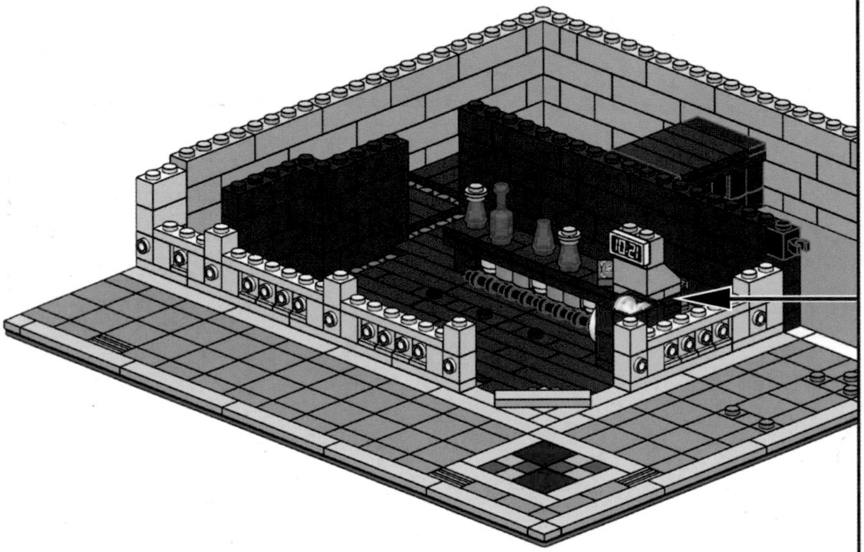

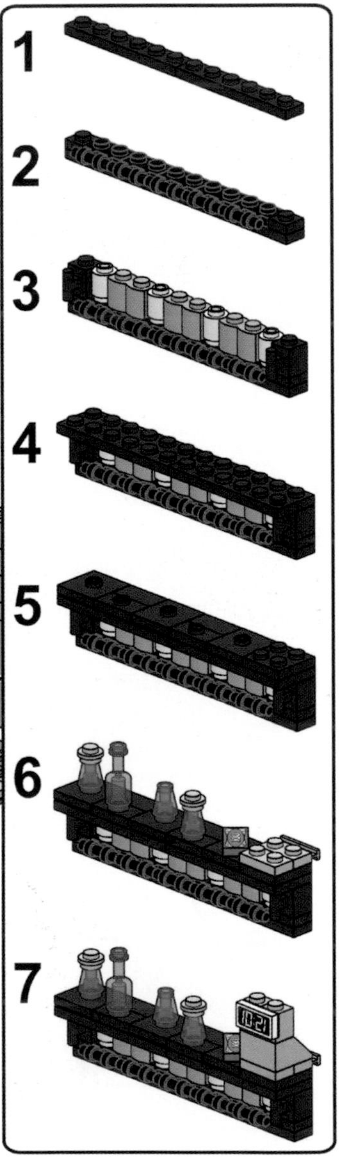

12

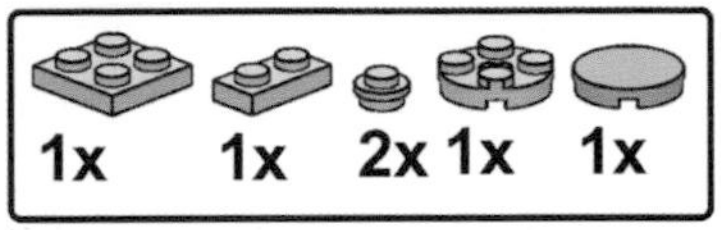

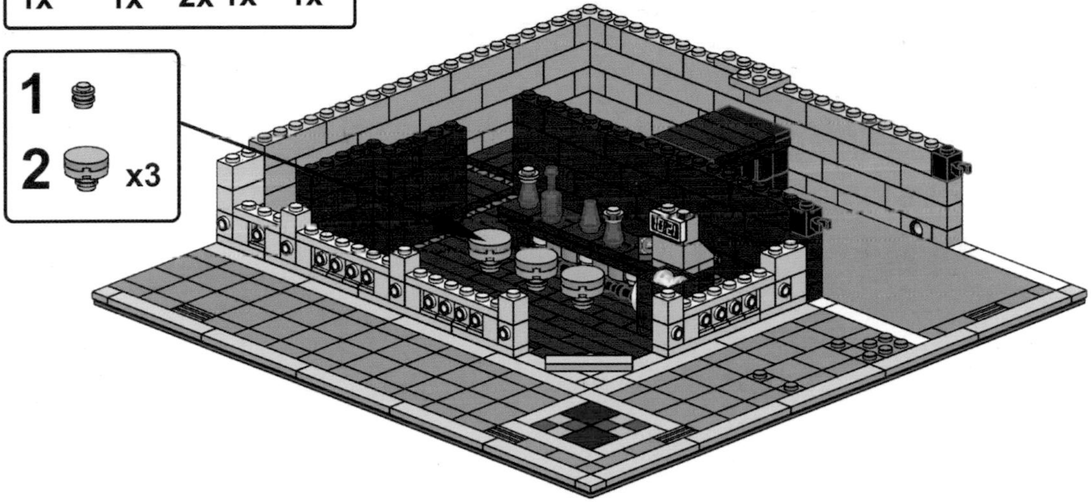

13

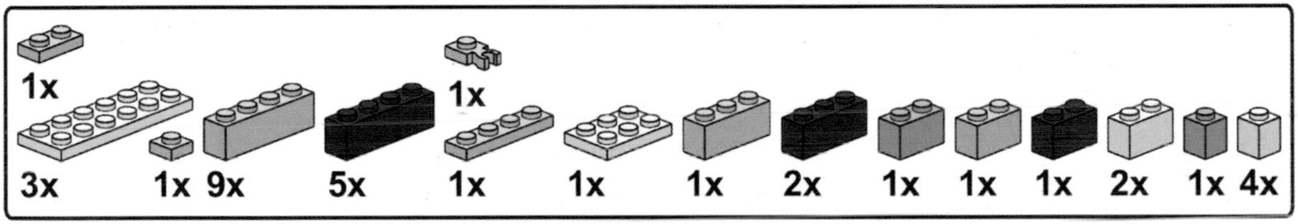

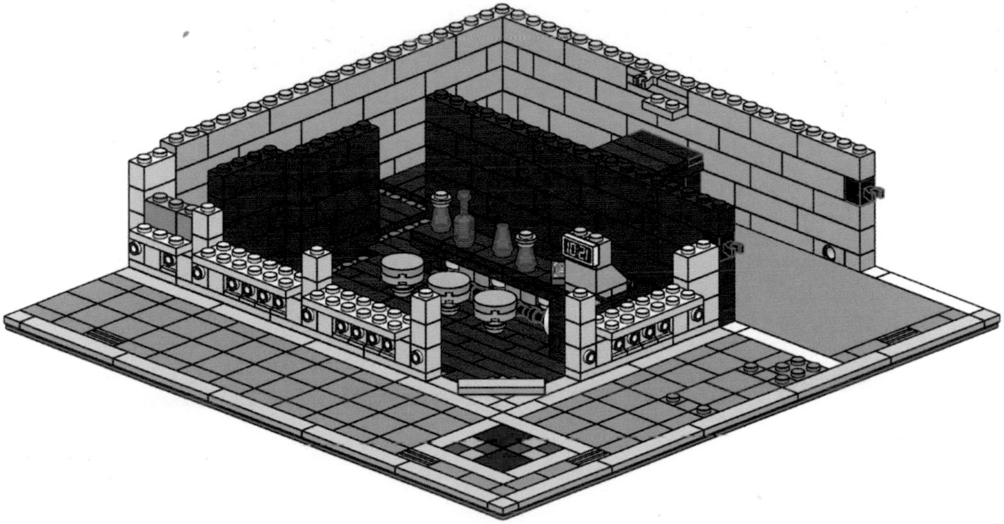

14

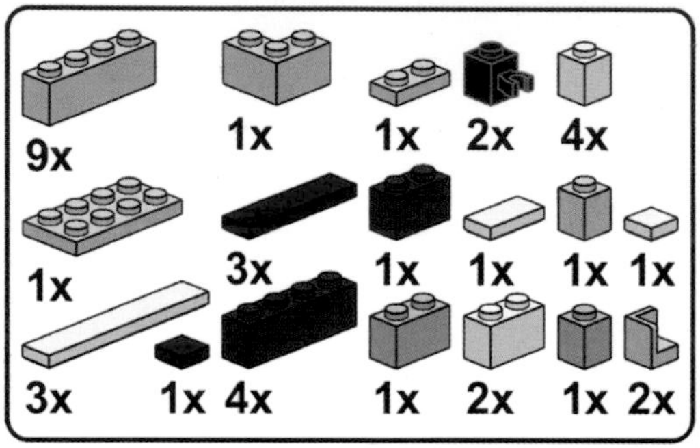

9x
1x
1x
2x
4x
1x
3x
1x
1x
1x
1x
3x
1x
4x
1x
2x
1x
2x

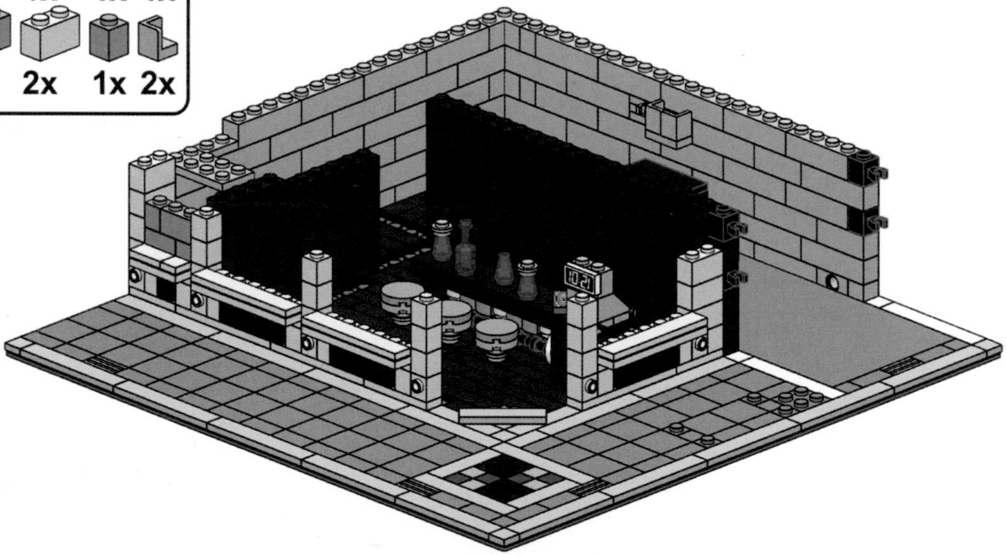

15

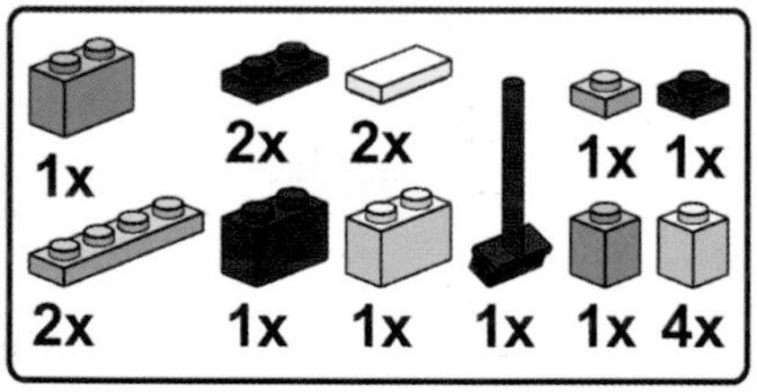

1x
2x
2x
1x
1x
2x
1x
1x
1x
1x
4x

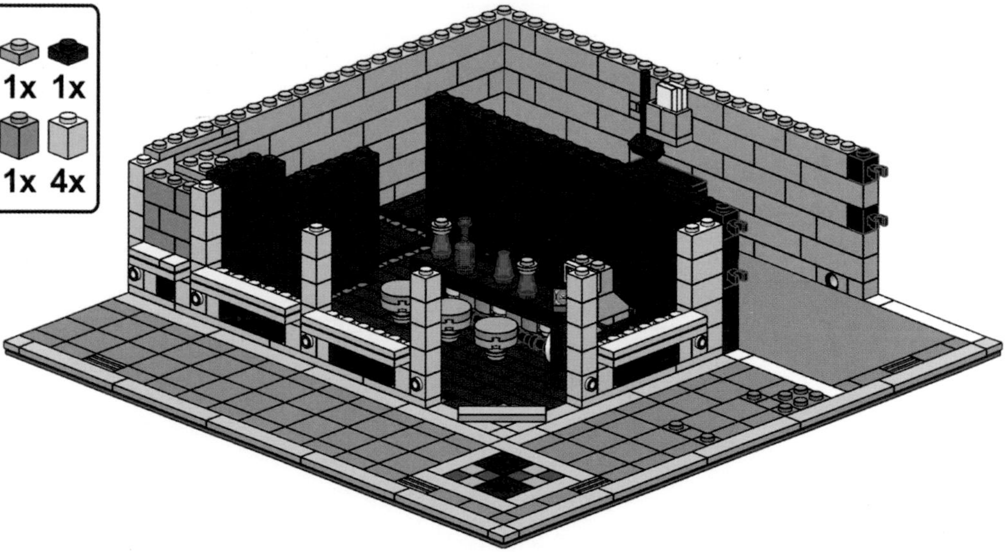

16

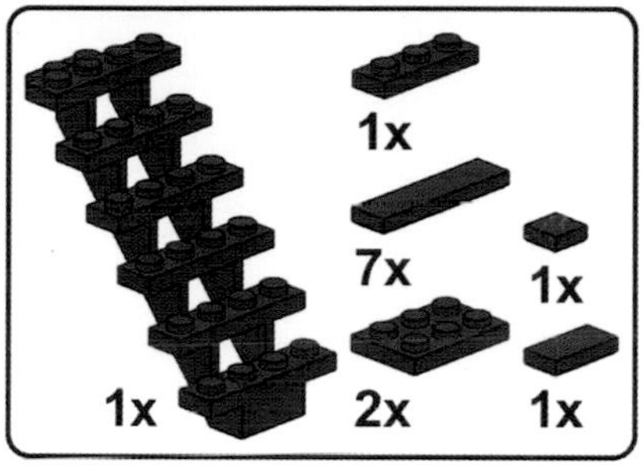

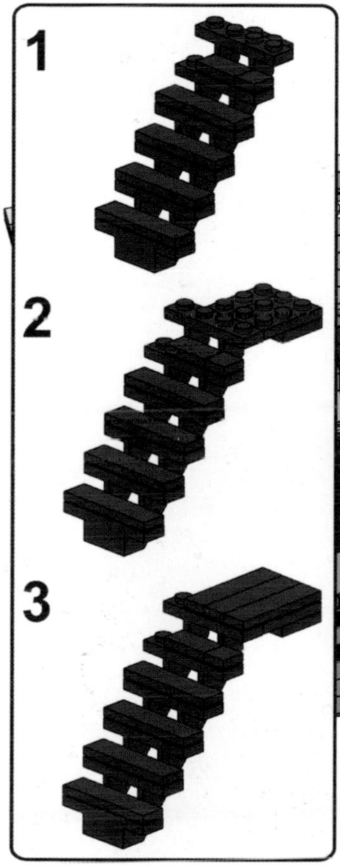

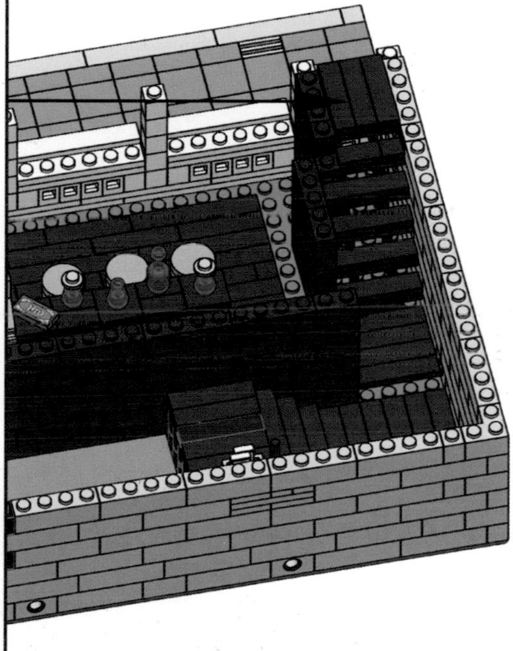

17

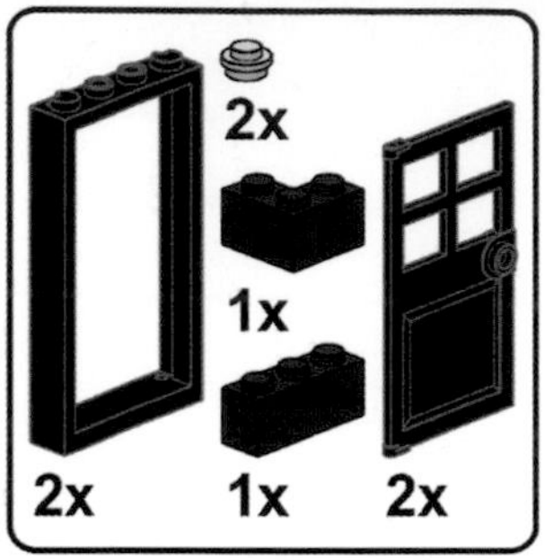
2x
1x
2x
1x
2x

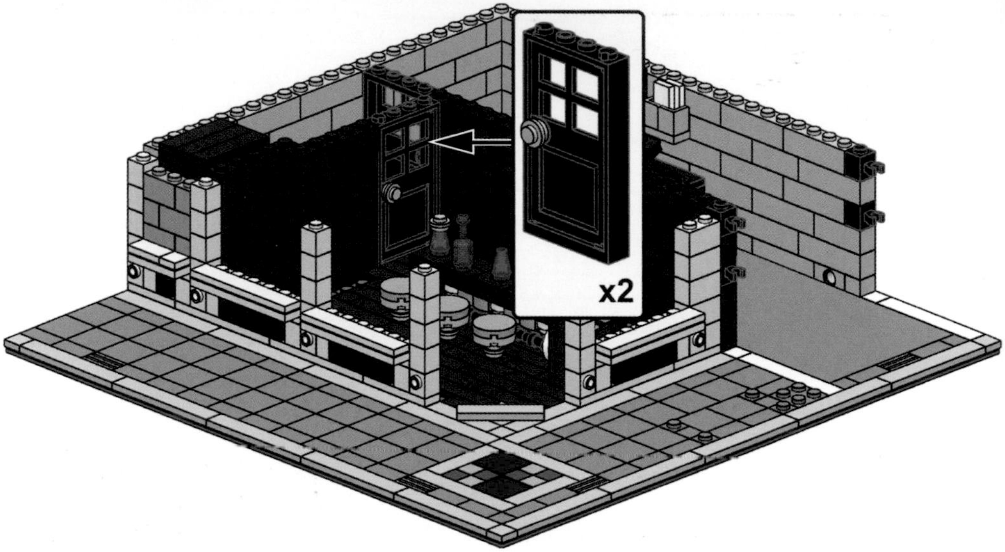
x2

18

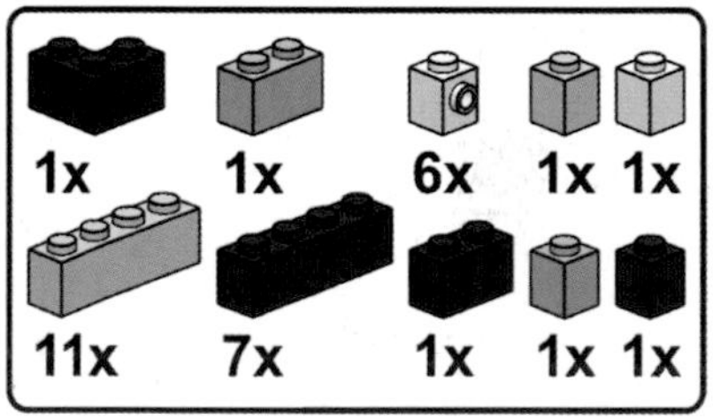
1x
1x
6x
1x
1x
11x
7x
1x
1x
1x

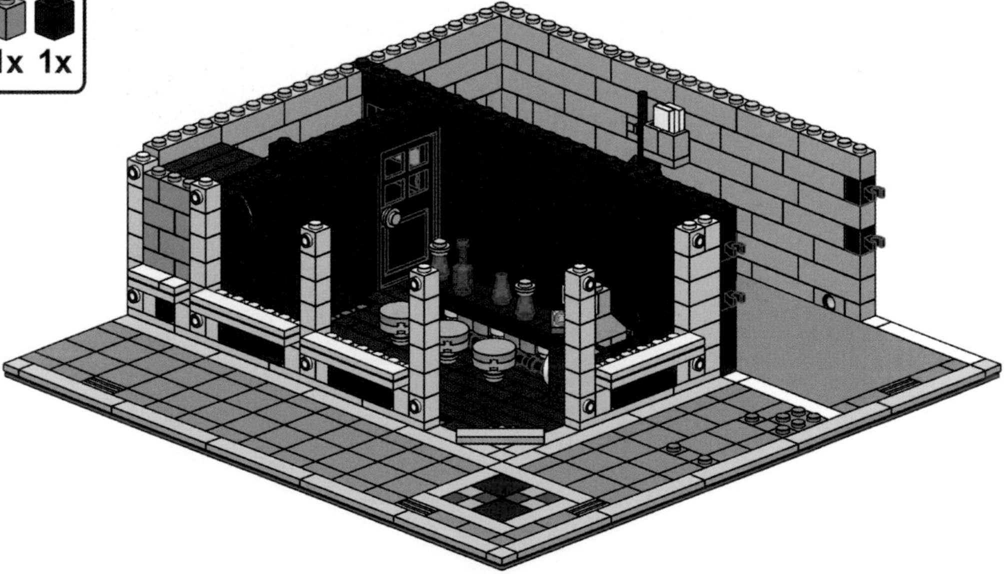

19

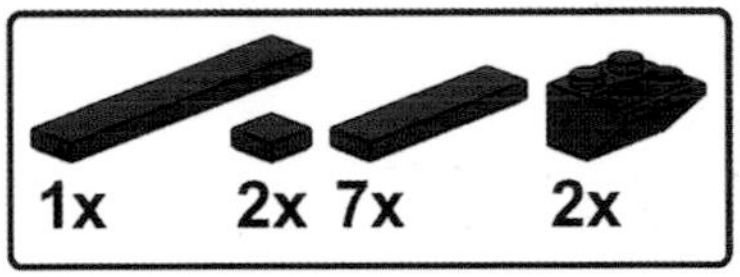

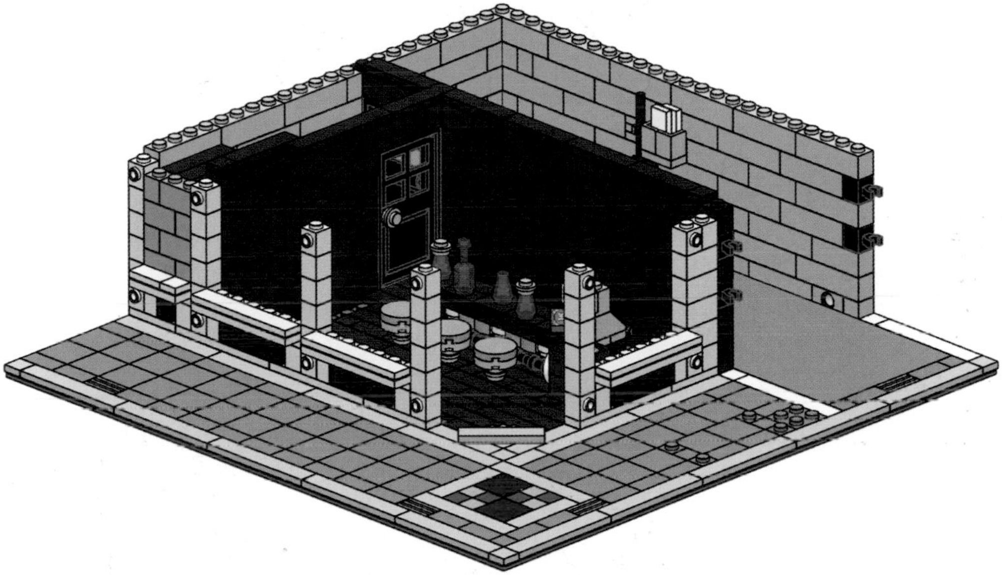

20

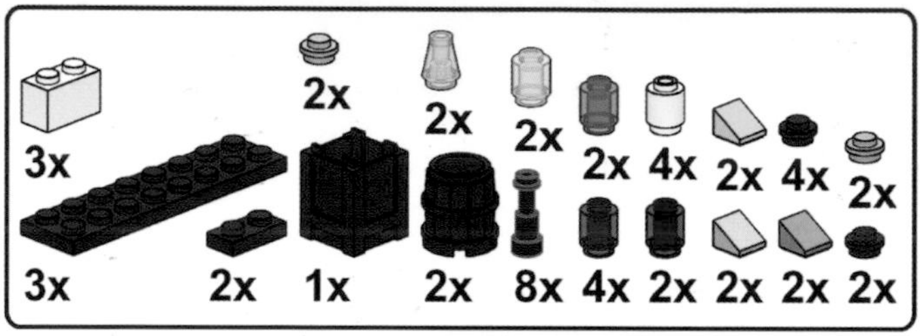

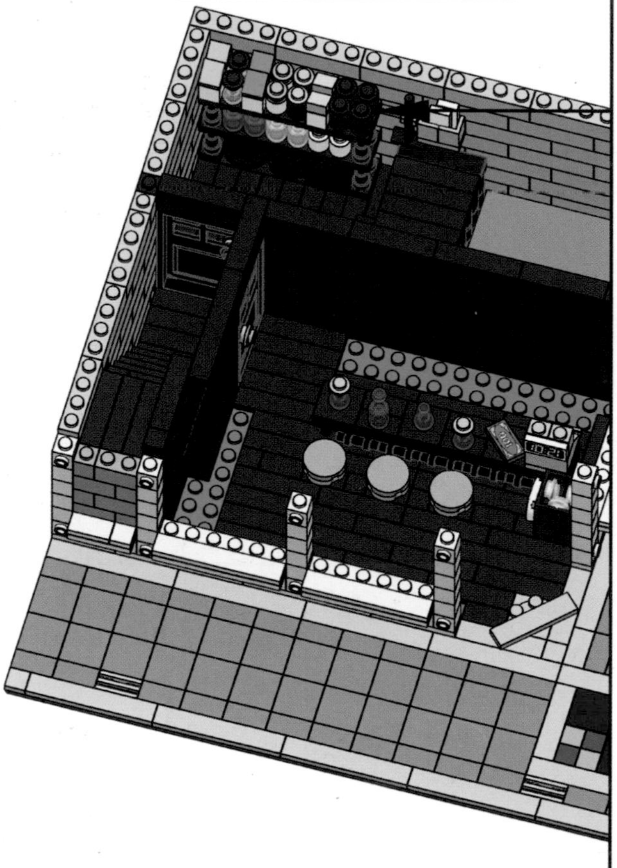

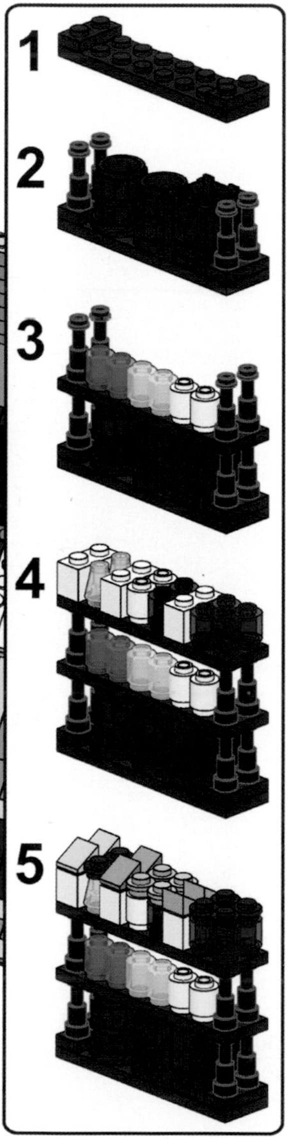

21

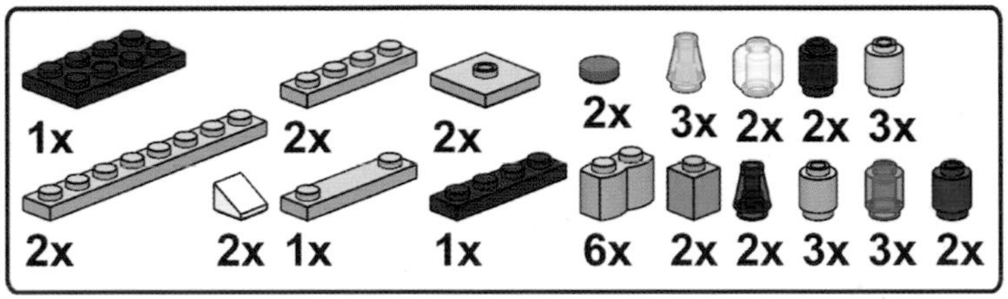

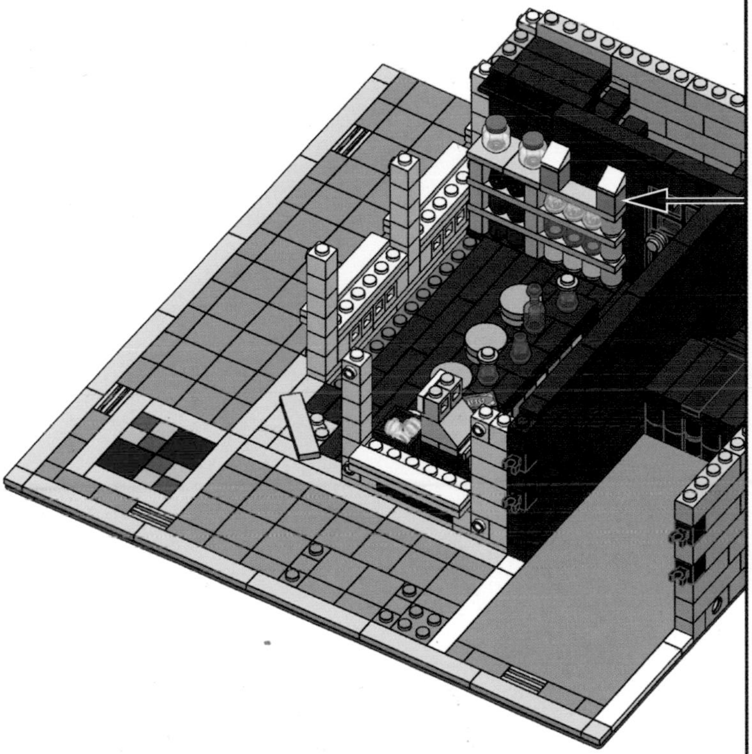

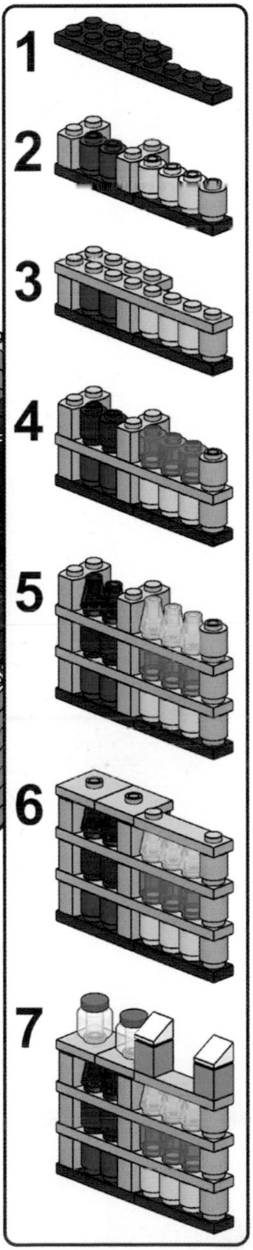

22

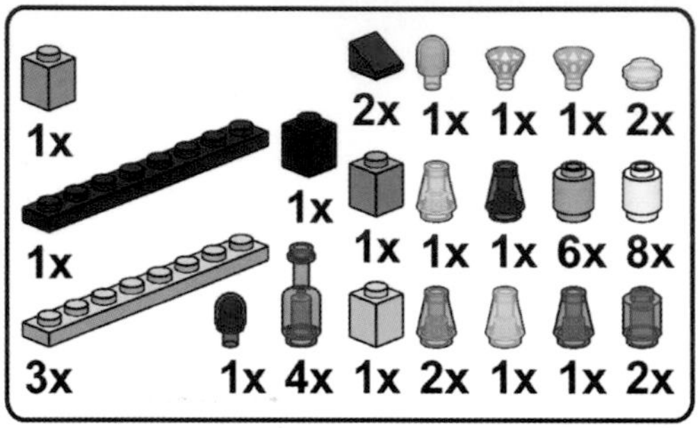
1x
2x 1x 1x 1x 2x
1x
1x
1x 1x 1x 6x 8x
3x
1x 4x 1x 2x 1x 1x 2x

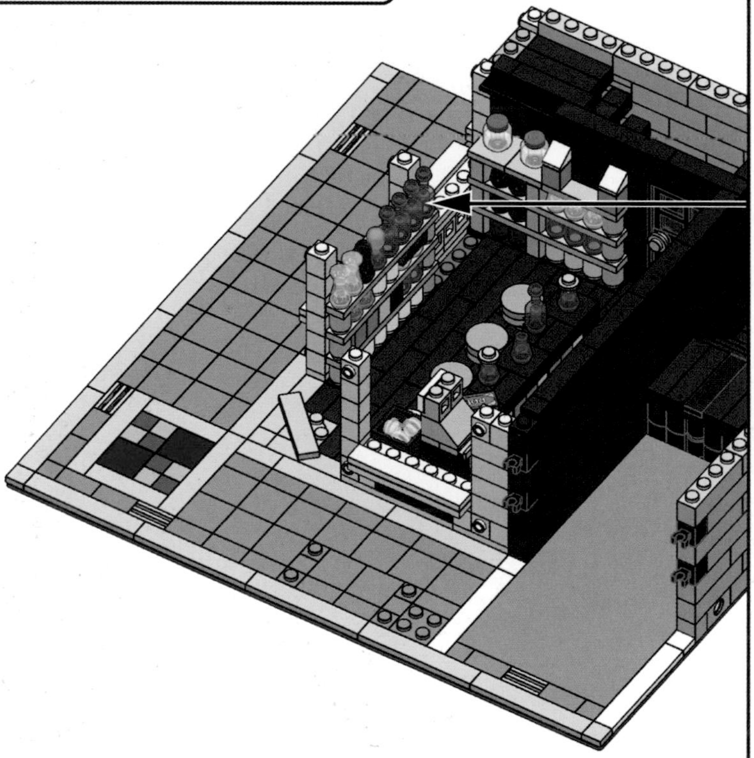

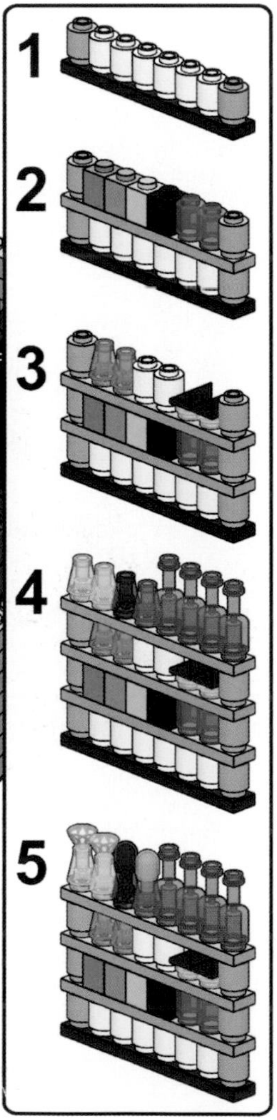
1
2
3
4
5

23

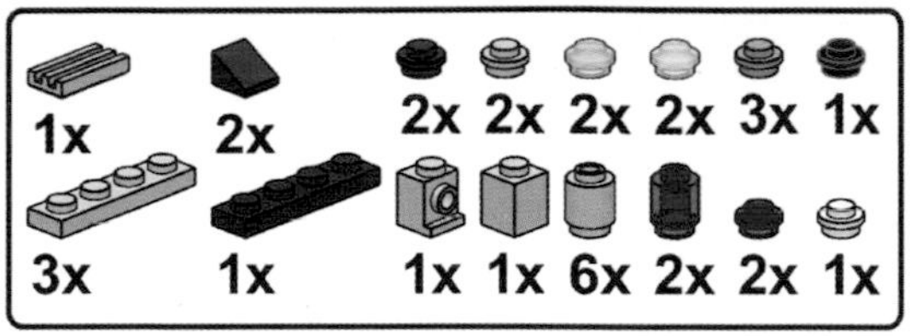

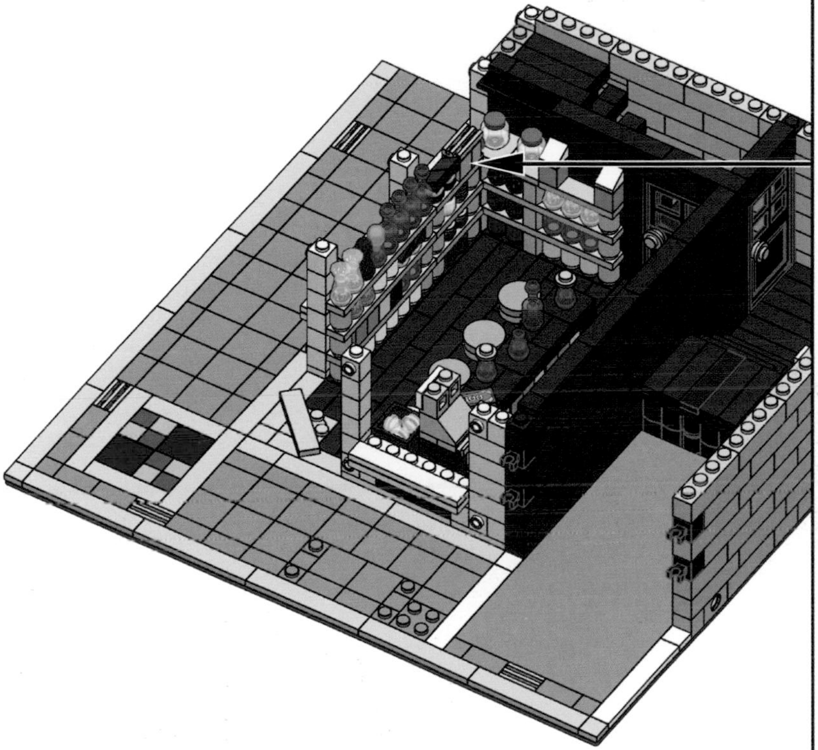

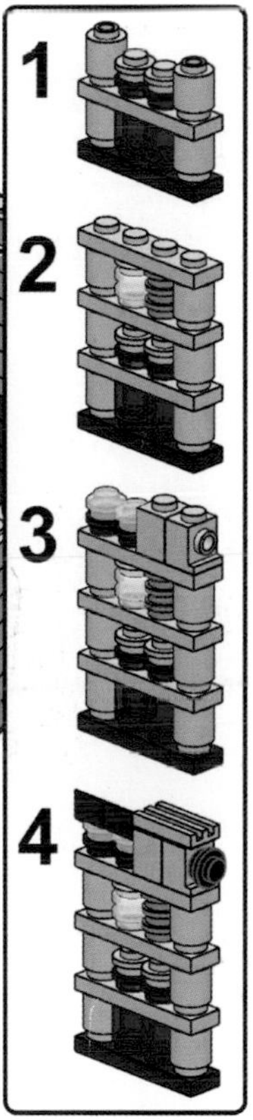

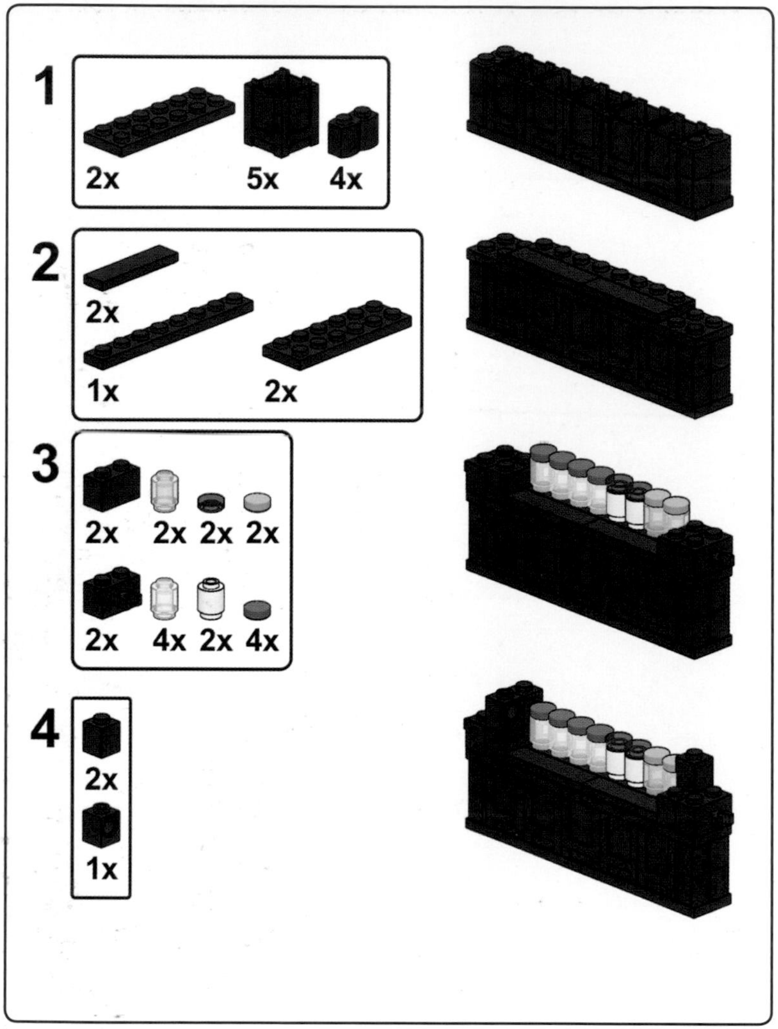
1
2x
5x
4x
2
2x
1x
2x
3
2x
2x
2x
2x
2x
4x
2x
4x
4
2x
1x

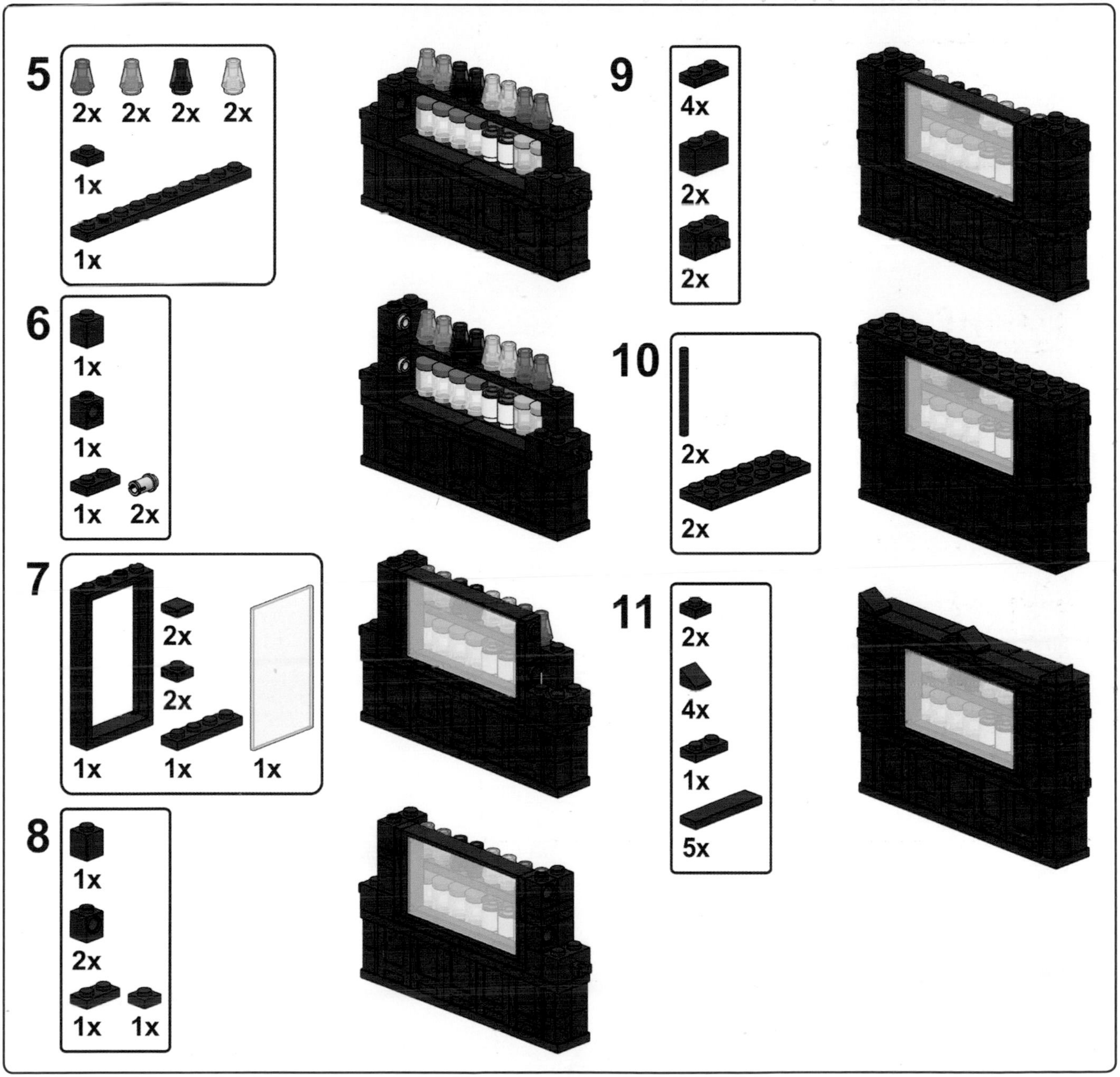
5
2x 2x 2x 2x
1x
1x
6
1x
1x
1x 2x
7
1x
2x
2x
1x
1x
8
1x
2x
1x 1x
9
4x
2x
2x
10
2x
2x
11
2x
4x
1x
5x

24

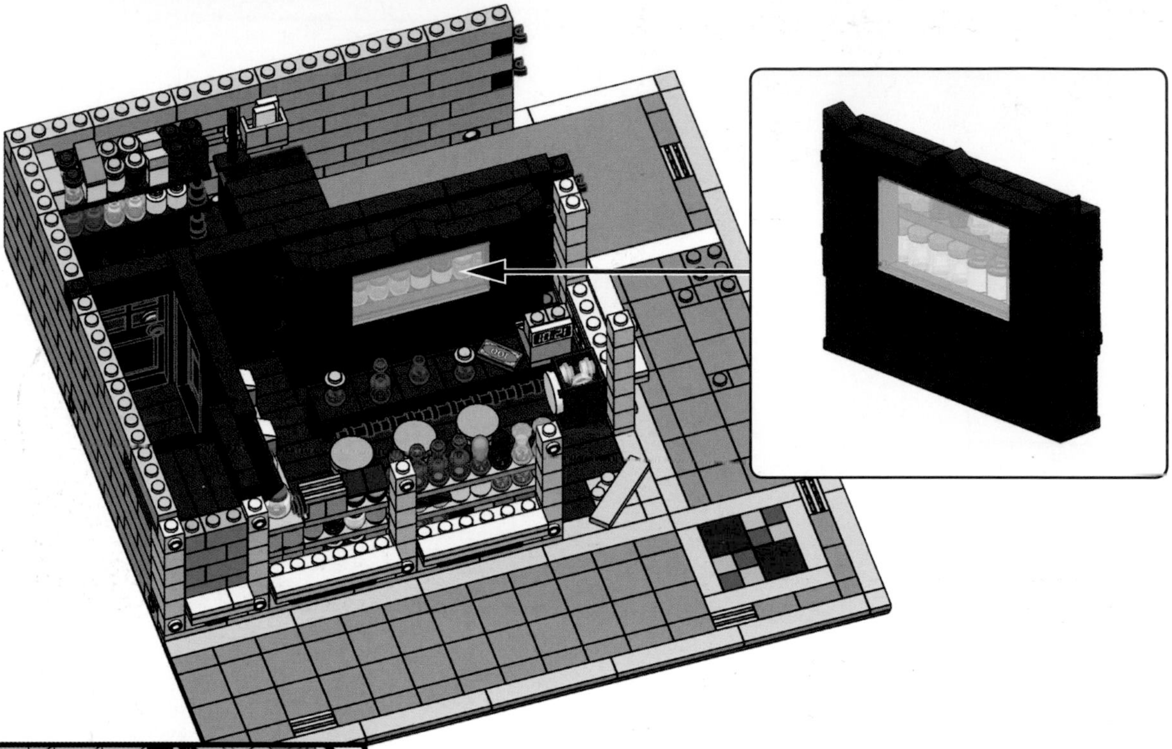

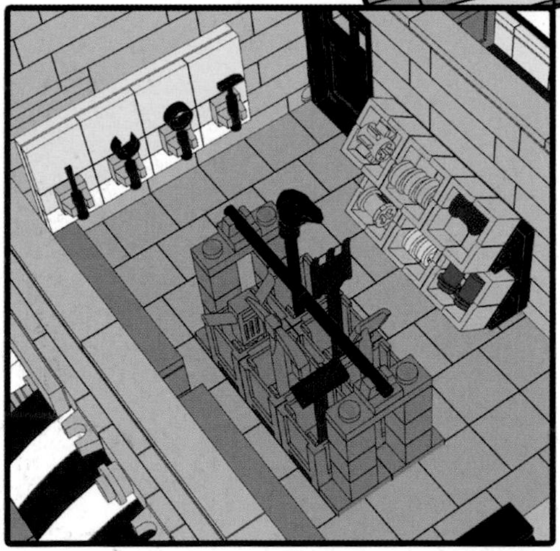

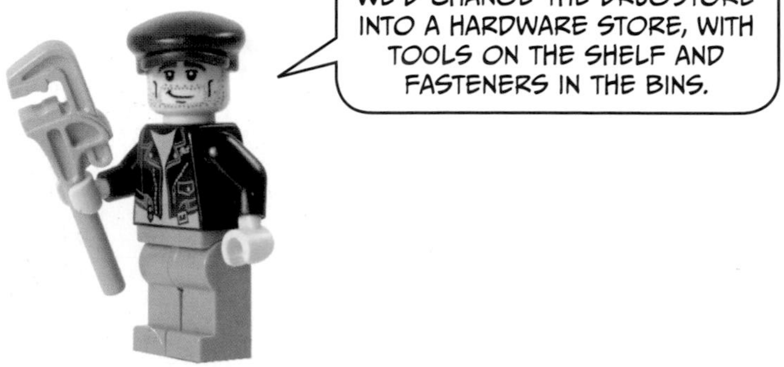
YOU CAN MAKE ANY TYPE OF STORE YOU WANT. HERE'S HOW WE'D CHANGE THE DRUGSTORE INTO A HARDWARE STORE, WITH TOOLS ON THE SHELF AND FASTENERS IN THE BINS.

25

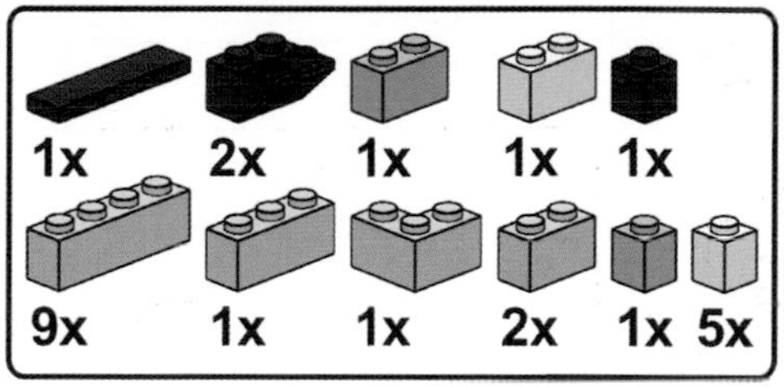
1x
2x
1x
1x
1x
9x
1x
1x
2x
1x
5x

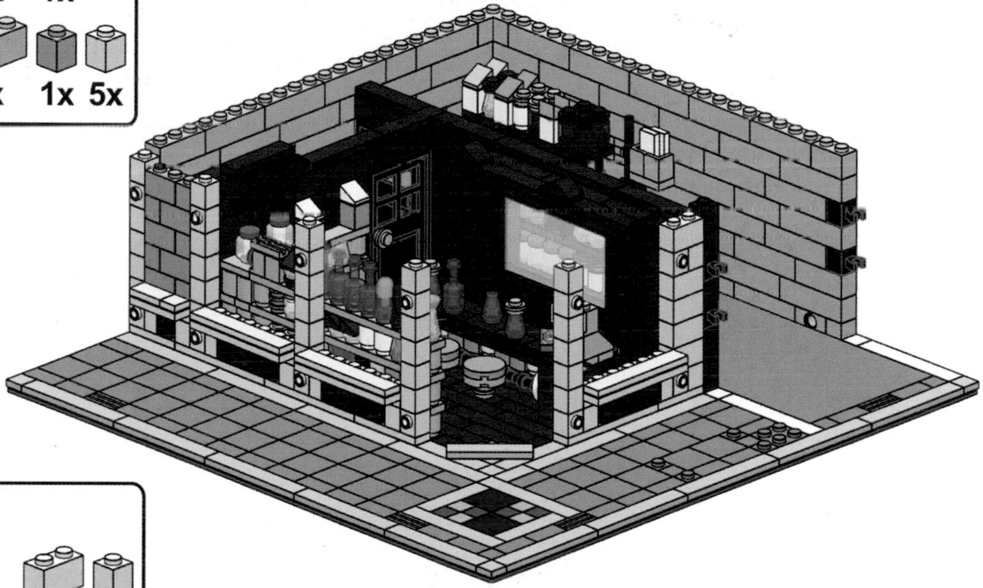

26

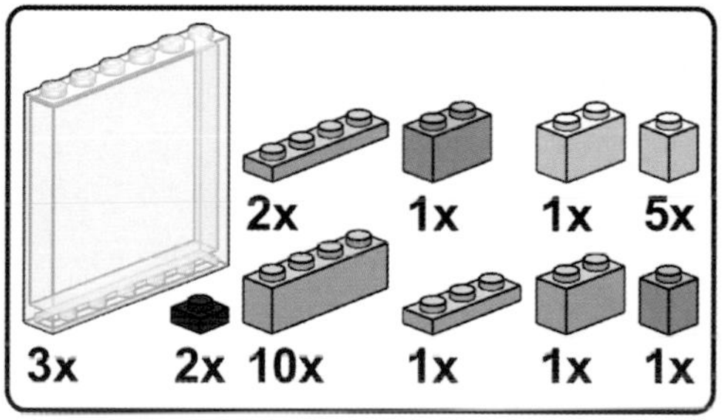
2x
1x
1x
5x
3x
2x
10x
1x
1x
1x

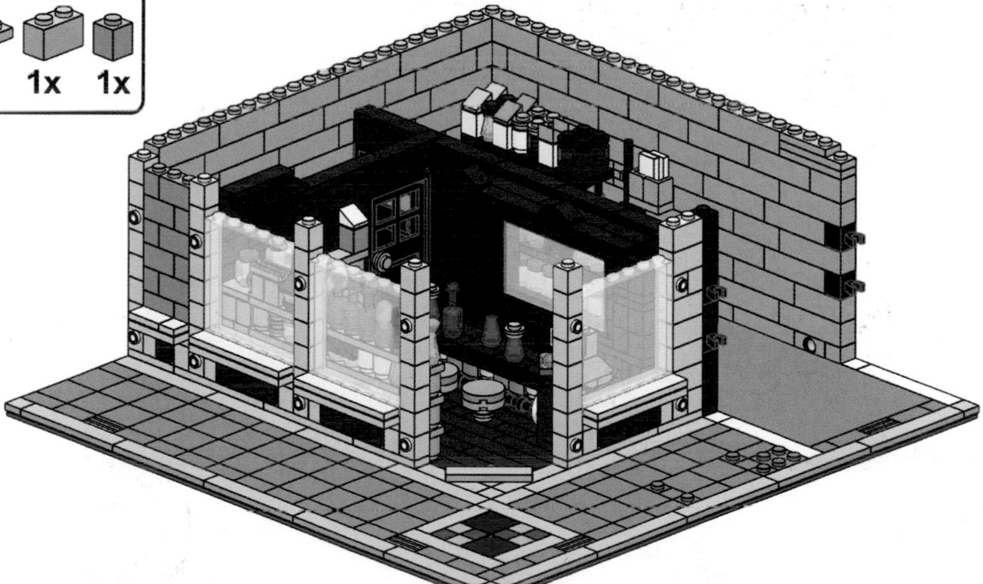

27

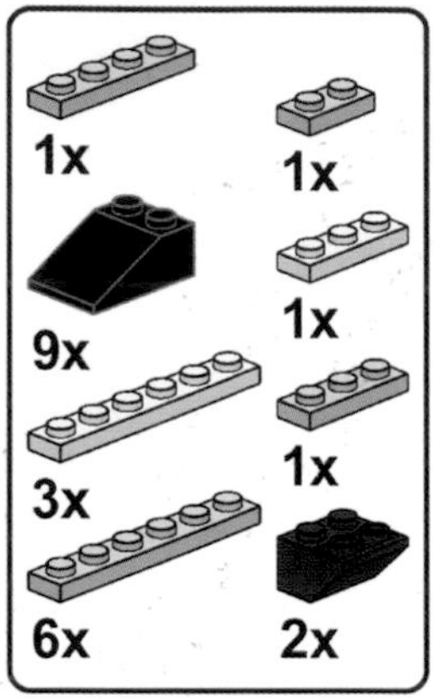
1x
1x
9x
1x
3x
1x
6x
2x

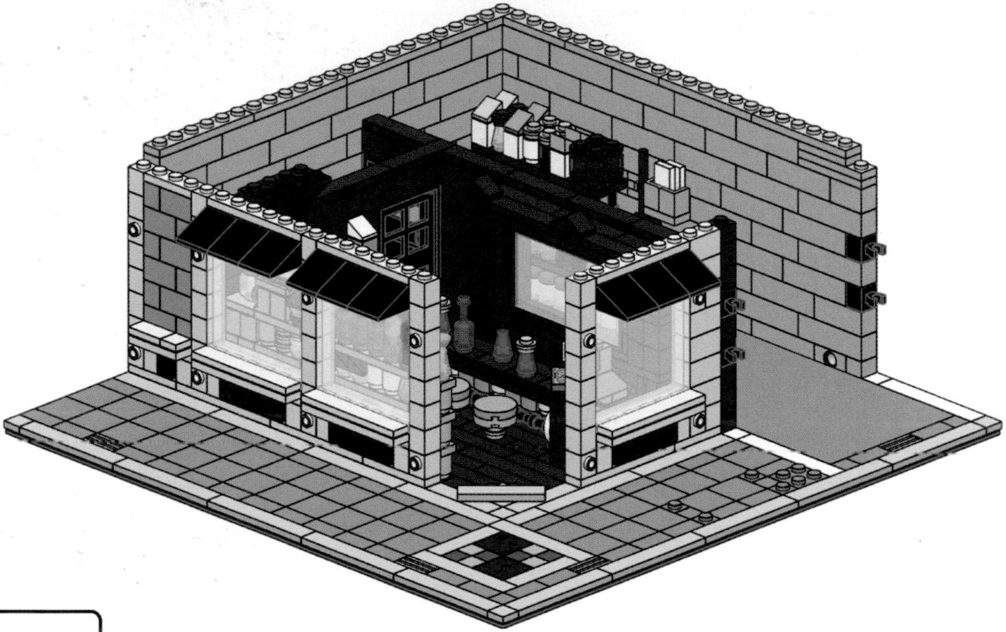

28

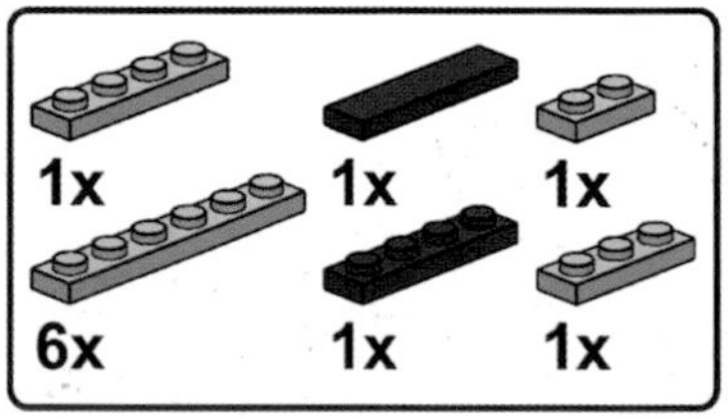
1x
1x
1x
6x
1x
1x

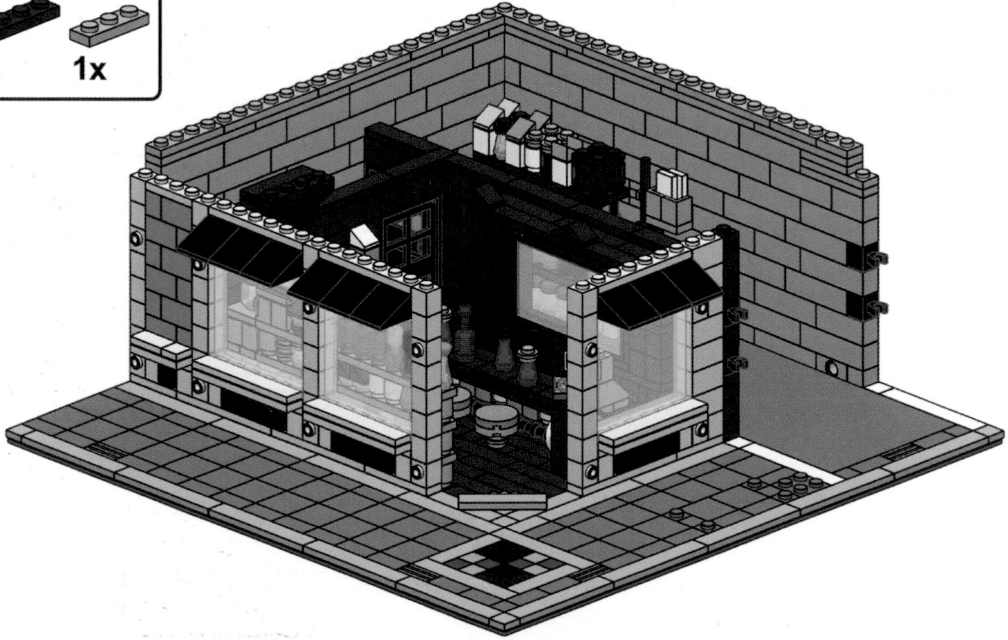

29

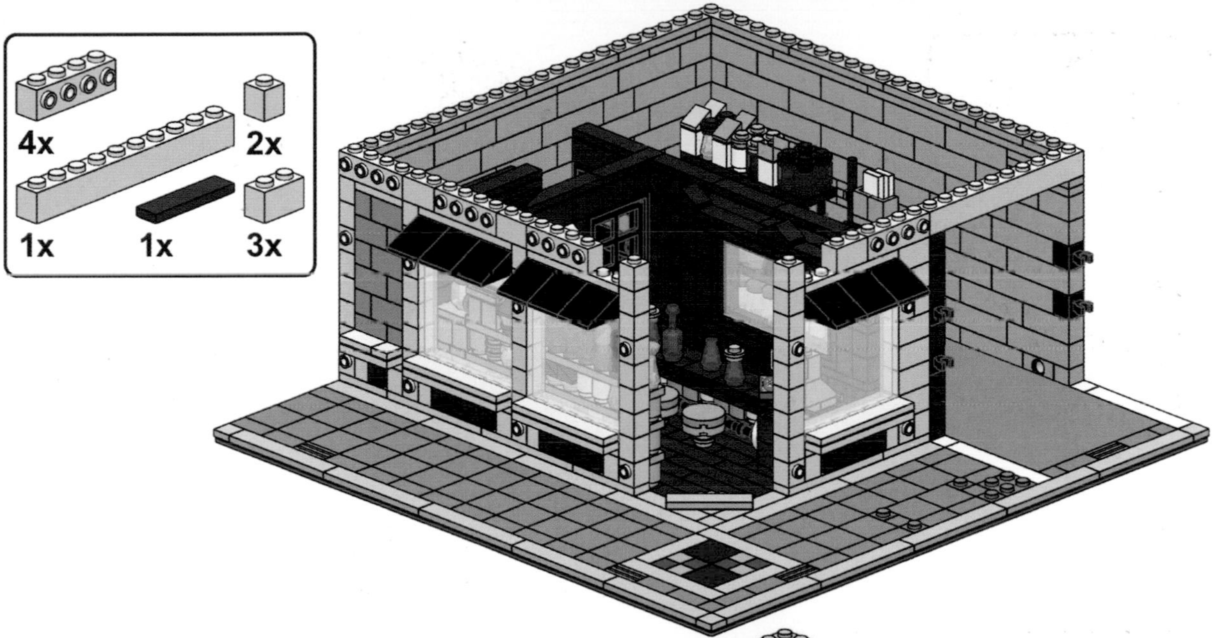
4x
2x
1x
1x
3x

30

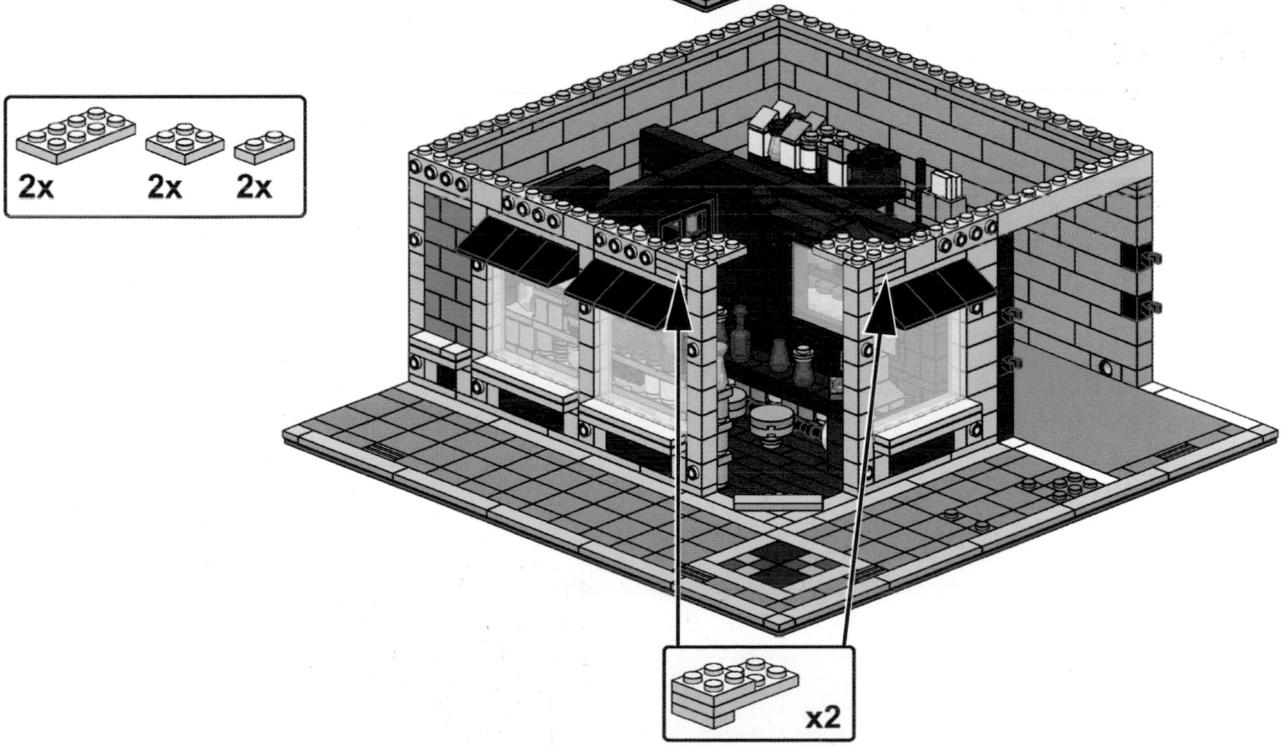
2x
2x
2x
x2

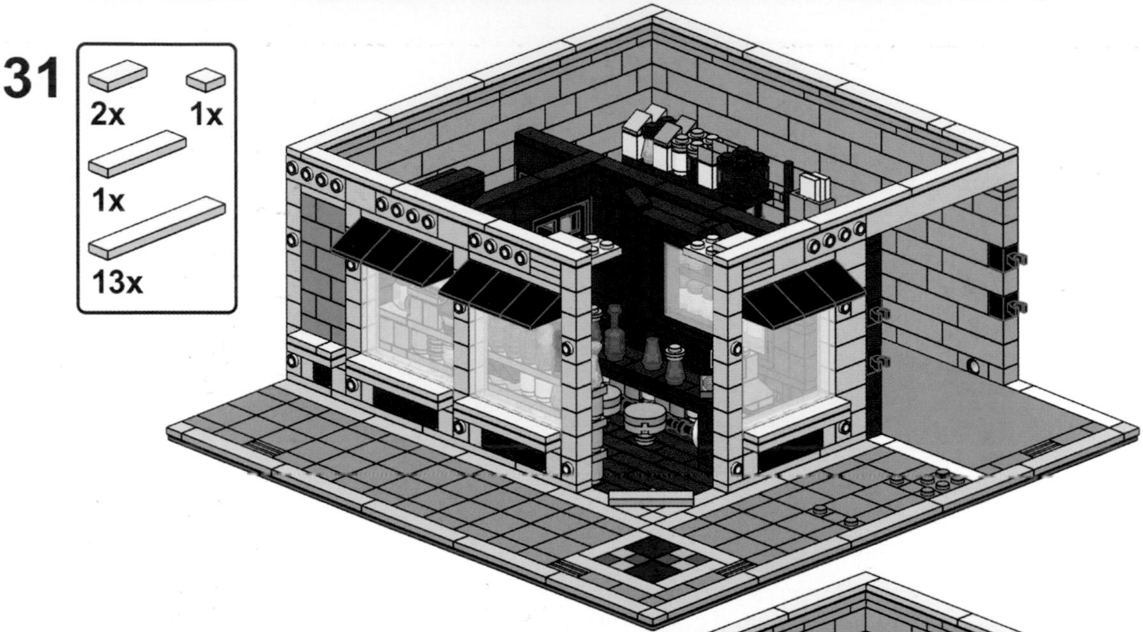

31
2x
1x
1x
13x

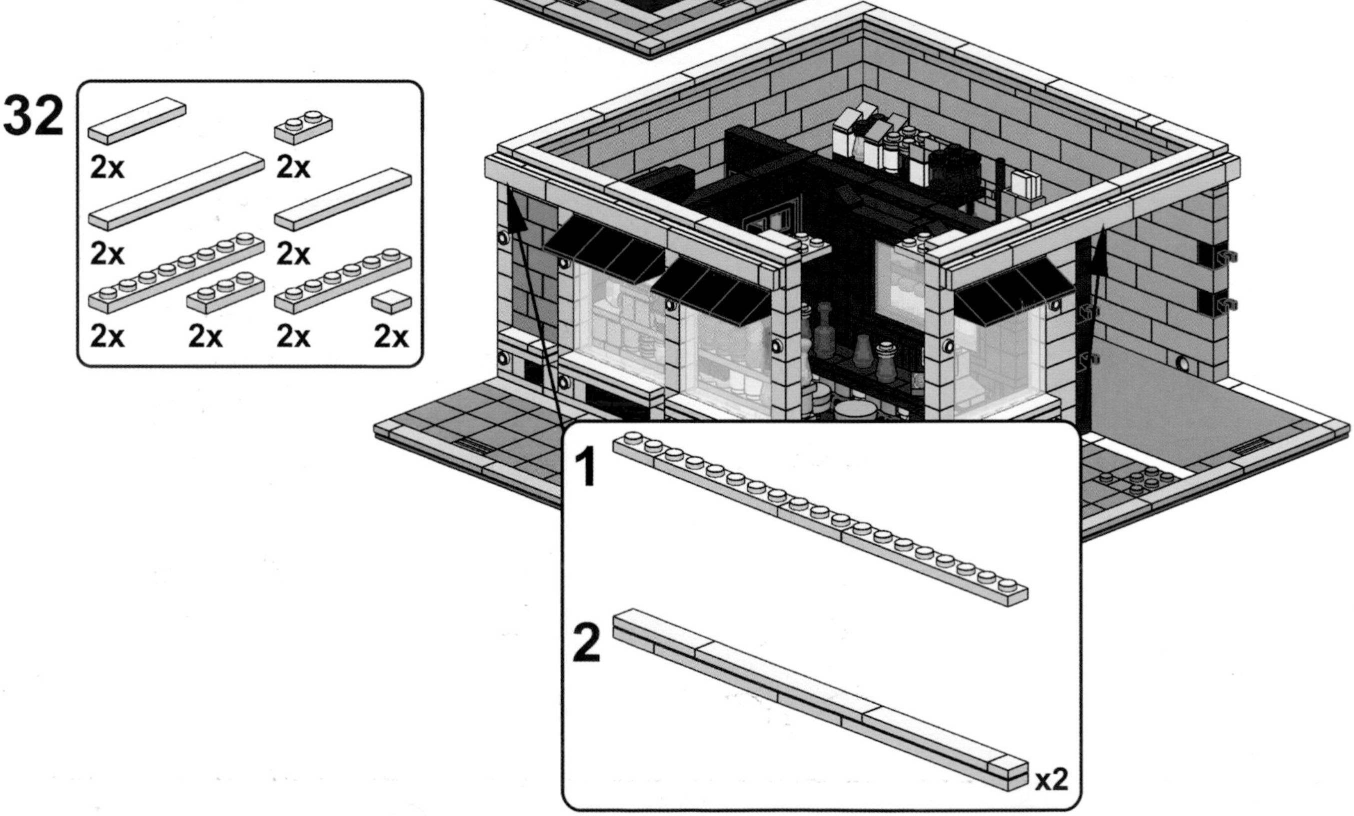

32
2x
2x
2x
2x
2x
2x
2x
2x
1
2
x2

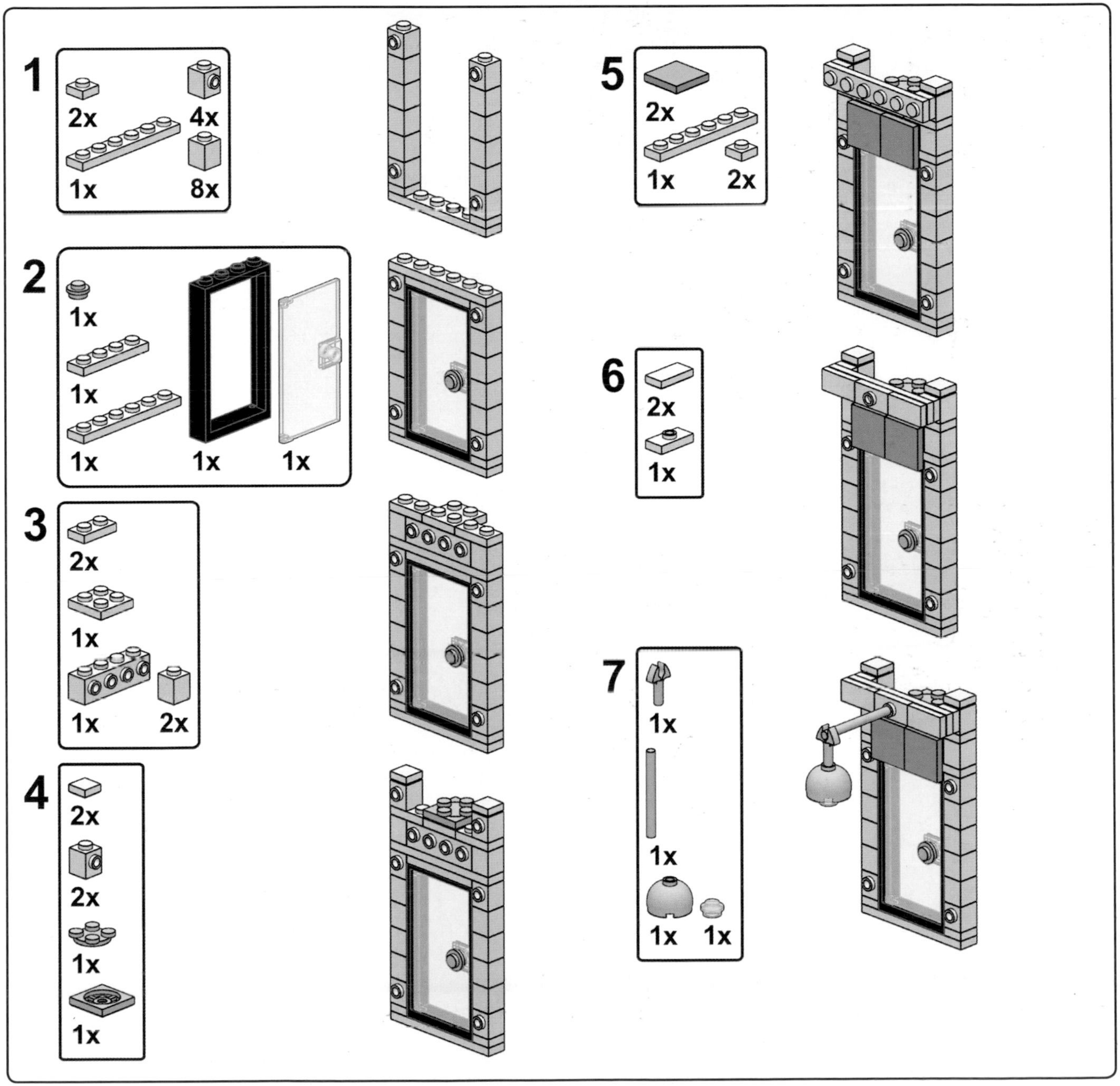
1
2x
4x
1x
8x
2
1x
1x
1x
1x
1x
3
2x
1x
1x
2x
4
2x
2x
1x
1x
5
2x
1x
2x
6
2x
1x
7
1x
1x
1x
1x

33

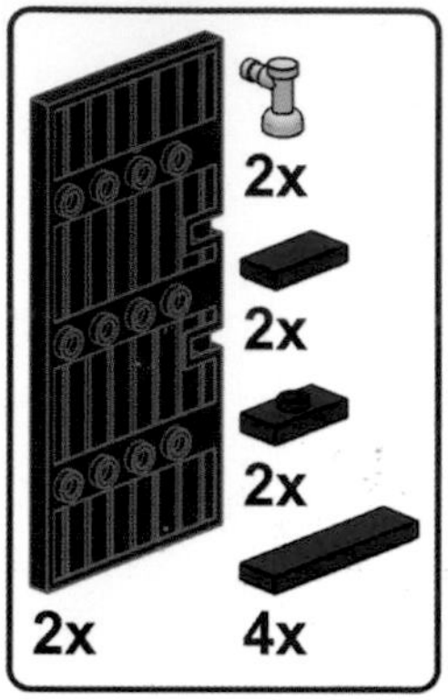
2x
2x
2x
2x
4x

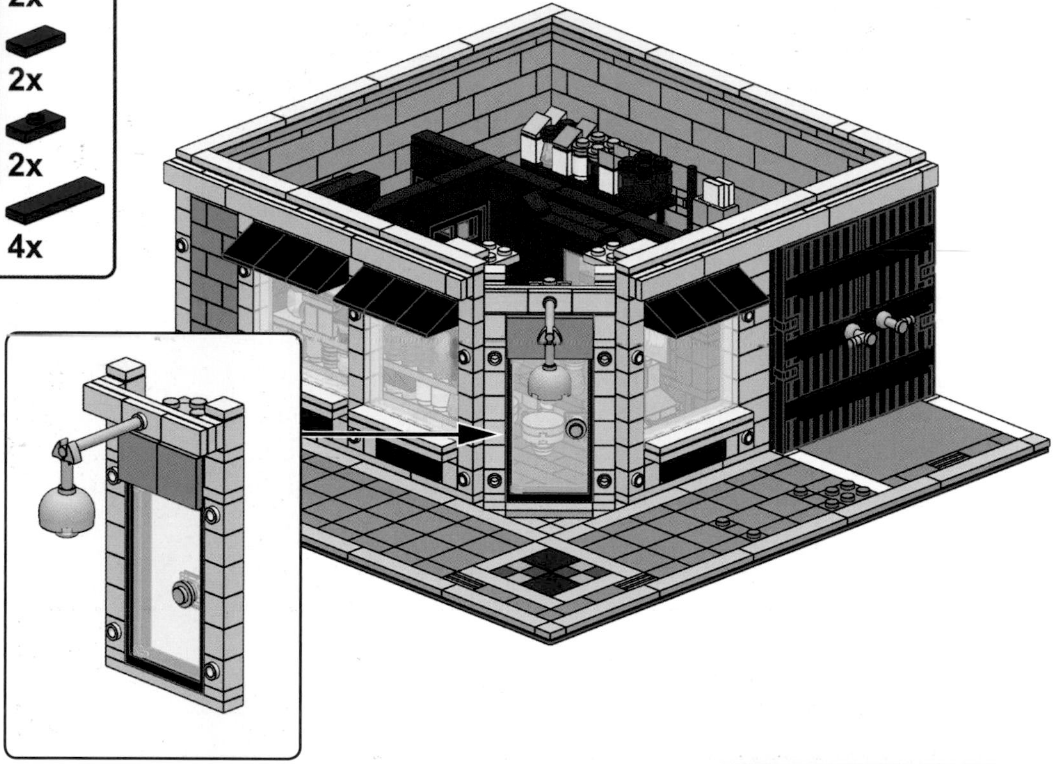

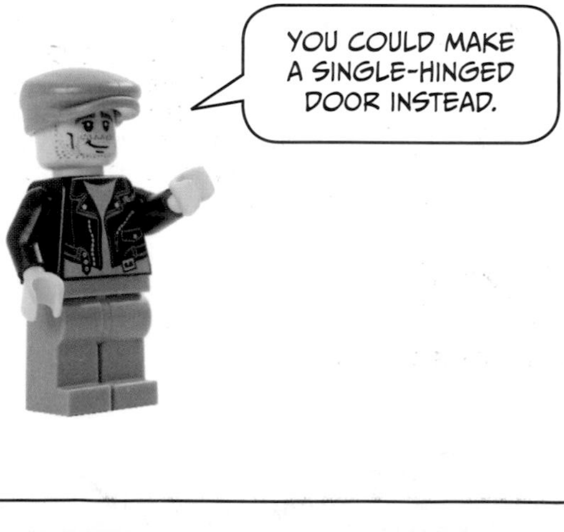
YOU COULD MAKE A SINGLE-HINGED DOOR INSTEAD.

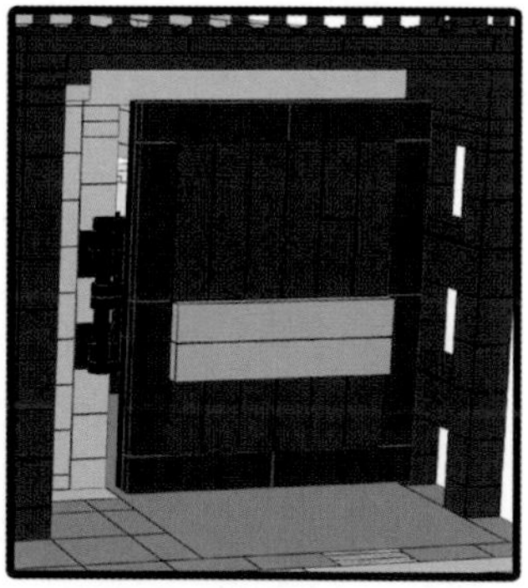

34

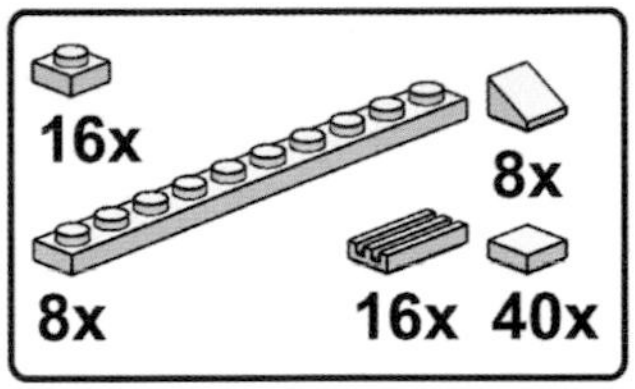
16x
8x
8x
16x
40x

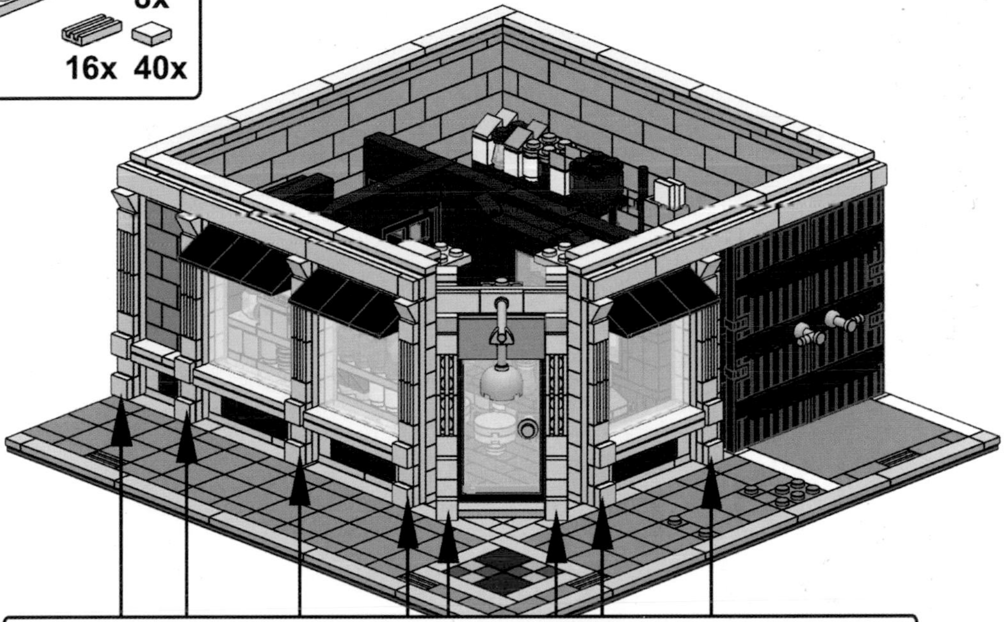

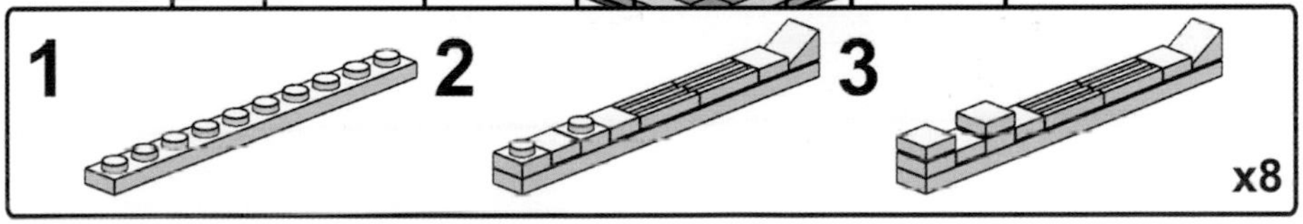
1
2
3
x8

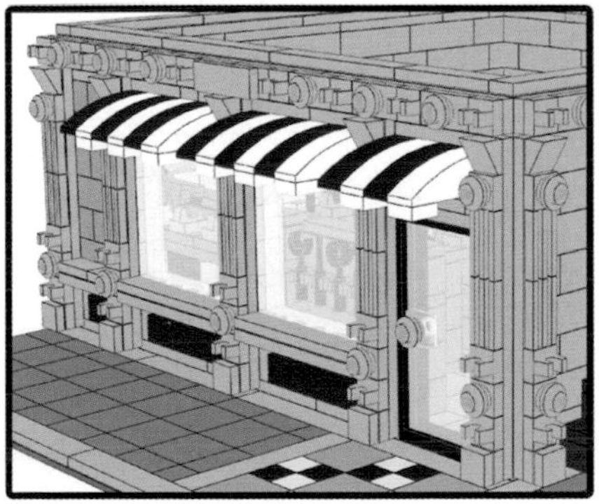

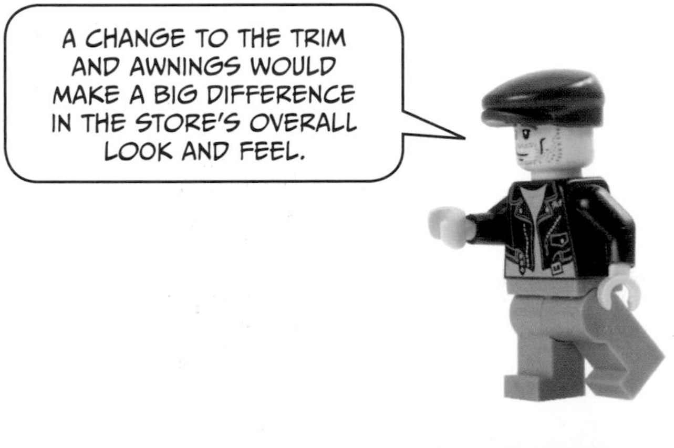
A CHANGE TO THE TRIM AND AWNINGS WOULD MAKE A BIG DIFFERENCE IN THE STORE'S OVERALL LOOK AND FEEL.

35

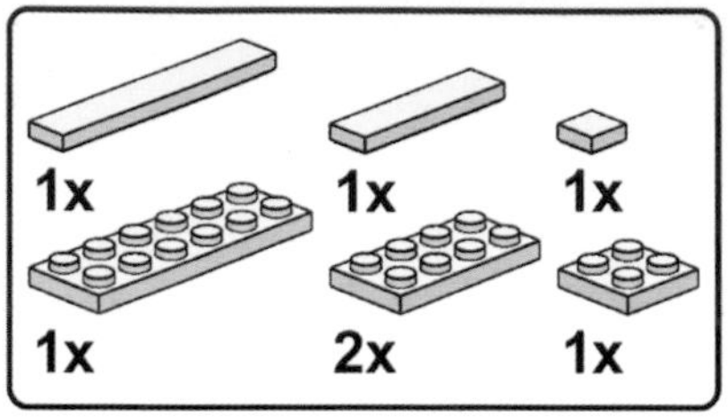
1x
1x
1x
1x
2x
1x

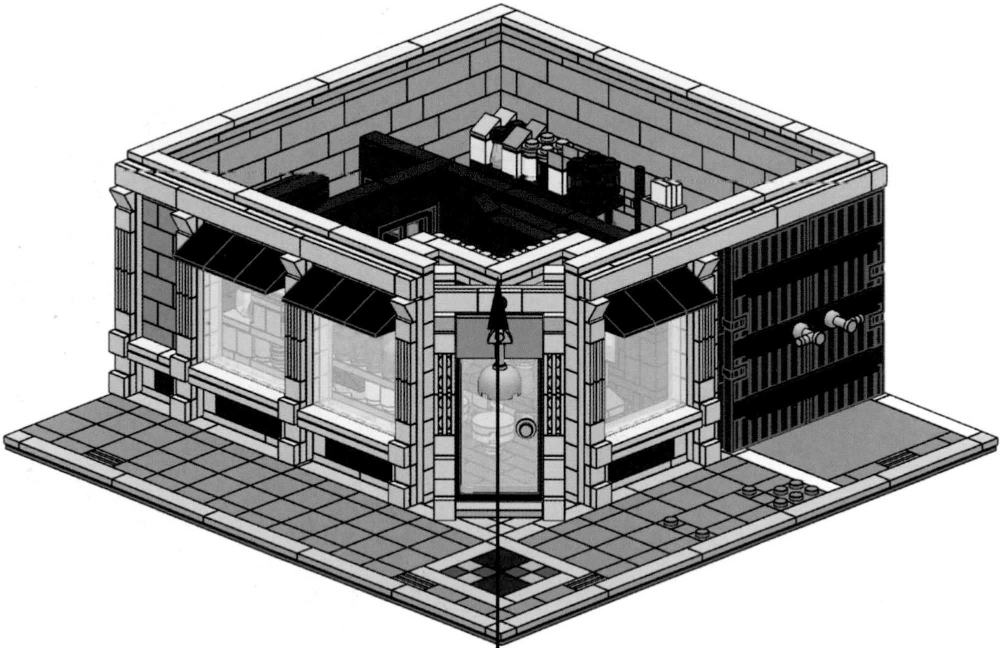

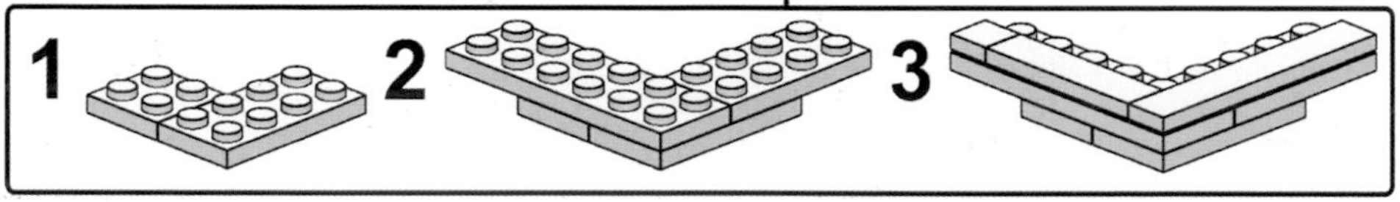
1
2
3

36

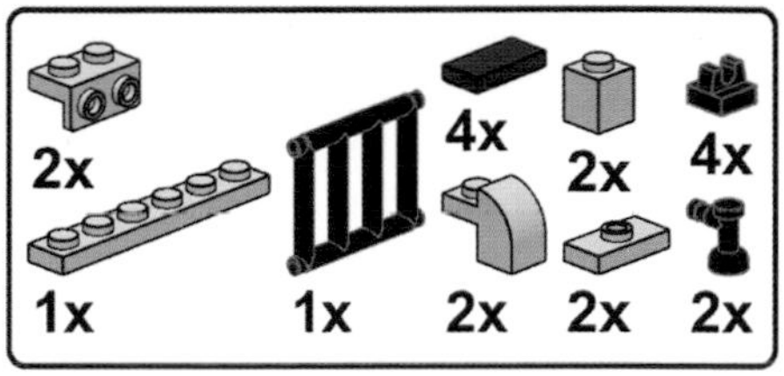

2x
4x
2x
4x
1x
1x
2x
2x
2x

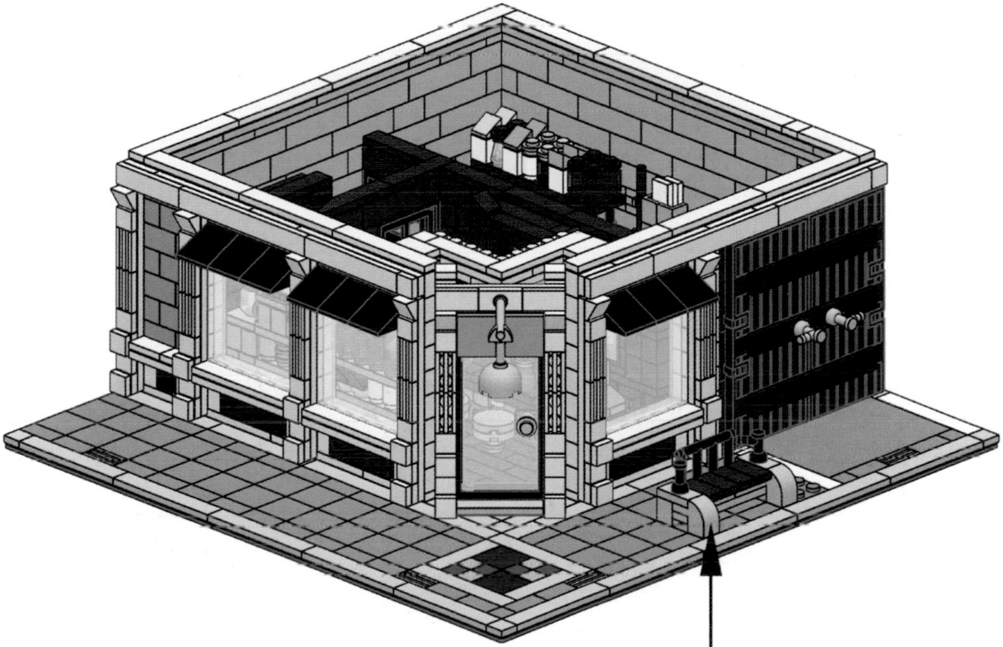

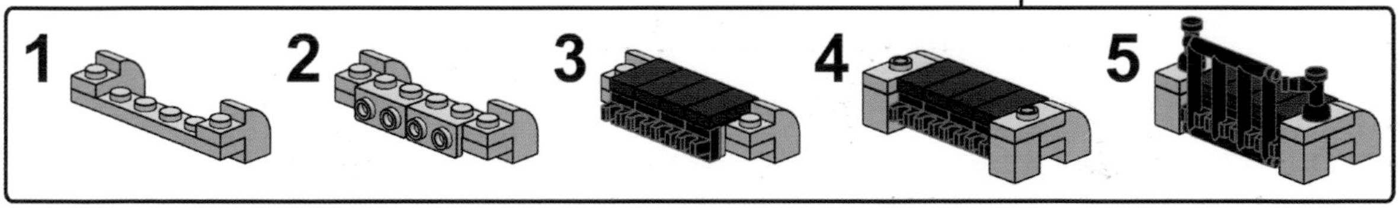

1
2
3
4
5

37

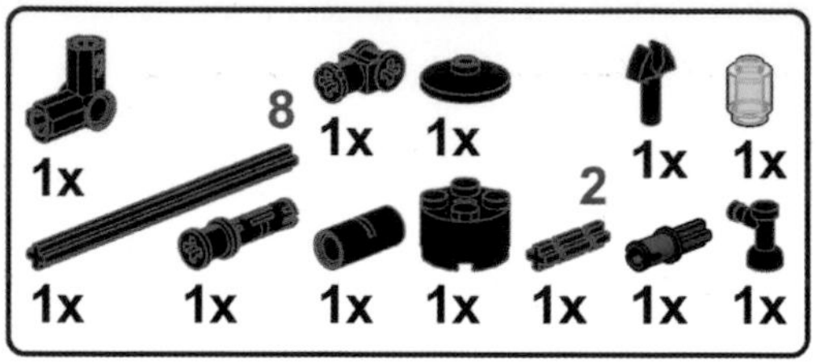
1x
8
1x
1x
1x
1x
2
1x
1x
1x
1x
1x
1x
1x
1x
1x

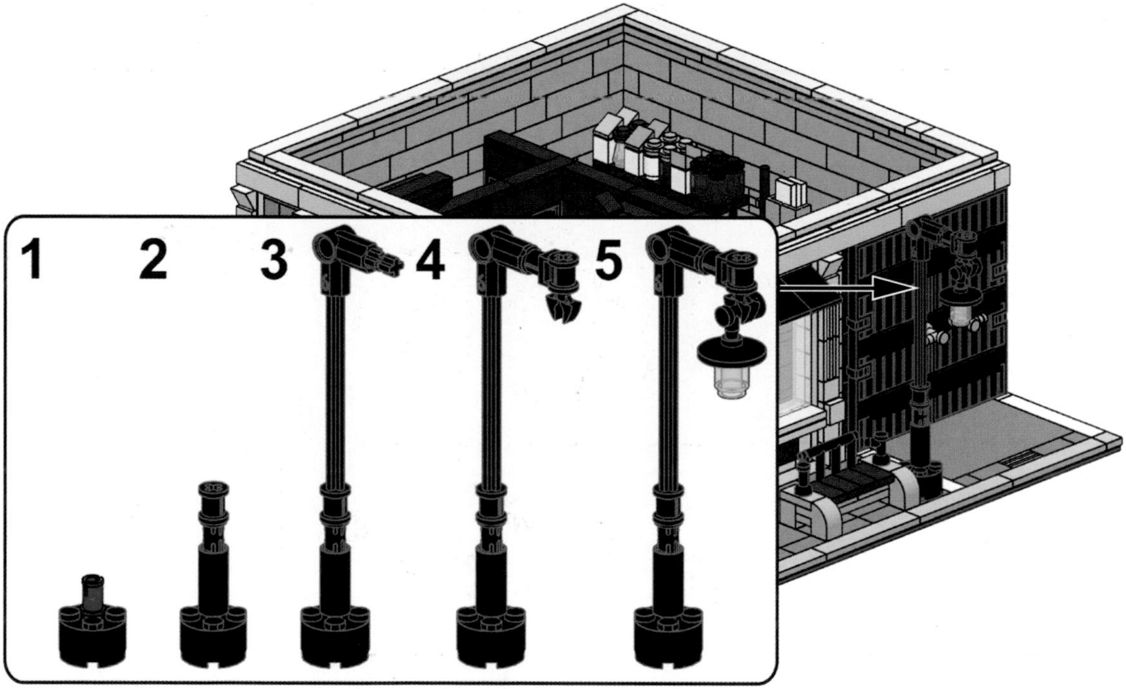
1
2
3
4
5

Second Floor

1

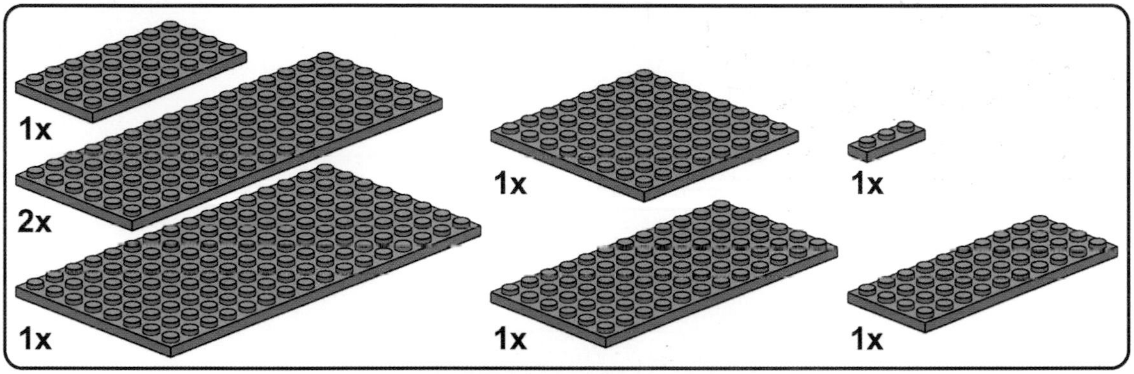

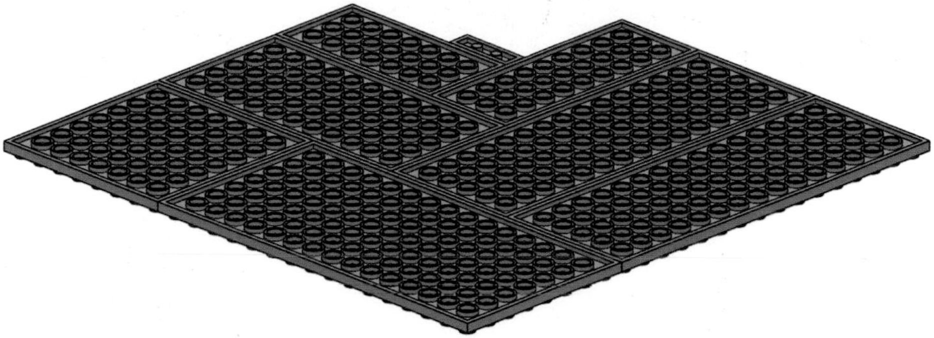

2

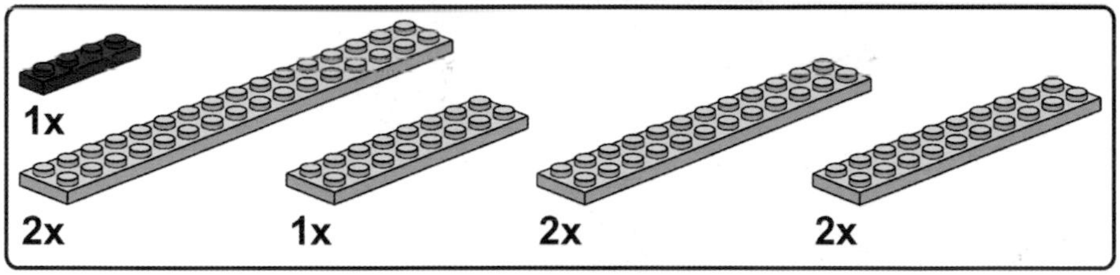

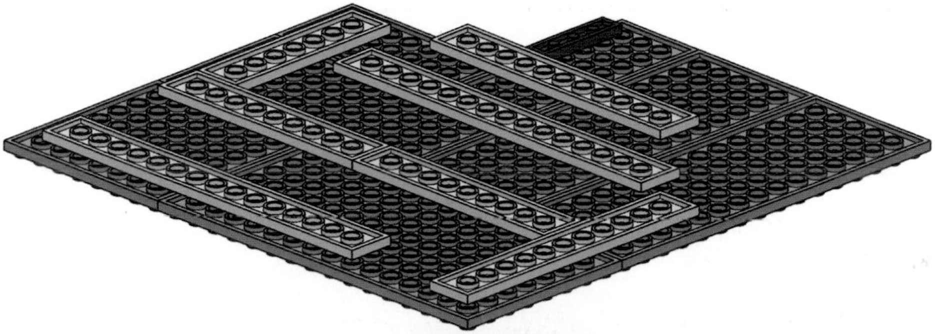

3

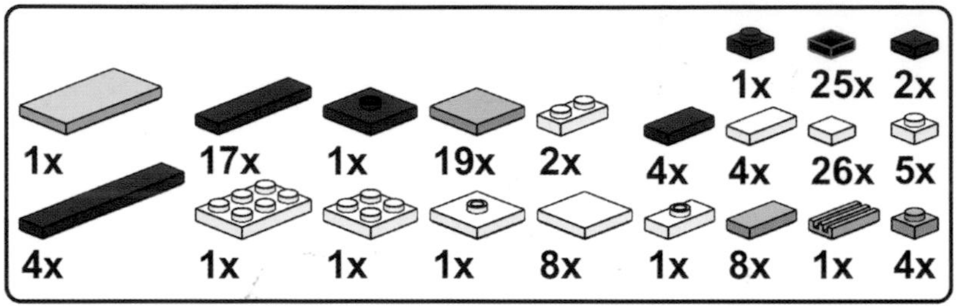
1x
17x
1x
19x
2x
4x
1x
25x
2x
4x
26x
5x
4x
1x
1x
1x
8x
1x
8x
1x
4x

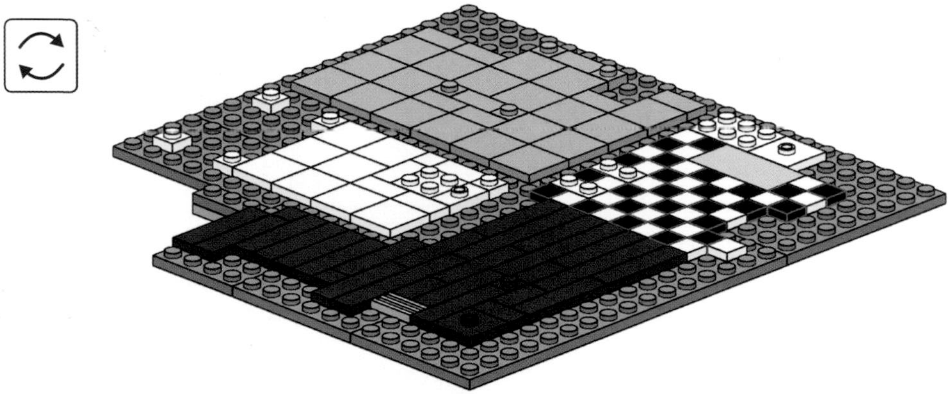

4

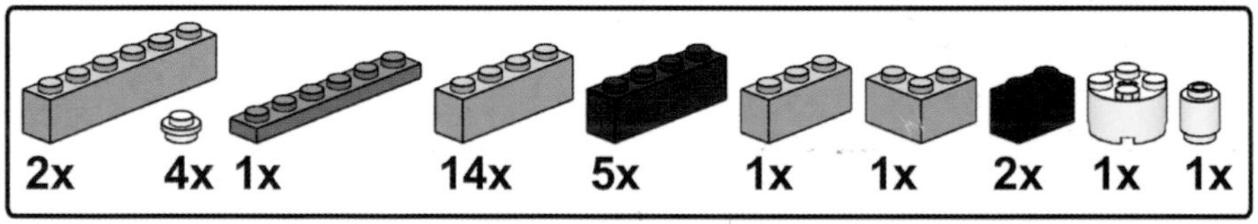
2x
4x
1x
14x
5x
1x
1x
2x
1x
1x

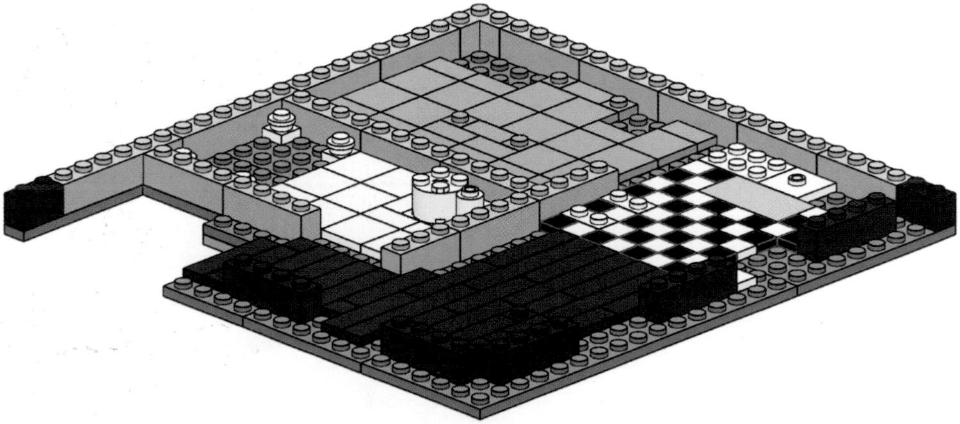

5

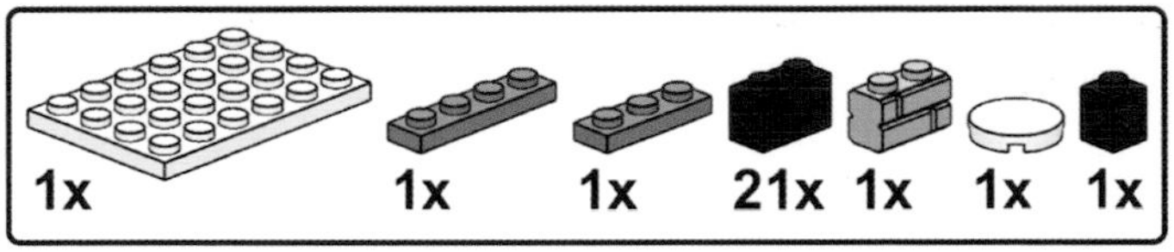
1x
1x
1x
21x
1x
1x
1x

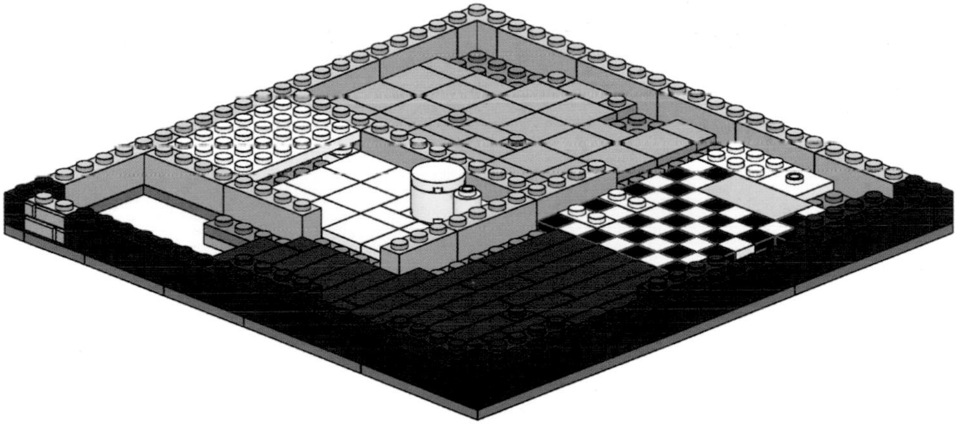

6

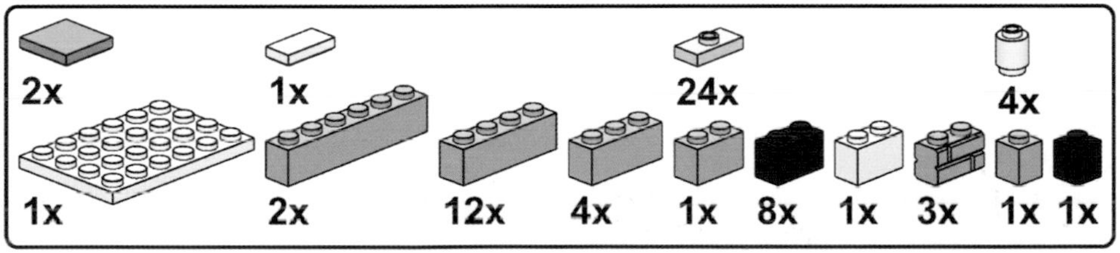
2x
1x
24x
4x
1x
2x
12x
4x
1x
8x
1x
3x
1x
1x

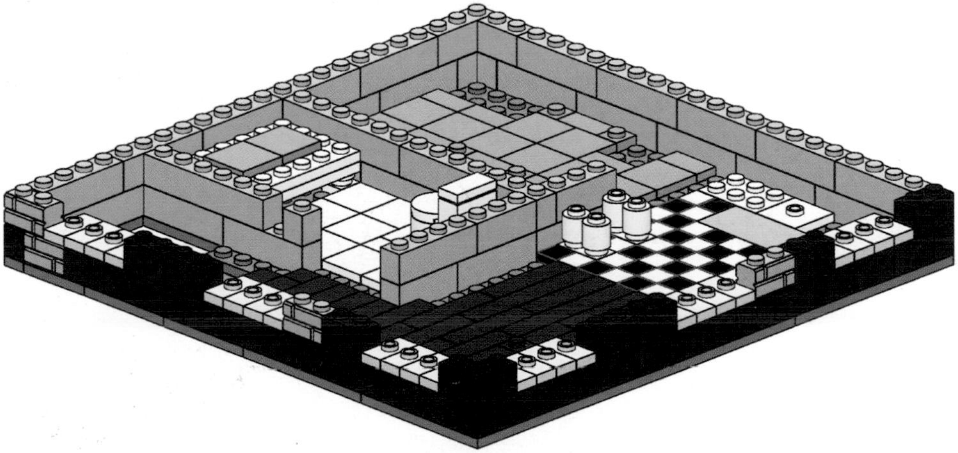

7

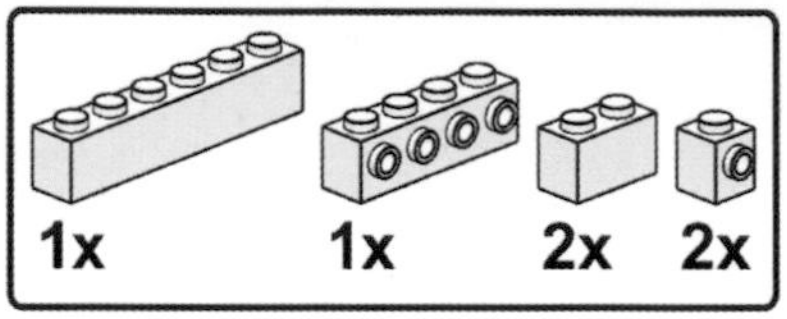
1x
1x
2x
2x

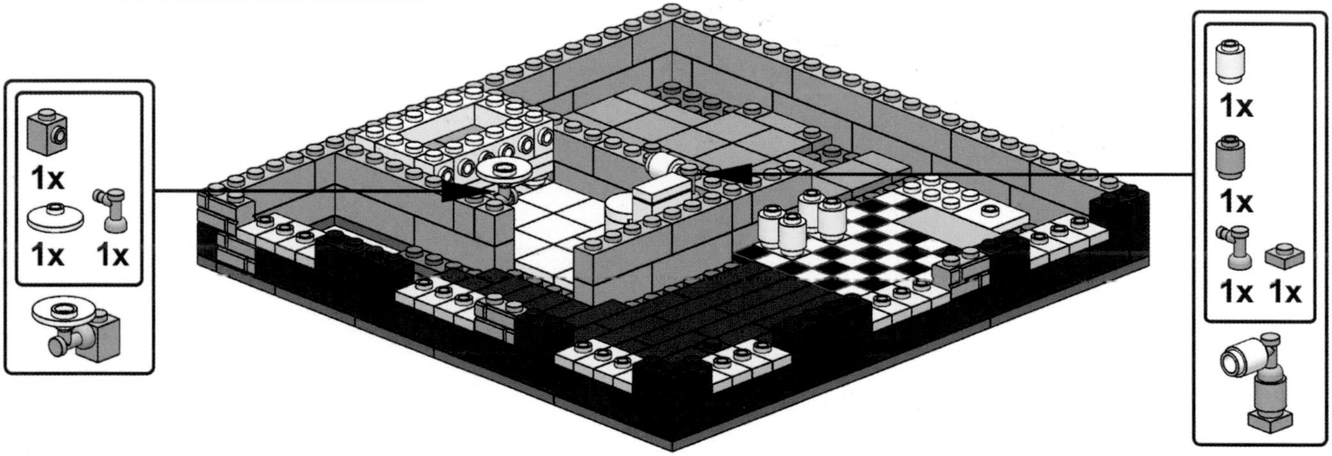
1x
1x 1x
1x
1x
1x 1x

8

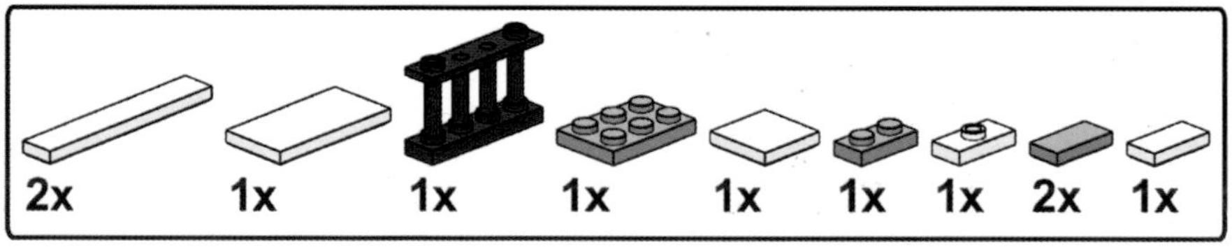
2x
1x
1x
1x
1x
1x
1x
2x
1x

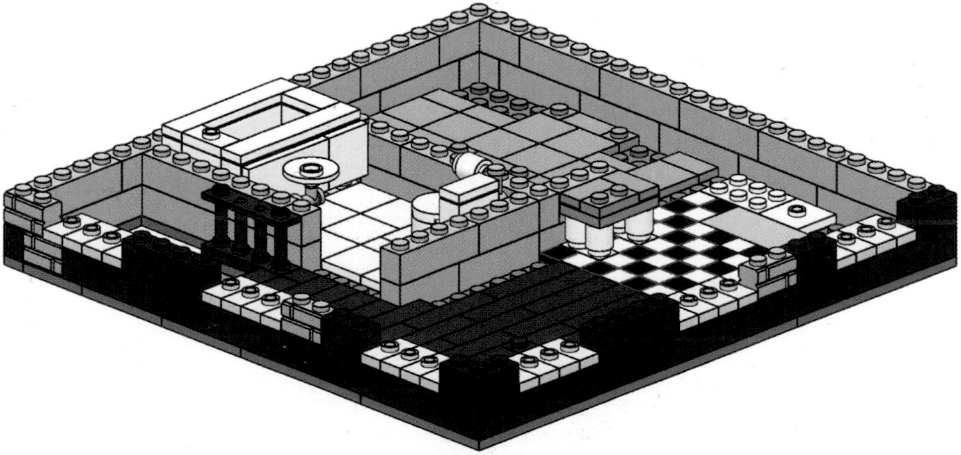

9

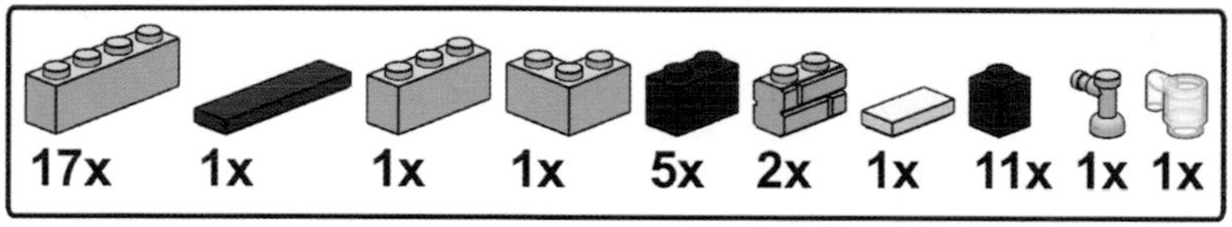
17x
1x
1x
1x
5x
2x
1x
11x
1x
1x

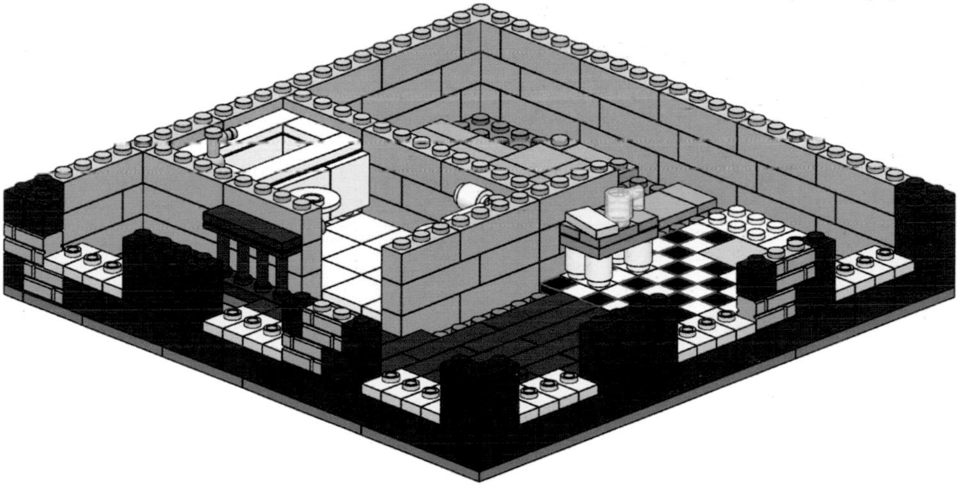

10

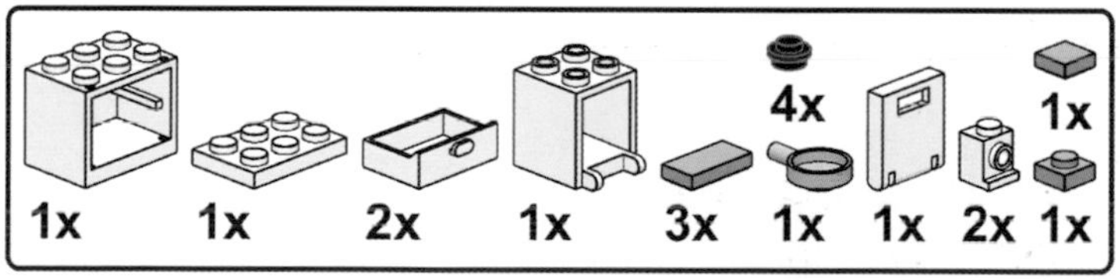
1x
1x
2x
1x
3x
4x
1x
1x
2x
1x
1x

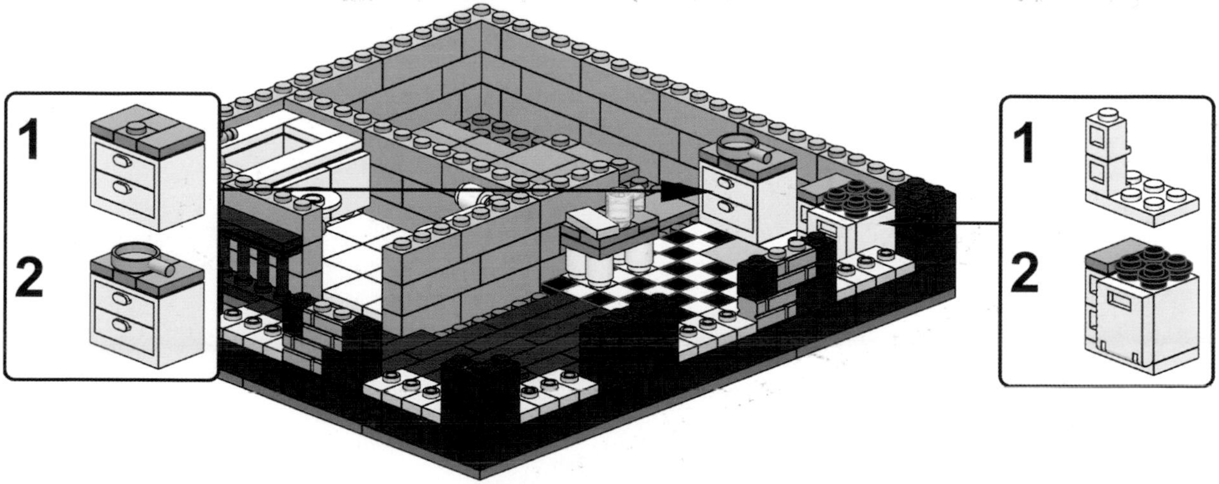
1
2
1
2

11

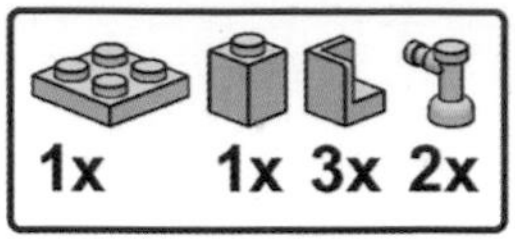
1x
1x 3x 2x

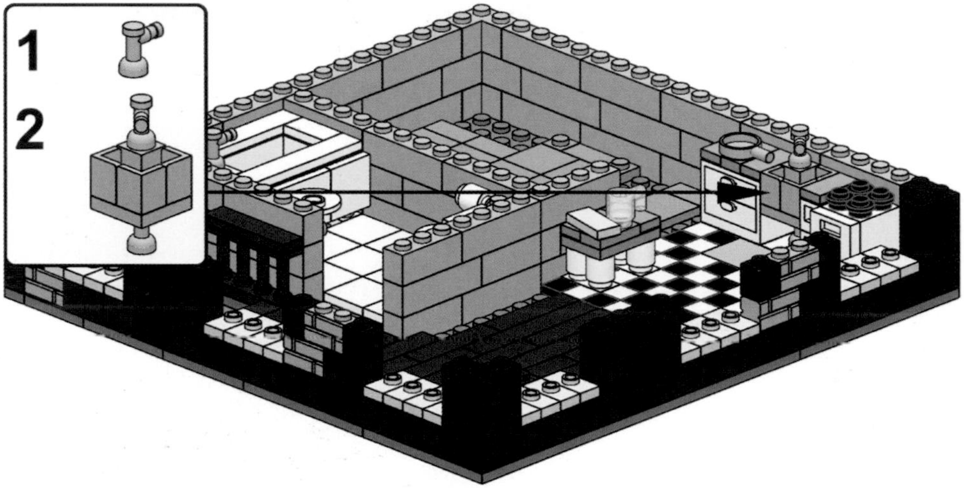
1
2

12

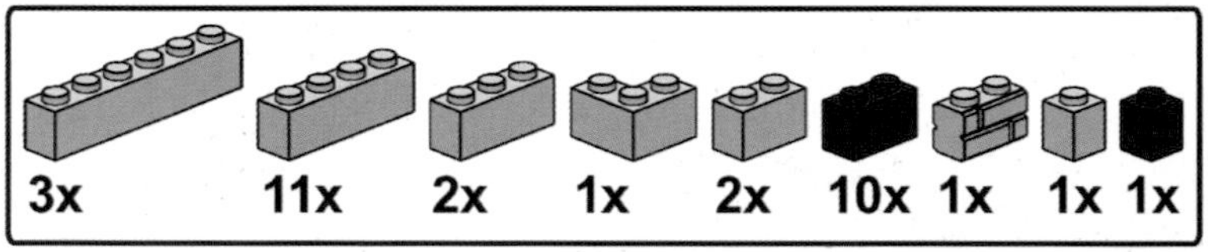
3x
11x
2x
1x
2x
10x 1x
1x 1x

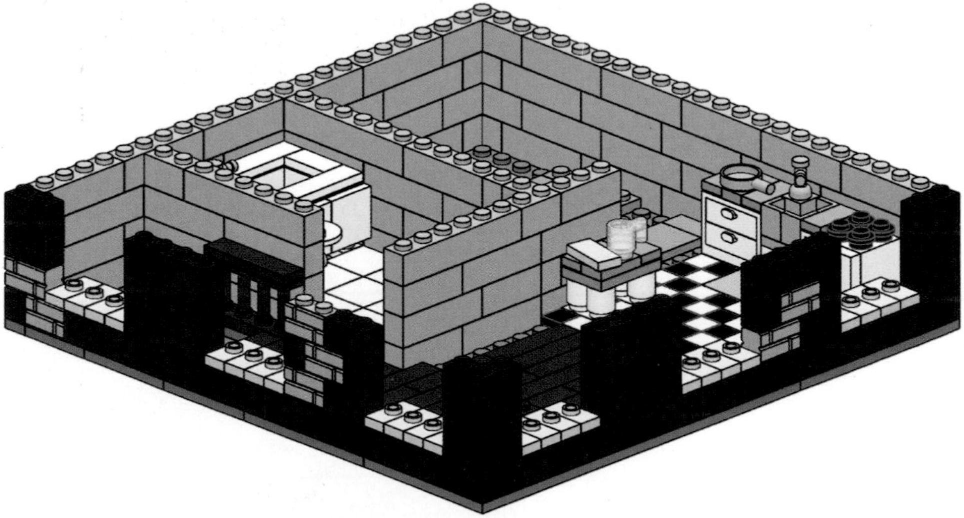

13

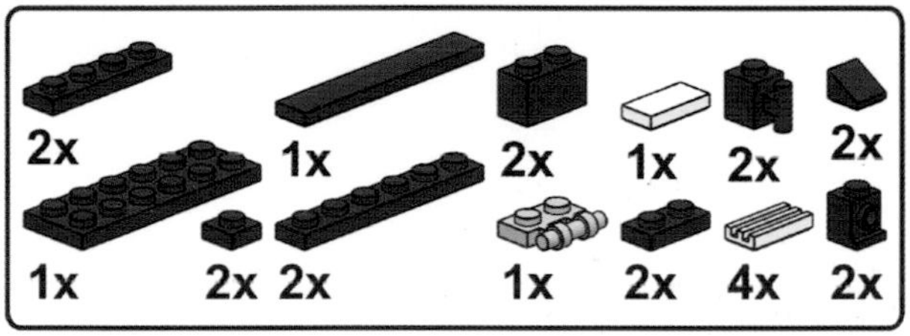
2x
1x
2x
1x
2x
2x
1x
2x
2x
1x
2x
4x
2x

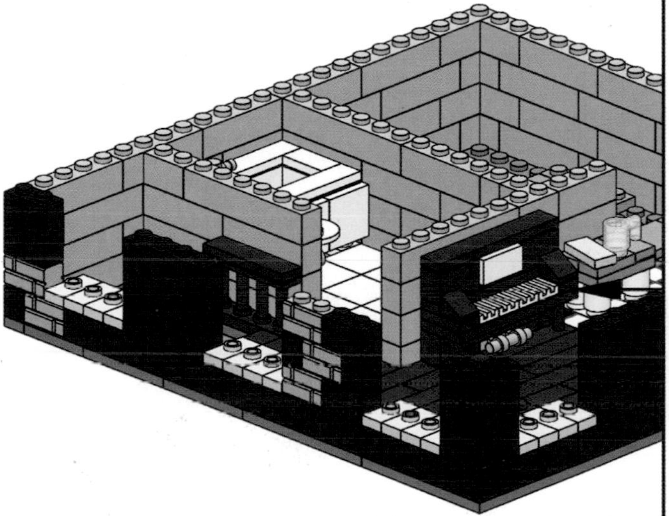

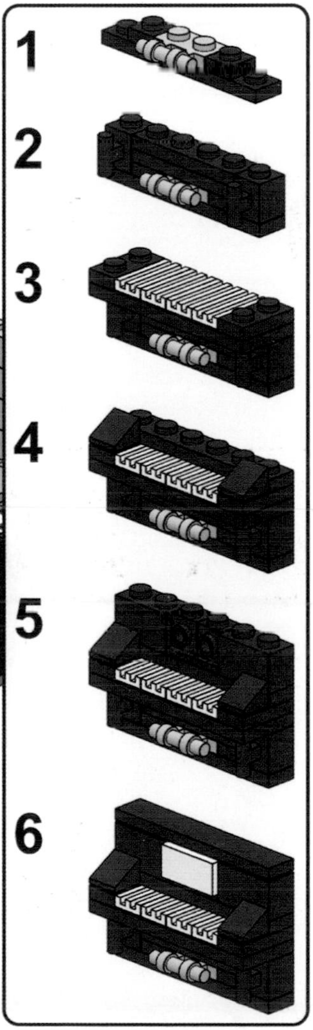
1
2
3
4
5
6

14

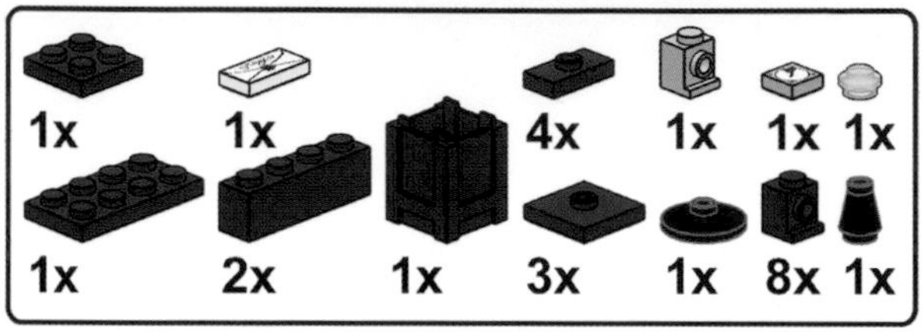
1x
1x
4x
1x
1x
1x
1x
2x
1x
3x
1x
8x
1x

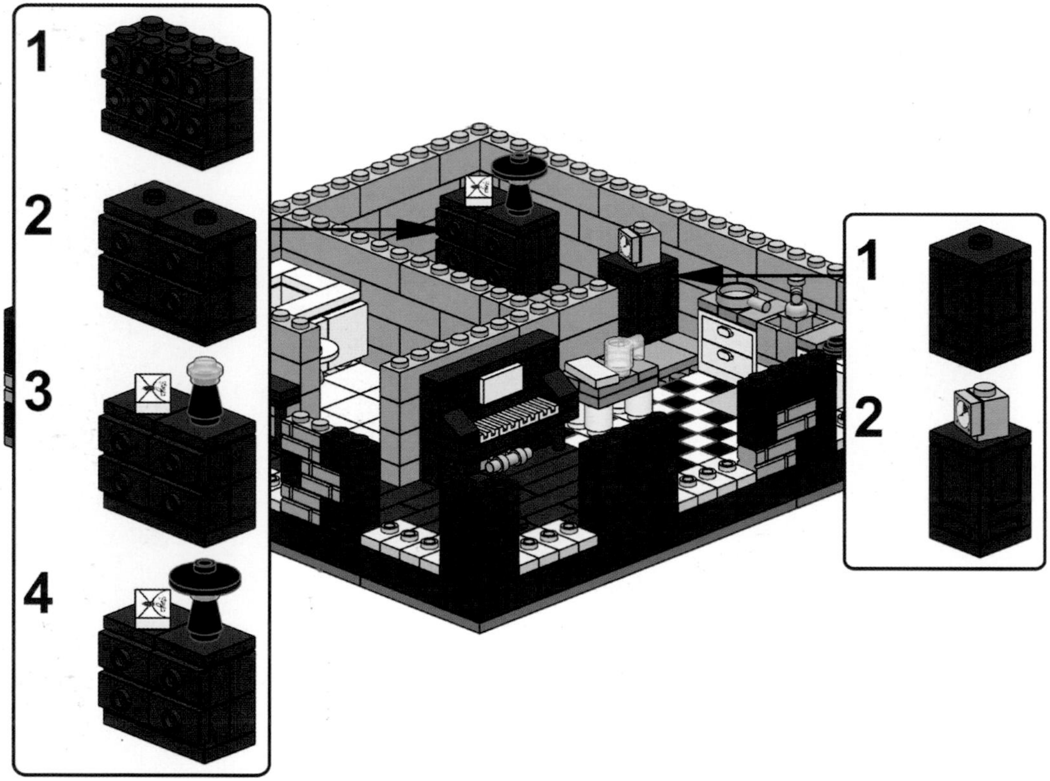
1
2
3
4
1
2

15

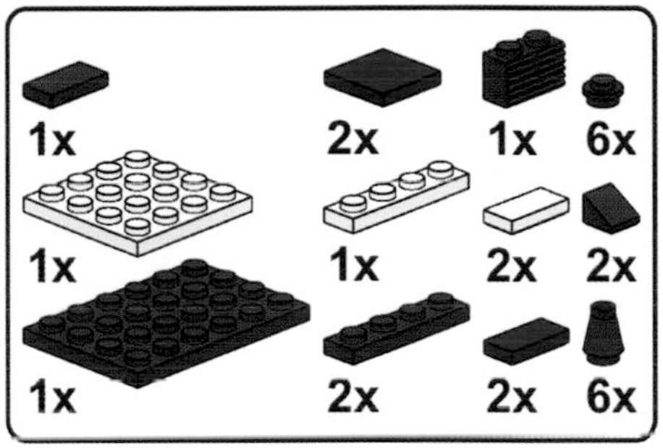

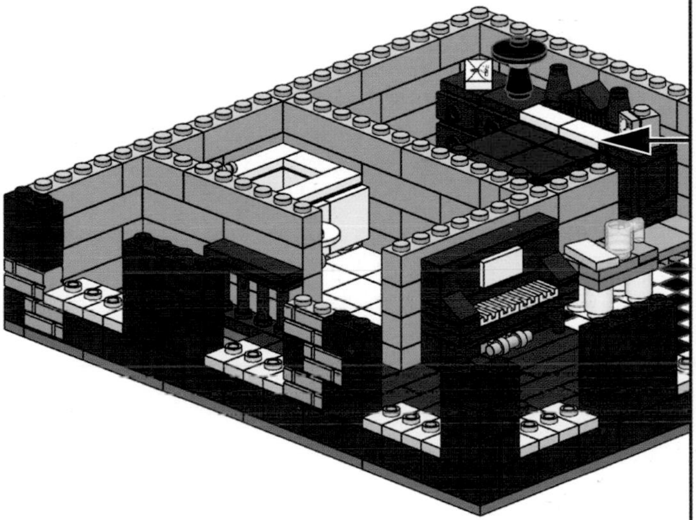

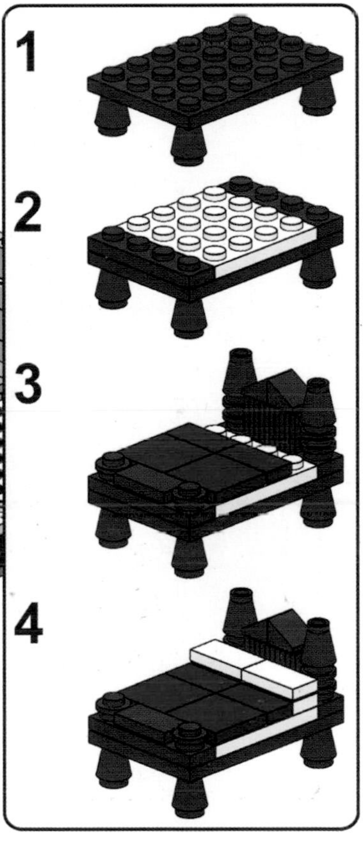

16

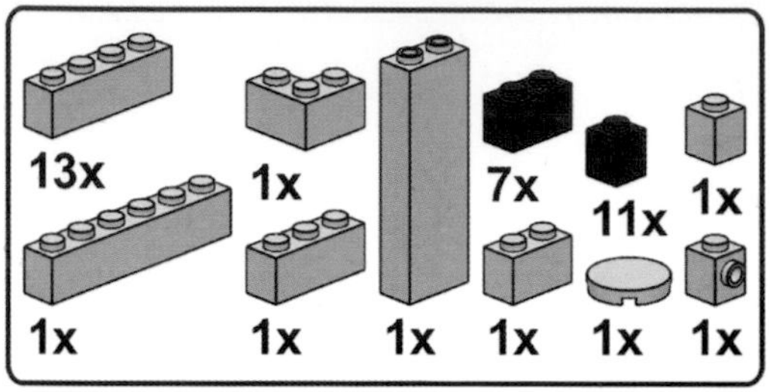
13x
1x
1x
1x
1x
7x
11x
1x
1x
1x
1x
1x

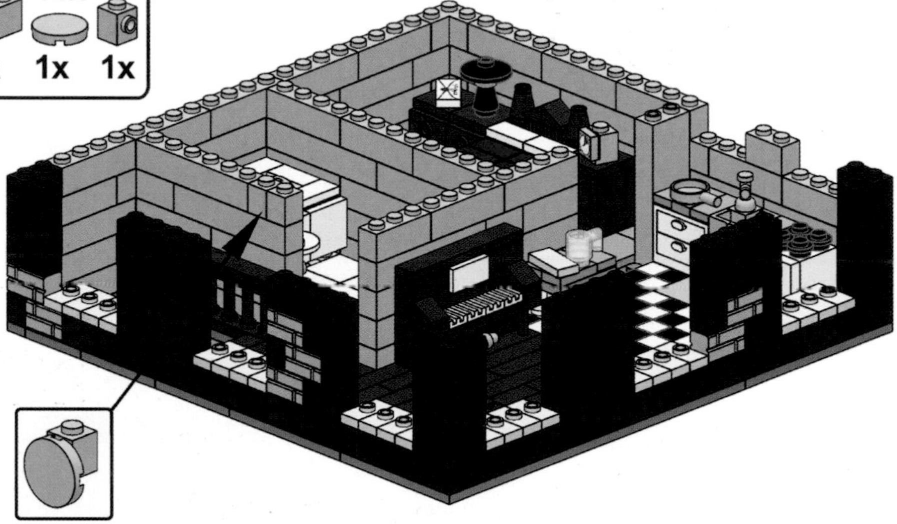

17

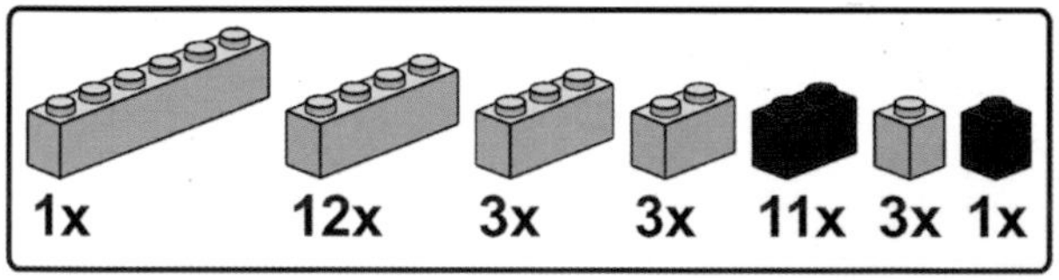
1x
12x
3x
3x
11x
3x
1x

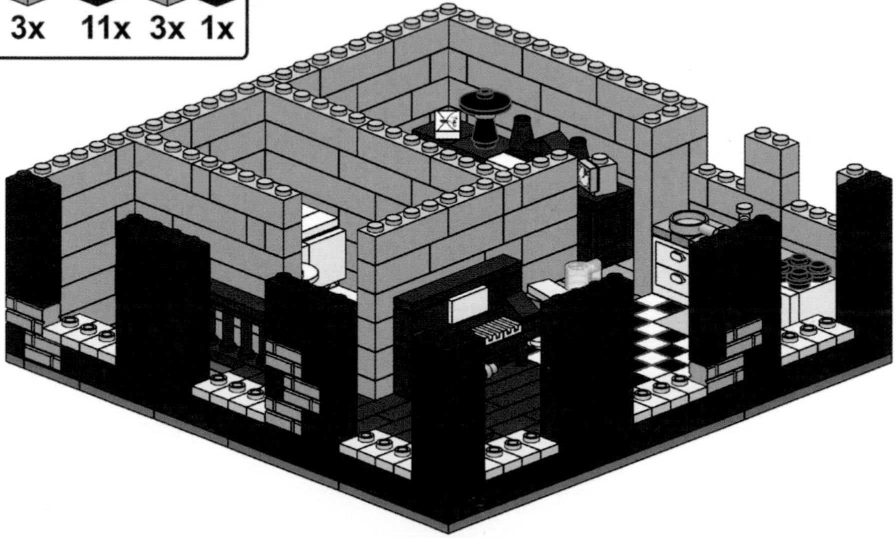

18

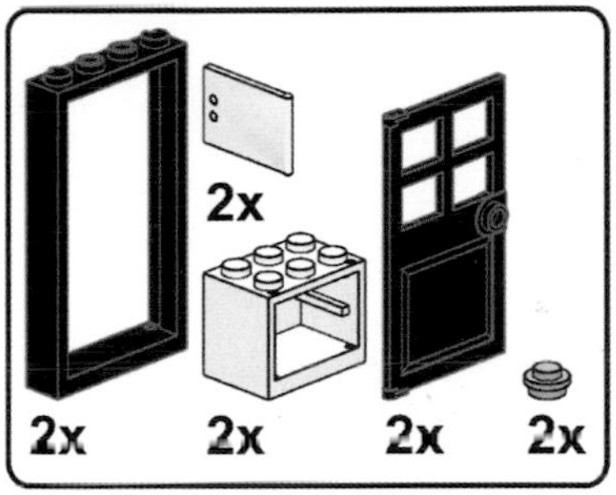
2x
2x
2x
2x
2x
2x

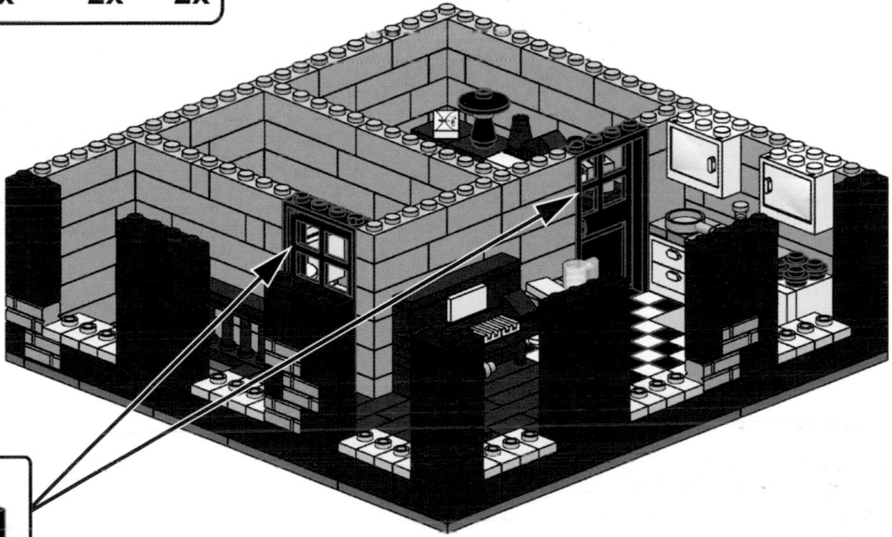

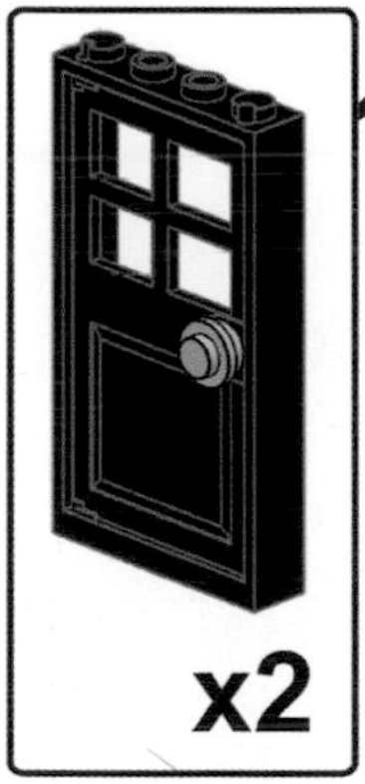
x2

19

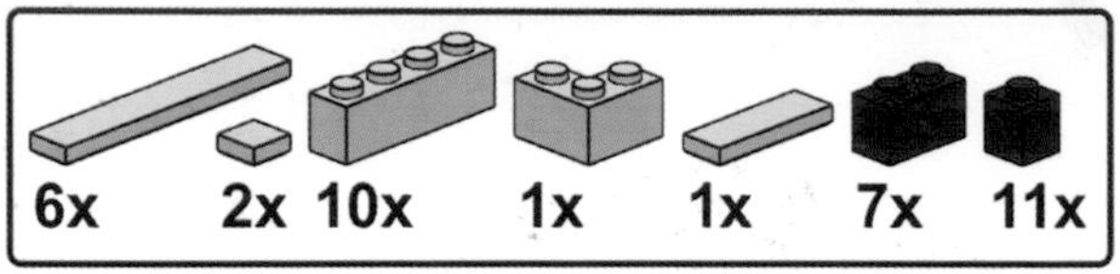
6x
2x
10x
1x
1x
7x
11x

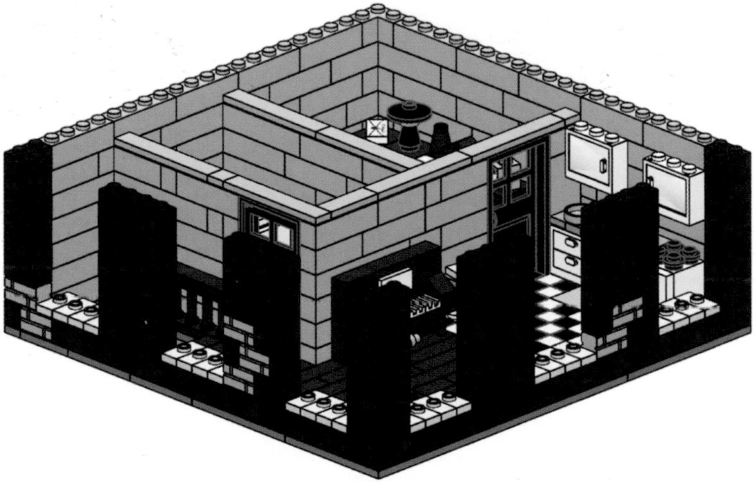

20

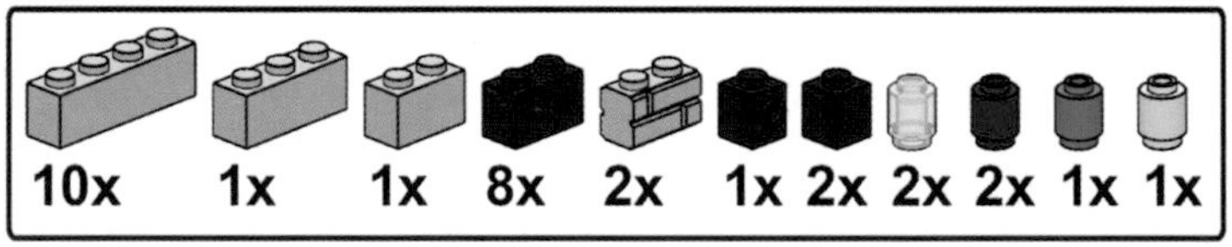
10x
1x
1x
8x
2x
1x
2x
2x
2x
1x
1x

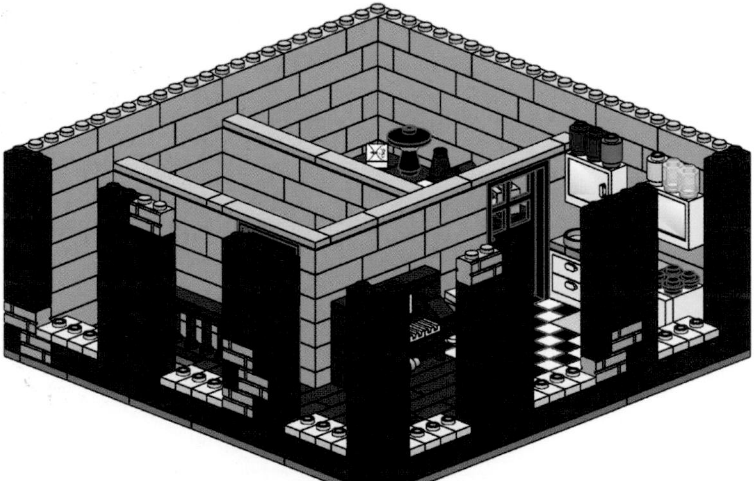

21

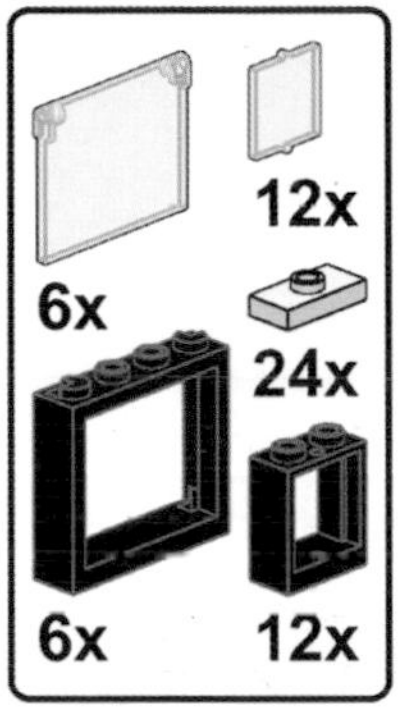
12x
6x
24x
6x
12x

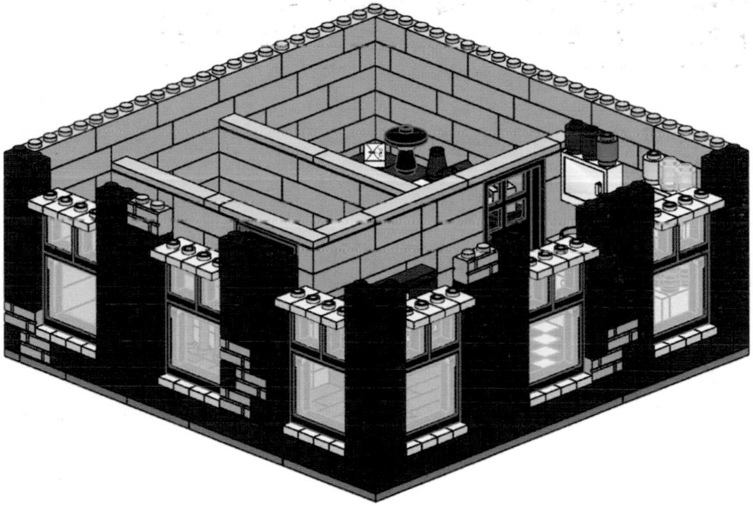

22

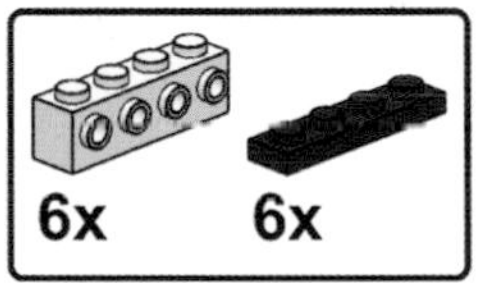
6x
6x

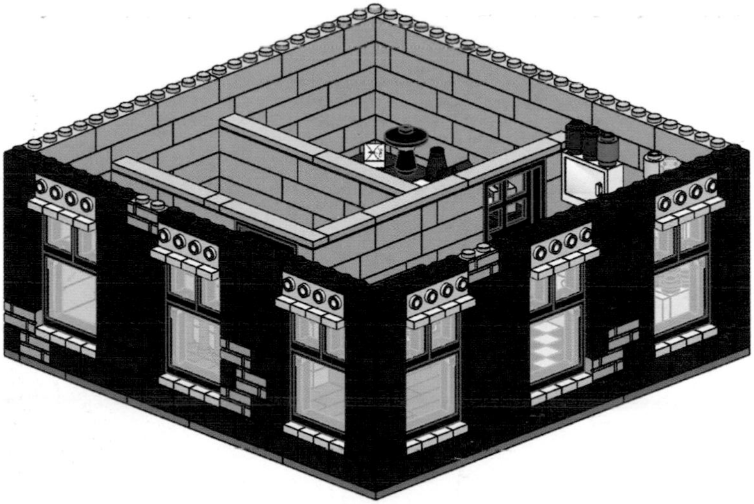

23

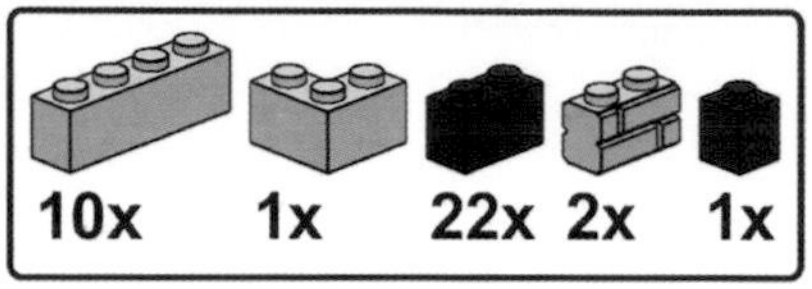
10x
1x
22x
2x
1x

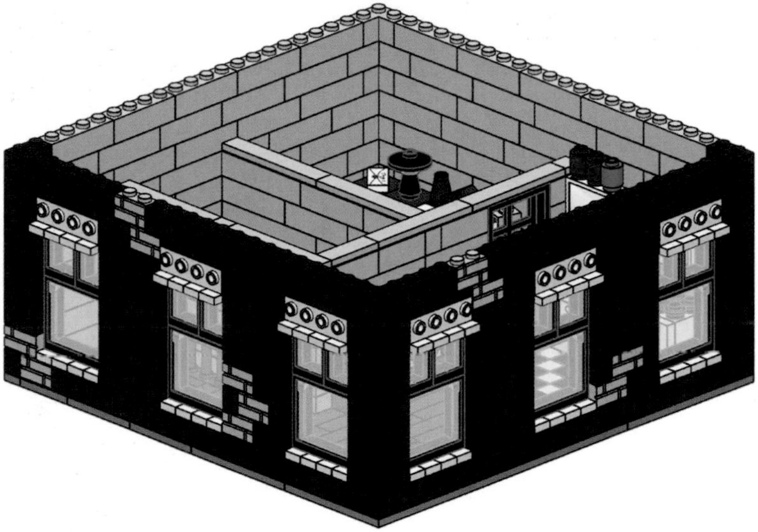

24

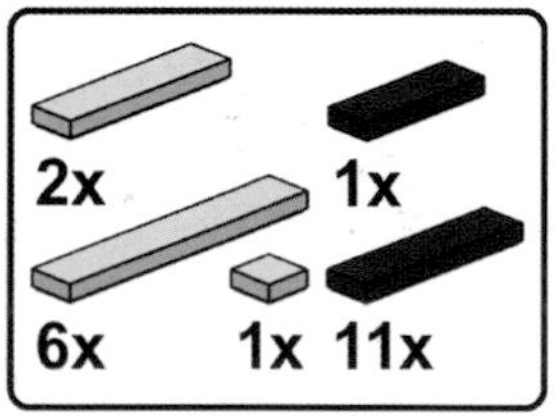
2x
1x
6x
1x
11x

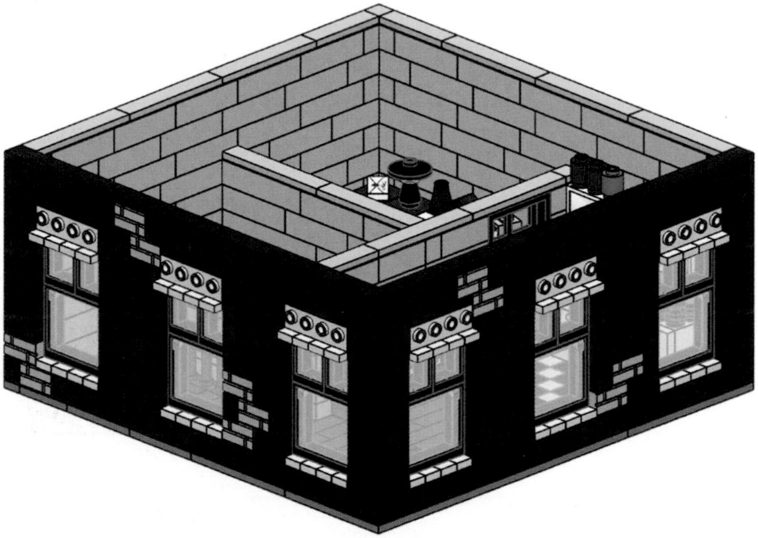

25

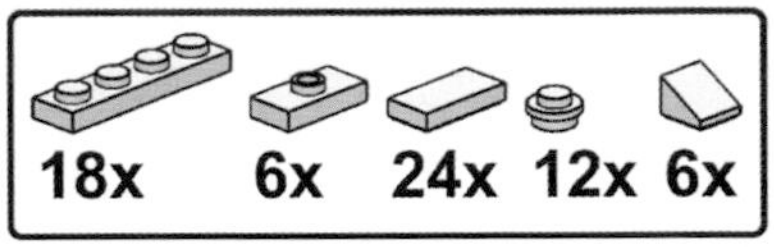
18x
6x
24x
12x
6x

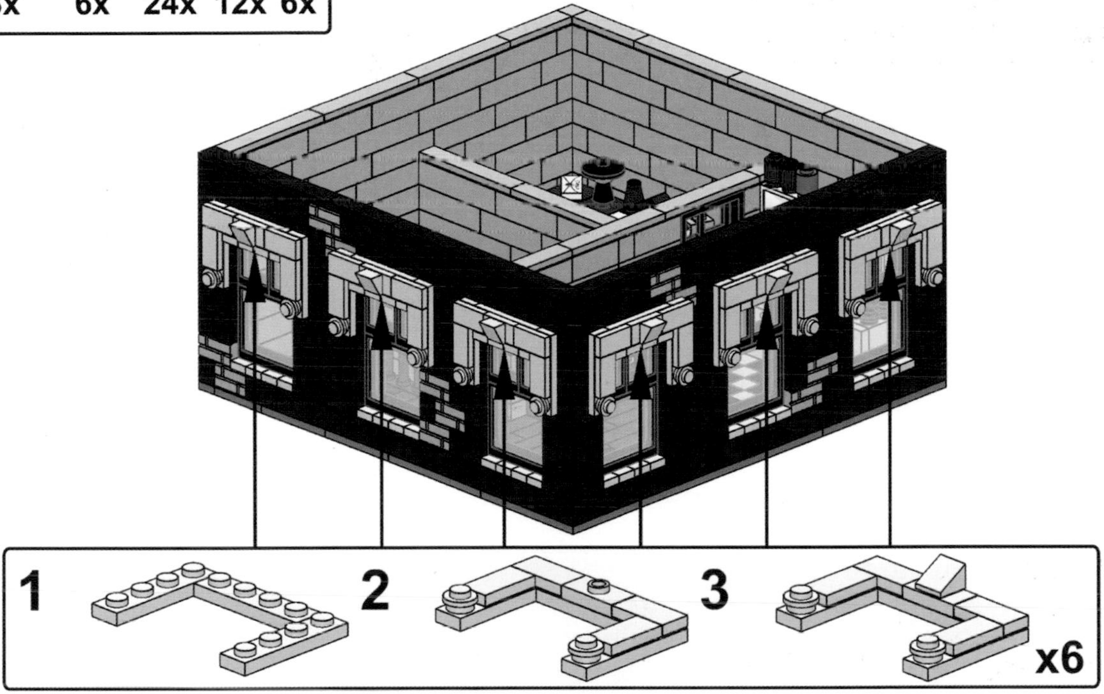
1
2
3
x6

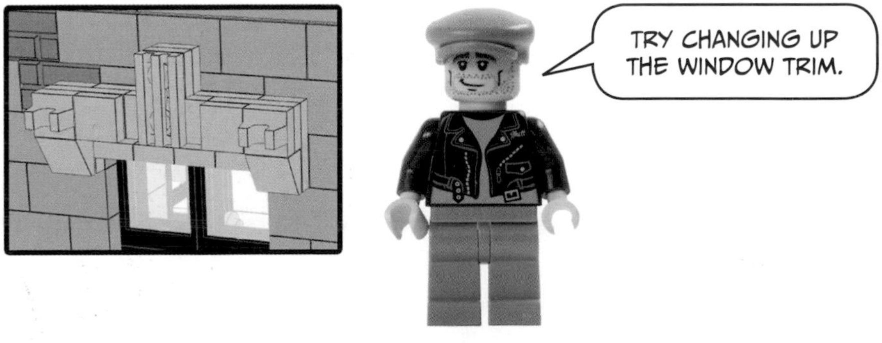
TRY CHANGING UP THE WINDOW TRIM.

26

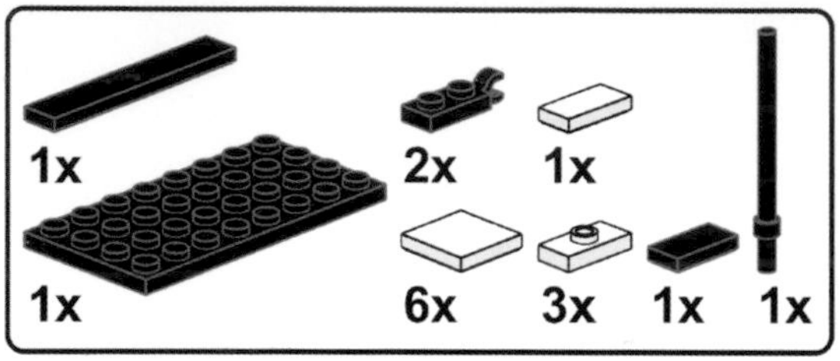

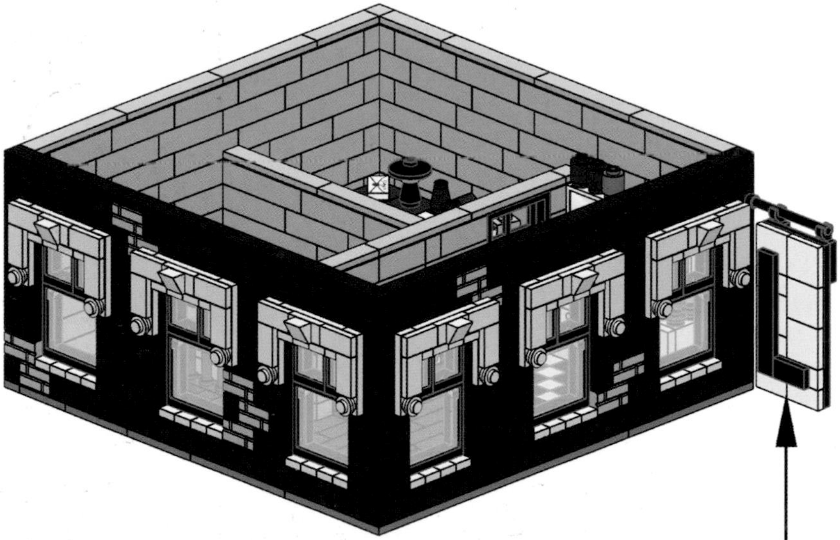

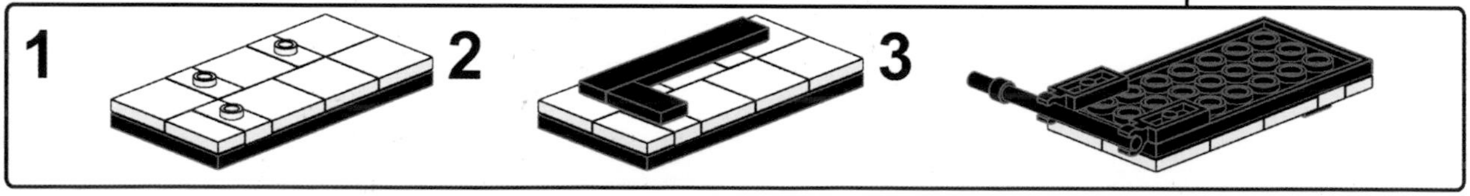

27

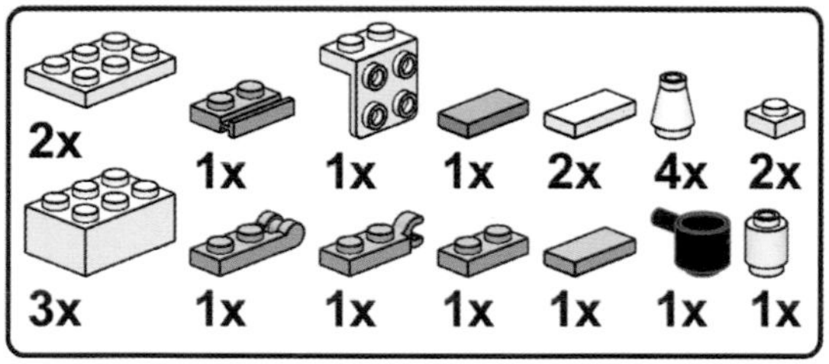
2x
1x
1x
1x
2x
4x
2x
3x
1x
1x
1x
1x
1x
1x

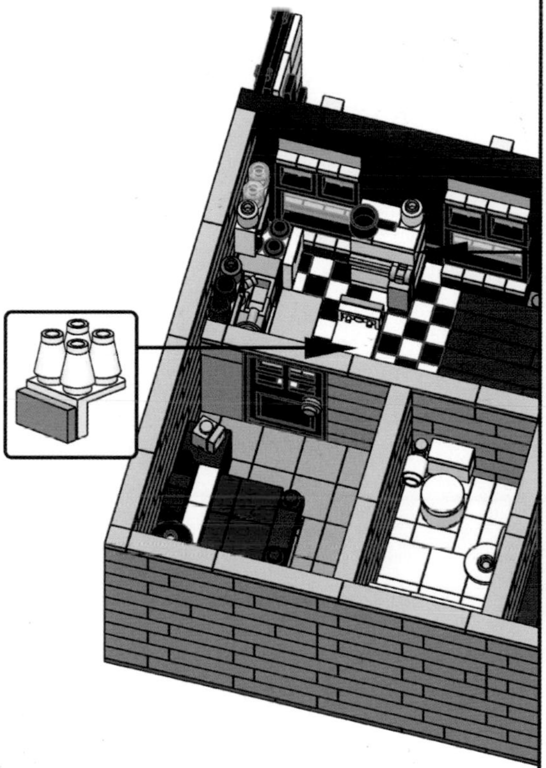

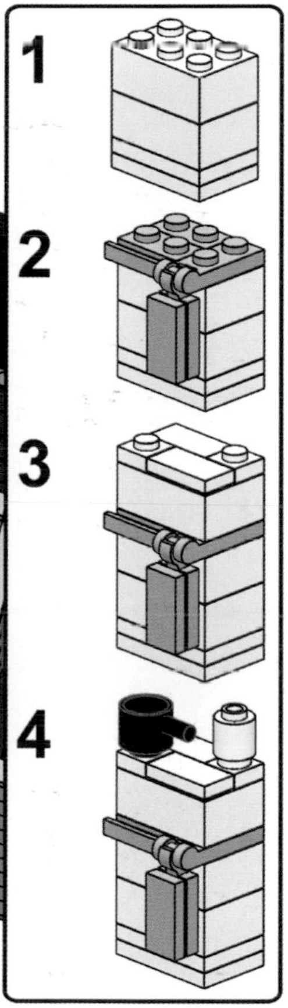
1
2
3
4

28

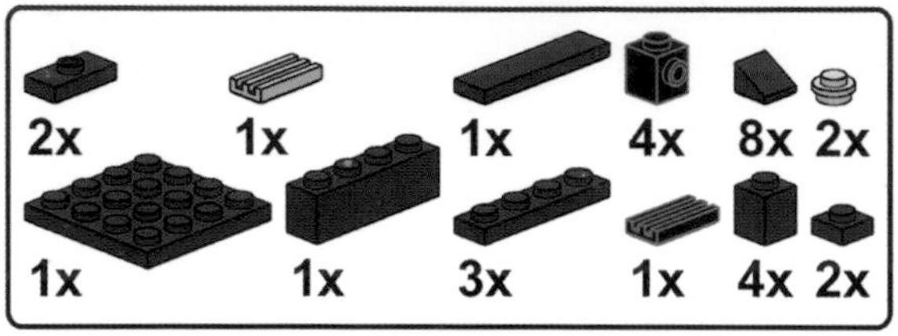
2x
1x
1x
4x
8x
2x
1x
1x
3x
1x
4x
2x

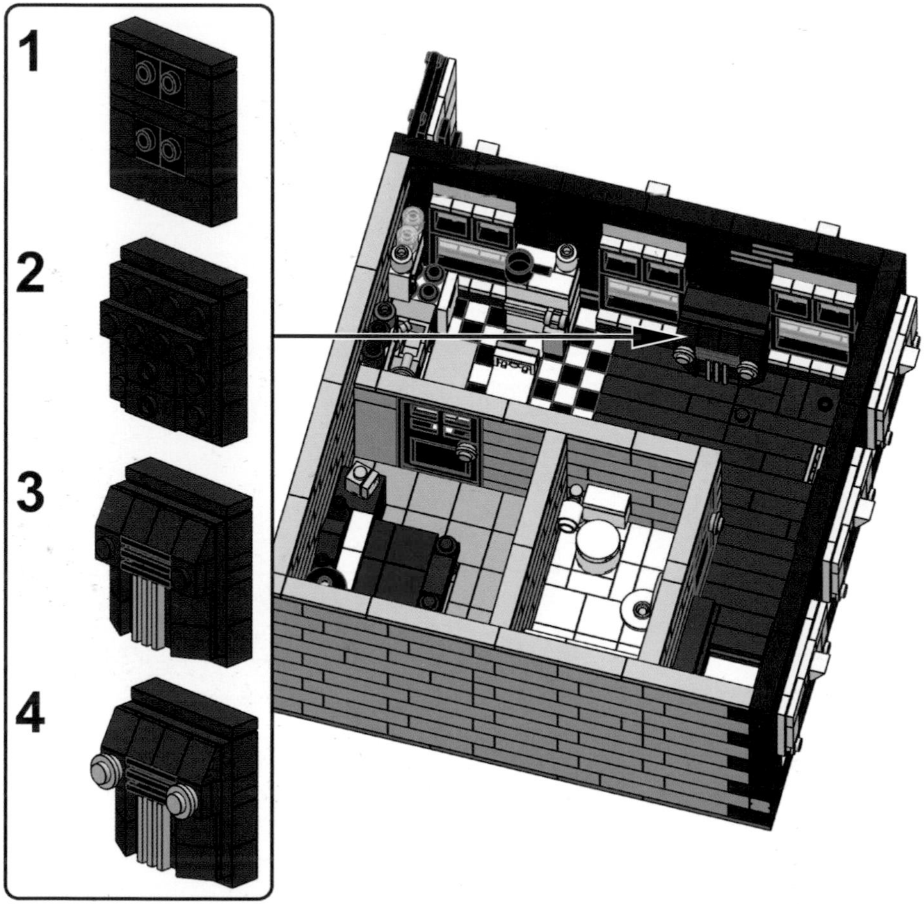
1
2
3
4

29

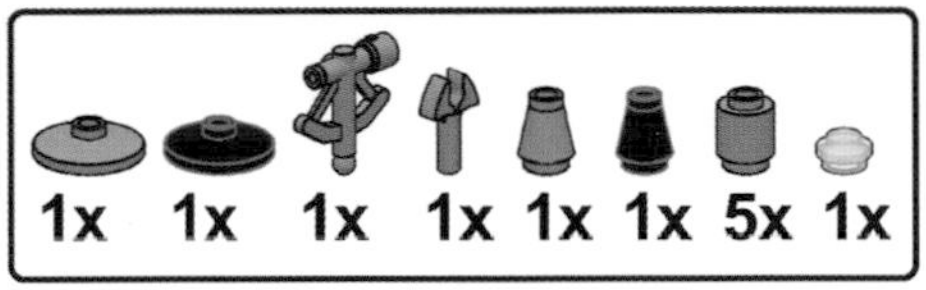
1x 1x 1x 1x 1x 1x 5x 1x

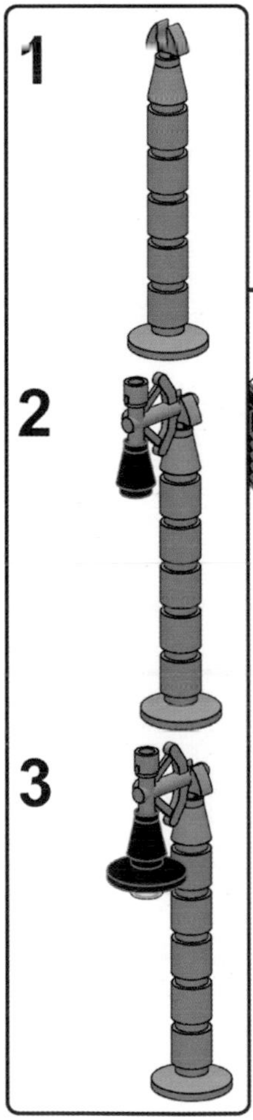
1
2
3

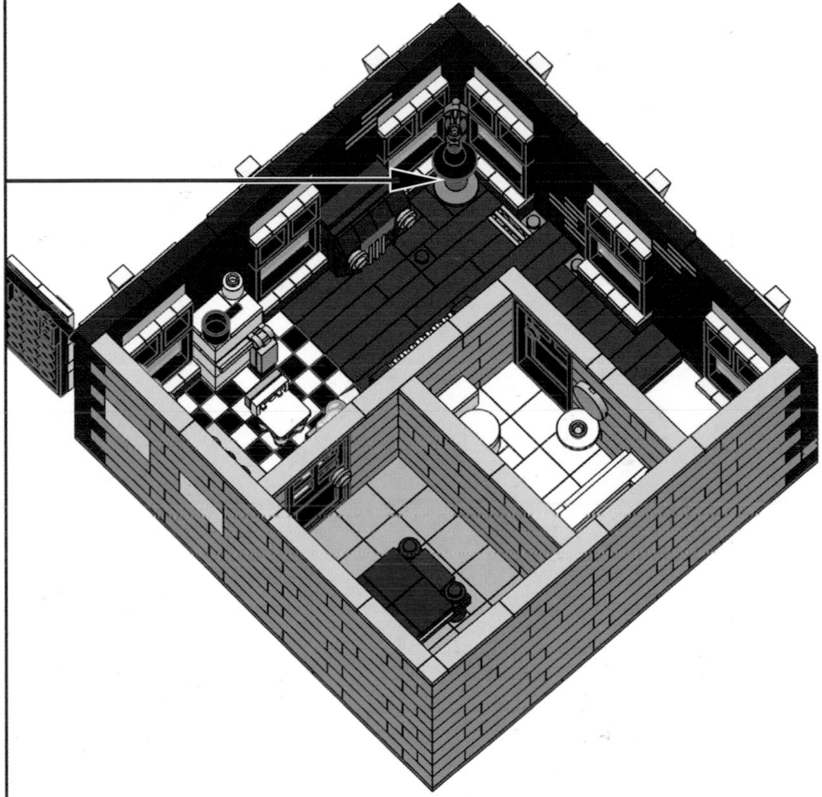

30

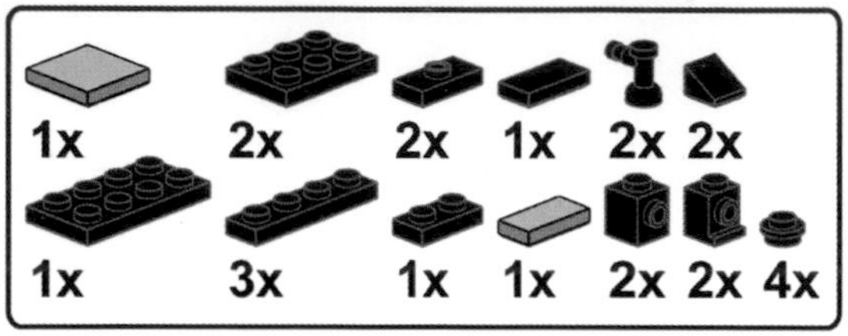
1x
2x
2x
1x
2x
2x
1x
3x
1x
1x
2x
2x
4x

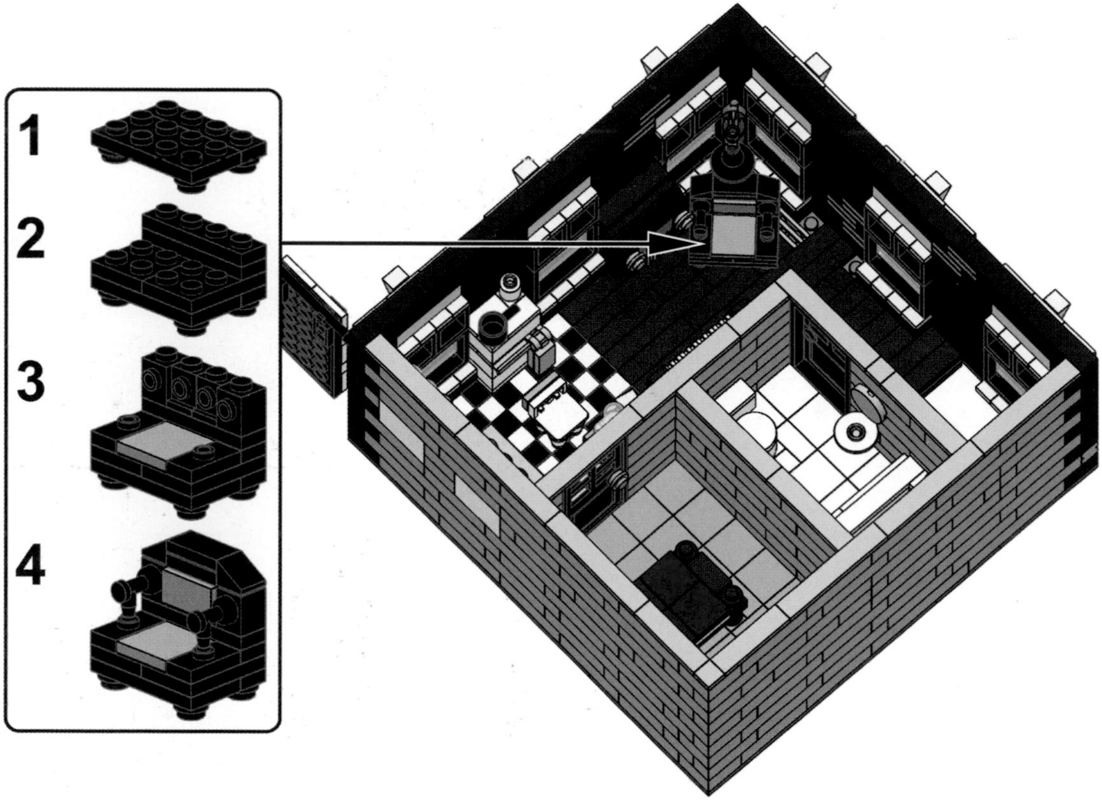
1
2
3
4

31

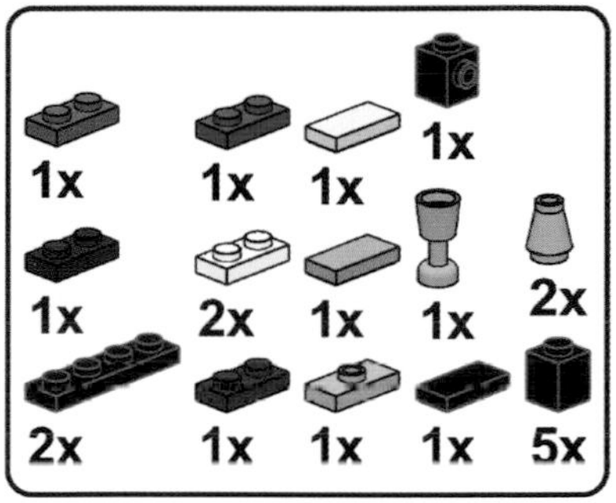
1x
1x
1x
1x
1x
2x
1x
1x
2x
2x
1x
1x
1x
5x

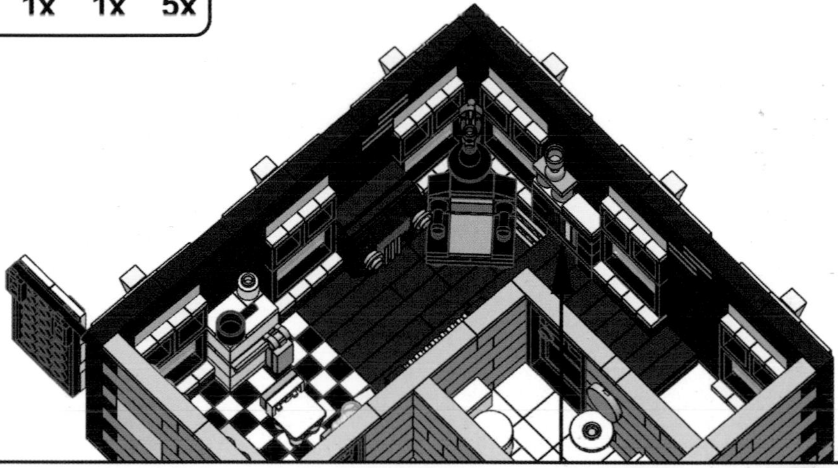

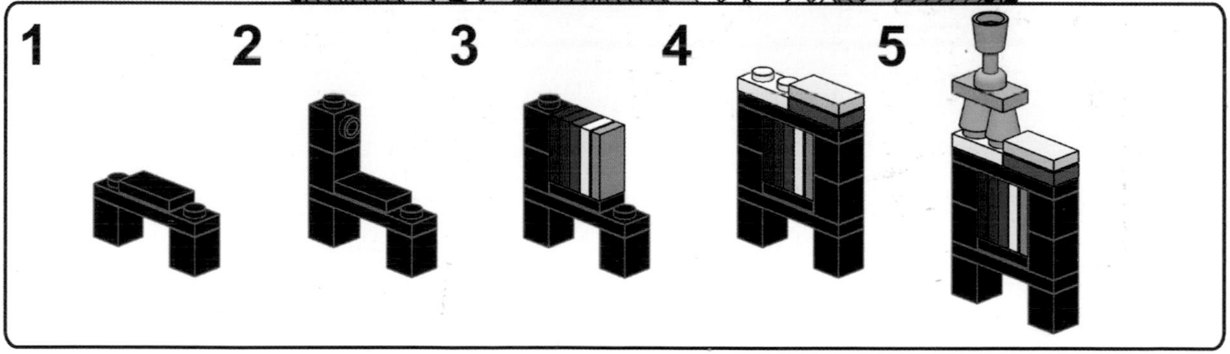
1
2
3
4
5

Roof

1

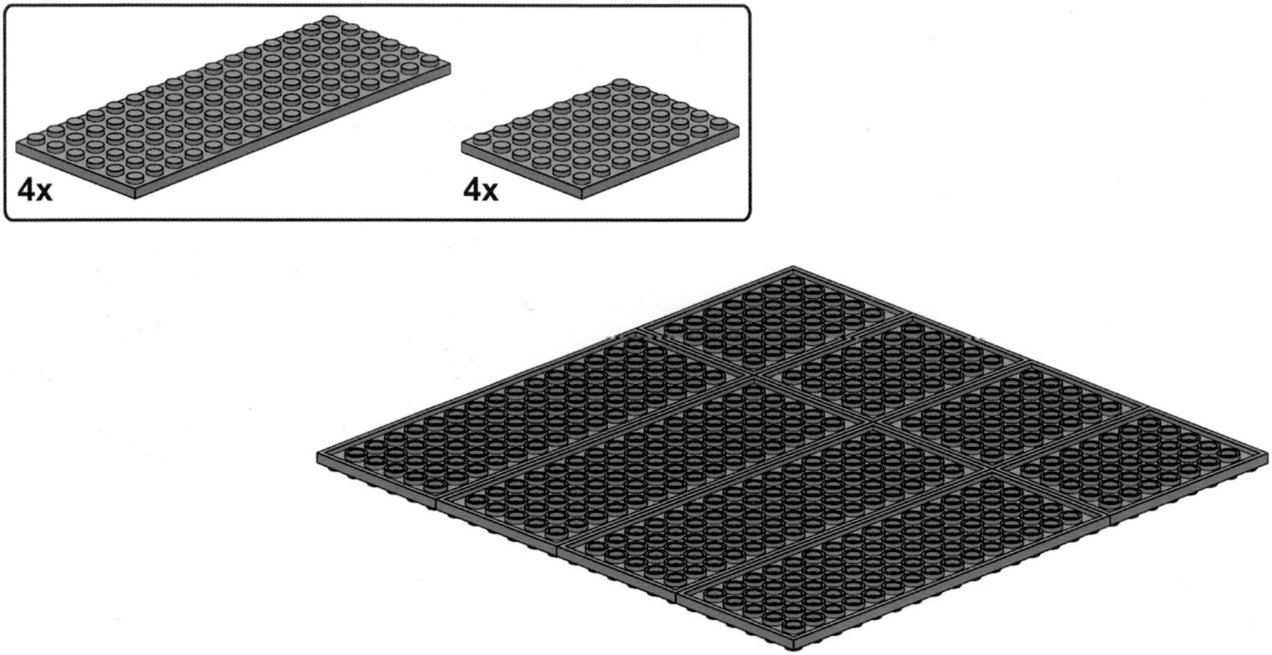

2

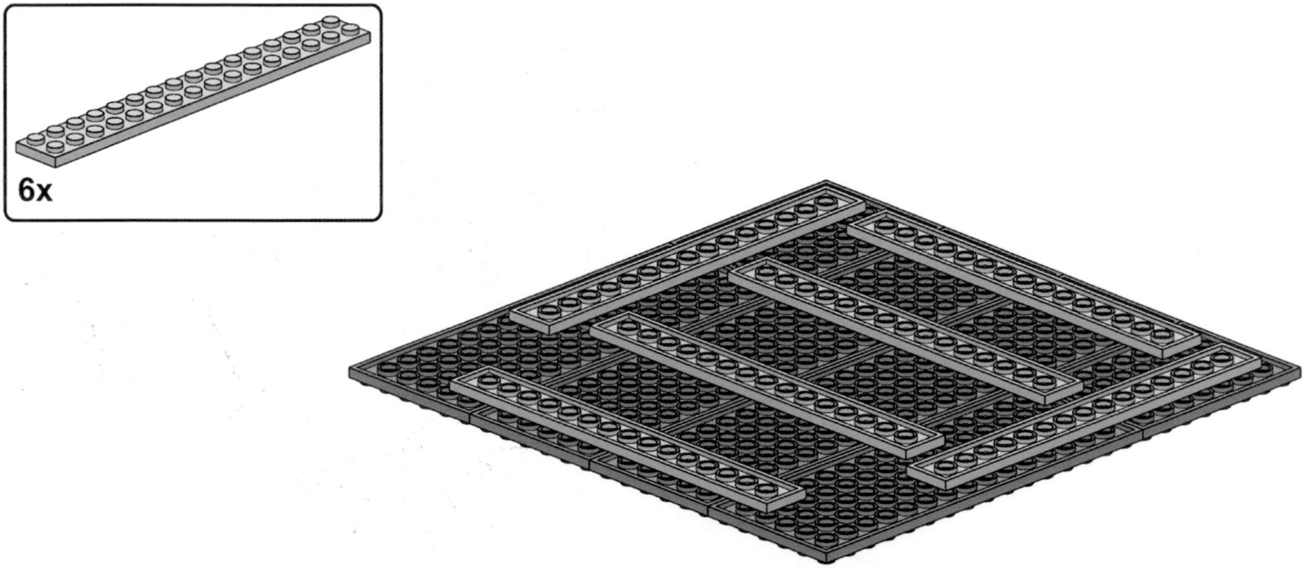

3

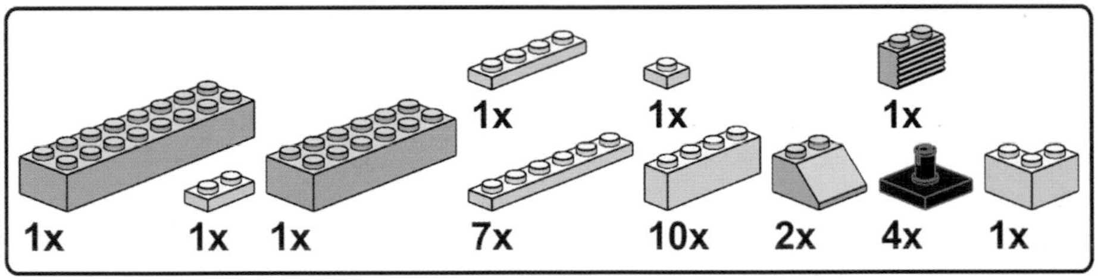
1x
1x
1x
1x
1x
1x
7x
10x
2x
4x
1x

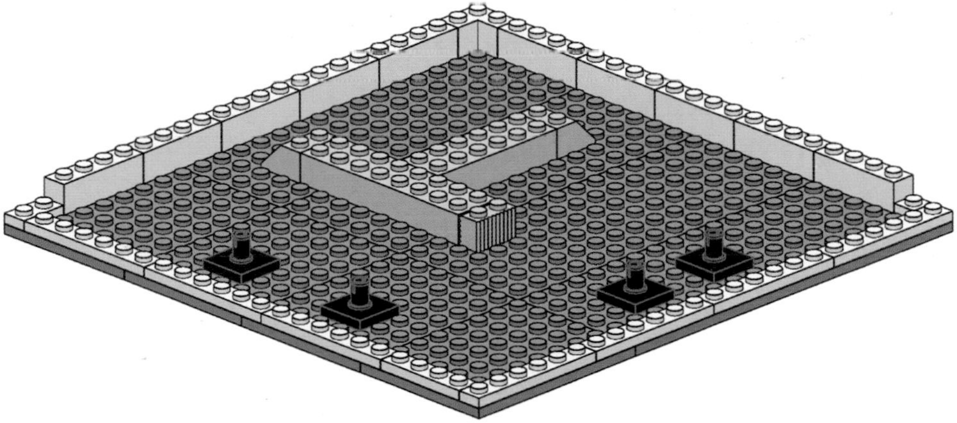

4

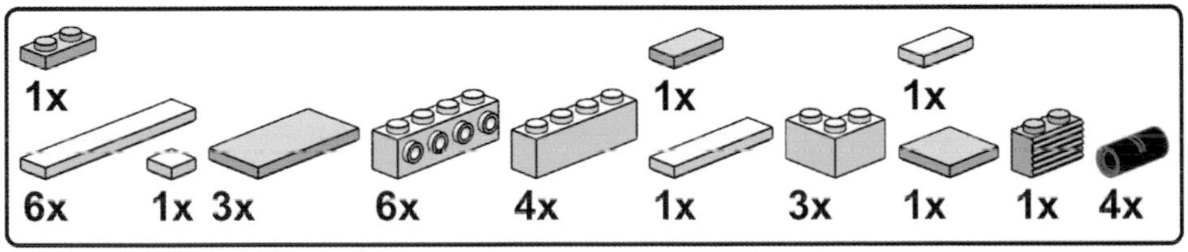
1x
1x
1x
6x
1x
3x
6x
4x
1x
3x
1x
1x
4x

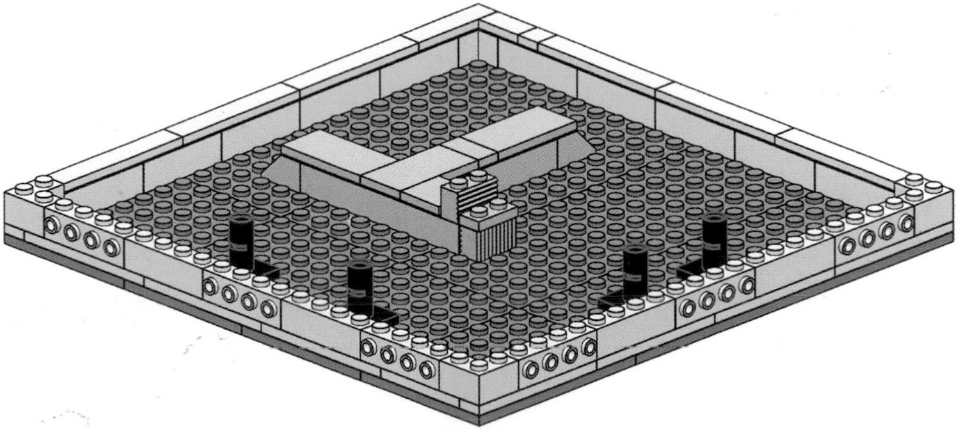

5

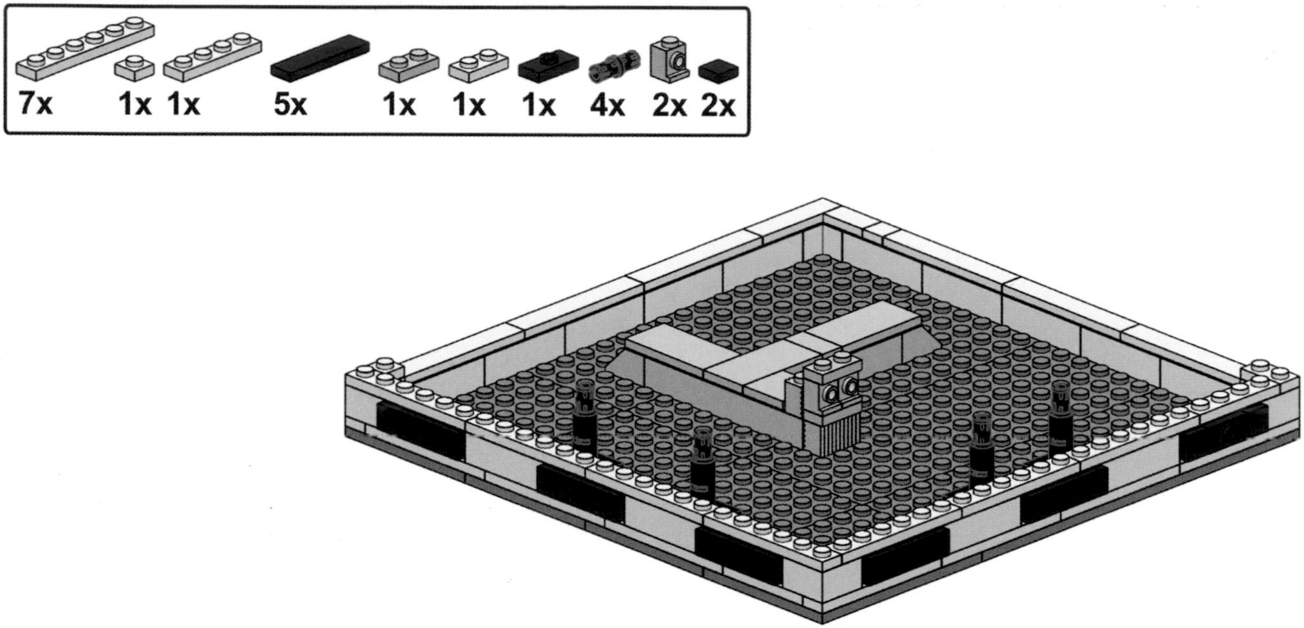
7x
1x 1x
5x
1x
1x
1x
4x
2x 2x

6

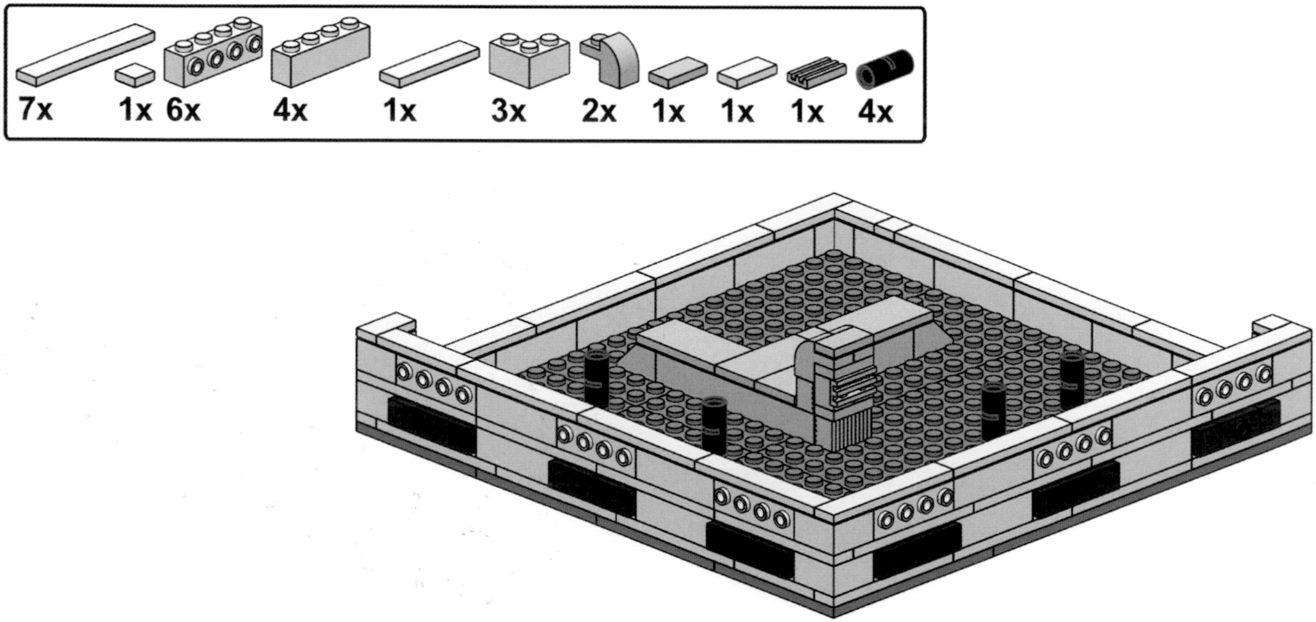
7x
1x 6x
4x
1x
3x
2x
1x
1x
1x
4x

7

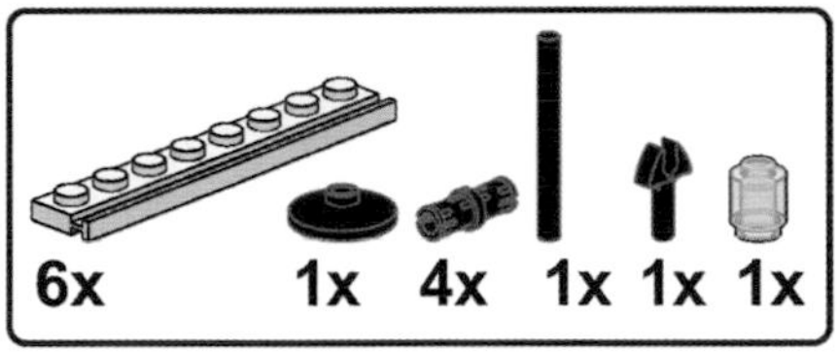
6x
1x
4x
1x
1x
1x

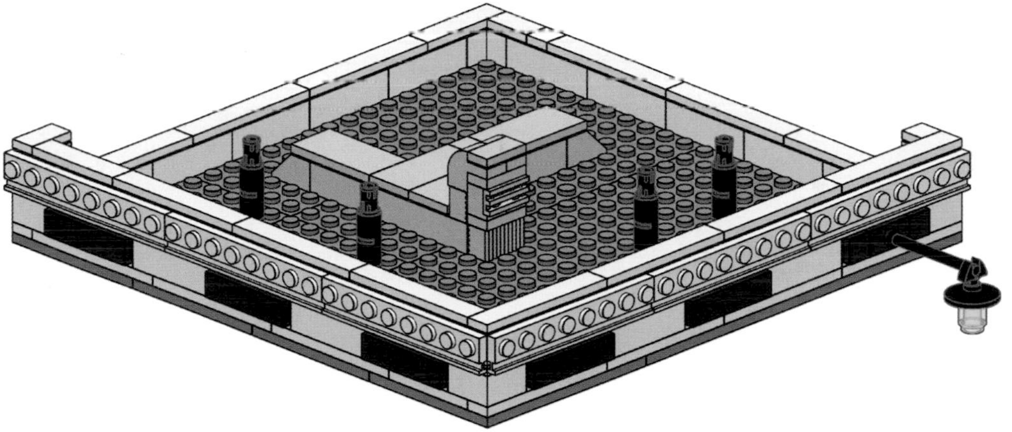

8

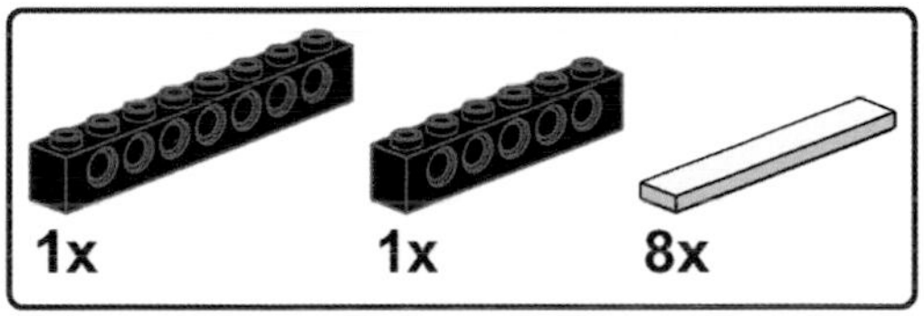
1x
1x
8x

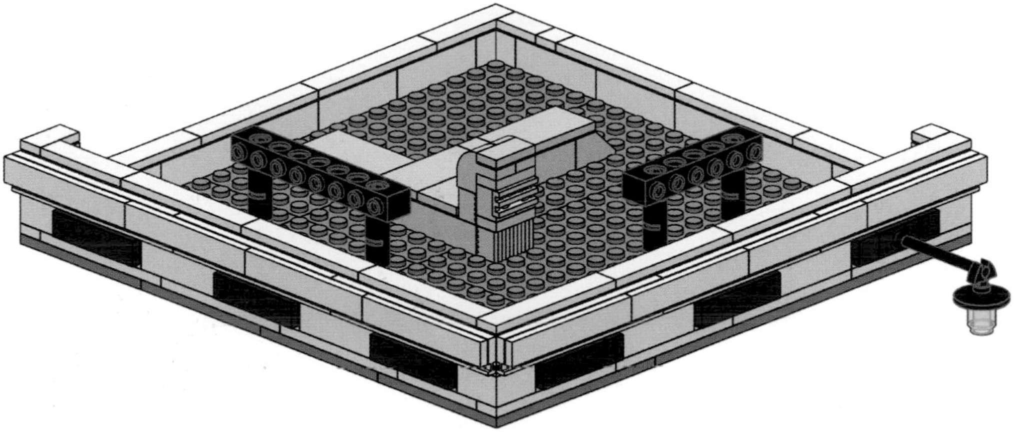

9

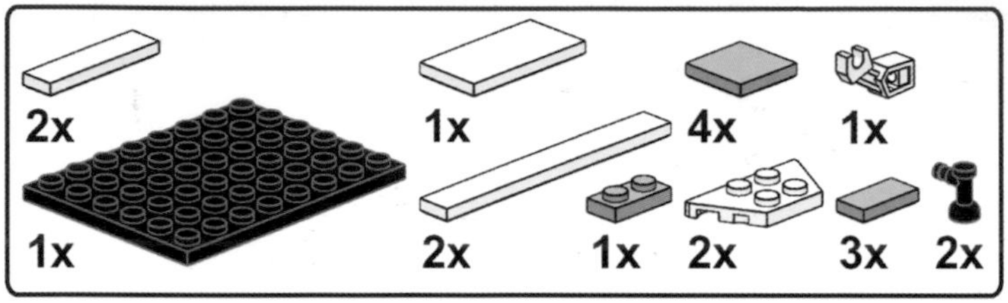
2x
1x
1x
2x
1x
4x
1x
1x
2x
3x
2x

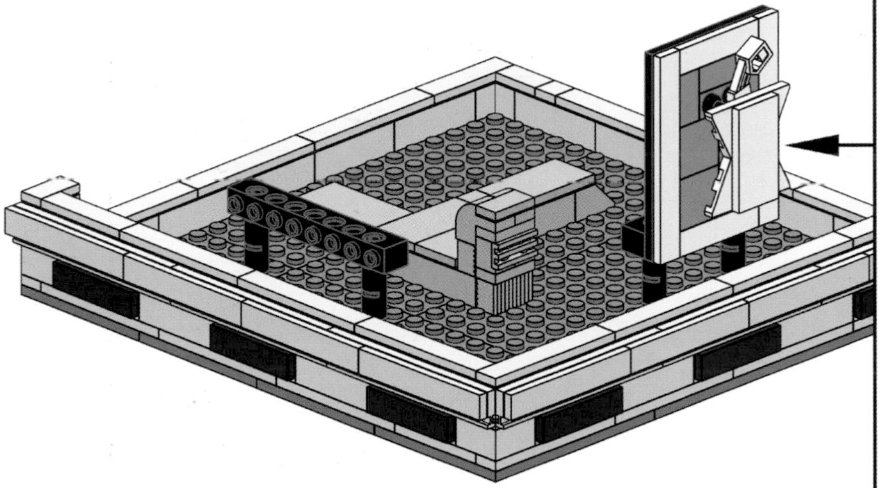

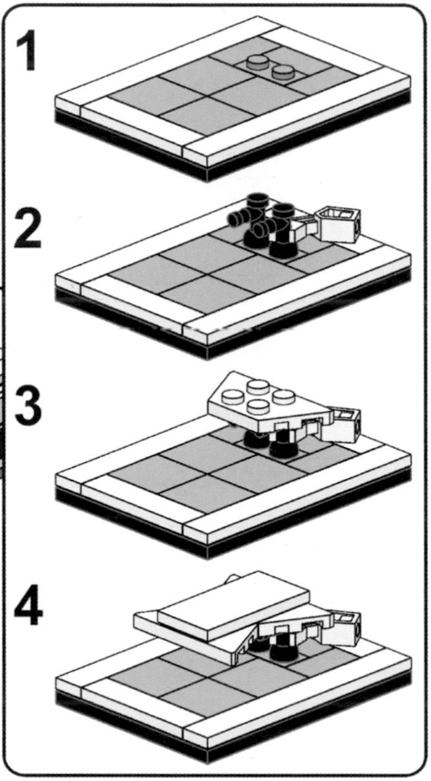
1
2
3
4

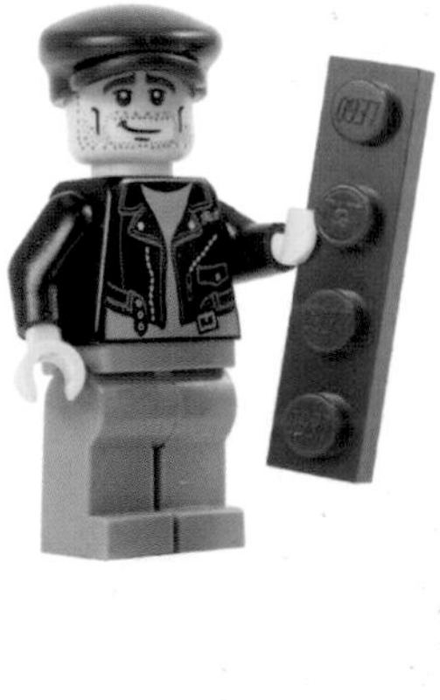

YOU COULD TURN THIS PLATE AROUND AND ATTACH IT TO TECHNIC BRICKS FOR A DIFFERENT LOOK TO THE TRIM.

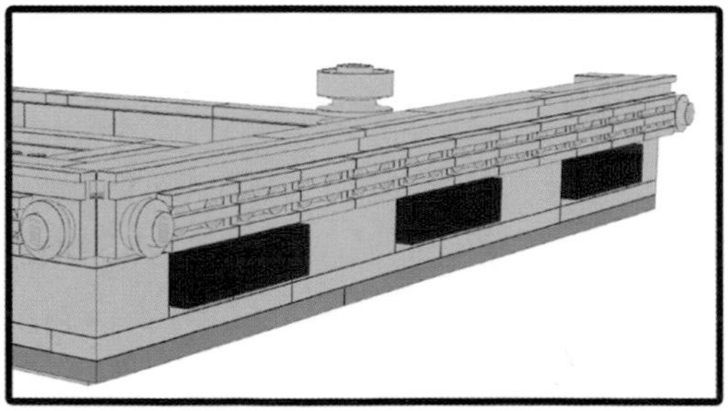

1

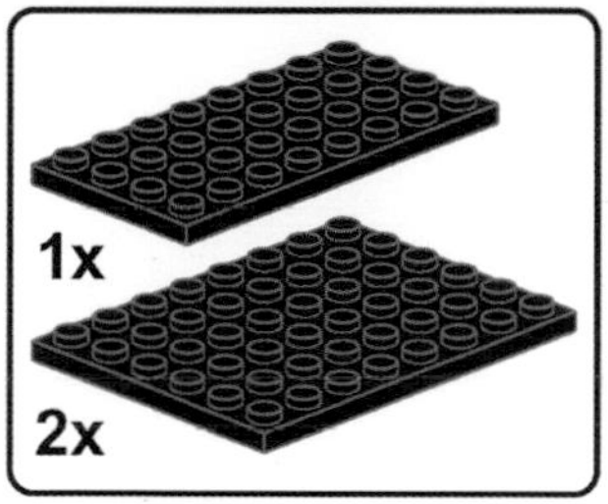

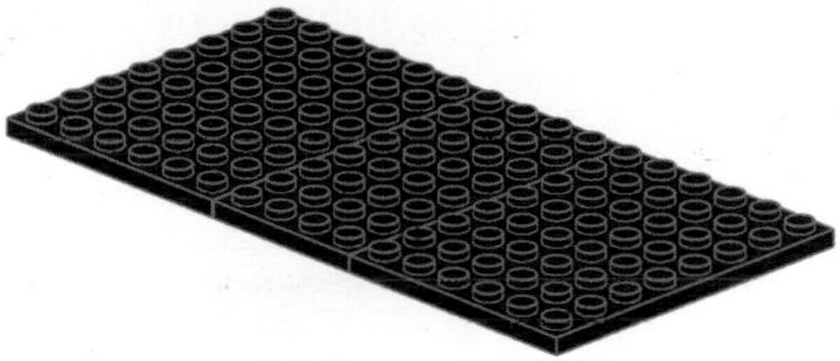

2

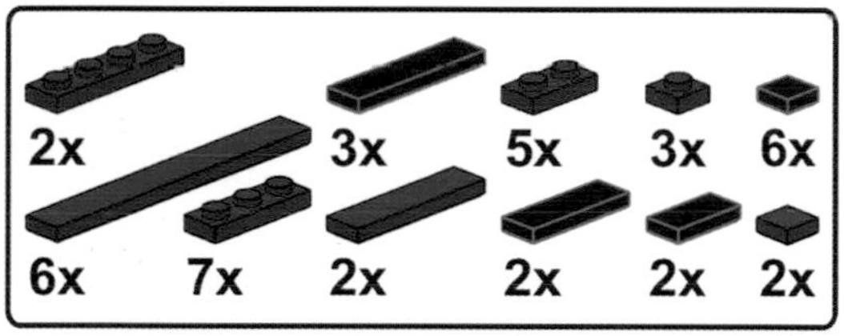

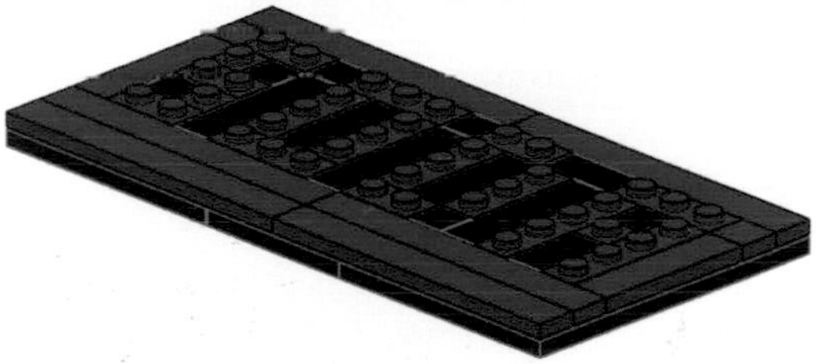

3

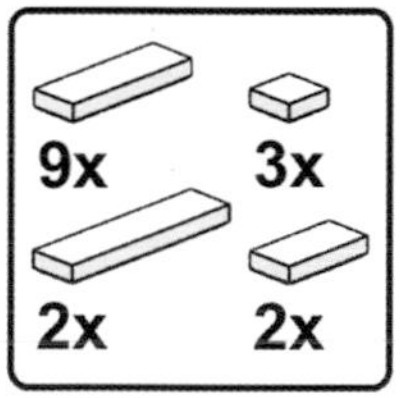

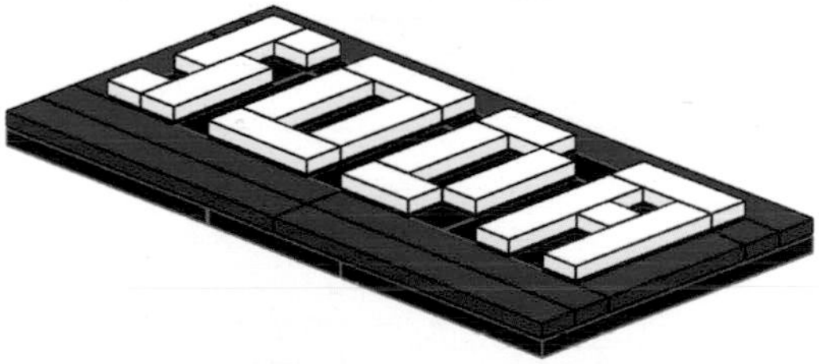

4

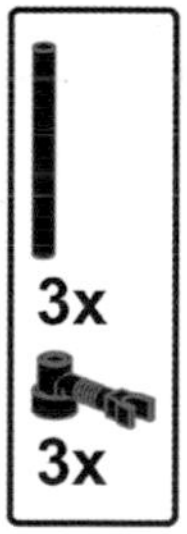

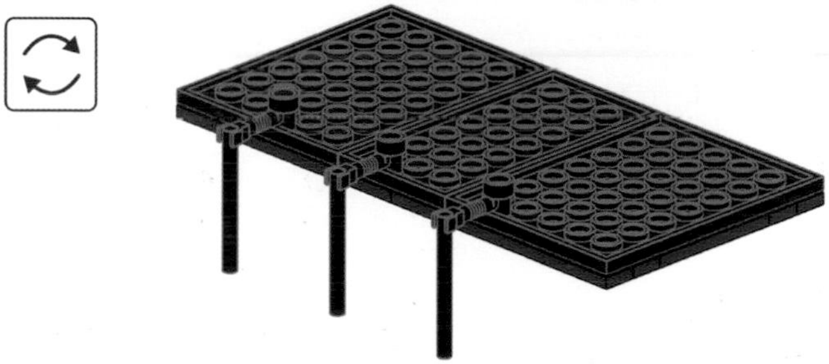

5

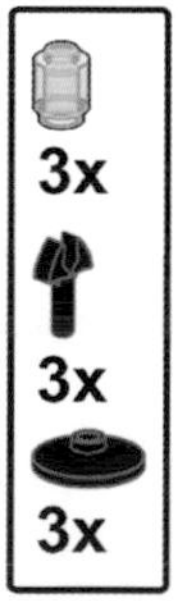

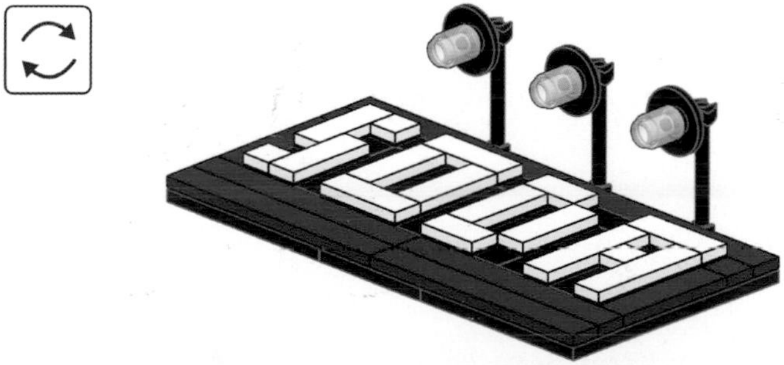

10

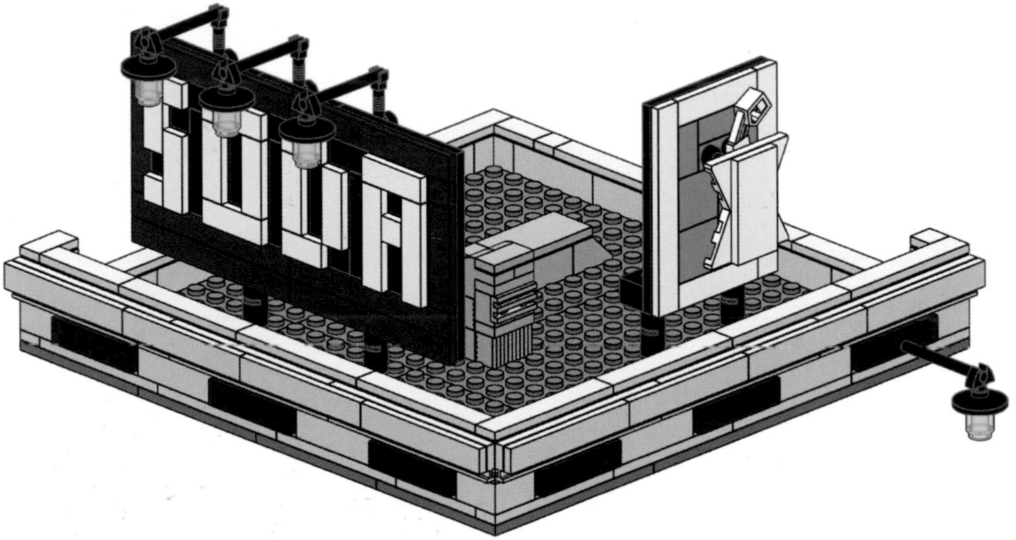

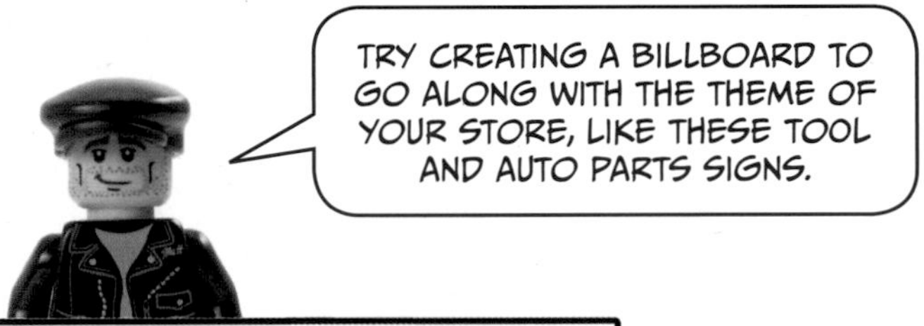
TRY CREATING A BILLBOARD TO GO ALONG WITH THE THEME OF YOUR STORE, LIKE THESE TOOL AND AUTO PARTS SIGNS.

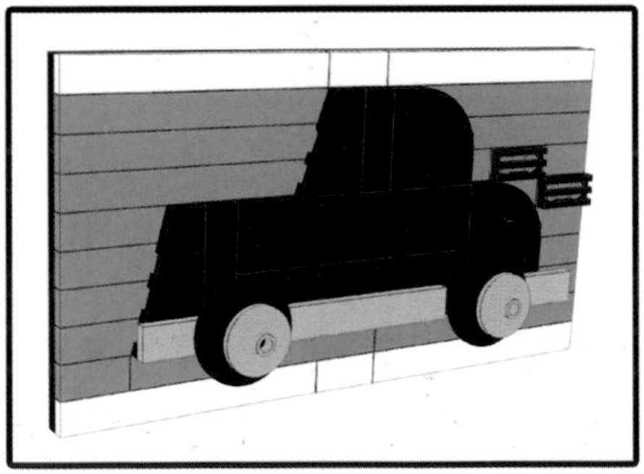

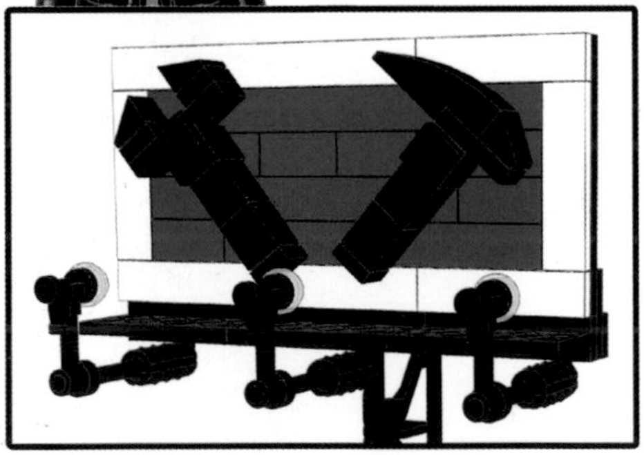

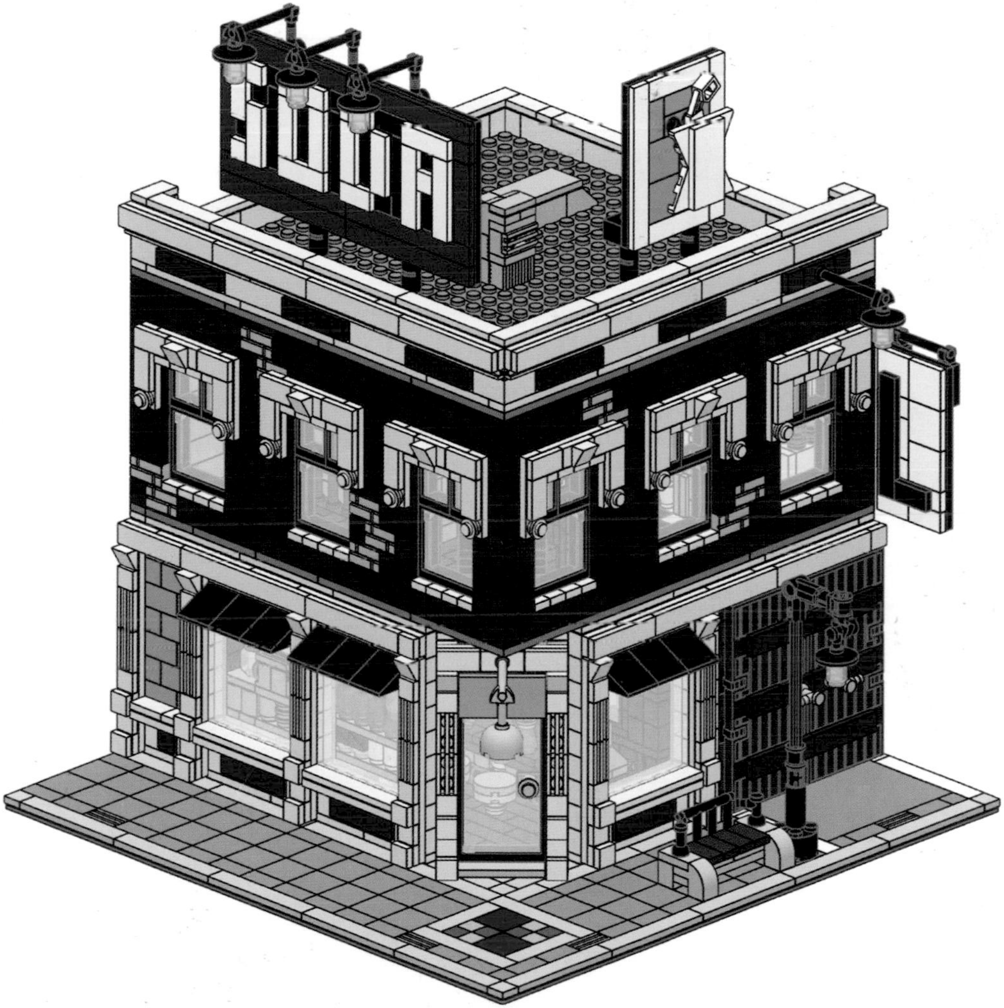
SODA

Houses

These three residential designs use the same base model as a starting point, which you'll build first. The exposed studs on the face of the building allow you to connect various facades.

Assembling the structural elements of your building separate from the decorative parts lets you really experiment with new techniques.

With the base complete, you'll see instructions for the Parisian Apartment (page 169) and Colonial Row House (page 177), which use the complete base structure in two very different styles. The Canal Ring House (page 184), built in the style of Amsterdam's Canal Ring district, uses the first two levels of the residential building but has a completely different third story and roof.

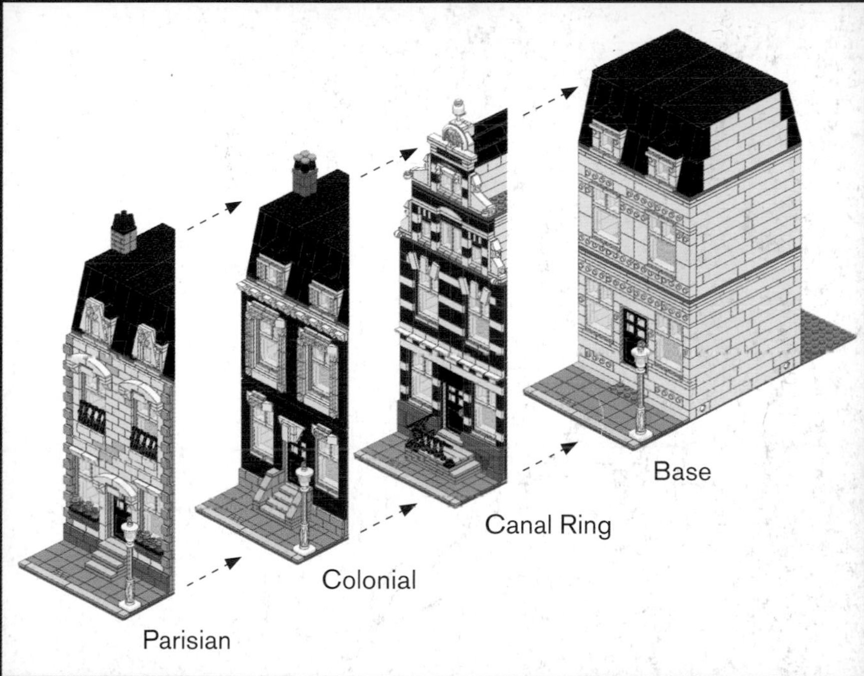
Parisian
Colonial
Canal Ring
Base

In this chapter you will find instructions for a base model with three instructions for different building facades.

Base

For a parts list you can download, visit *http://nostarch.com/legoneighborhood/*.

Bill of Materials

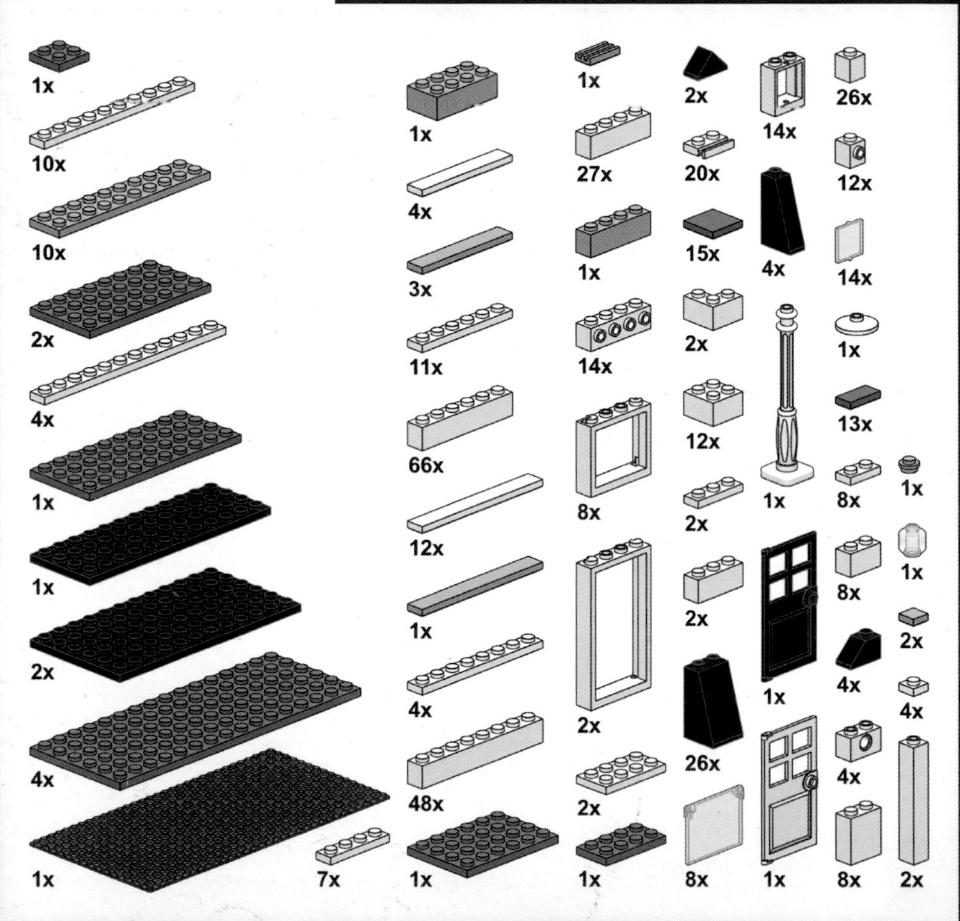

1x
10x
10x
2x
4x
1x
1x
2x
4x
1x
7x
1x
4x
3x
11x
66x
12x
1x
4x
48x
1x
1x
27x
1x
14x
8x
2x
2x
1x
2x
20x
15x
2x
12x
2x
2x
26x
8x
14x
4x
1x
1x
1x
26x
12x
14x
1x
13x
8x
8x
4x
4x
8x
1x
1x
2x
4x
2x

First Floor

1

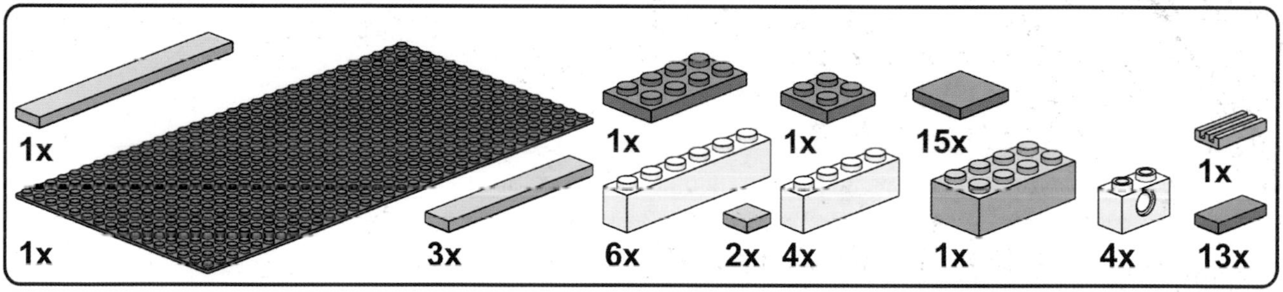
1x
1x
1x
1x
15x
1x
3x
6x
2x
4x
1x
4x
13x

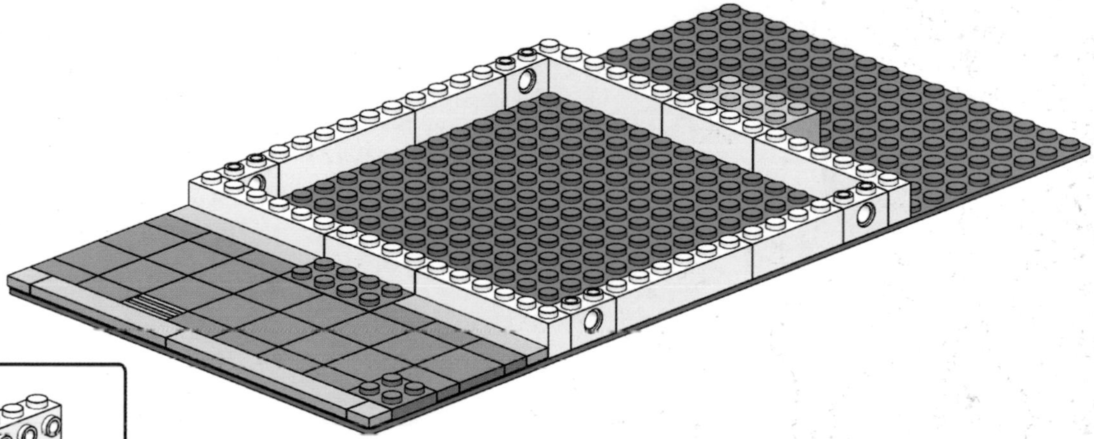

2

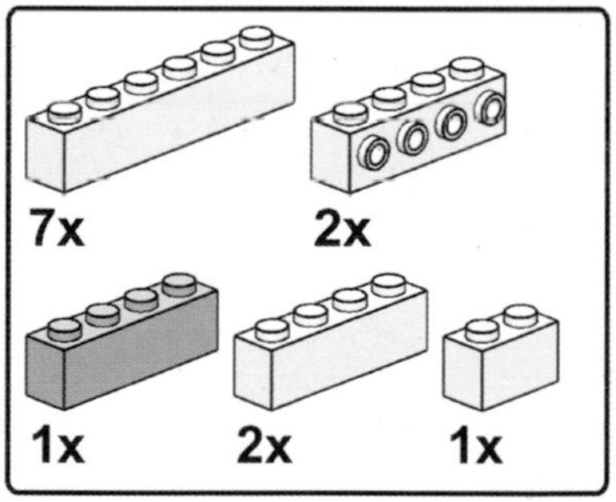
7x
2x
1x
2x
1x

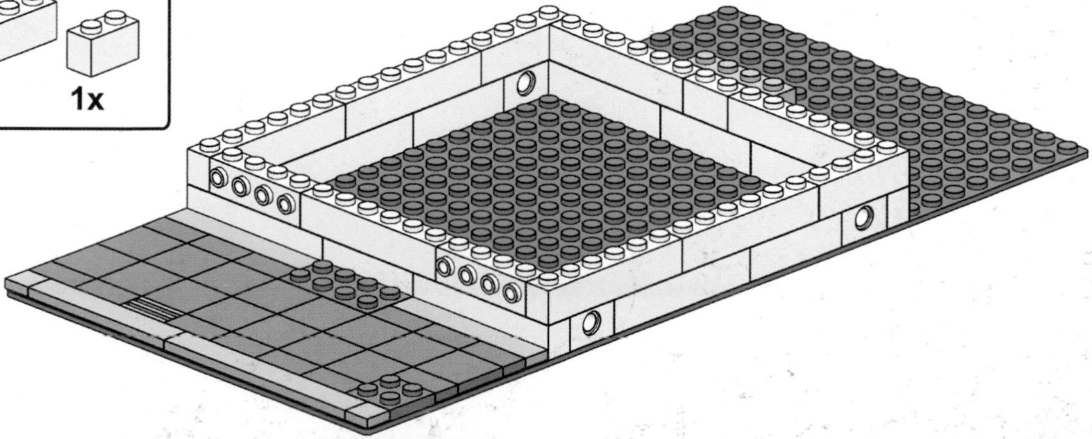

3

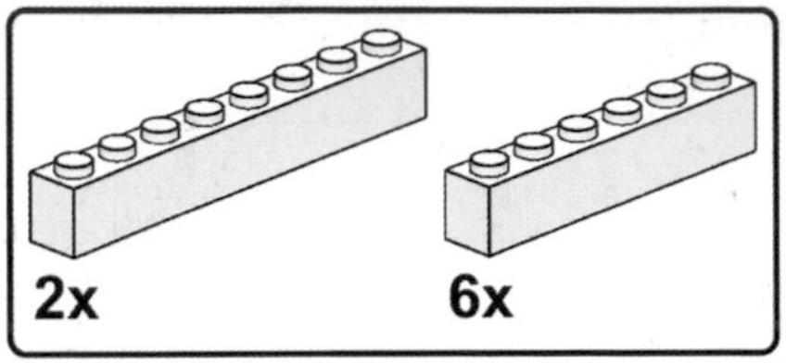
2x
6x

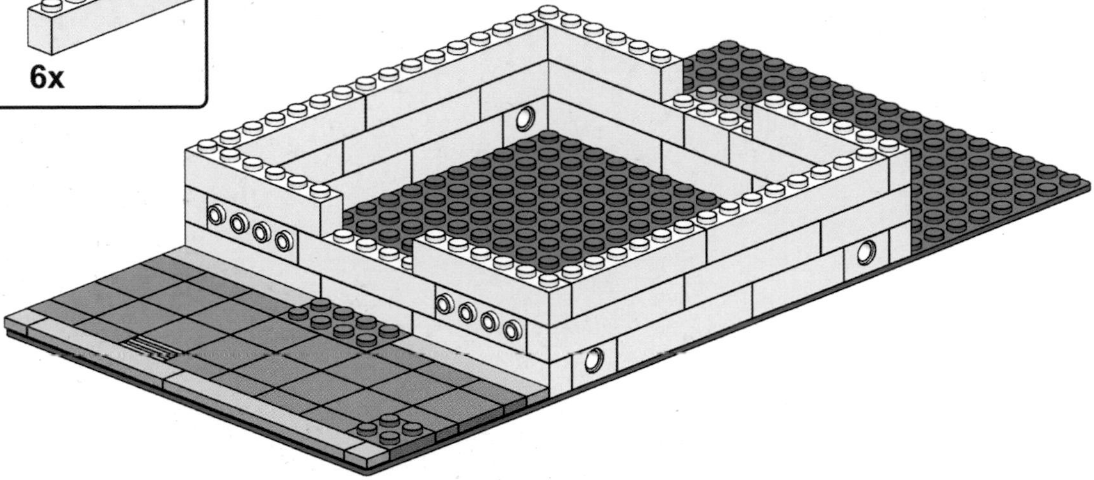

4

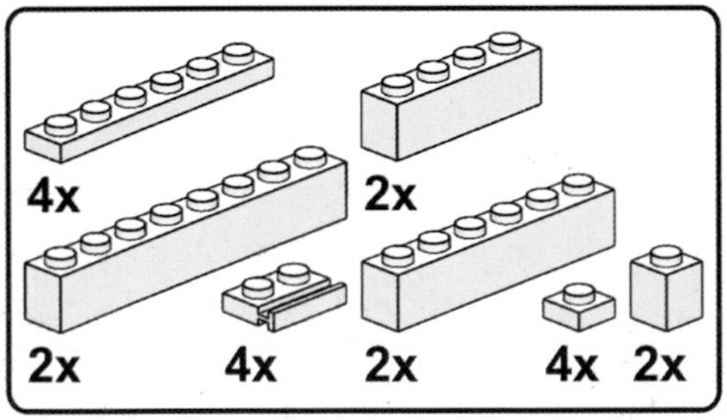
4x
2x
2x
4x
2x
4x
2x

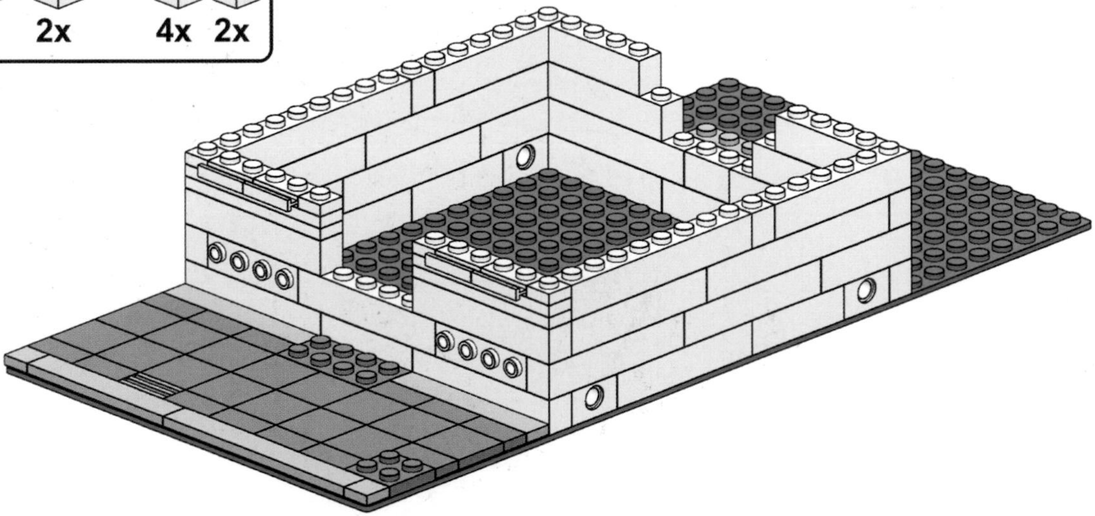

5

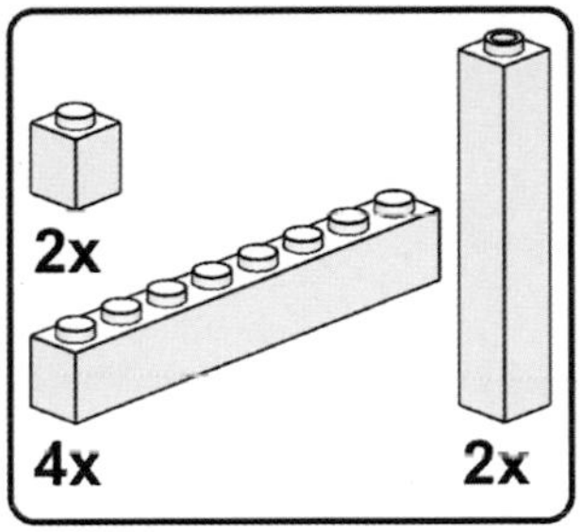
2x
4x
2x

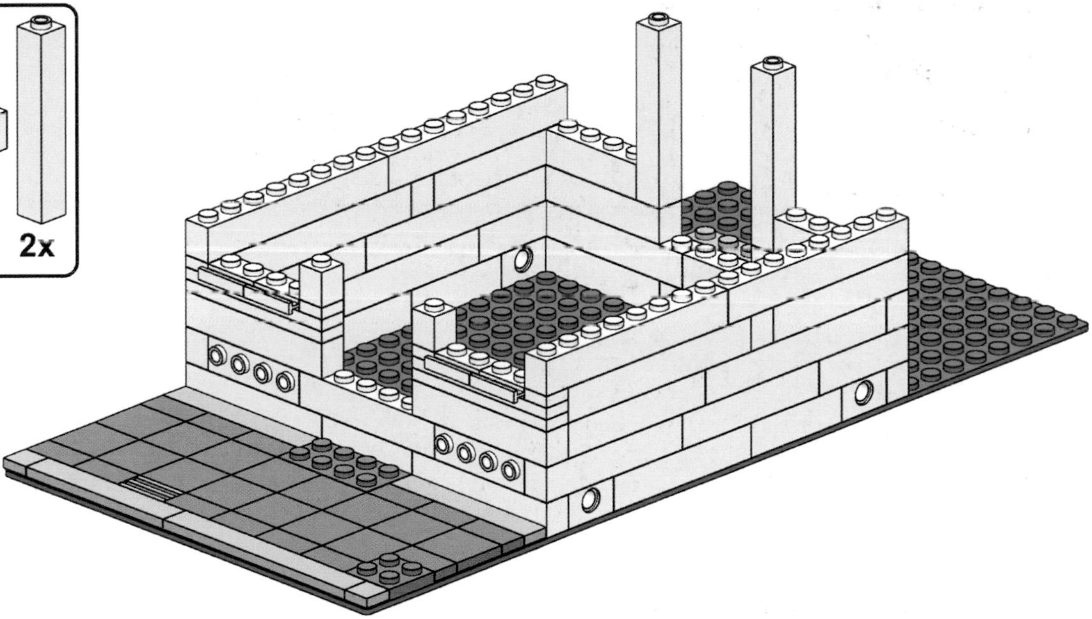

6

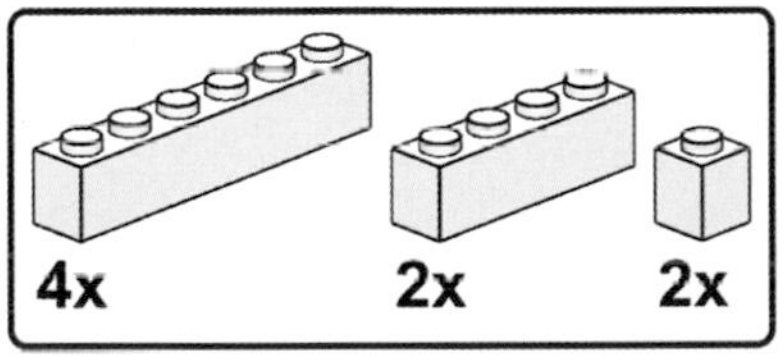
4x
2x
2x

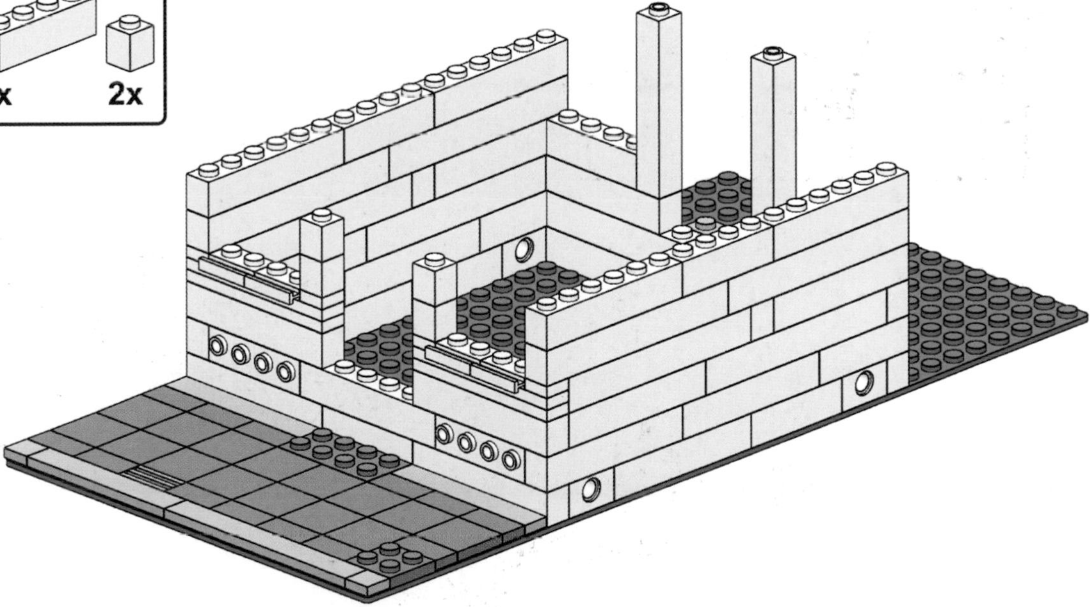

7

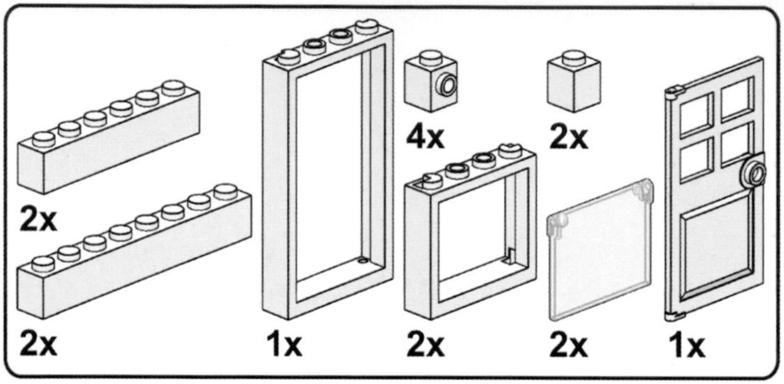
2x
2x
1x
4x
2x
2x
2x
1x

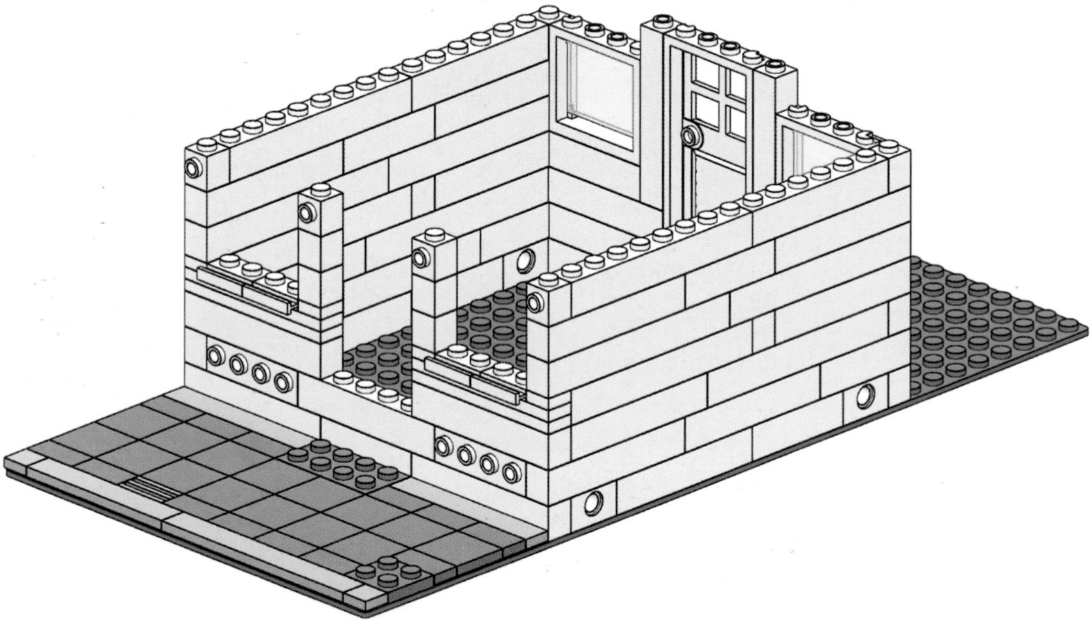

8

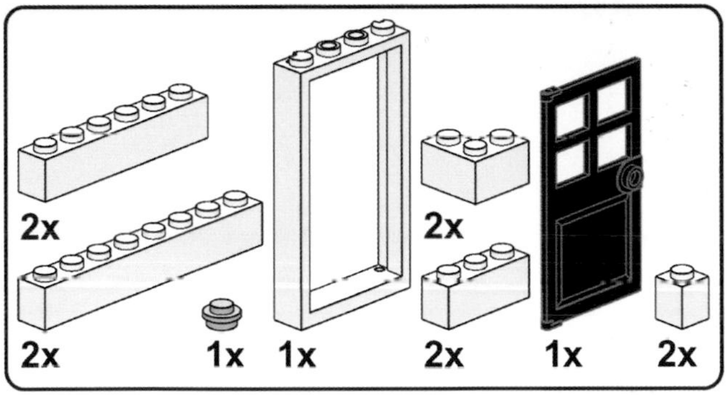
2x
2x
1x
1x
2x
2x
1x
2x

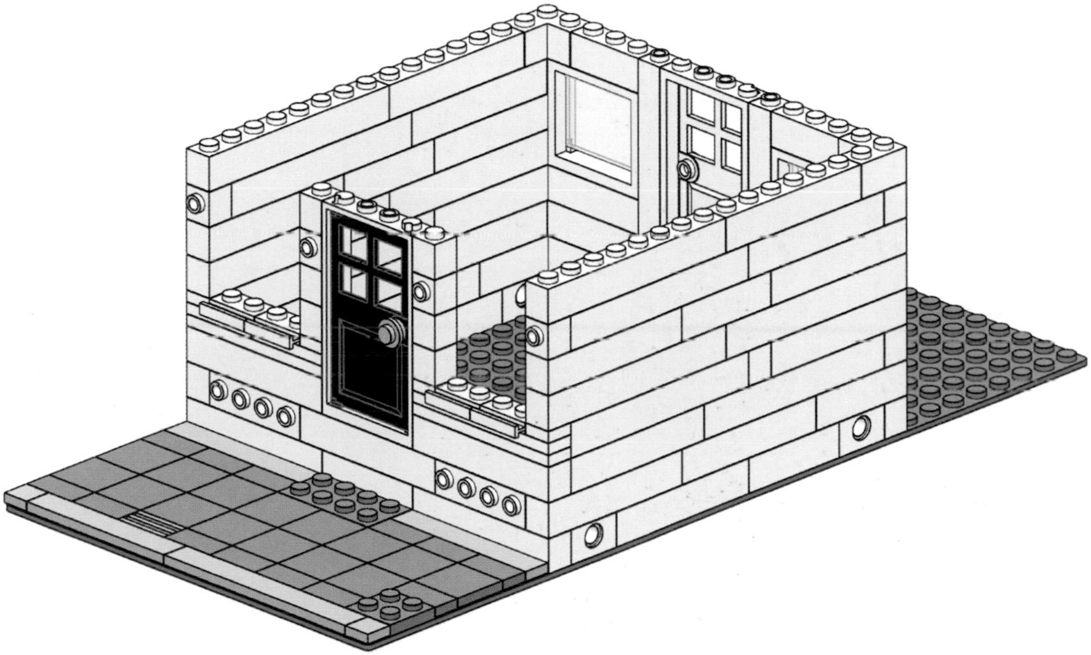

9

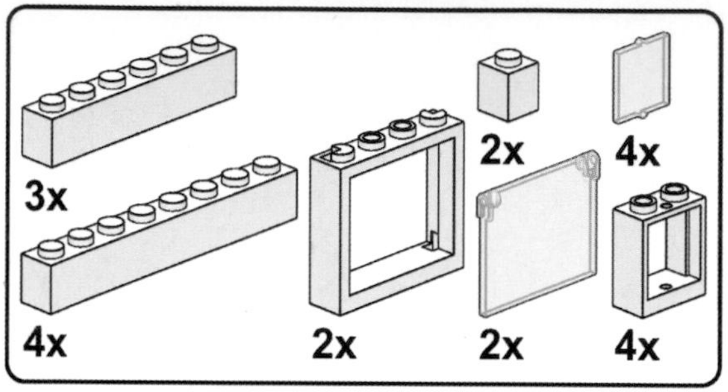
3x
4x
2x
2x
4x
2x
2x
4x

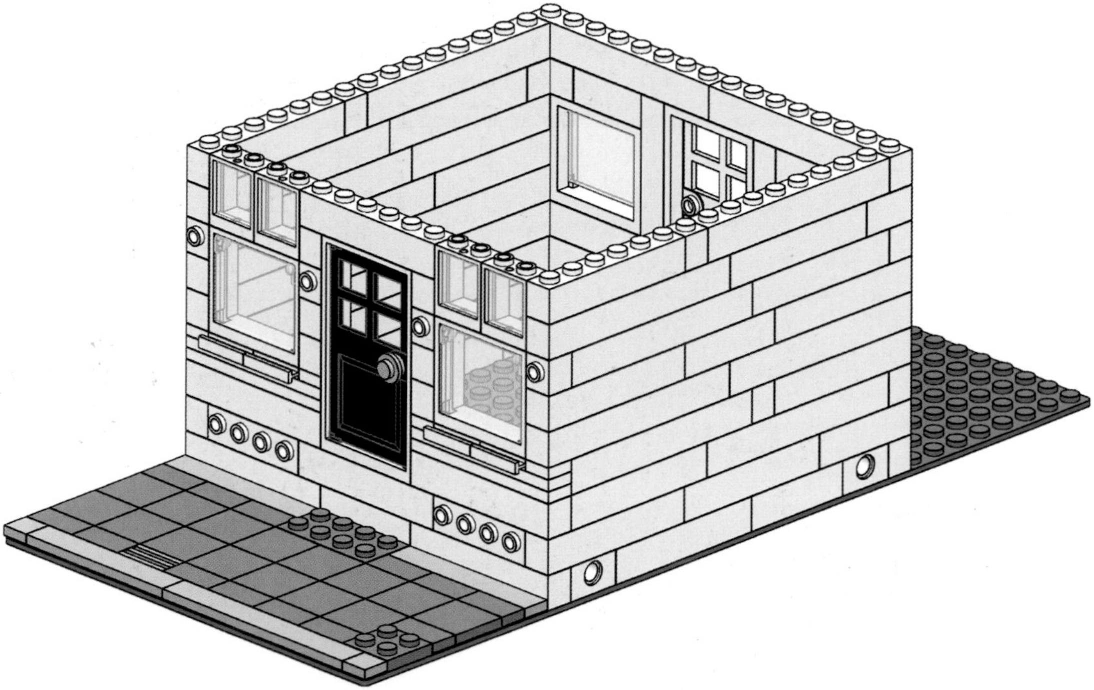

10

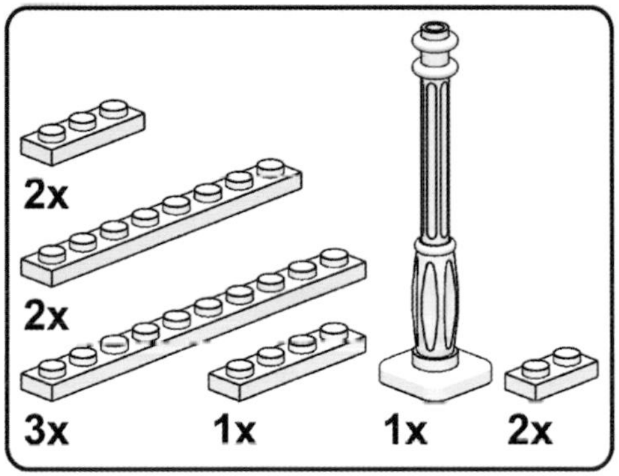
2x
2x
3x
1x
1x
2x

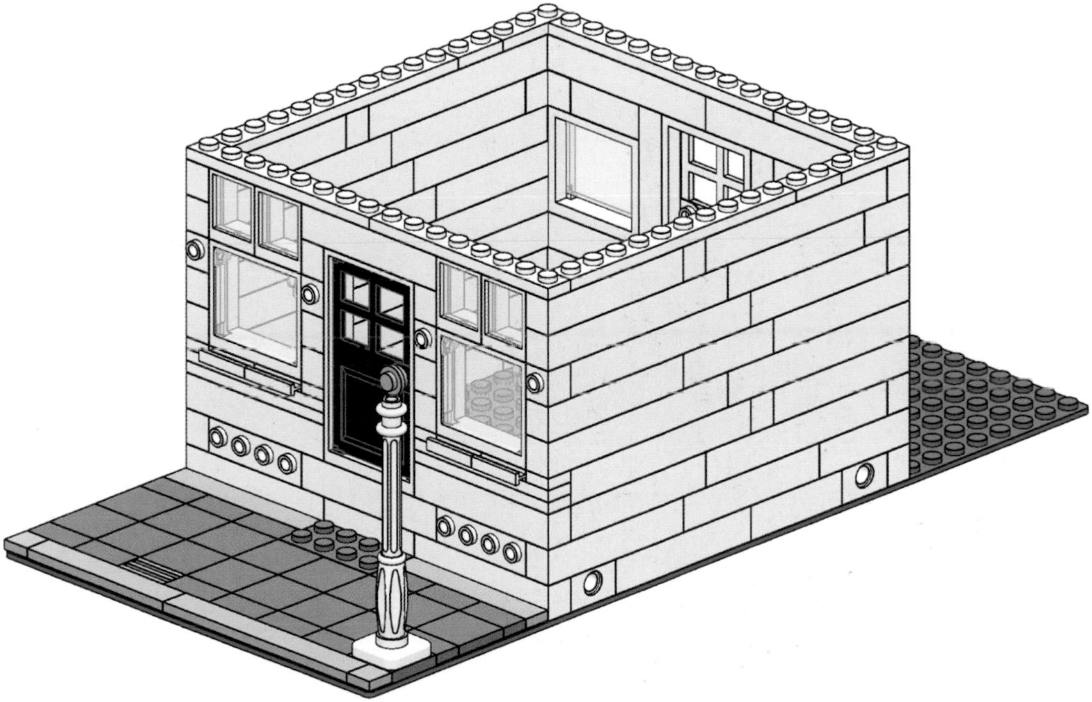

11

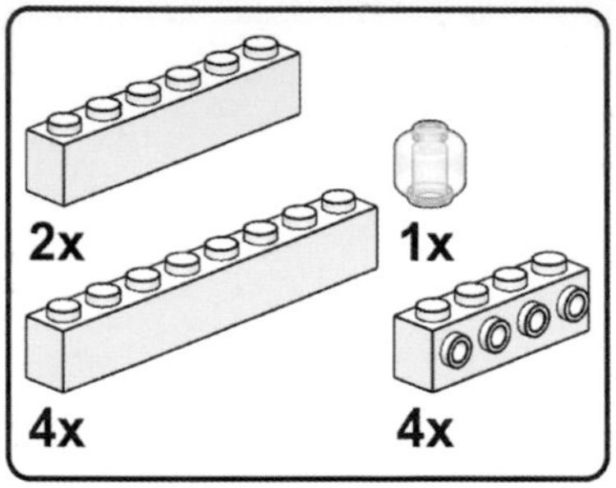

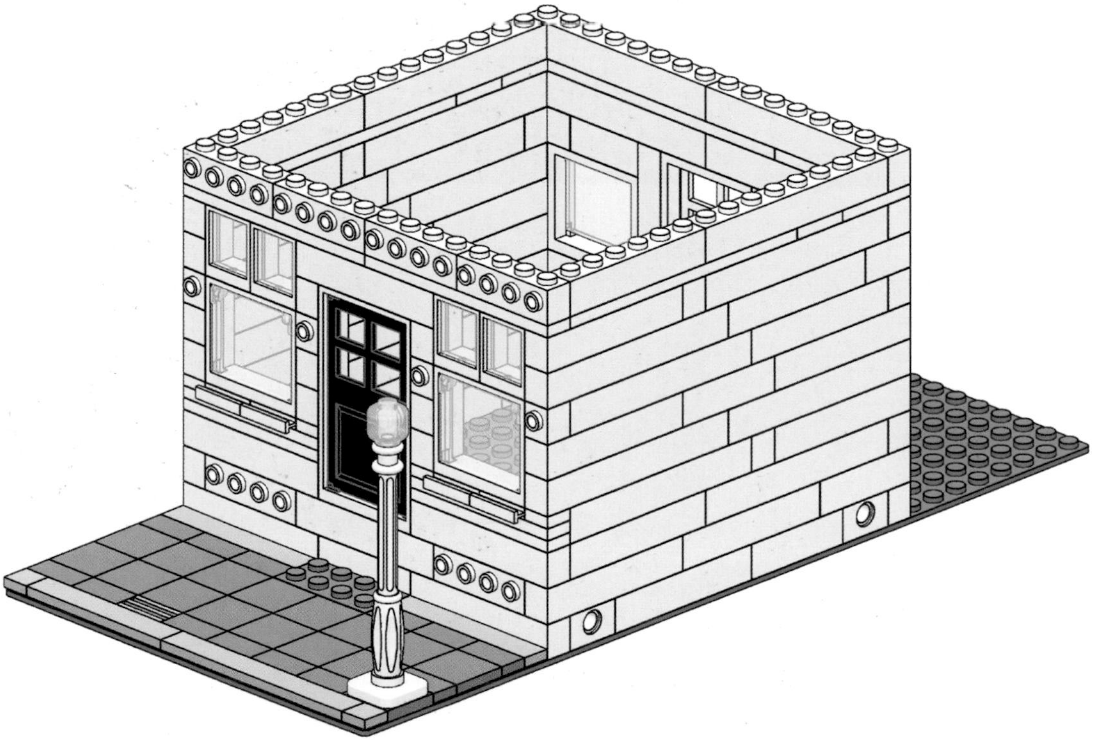

12

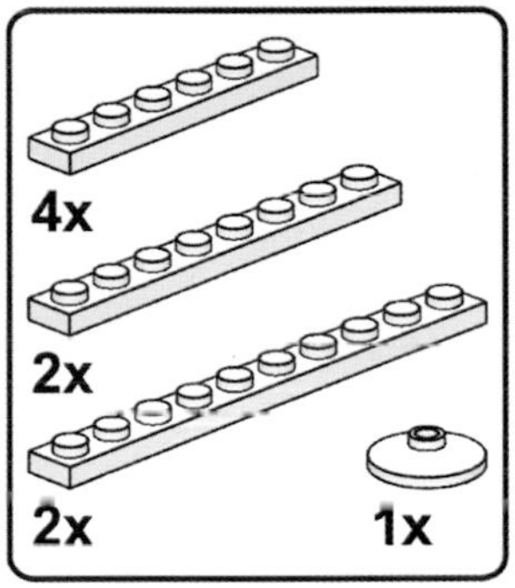

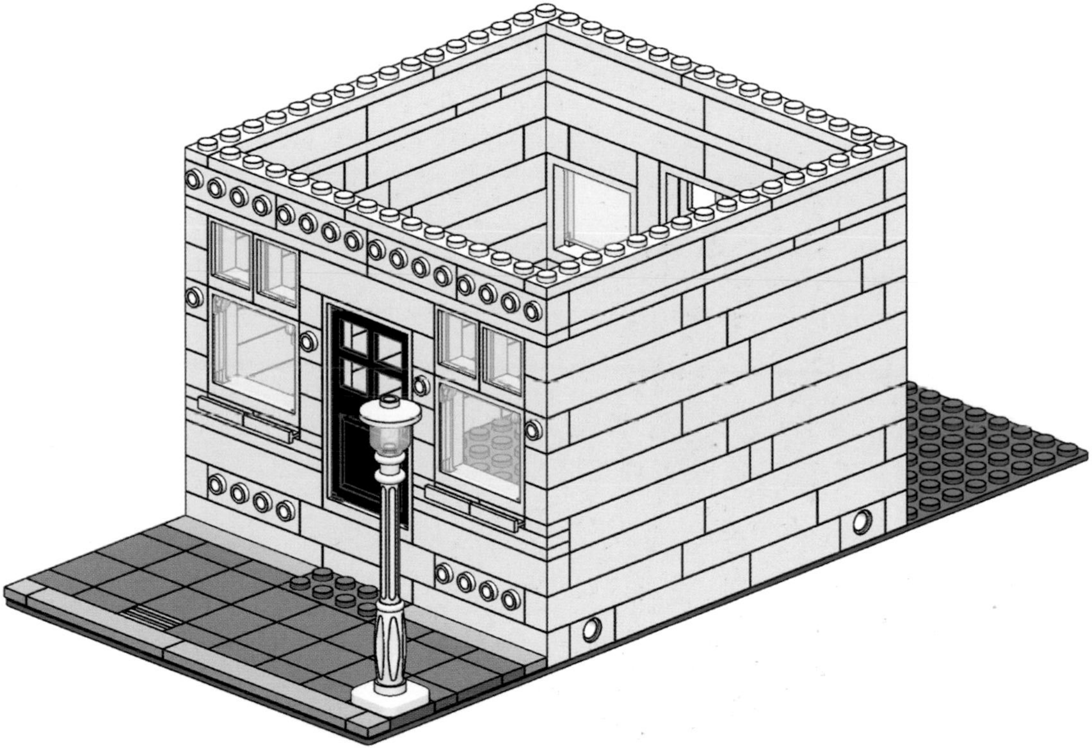

13

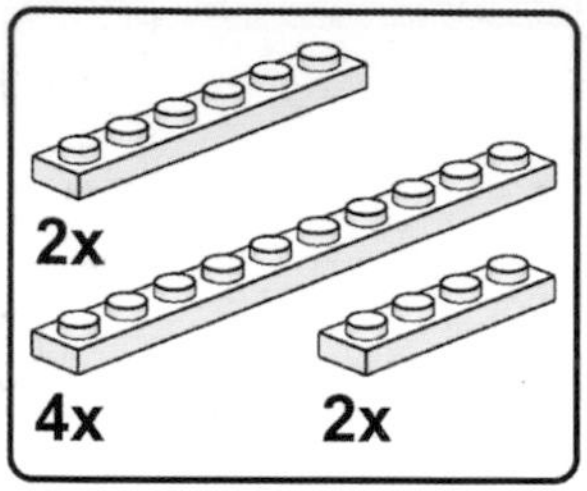

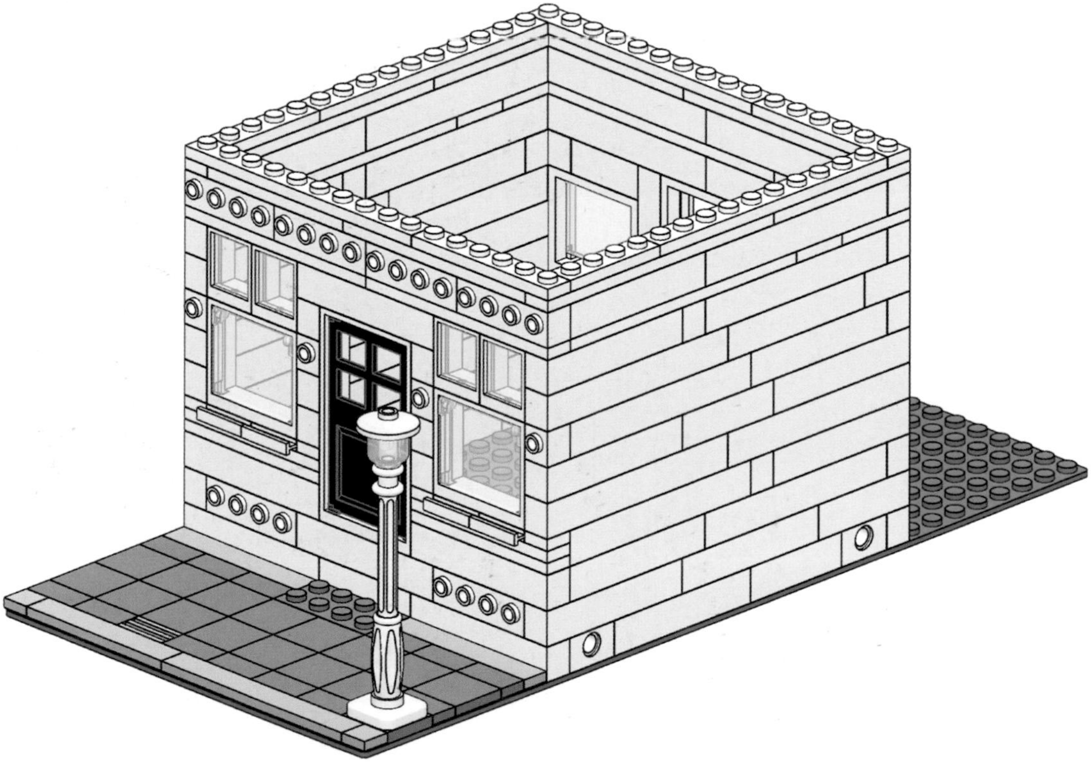

14

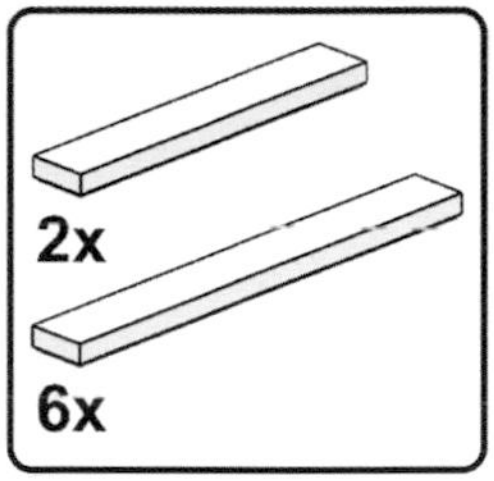

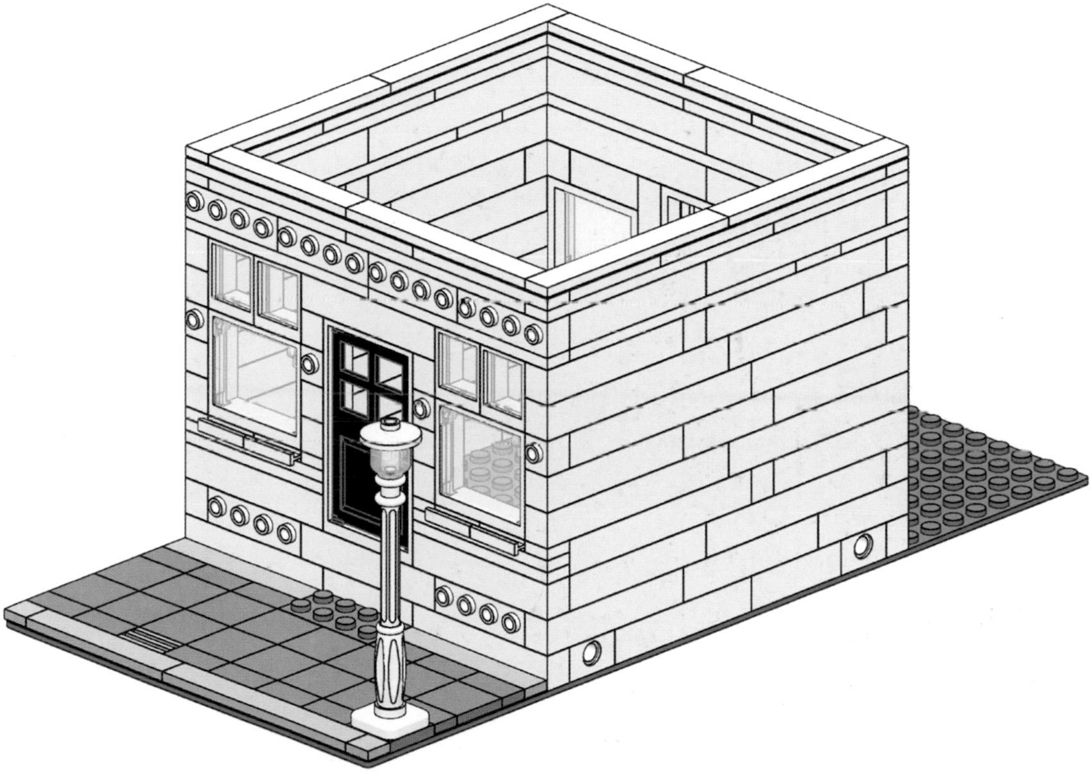

Second Floor

1

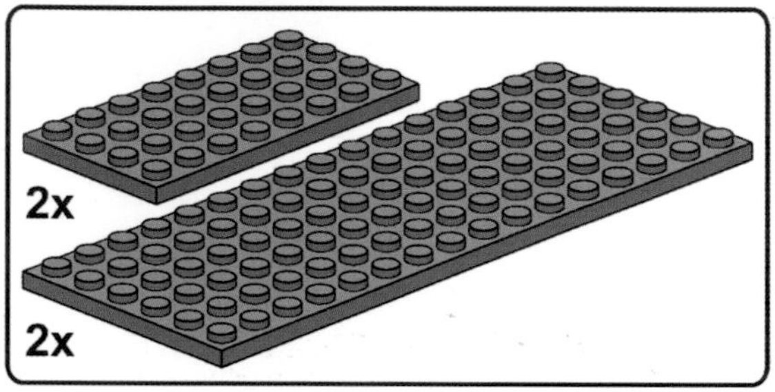

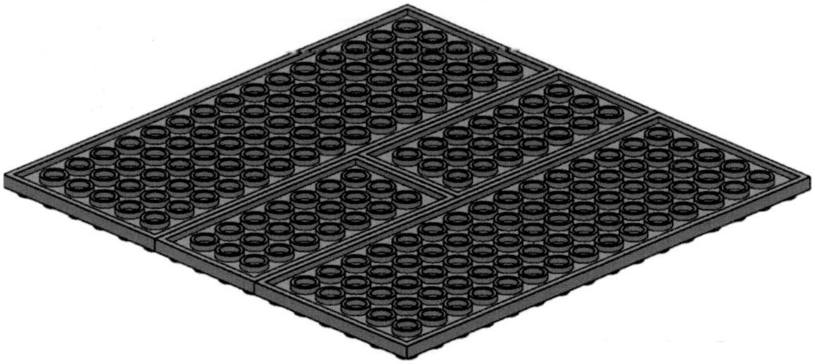

2

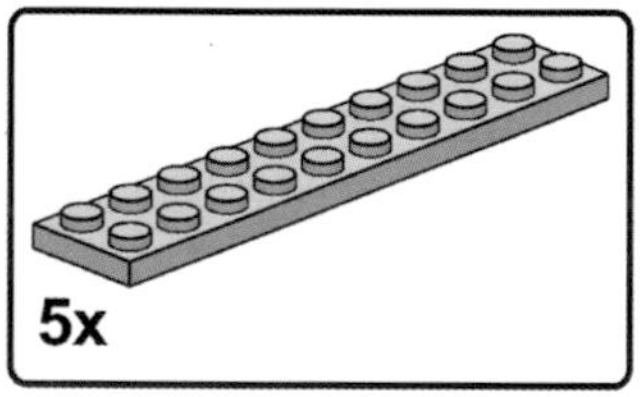

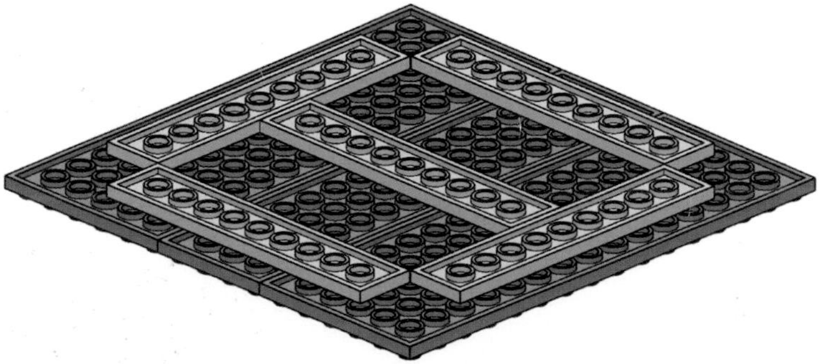

3

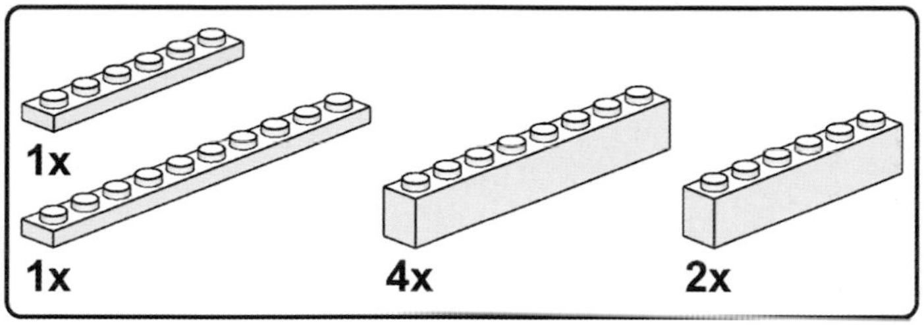
1x
1x
4x
2x

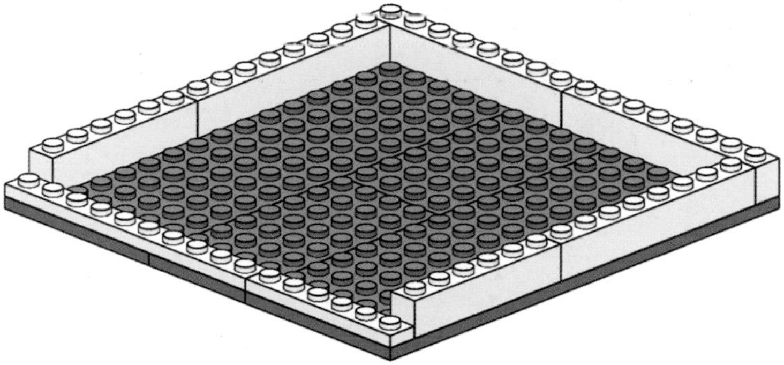

4

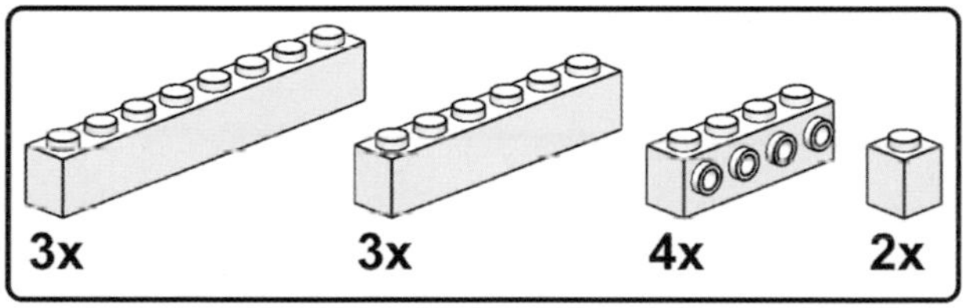
3x
3x
4x
2x

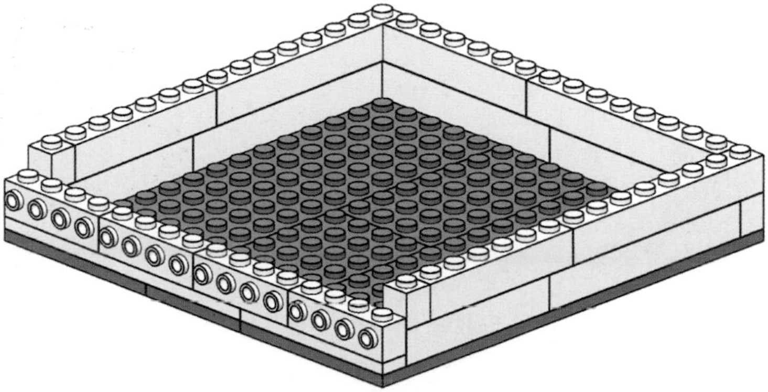

5

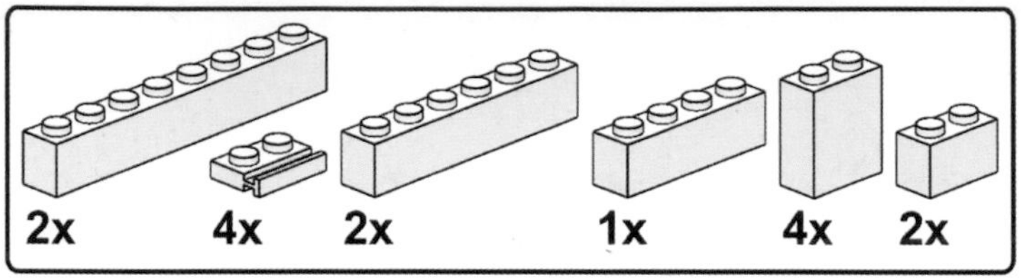
2x
4x
2x
1x
4x
2x

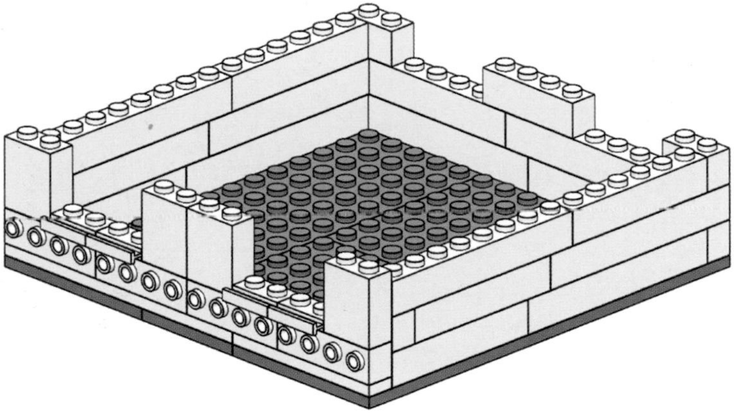

6

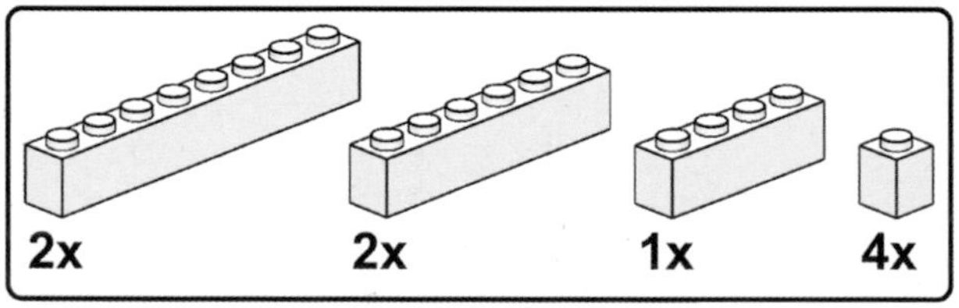
2x
2x
1x
4x

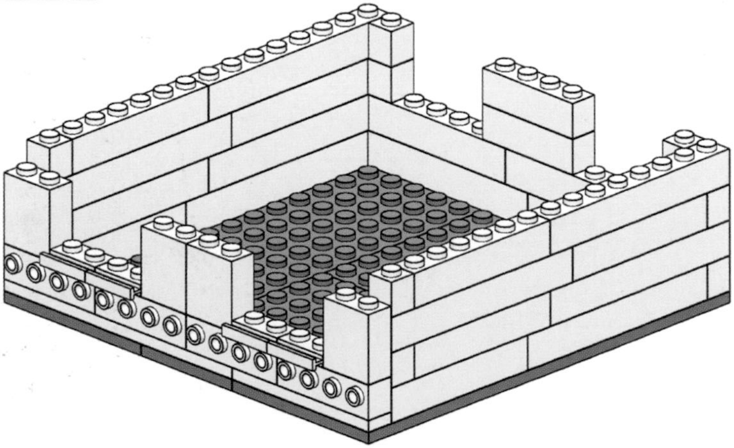

7

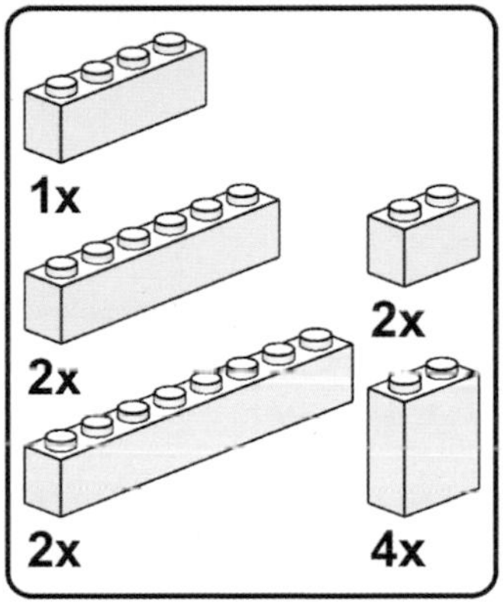
1x
2x
2x
2x
2x
4x

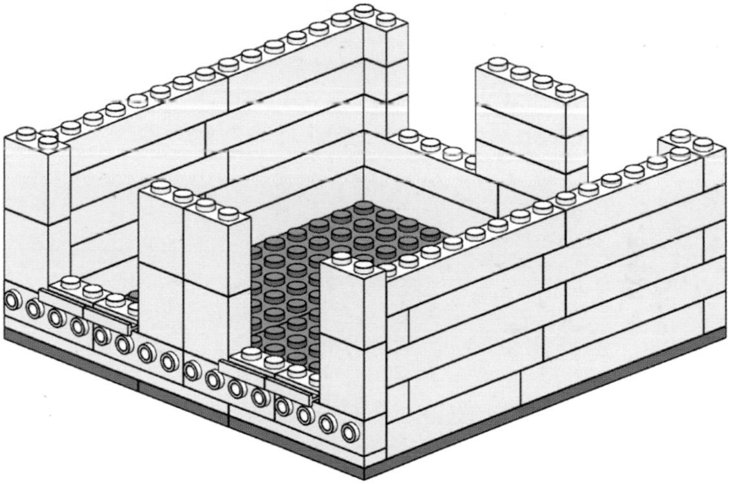

8

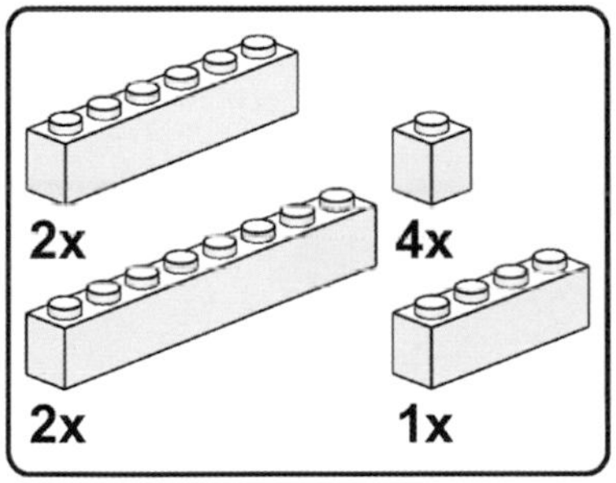
2x
4x
2x
1x

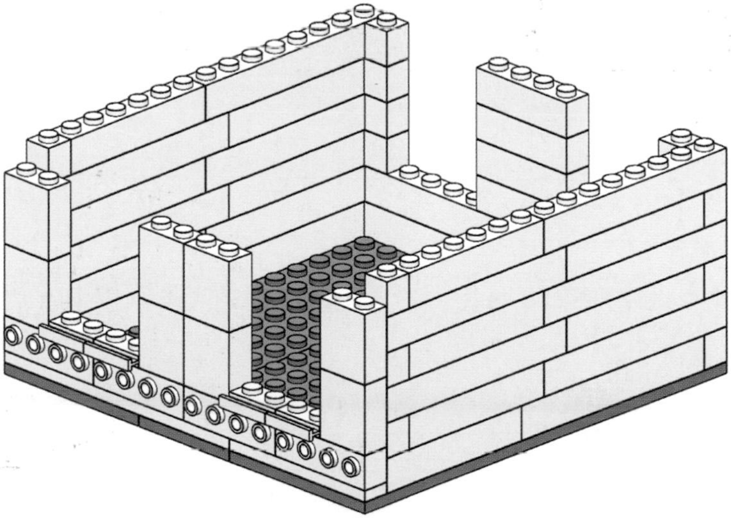

9

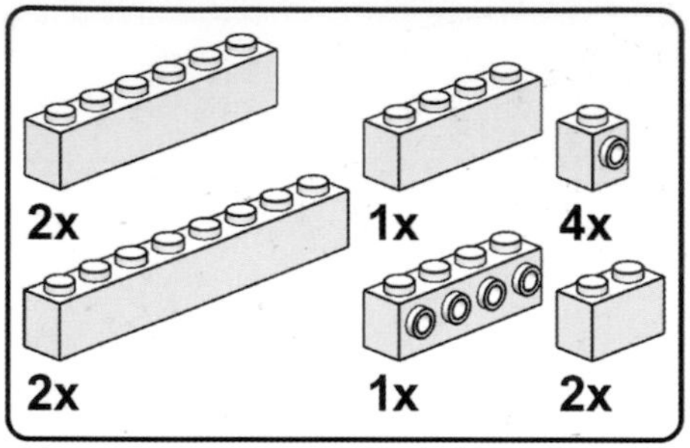
2x
1x
4x
2x
1x
2x

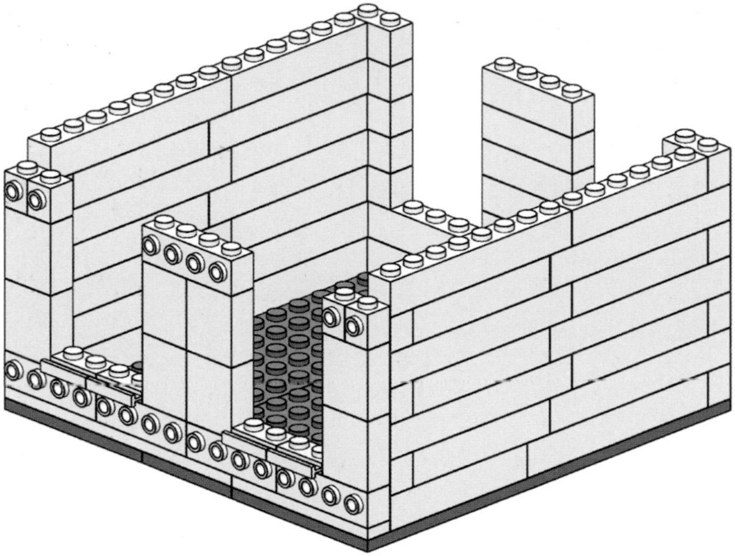

10

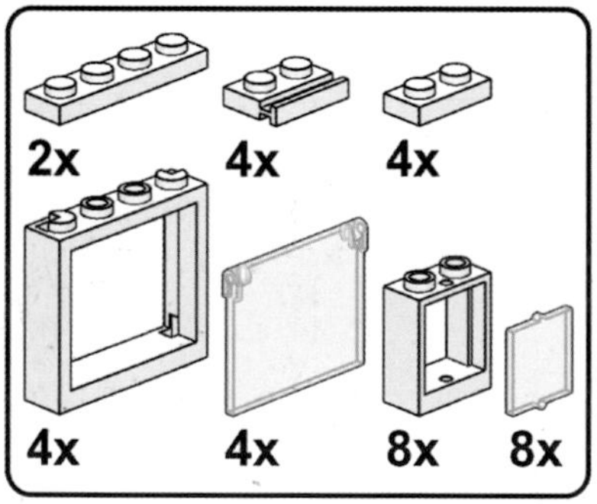
2x
4x
4x
4x
4x
8x
8x

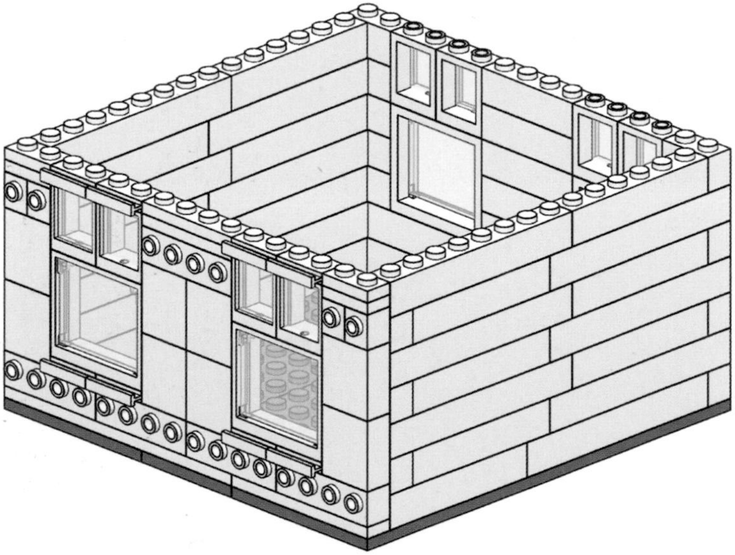

11

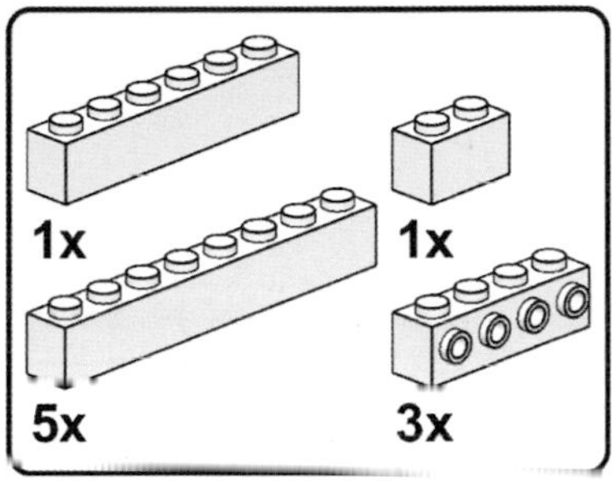
1x
1x
5x
3x

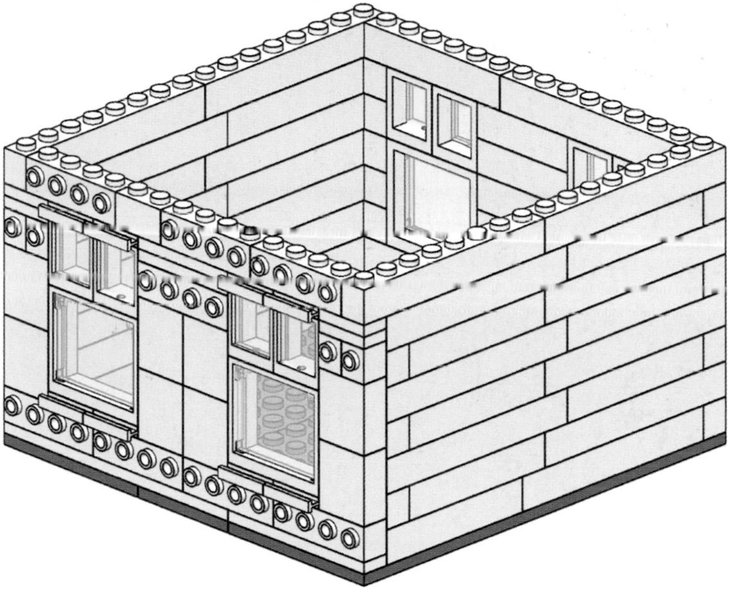

12

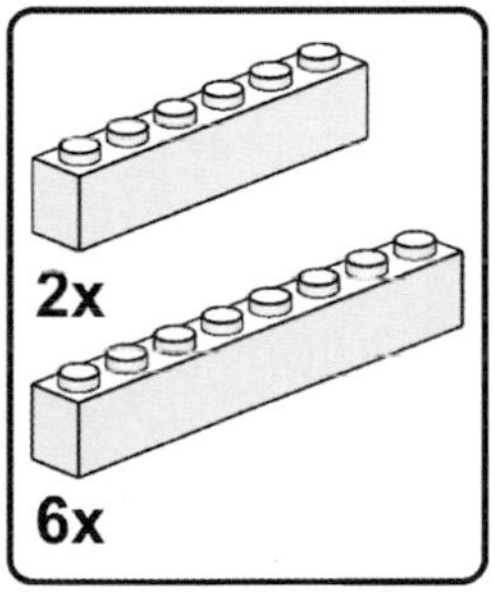
2x
6x

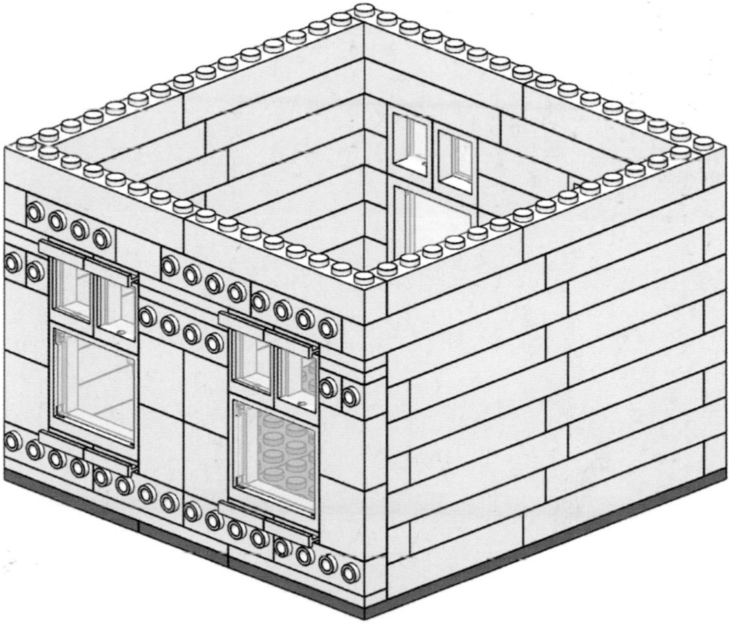

13

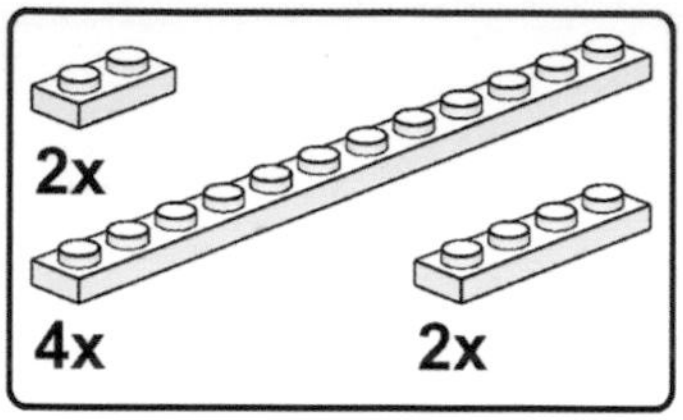
2x
4x
2x

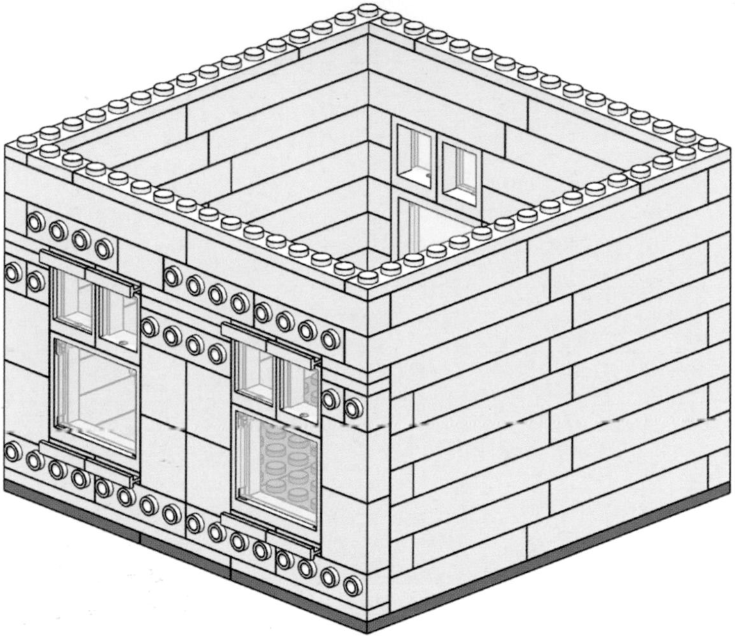

14

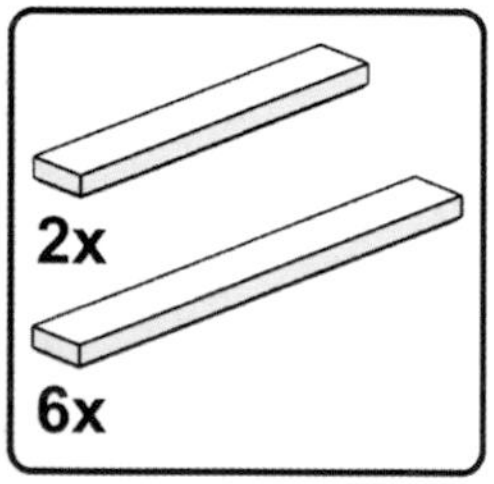
2x
6x

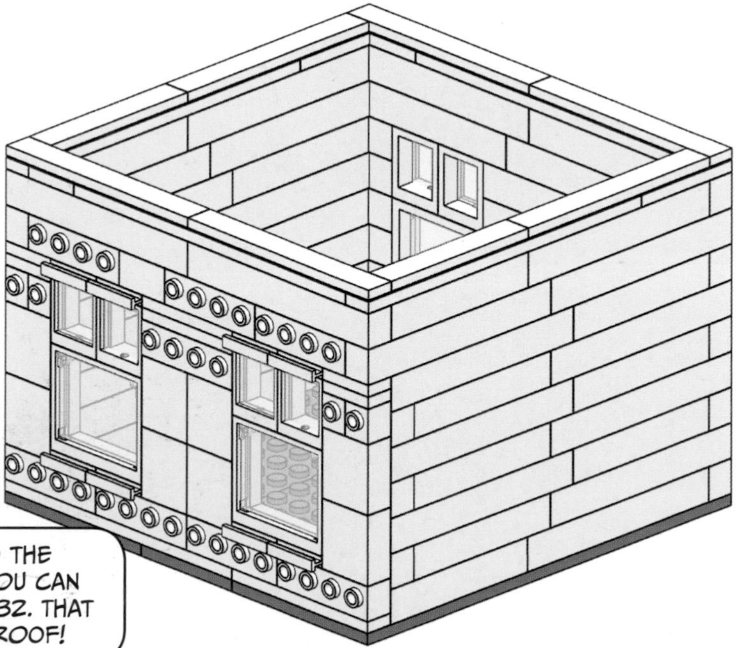

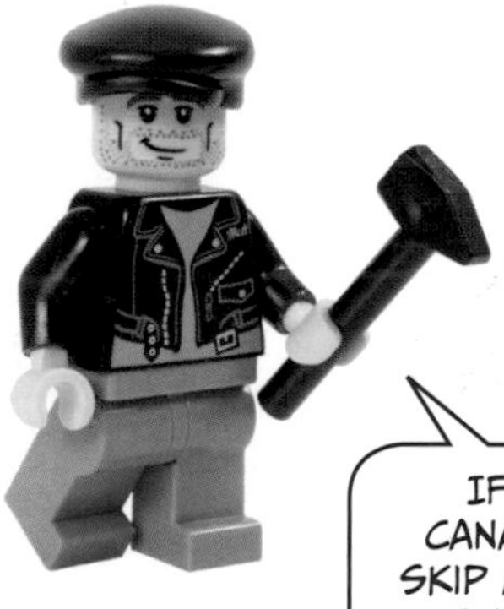
IF YOU'RE BUILDING THE CANAL RING HOUSE, YOU CAN SKIP AHEAD TO PAGE 182. THAT ONE HAS A CUSTOM ROOF!

Roof

1

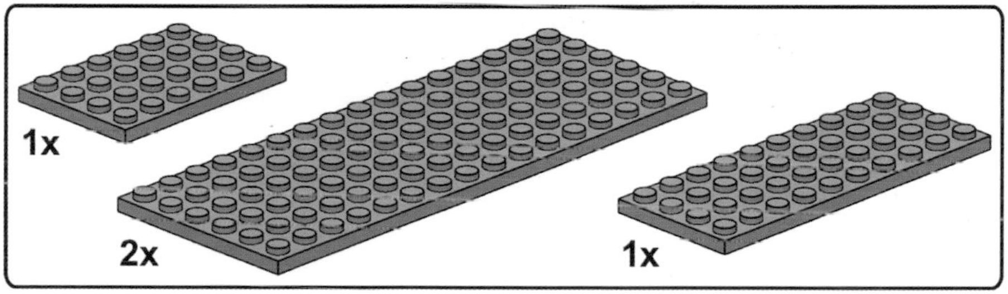

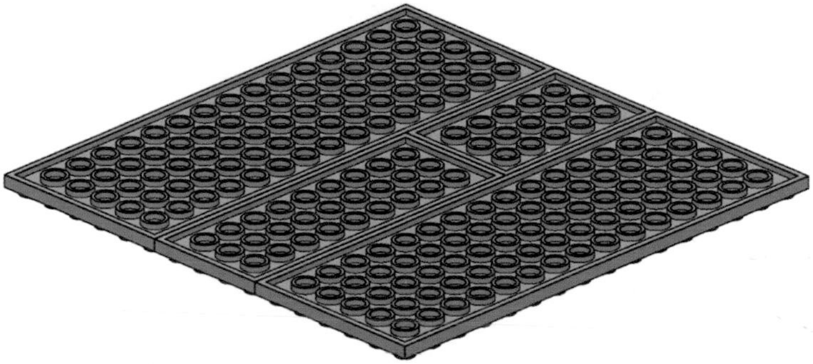

2

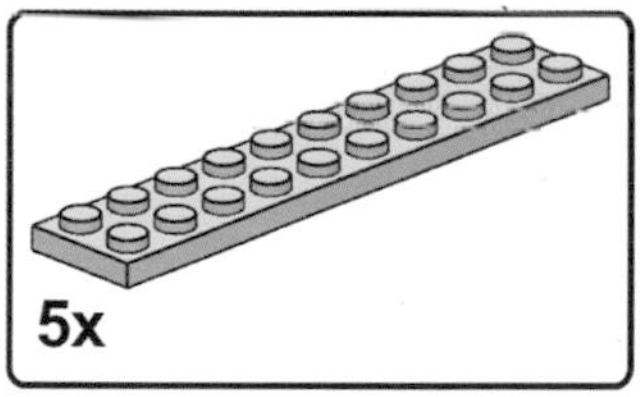

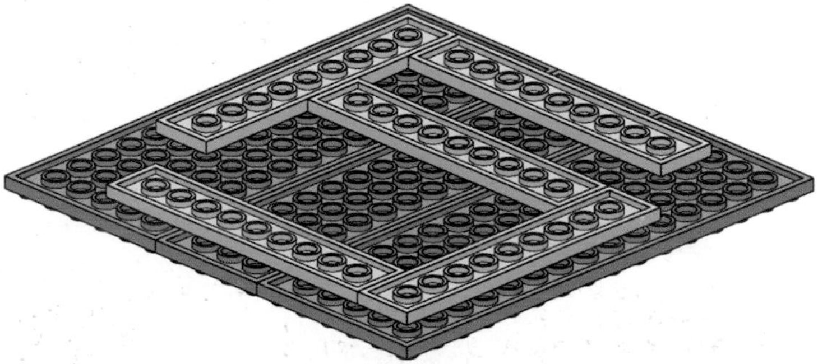

3

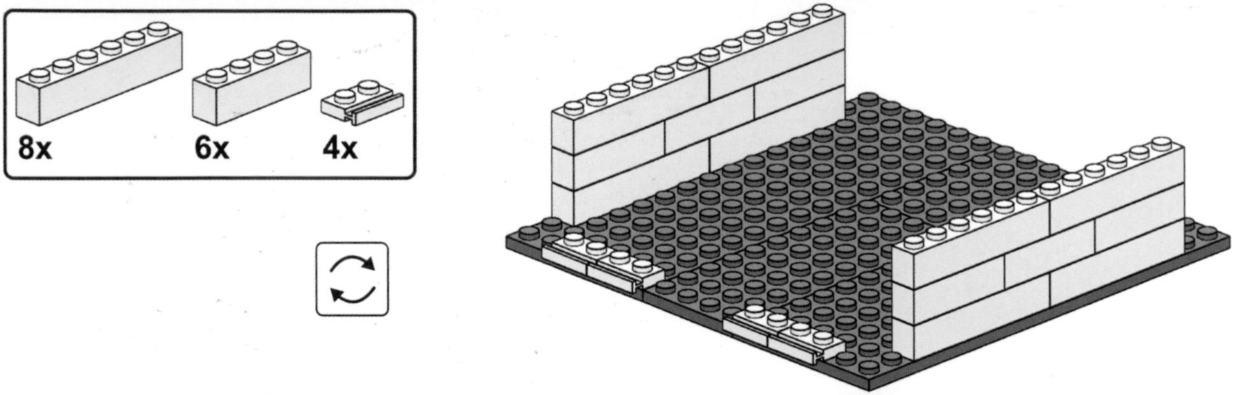
8x
6x
4x

4

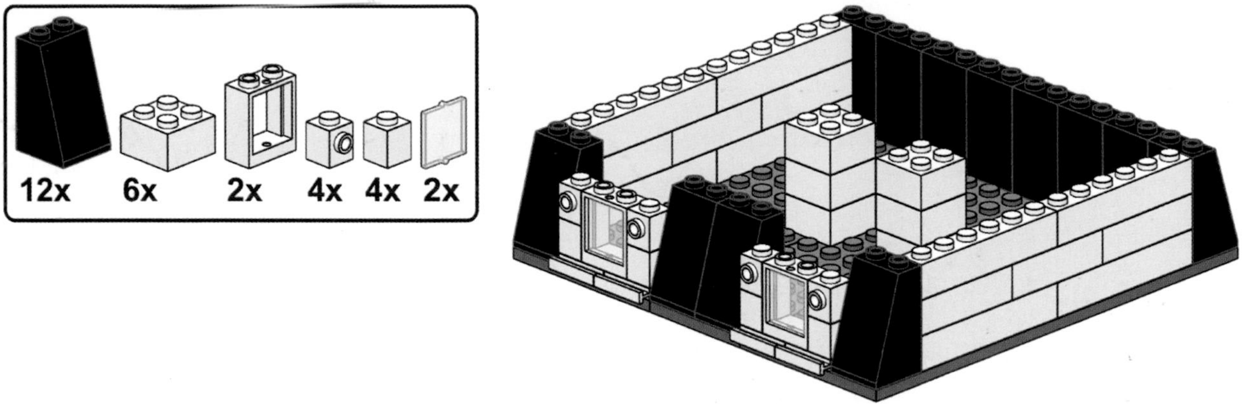
12x
6x
2x
4x
4x
2x

5

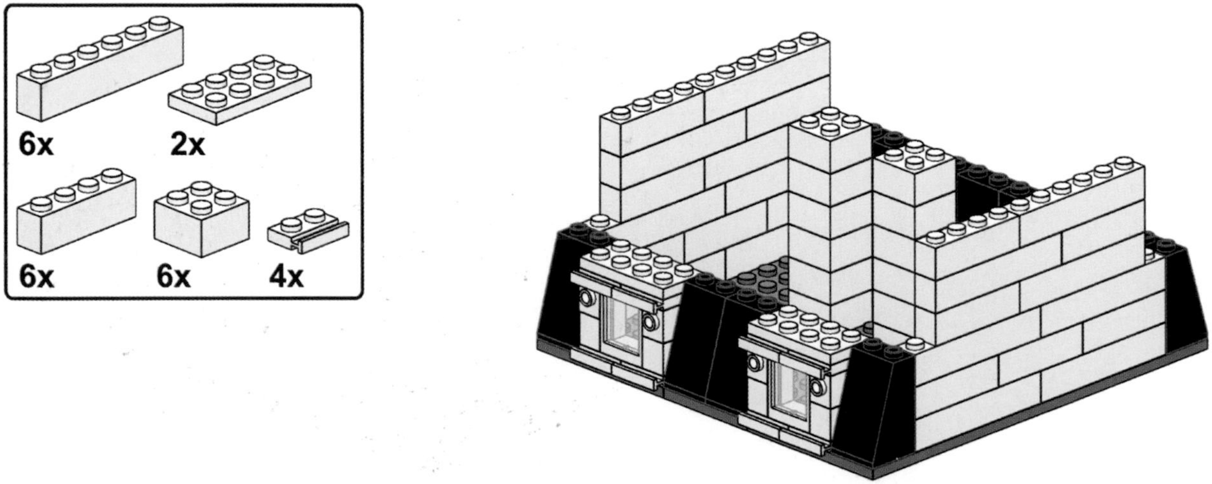
6x
2x
6x
6x
4x

6

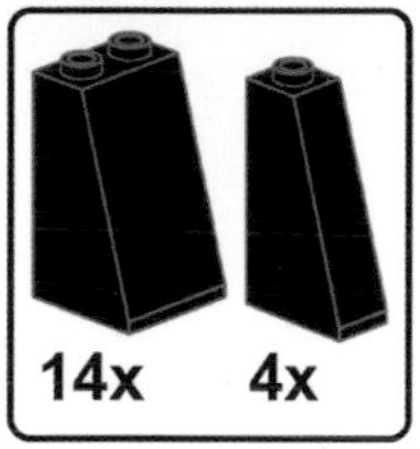
14x
4x

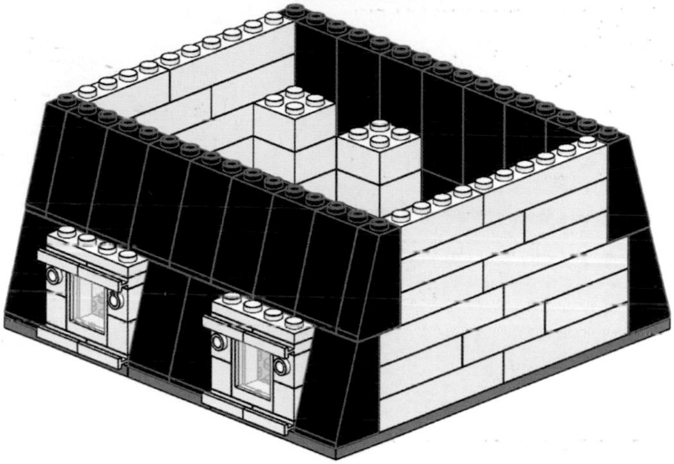

7

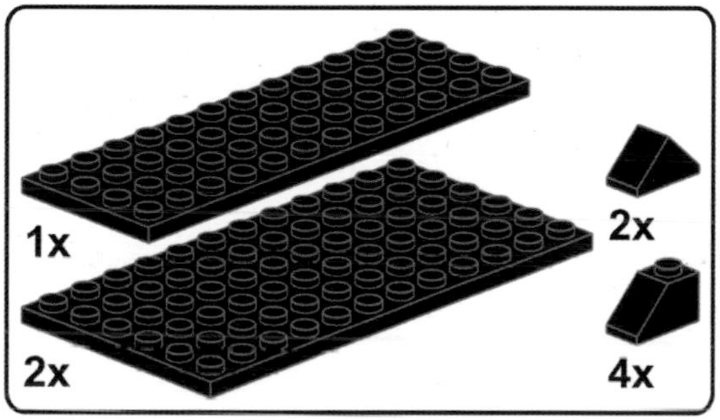
1x
2x
2x
4x

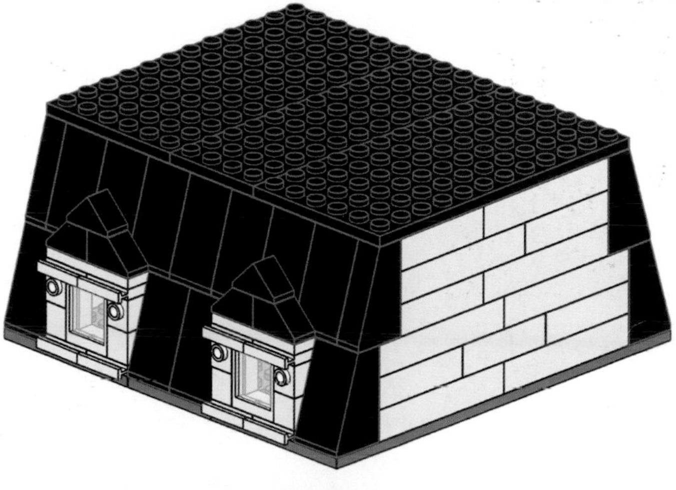

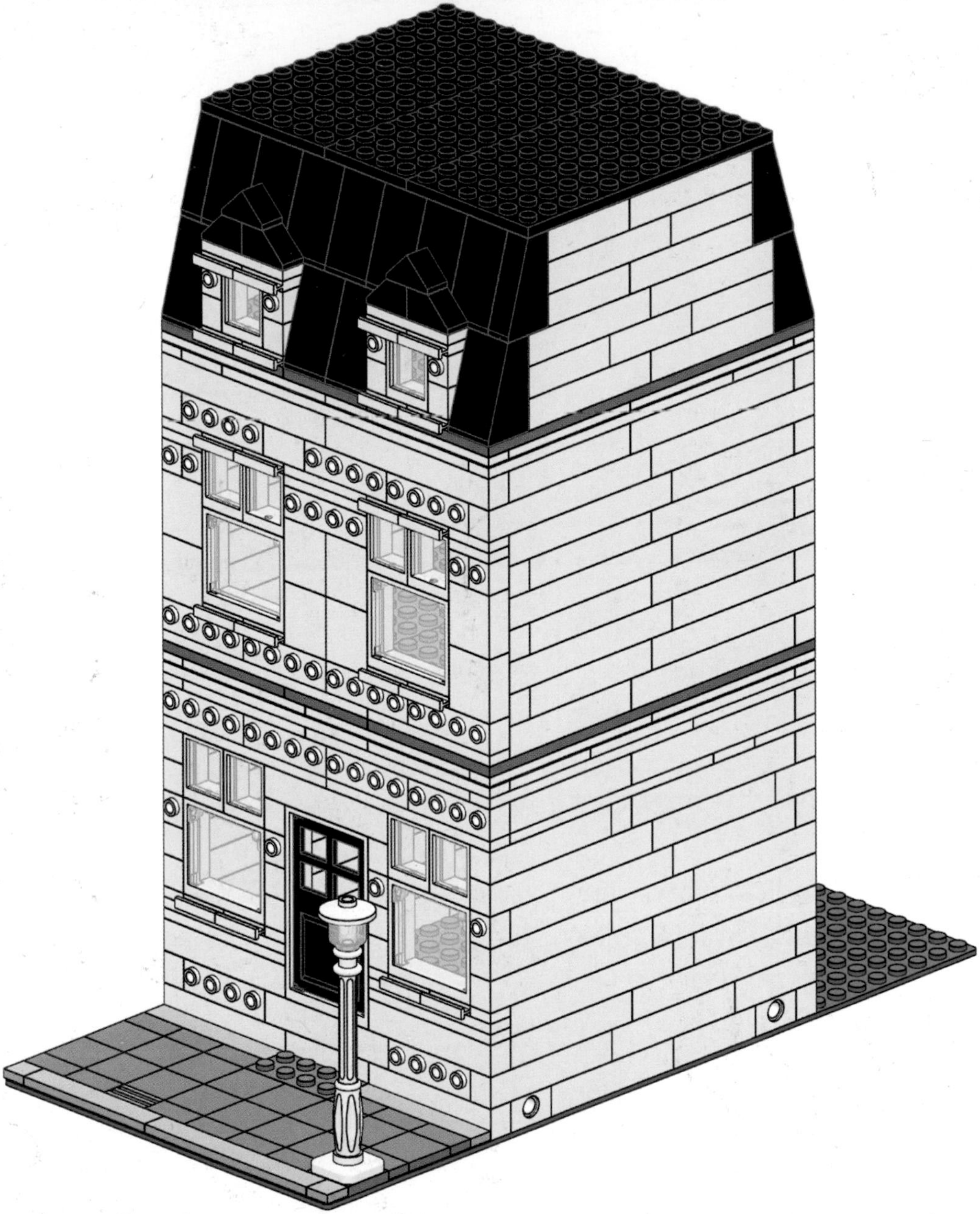

Parisian Apartment

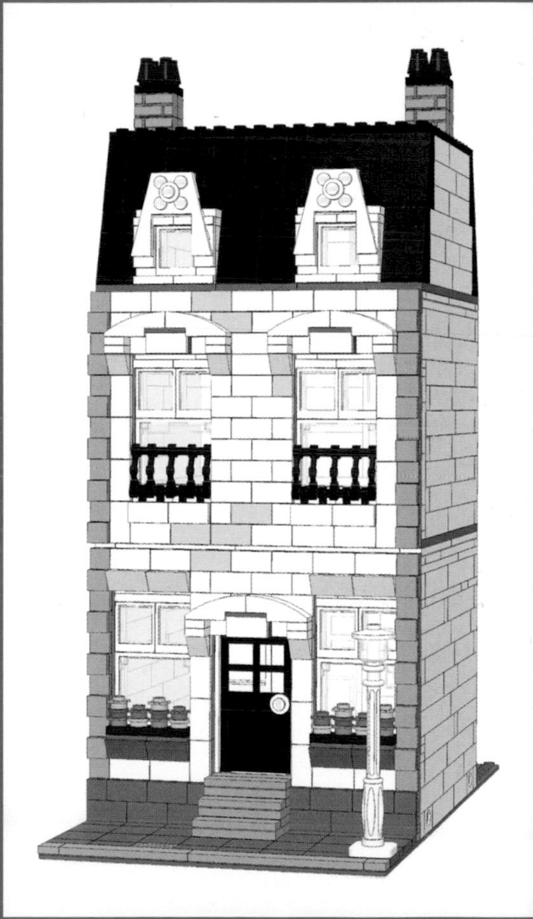

Bill of Materials

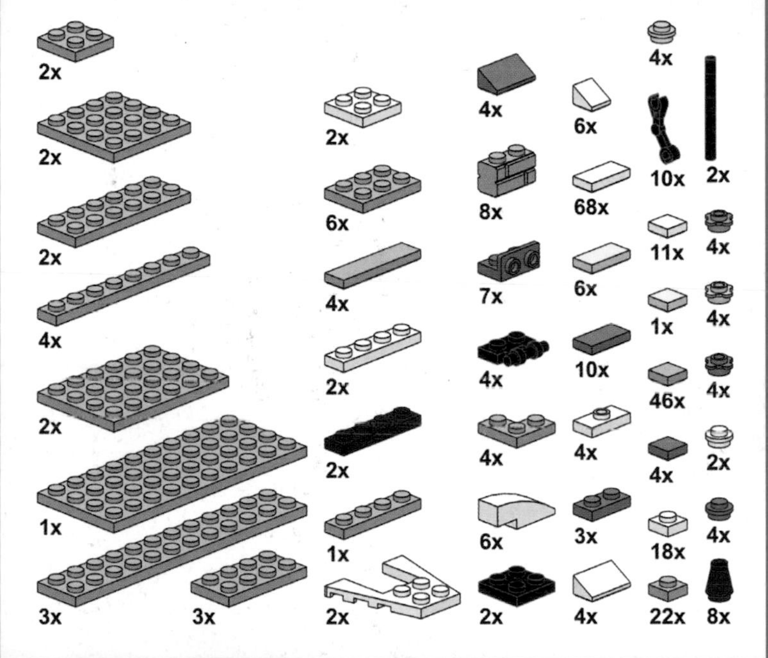

1

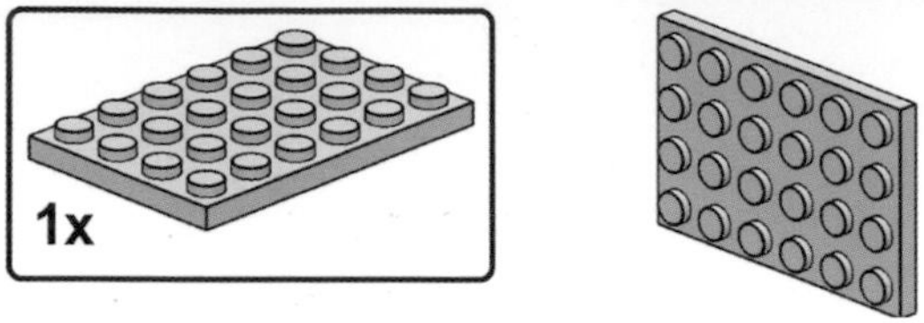
1x

2

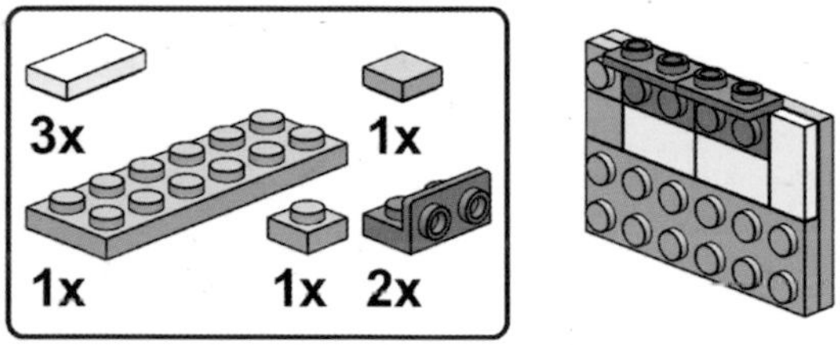
3x
1x
1x
1x 2x

3

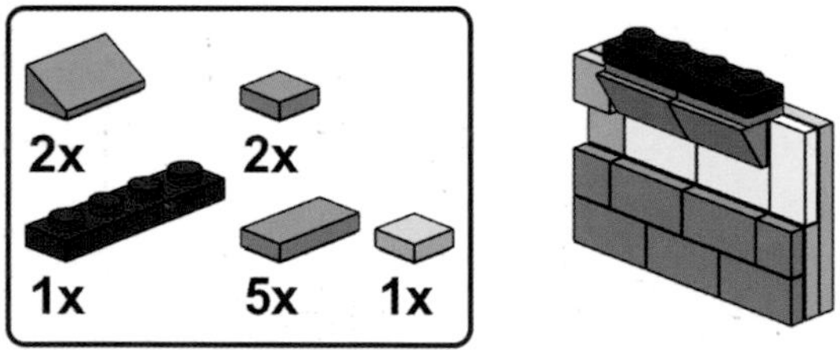
2x
2x
1x
5x
1x

4

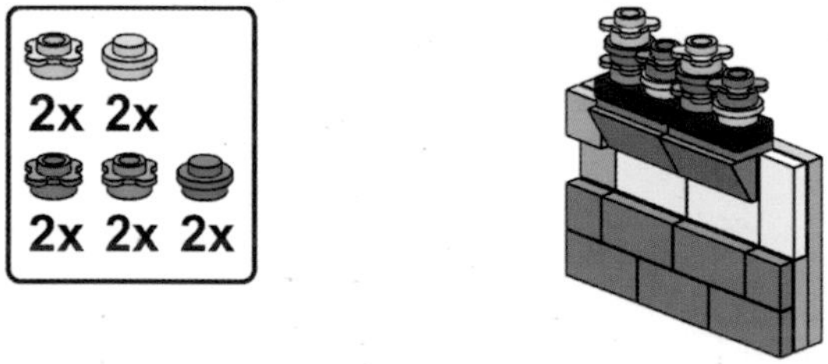
2x 2x
2x 2x 2x

1

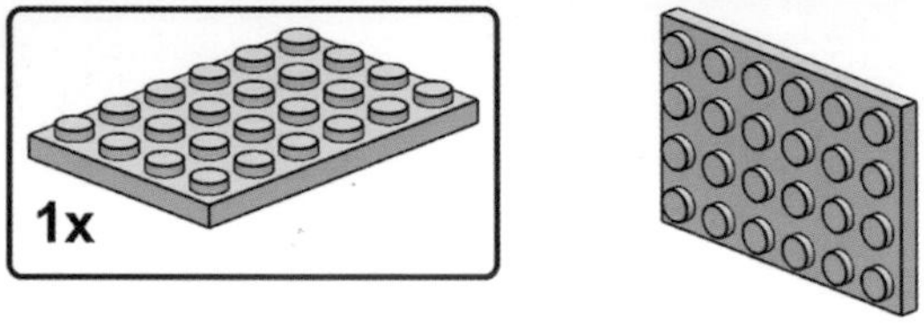
1x

2

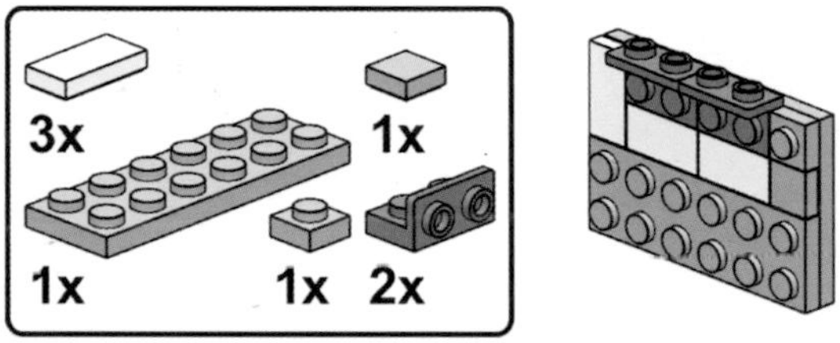
3x
1x
1x
1x 2x

3

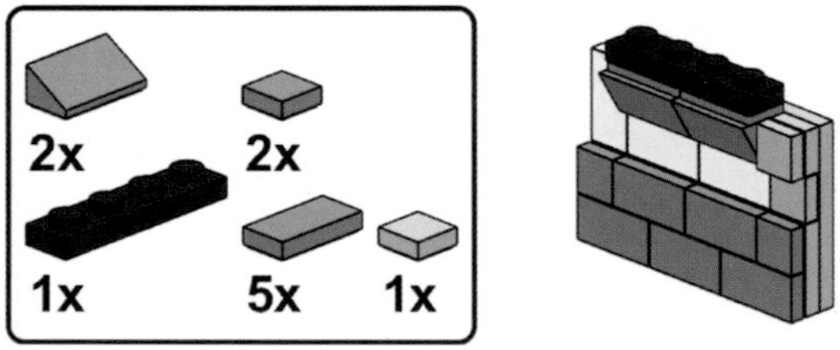
2x
2x
1x
5x
1x

4

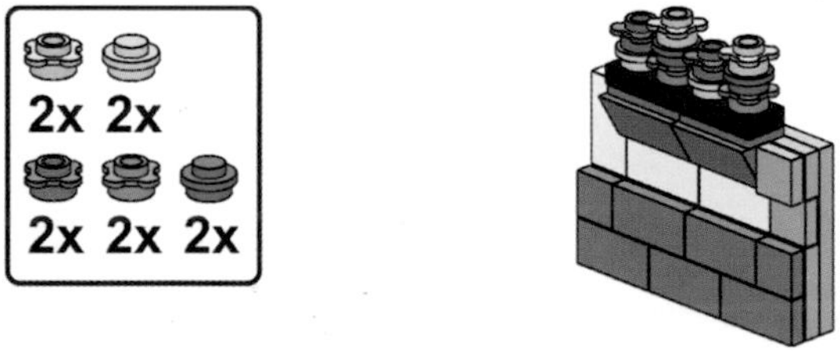
2x 2x
2x 2x 2x

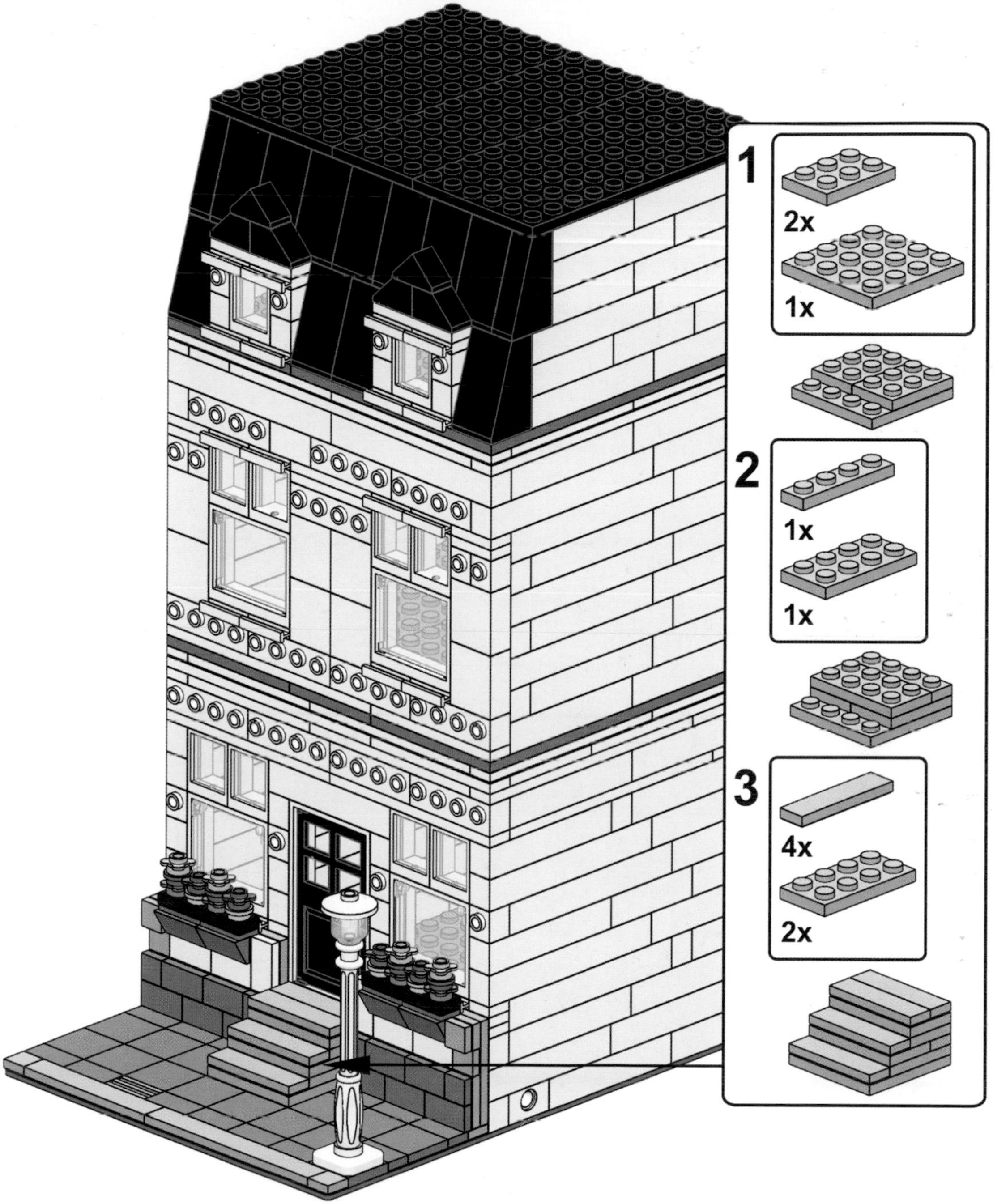
1
2x
1x
2
1x
1x
3
4x
2x

1

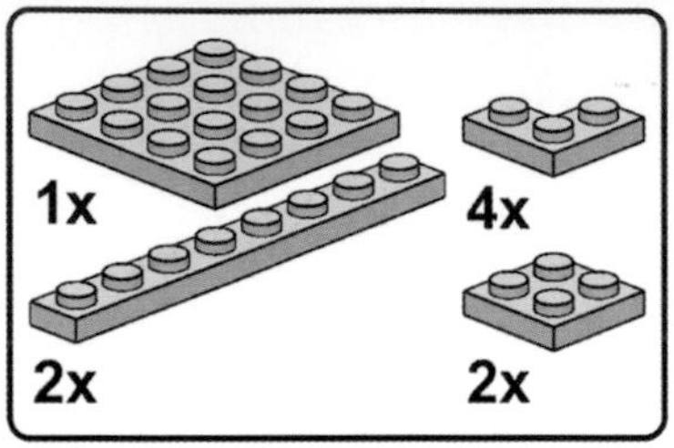
1x
4x
2x
2x

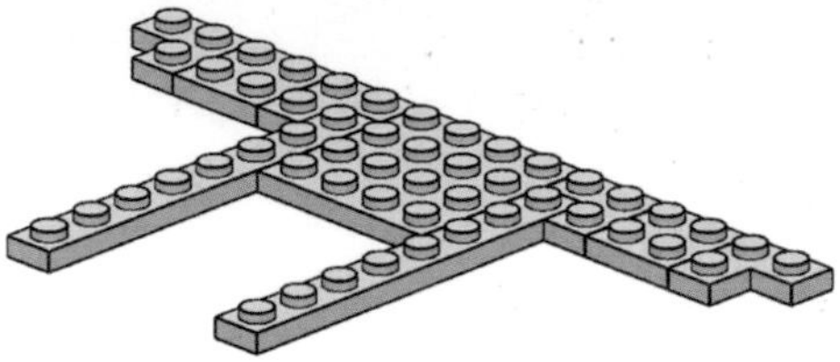

2

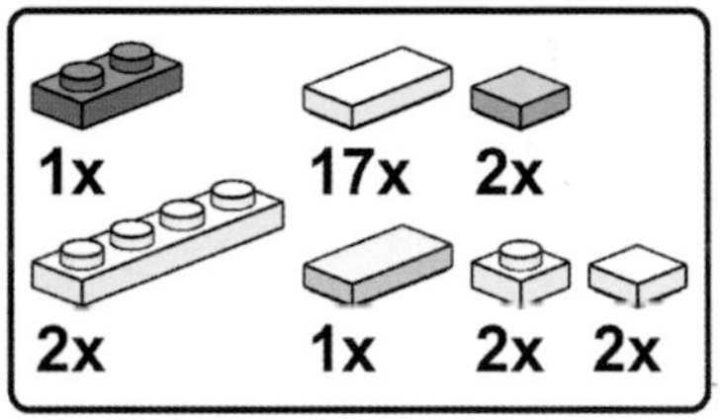
1x
17x
2x
2x
1x
2x
2x

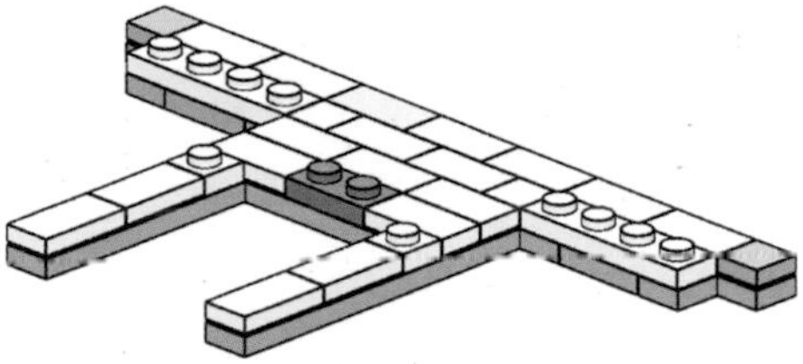

3

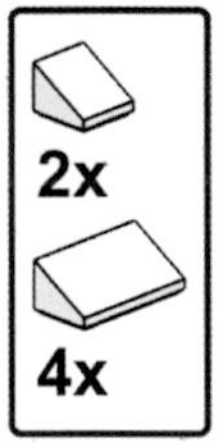
2x
4x

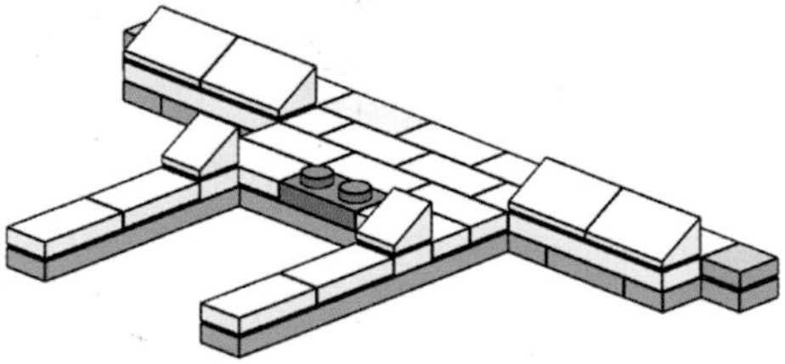

4

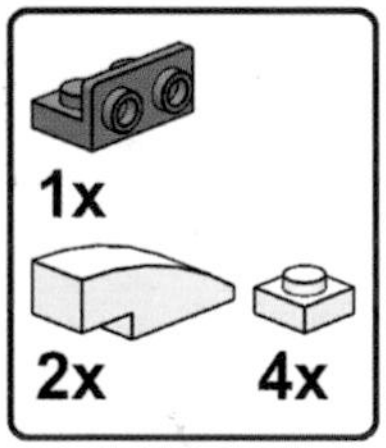
1x
2x
4x

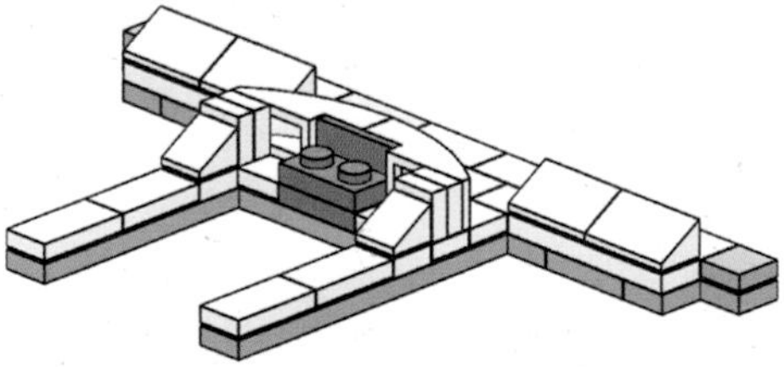

5

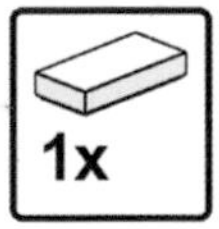
1x

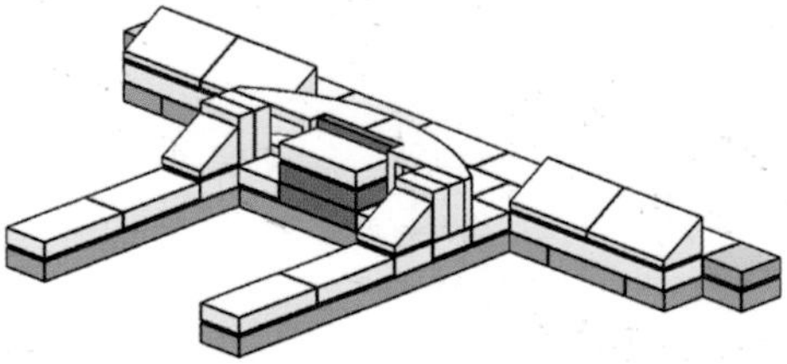

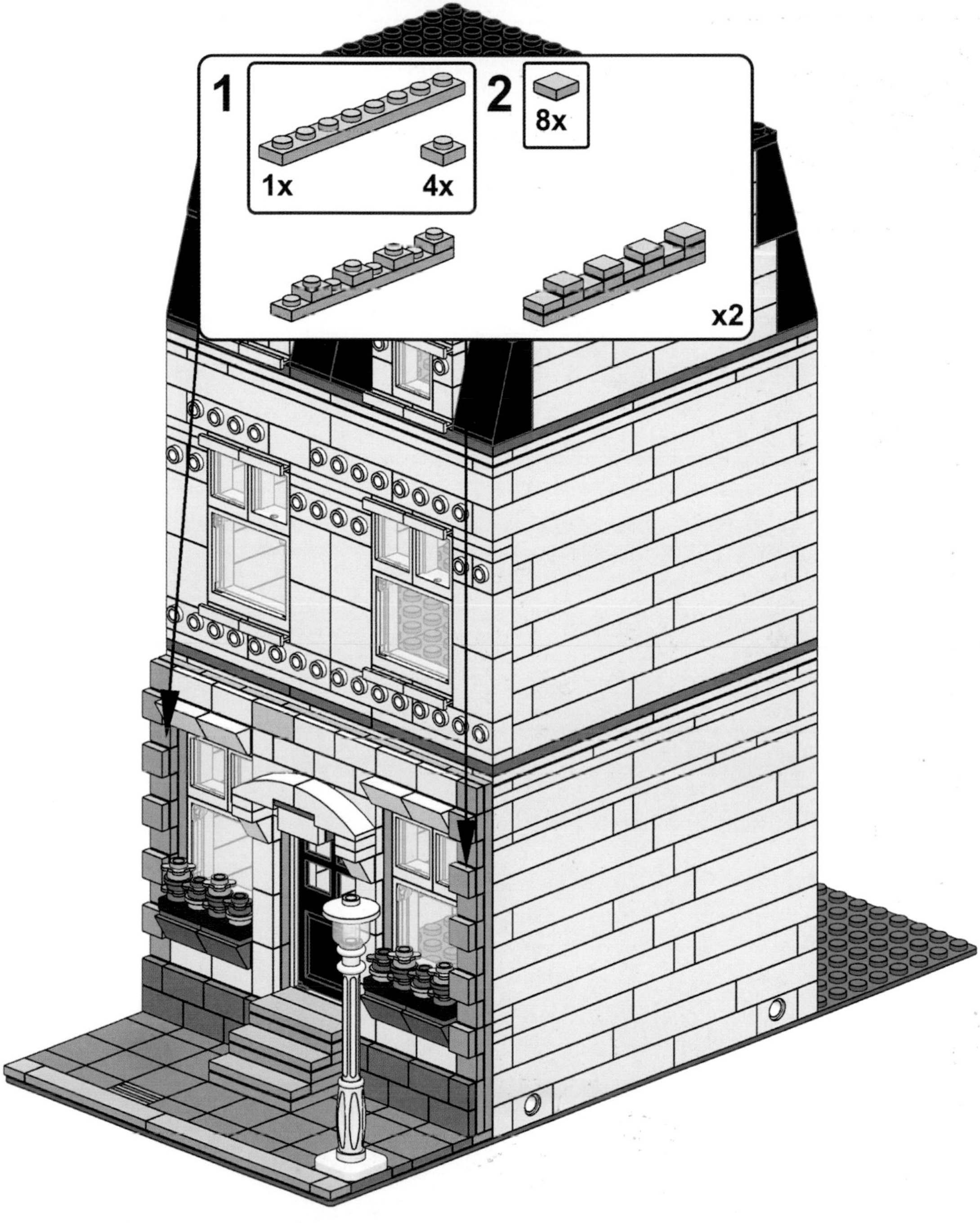
1
1x
4x
2
8x
x2

1

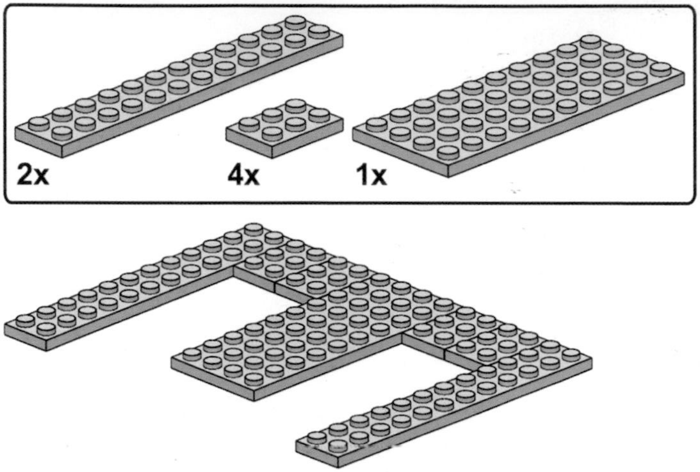
2x
4x
1x

2

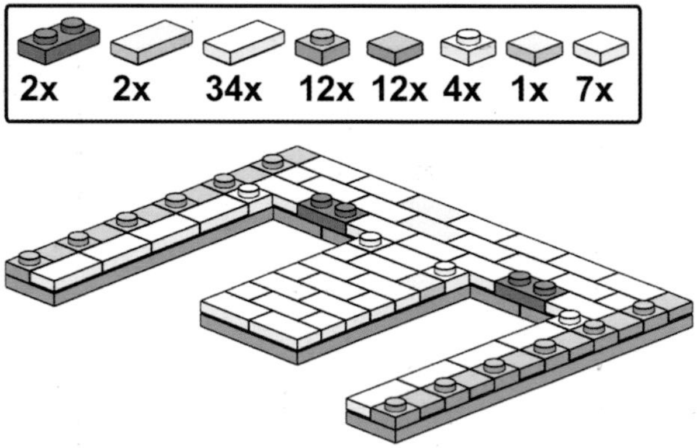
2x
2x
34x
12x
12x
4x
1x
7x

3

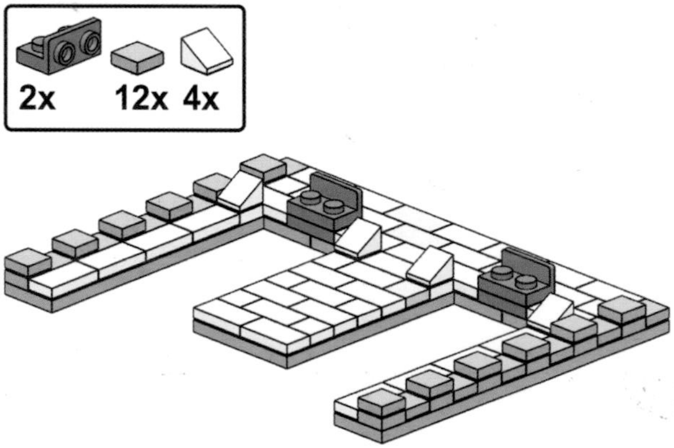
2x
12x
4x

4

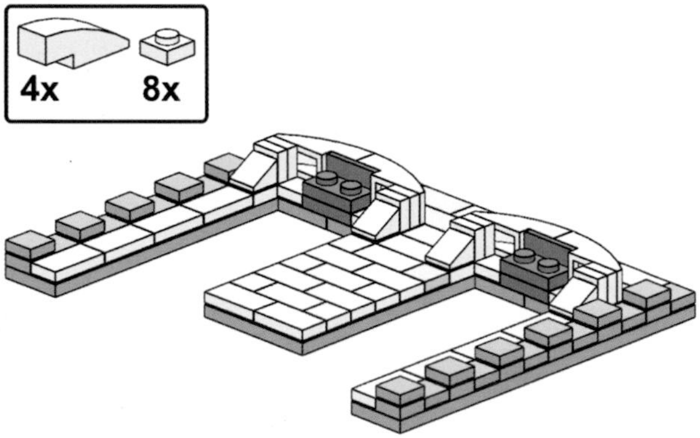
4x
8x

5

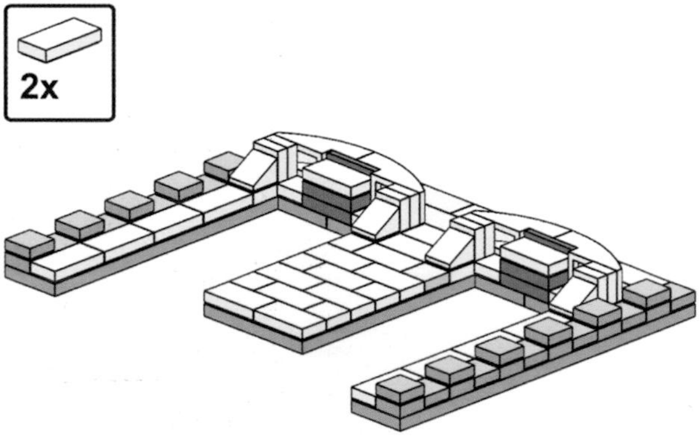
2x

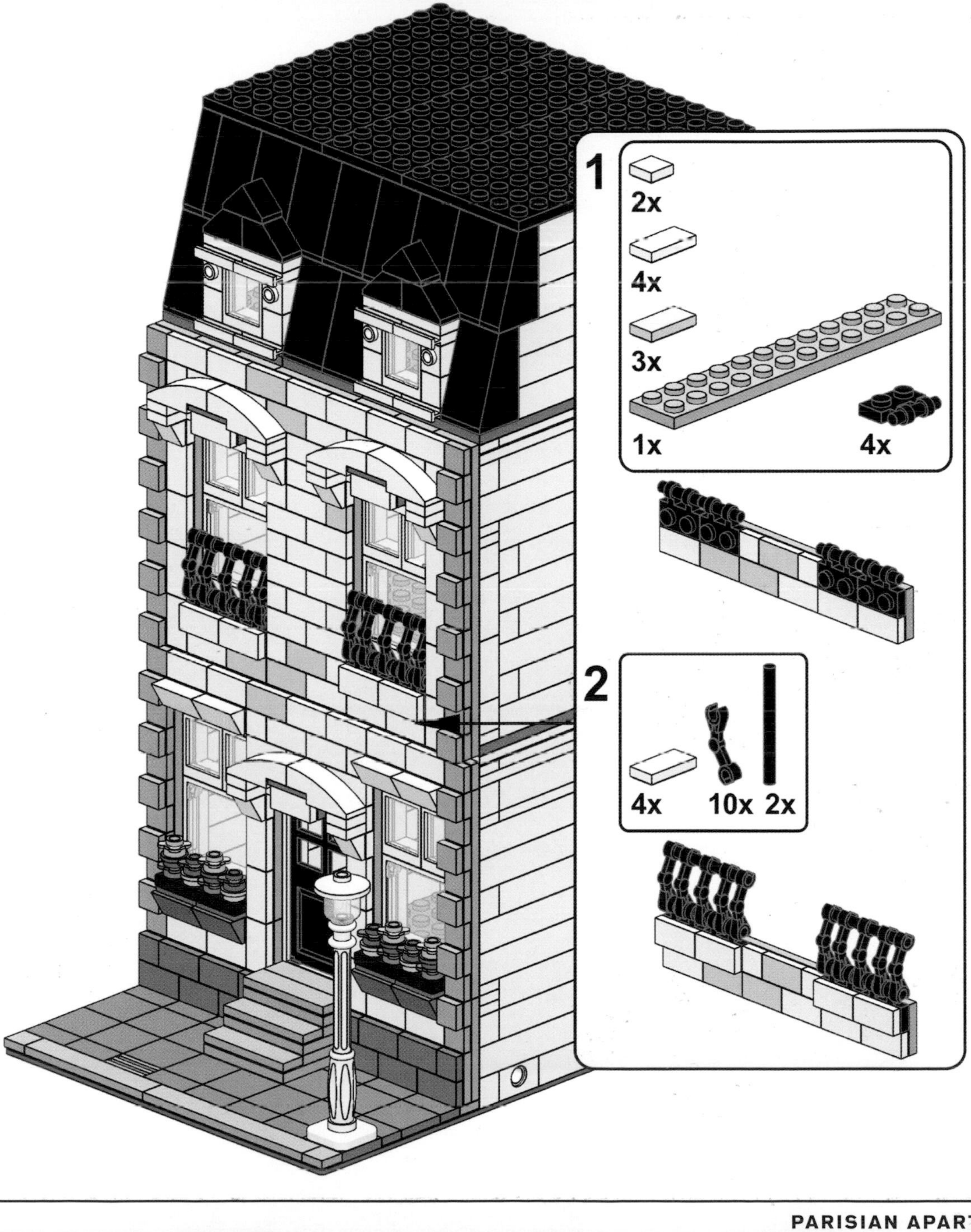
1
2x
4x
3x
1x
4x
2
4x
10x
2x

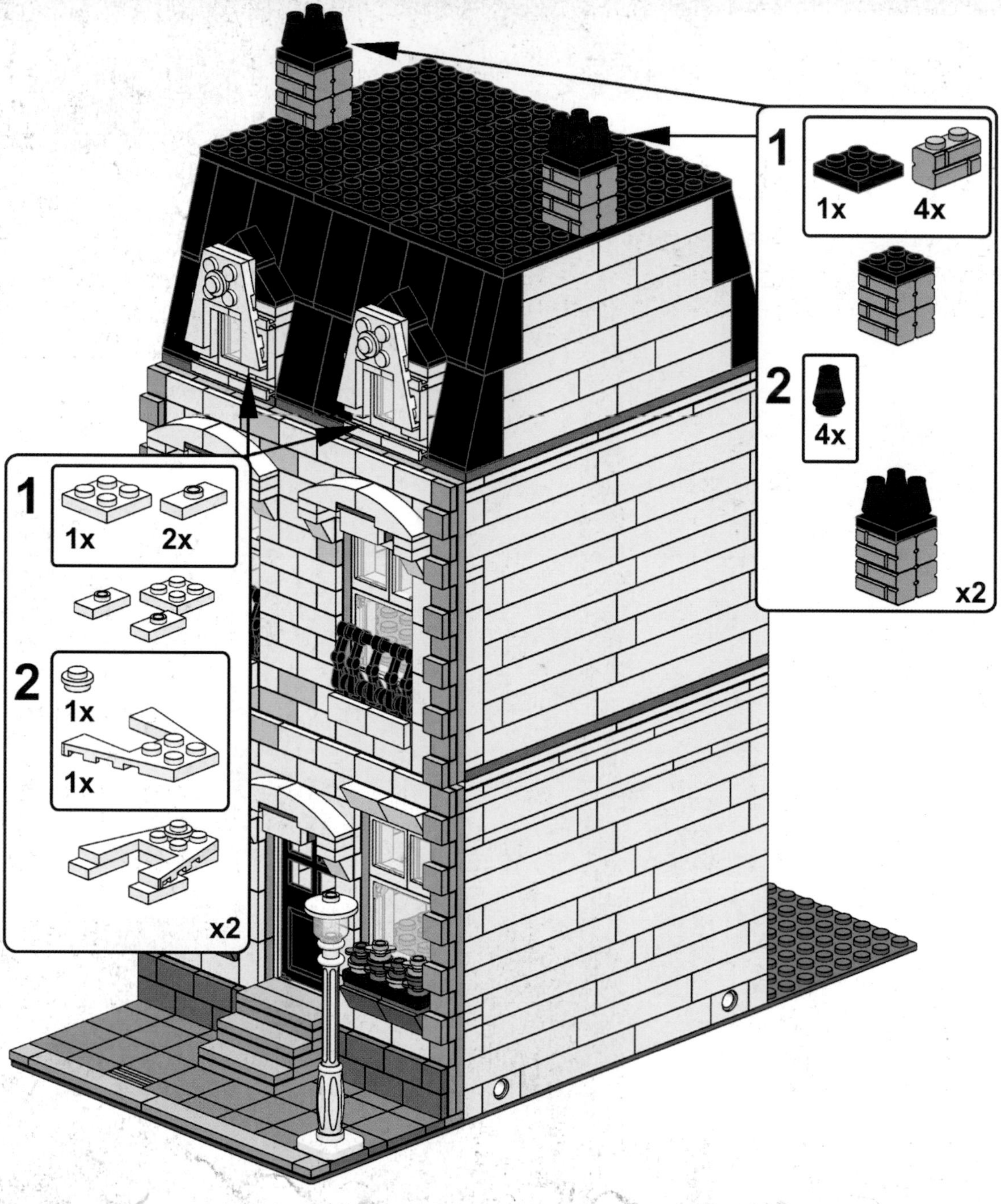
1
1x
2x
2
1x
1x
x2
1
1x
4x
2
4x
x2

Colonial Row House

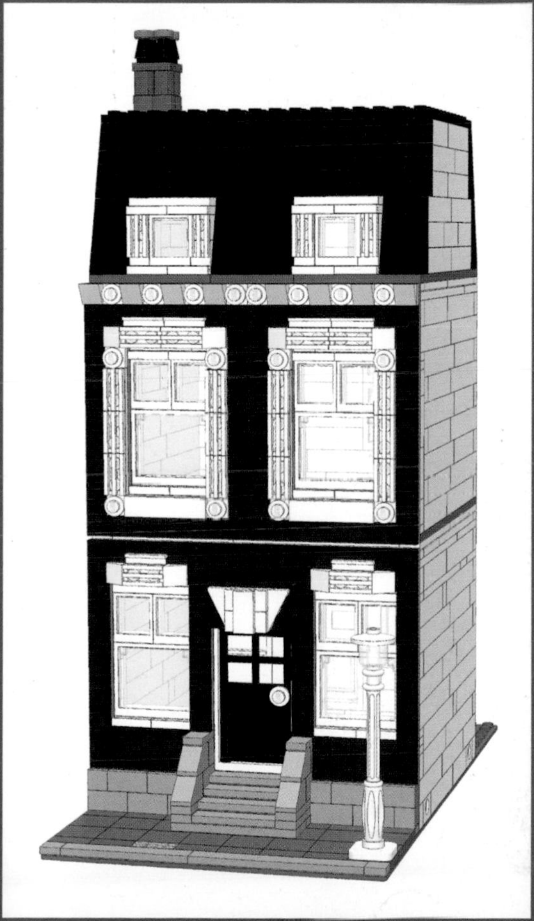

Bill of Materials

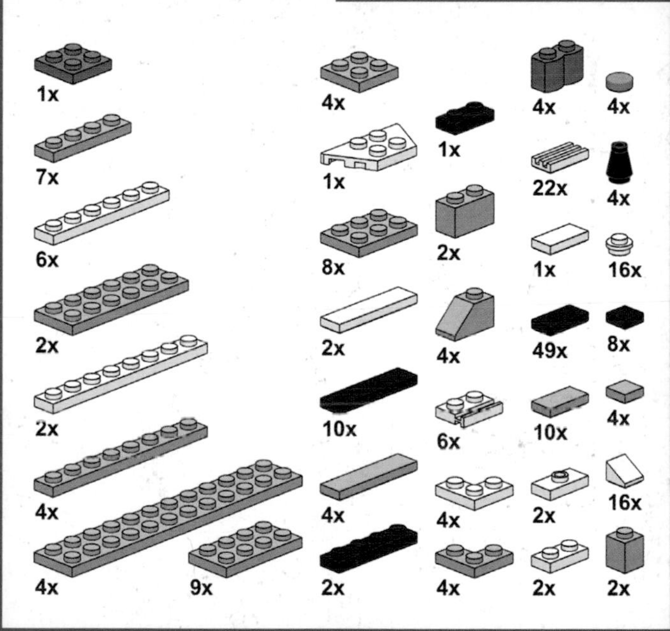

1x
7x
6x
2x
2x
4x
4x
9x
4x
1x
8x
2x
10x
4x
2x
1x
2x
4x
6x
4x
4x
4x
22x
1x
49x
10x
2x
2x
4x
4x
16x
8x
4x
16x
2x

1

2x

2

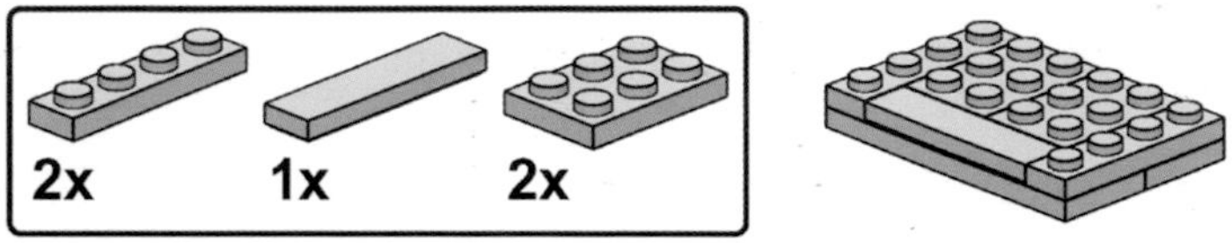
2x
1x
2x

3

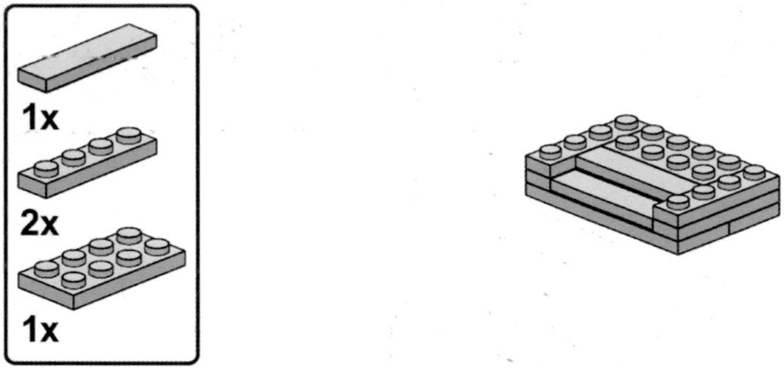
1x
2x
1x

4

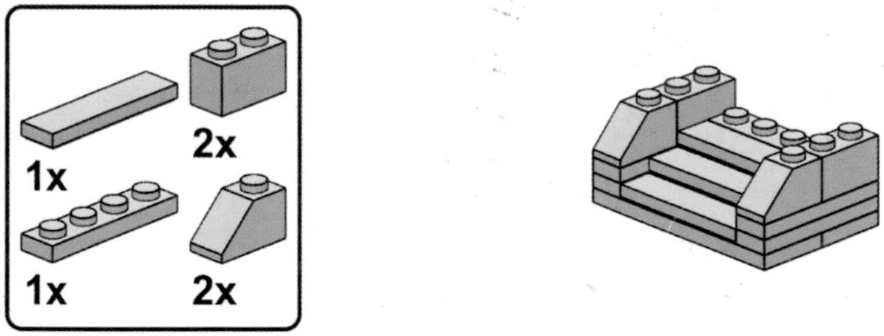
2x
1x
1x
2x

5

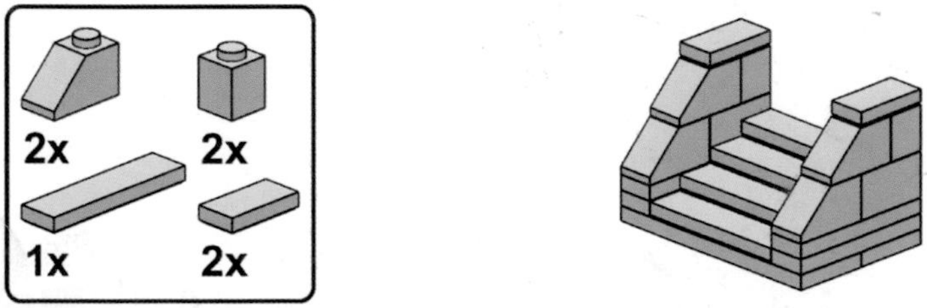
2x
2x
1x
2x

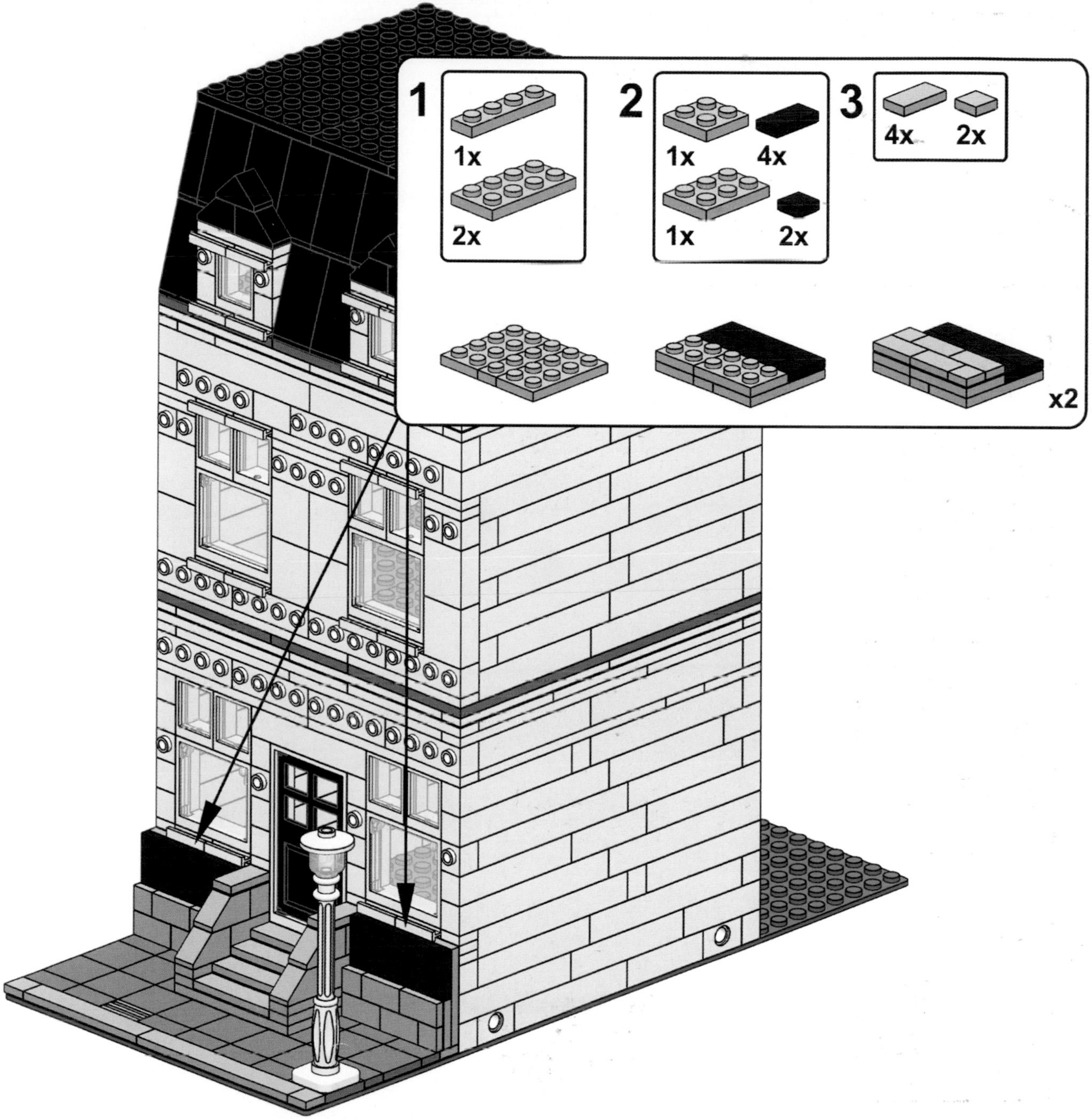
1
1x
2x
2
1x
4x
1x
2x
3
4x
2x
x2

1

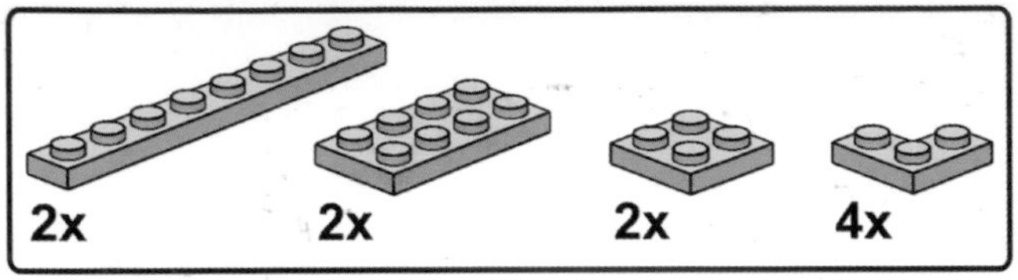
2x
2x
2x
4x

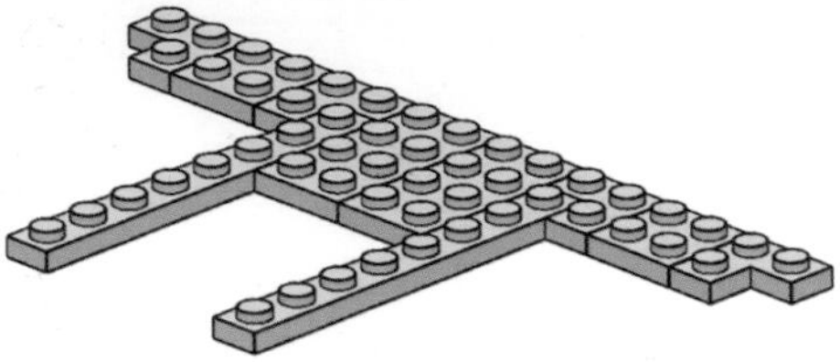

2

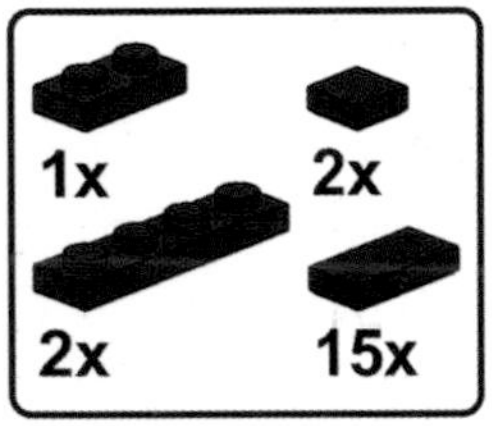
1x
2x
2x
15x

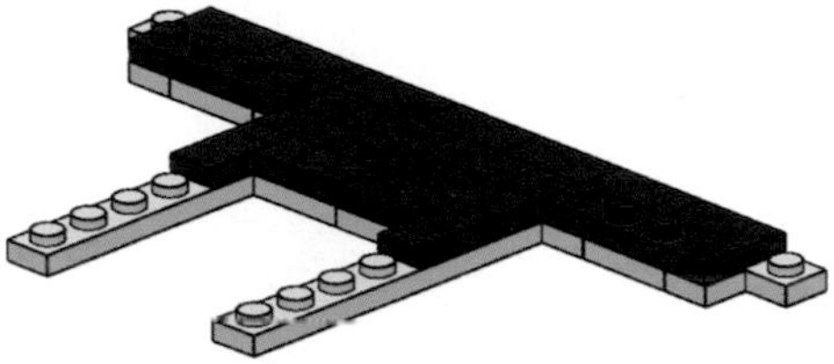

3

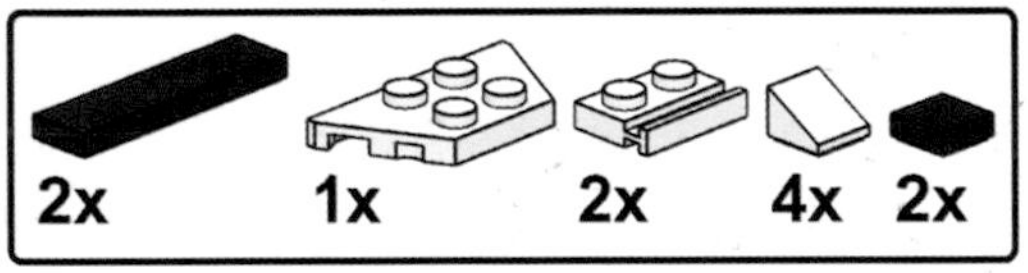
2x
1x
2x
4x
2x

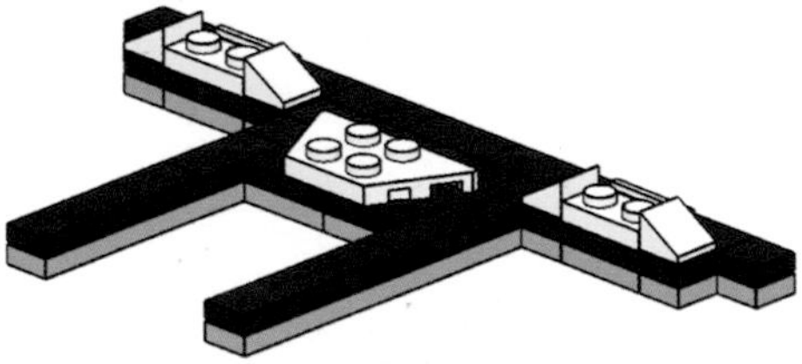

4

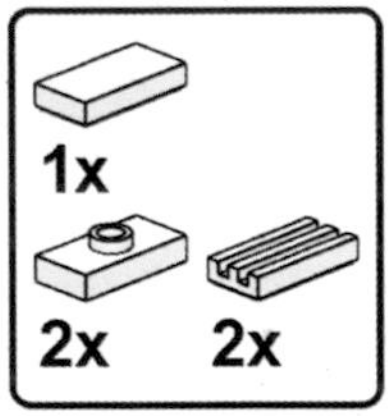
1x
2x
2x

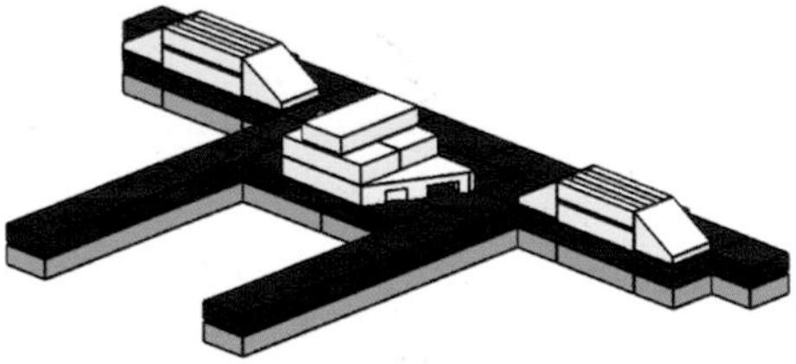

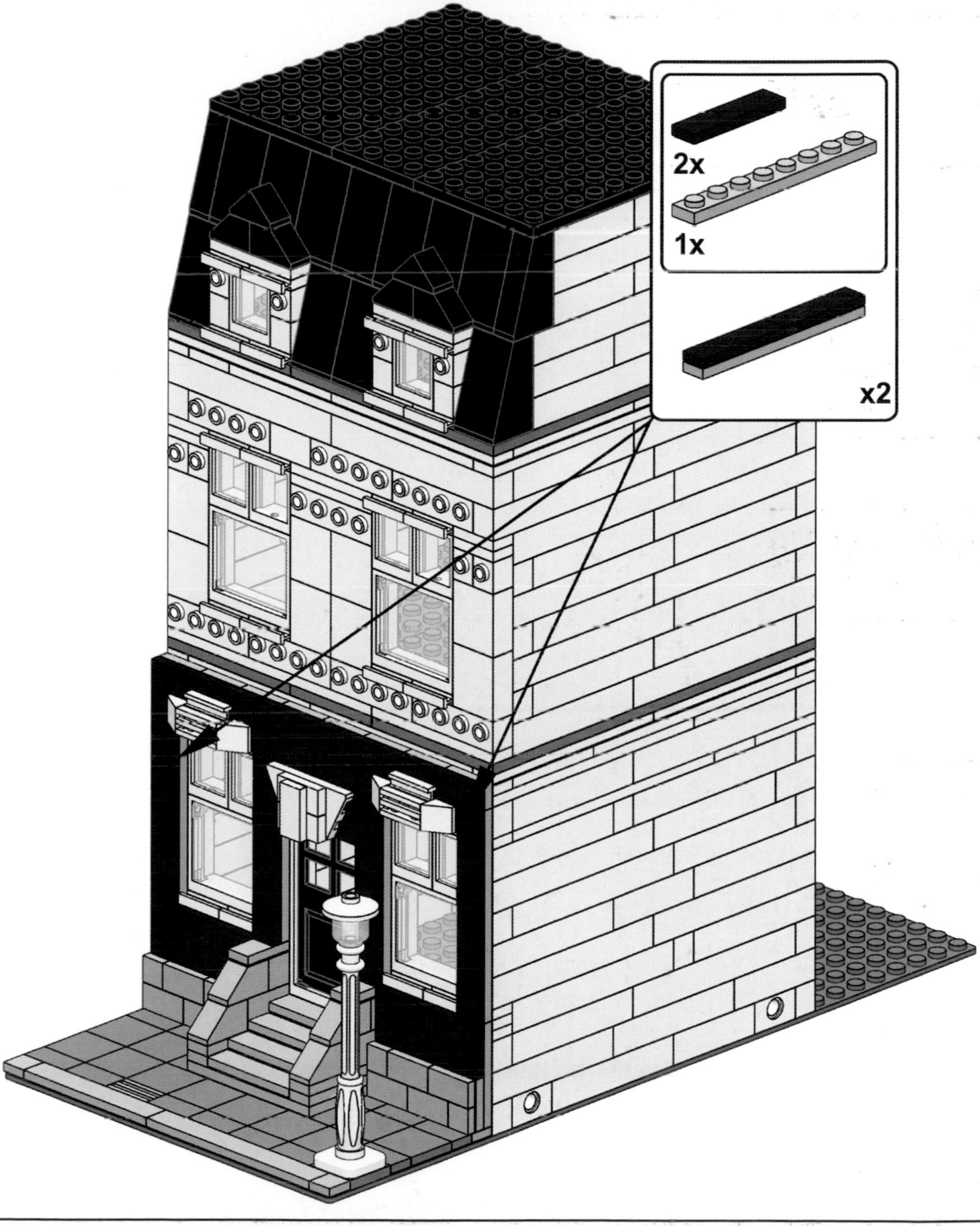
2x
1x
x2

1

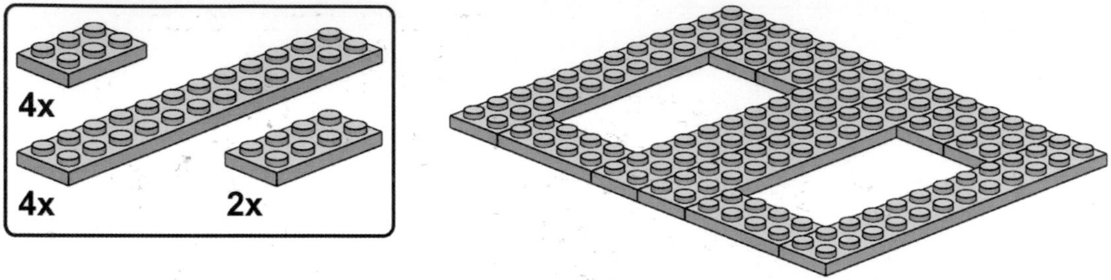
4x
4x
2x

2

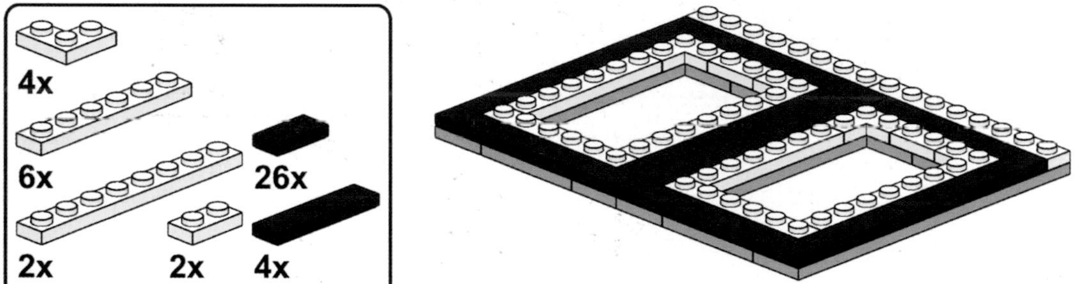
4x
6x
26x
2x
2x
4x

3

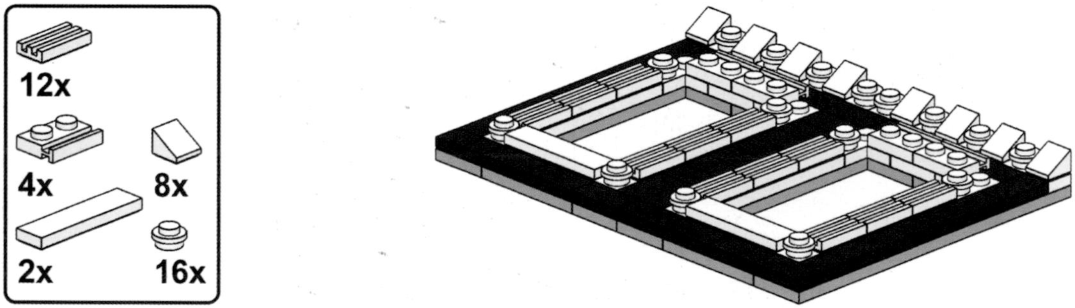
12x
4x
8x
2x
16x

4

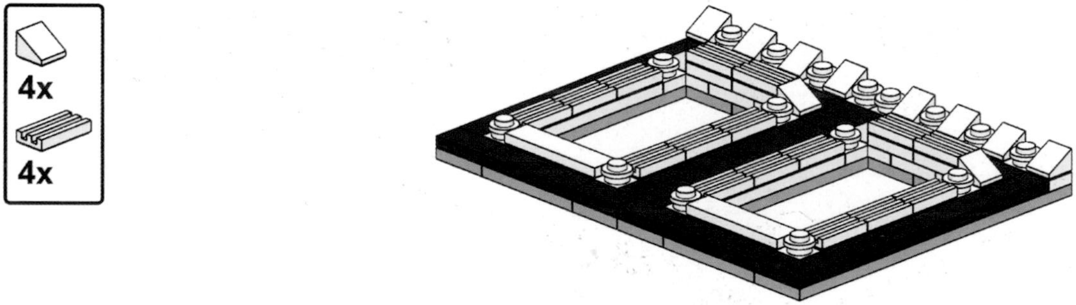
4x
4x

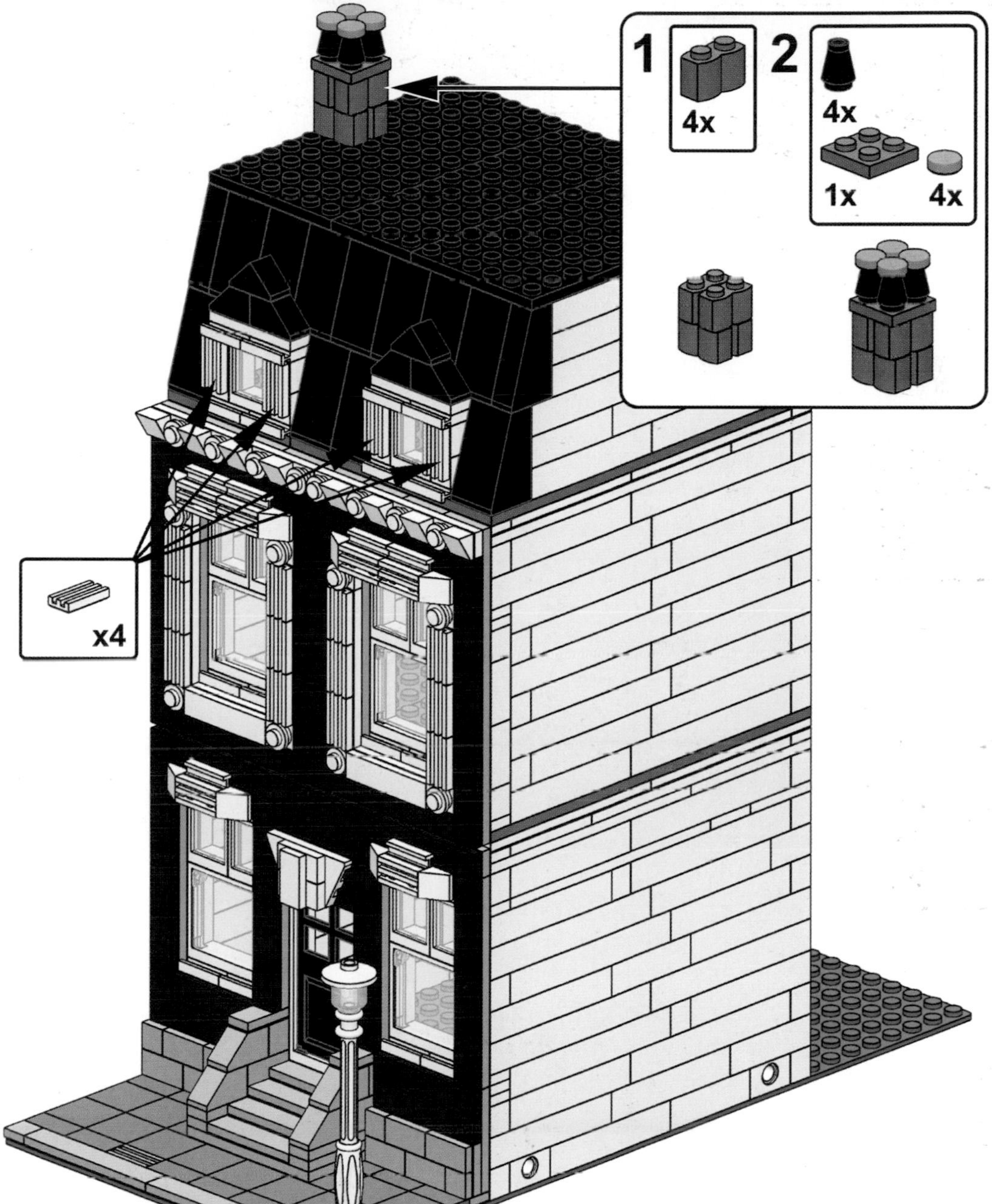
1
4x
2
4x
1x
4x
x4

Canal Ring House

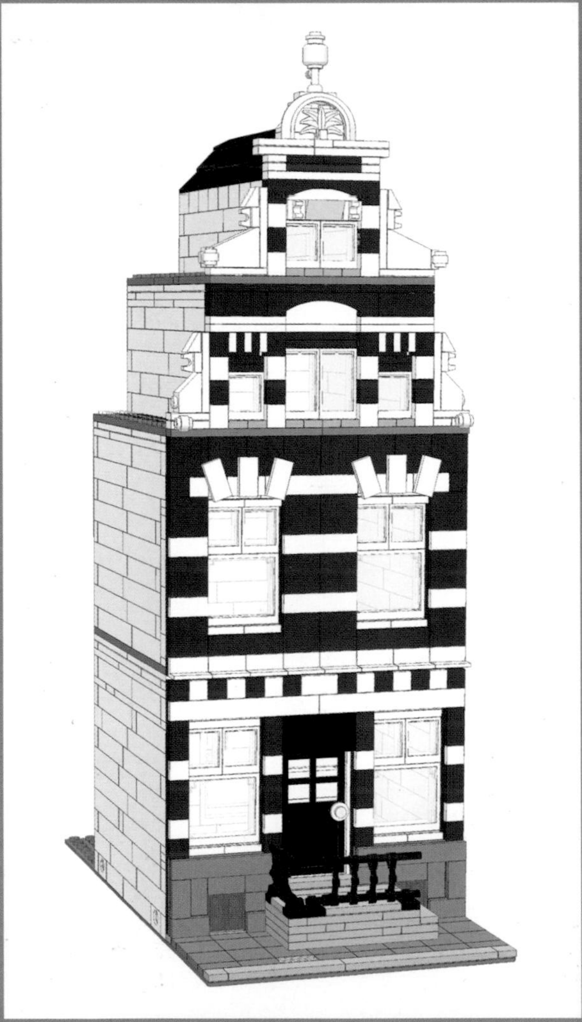

Bill of Materials

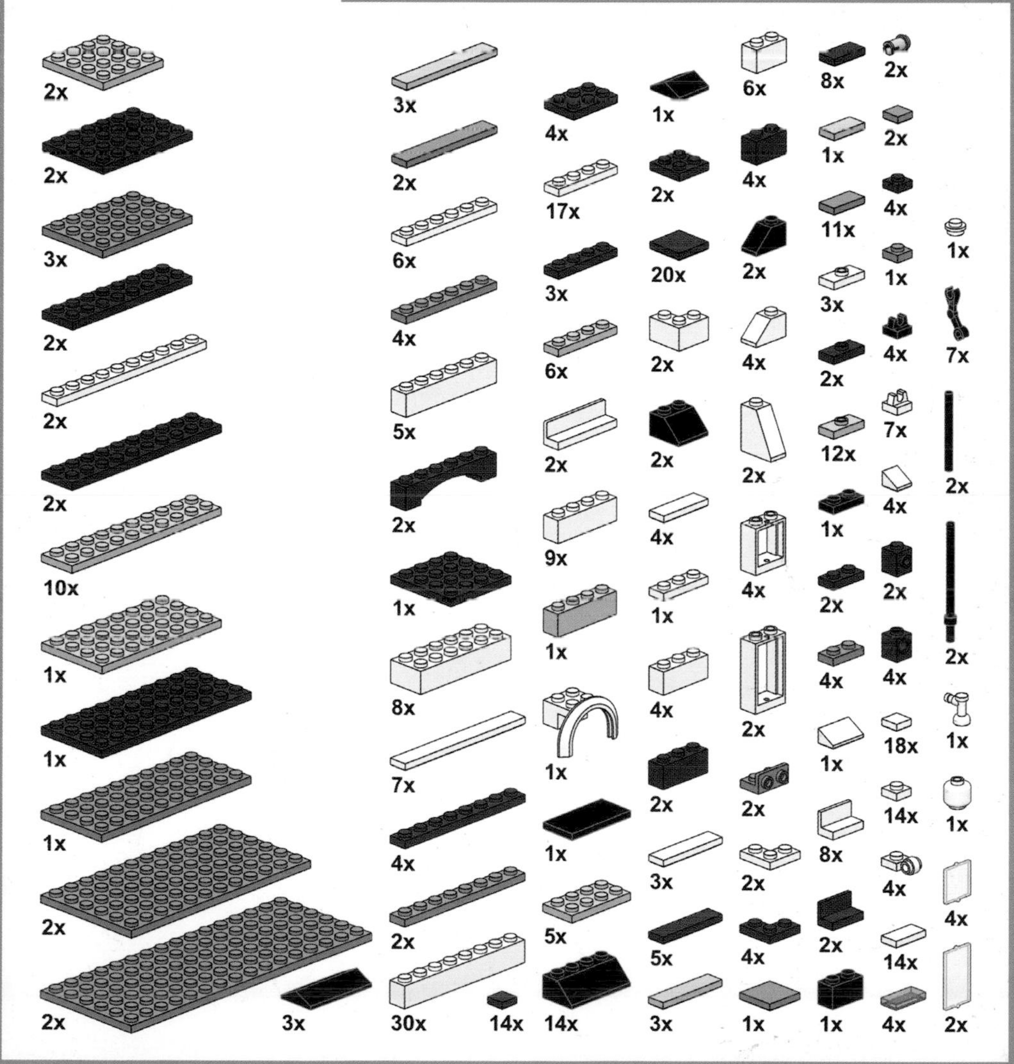

1

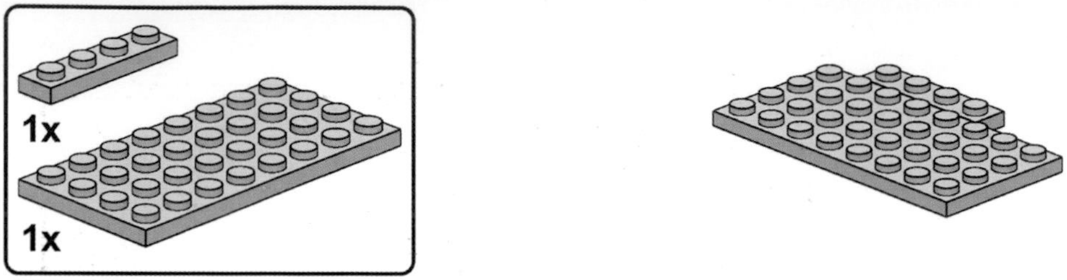

2

3

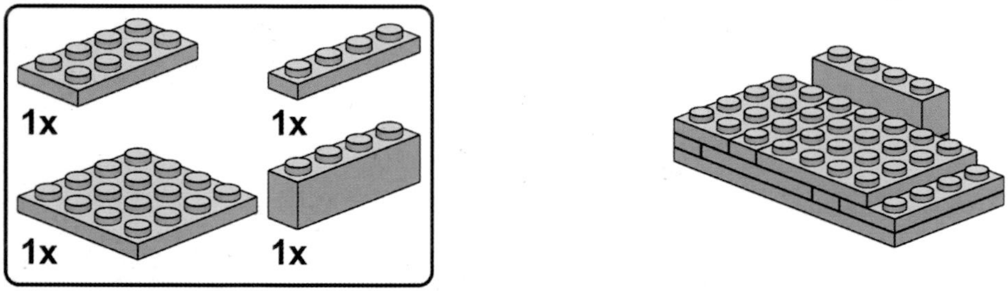

4

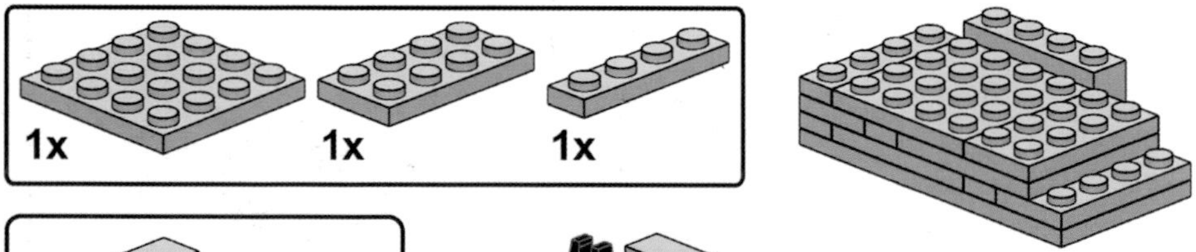

5

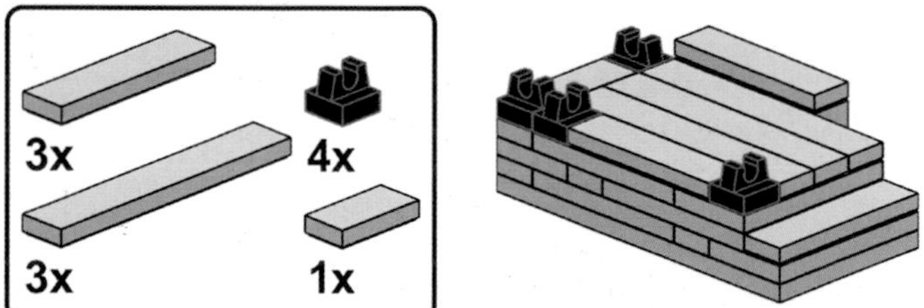

6

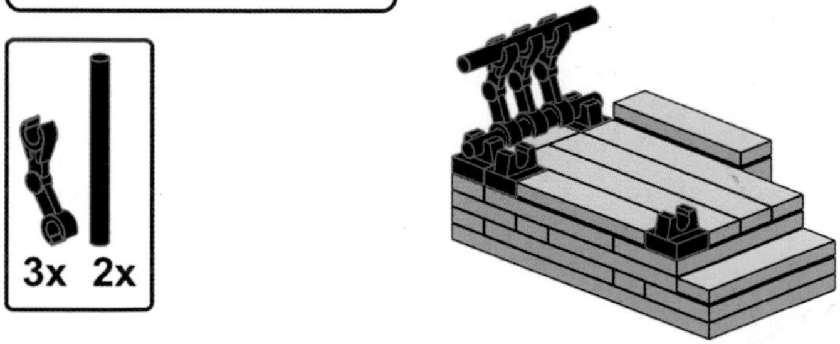

7

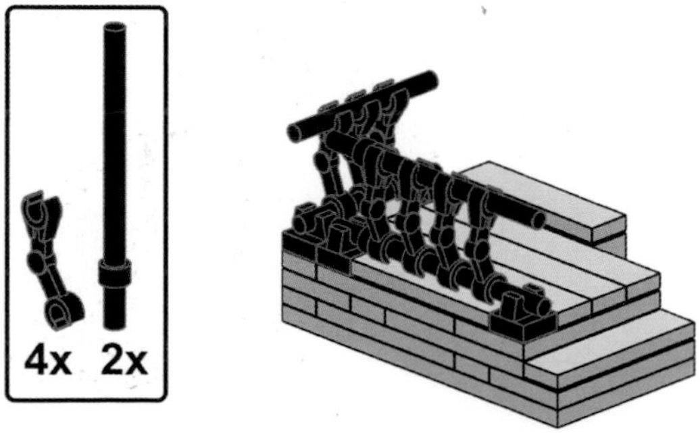

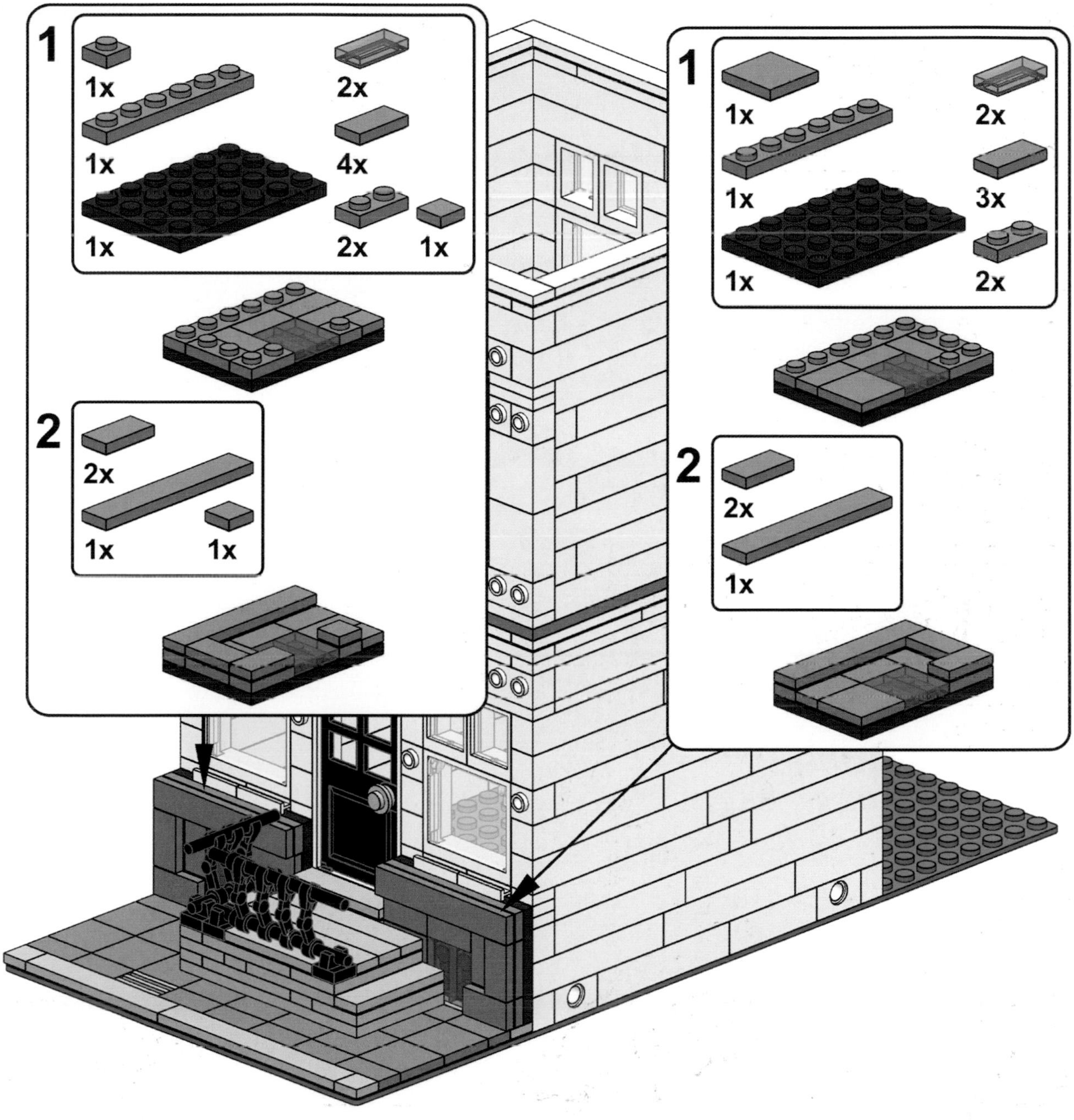
1
1x
2x
1x
4x
1x
2x
1x
2
2x
1x
1x
1
1x
2x
1x
3x
1x
2x
2
2x
1x

1

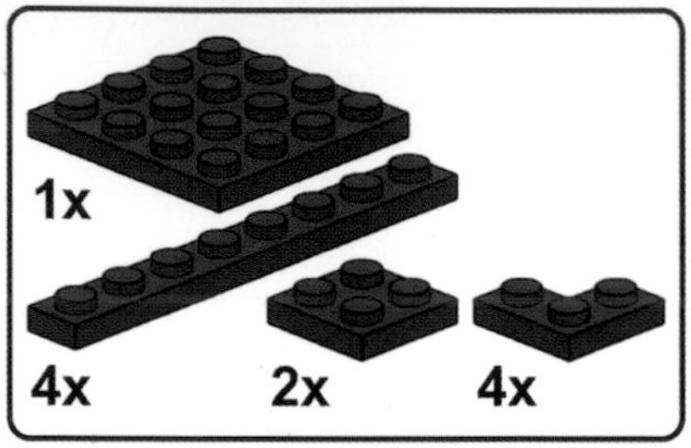
1x
4x
2x
4x

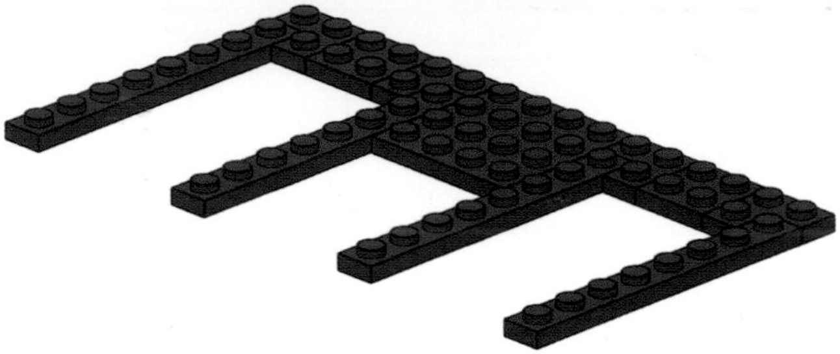

2

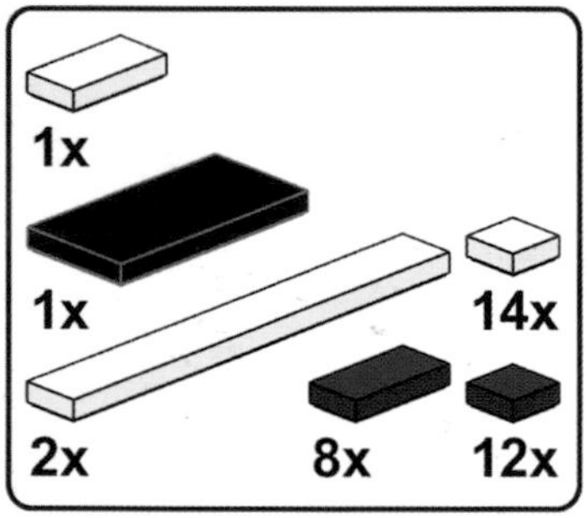
1x
1x
14x
2x
8x
12x

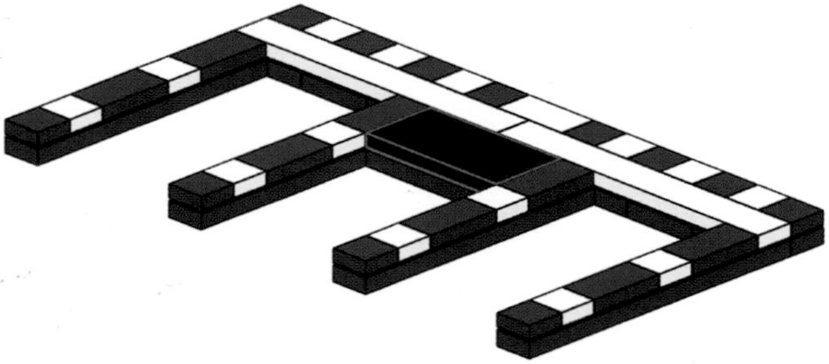

1

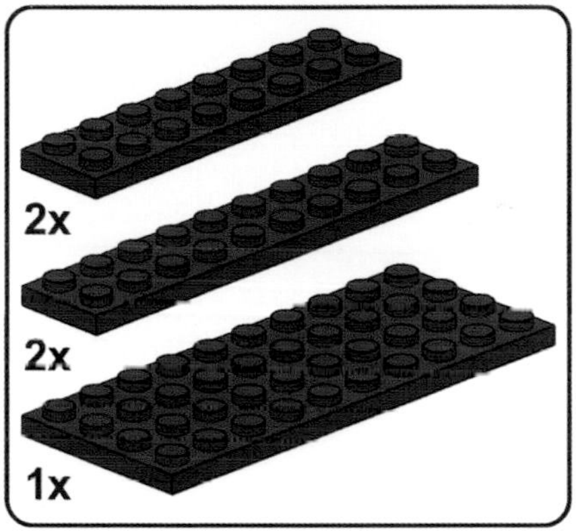
2x
2x
1x

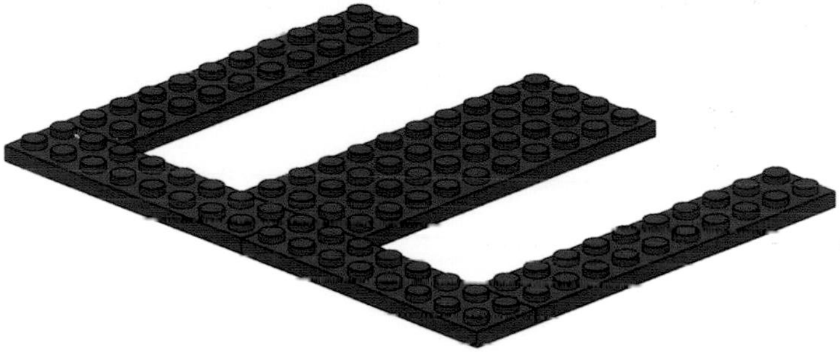

2

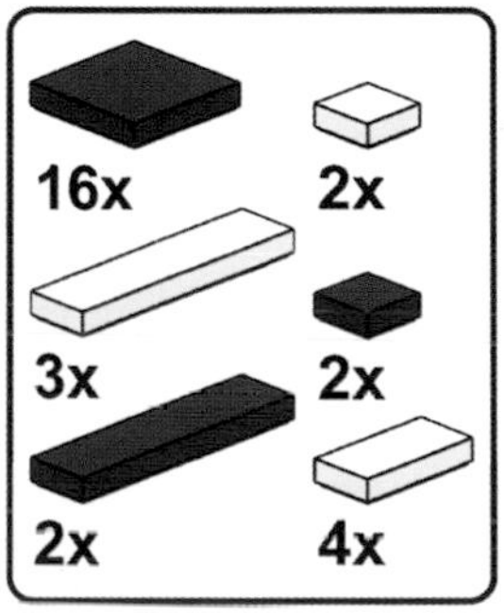
16x
2x
3x
2x
2x
4x

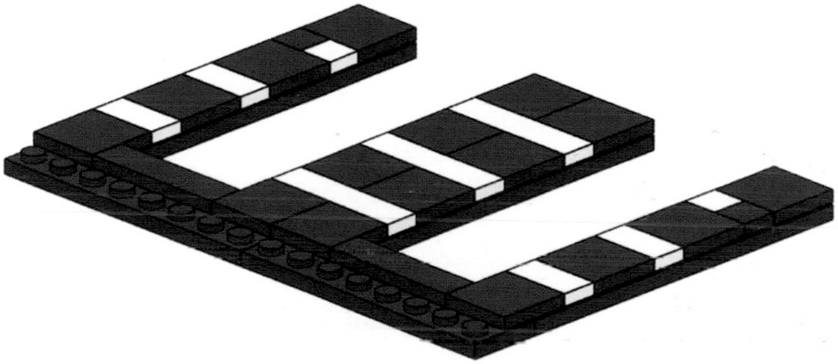

3

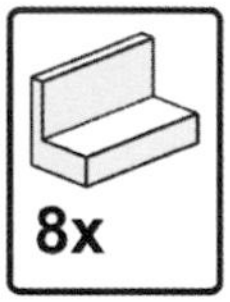
8x

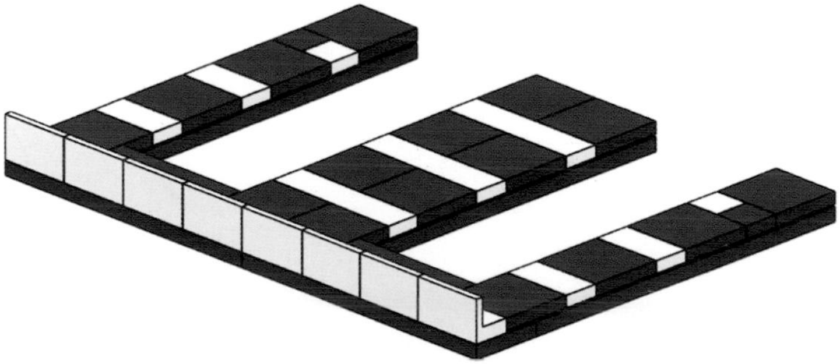

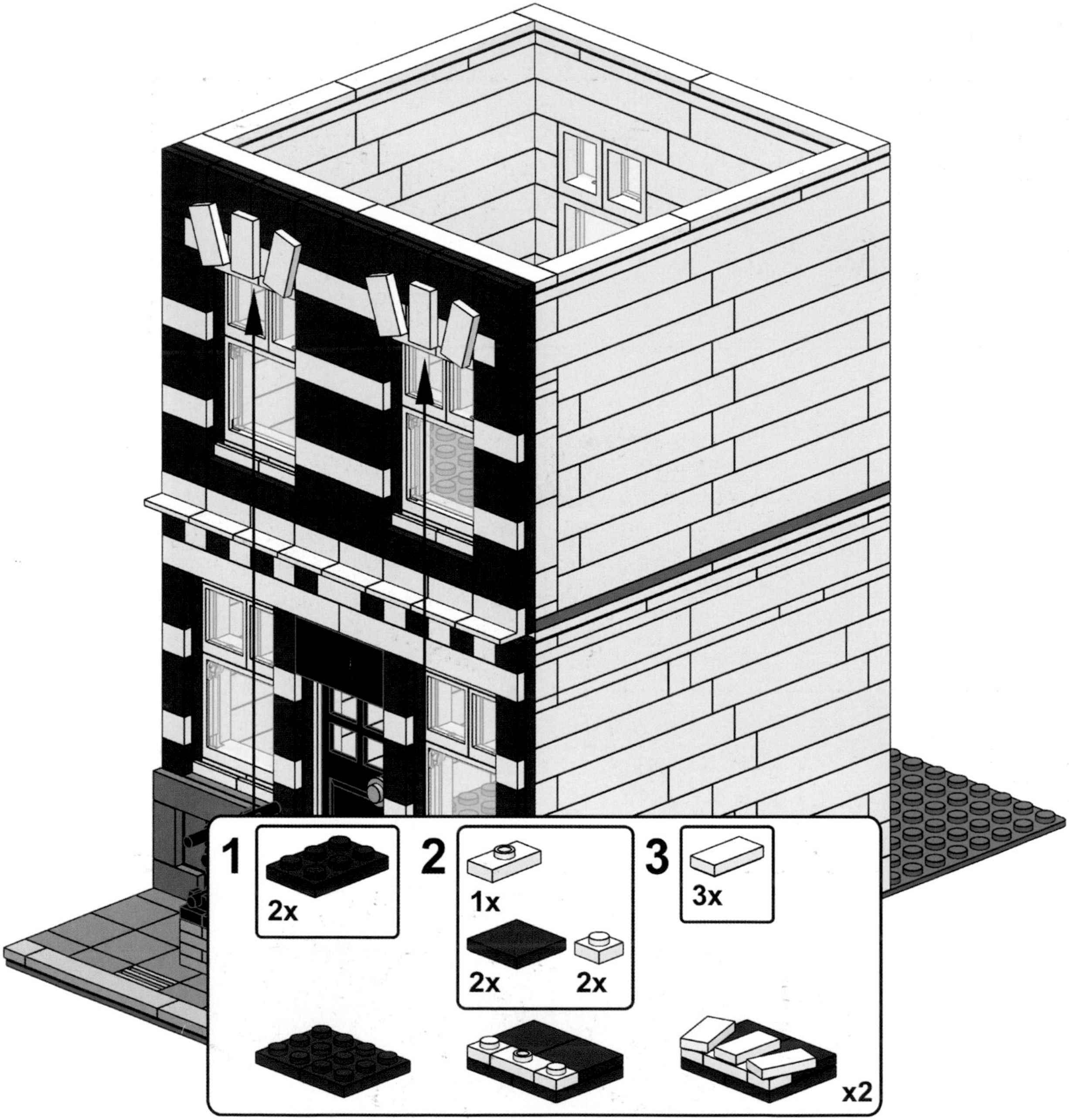
1
2x
2
1x
2x
2x
3
3x
x2

Third Floor

1

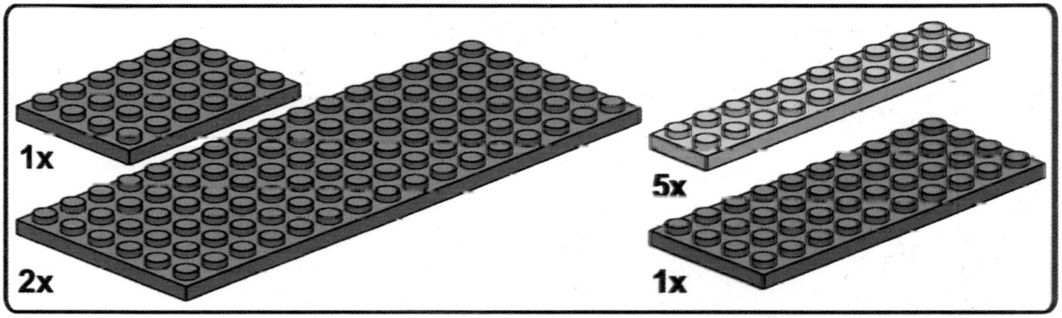
1x
2x
5x
1x

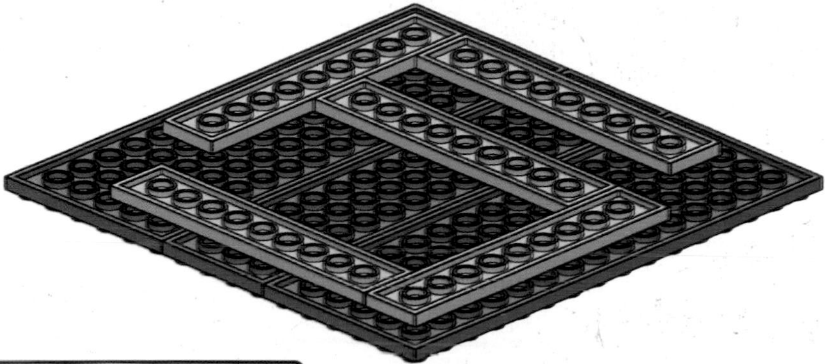

2

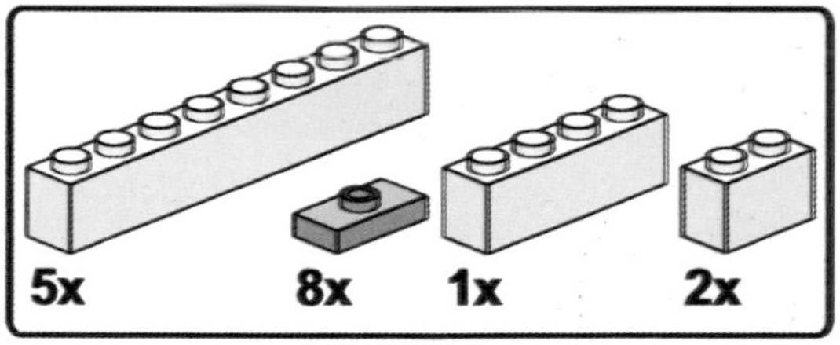
5x
8x
1x
2x

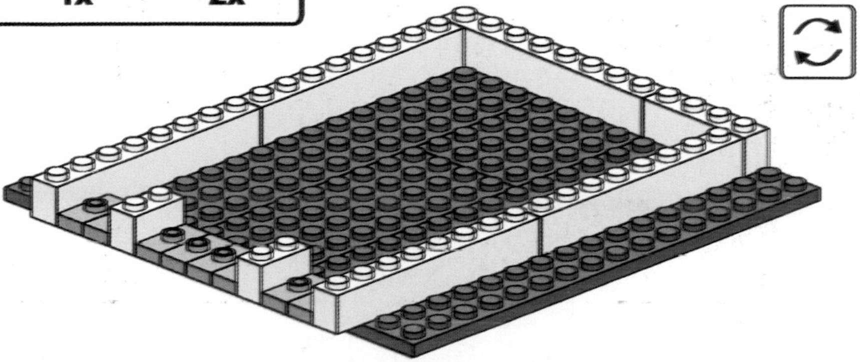

3

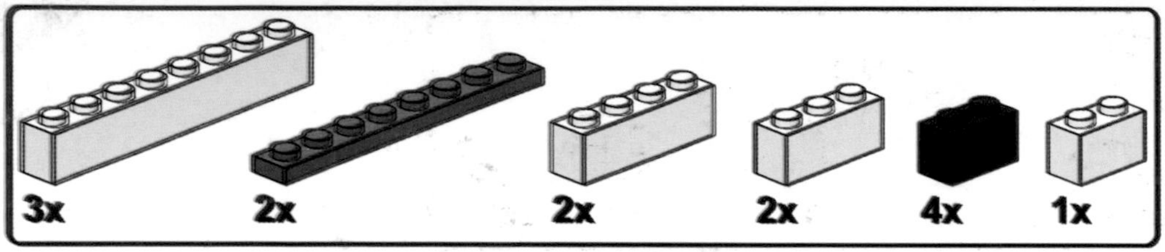
3x
2x
2x
2x
4x
1x

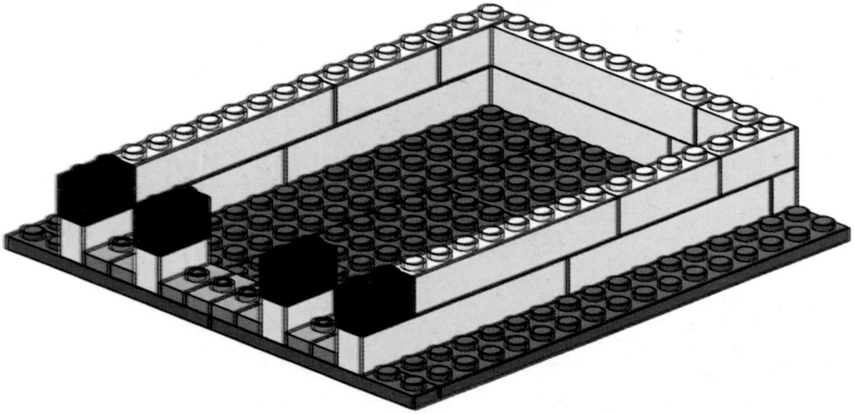

4

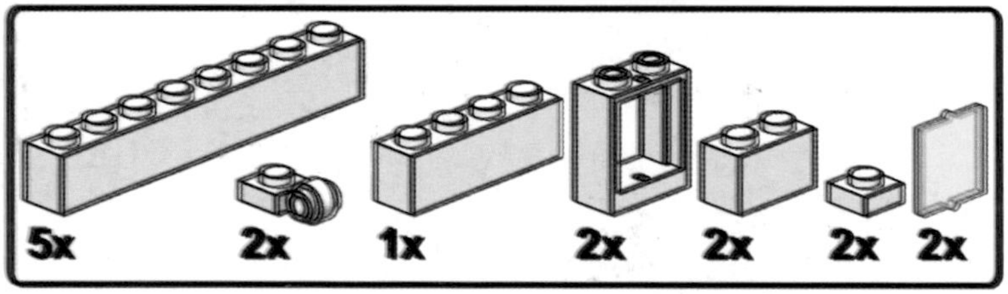
5x
2x
1x
2x
2x
2x
2x

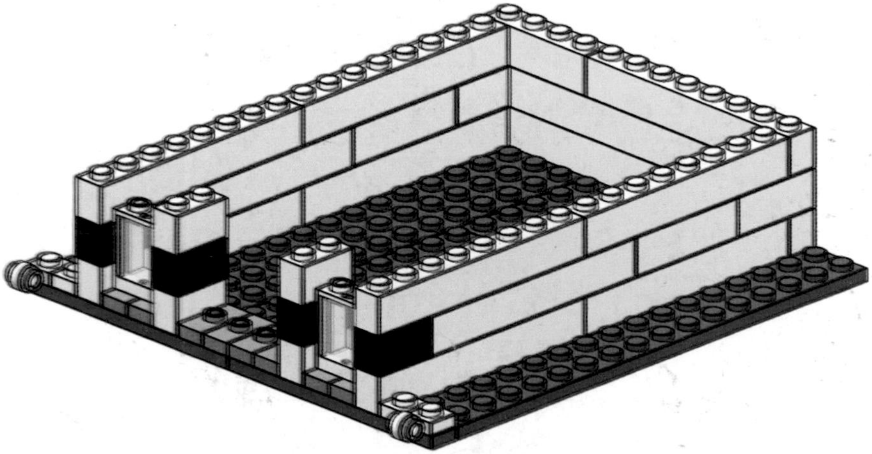

5

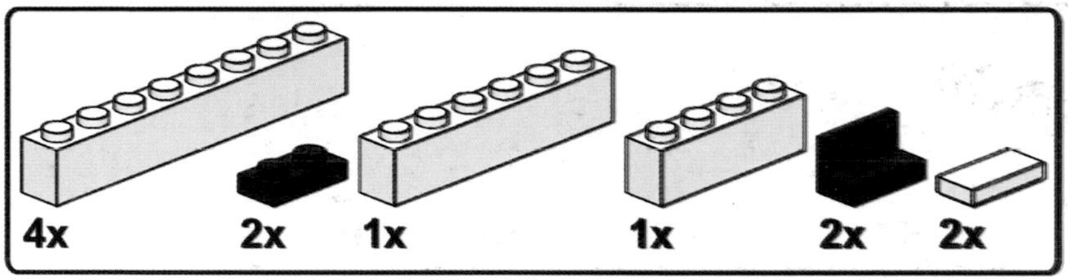
4x
2x
1x
1x
2x
2x

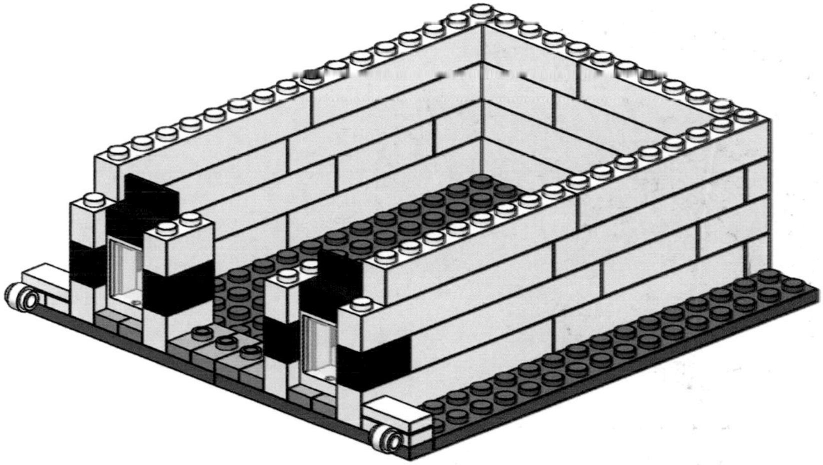

6

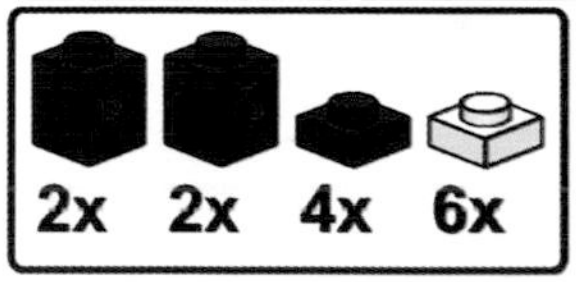
2x
2x
4x
6x

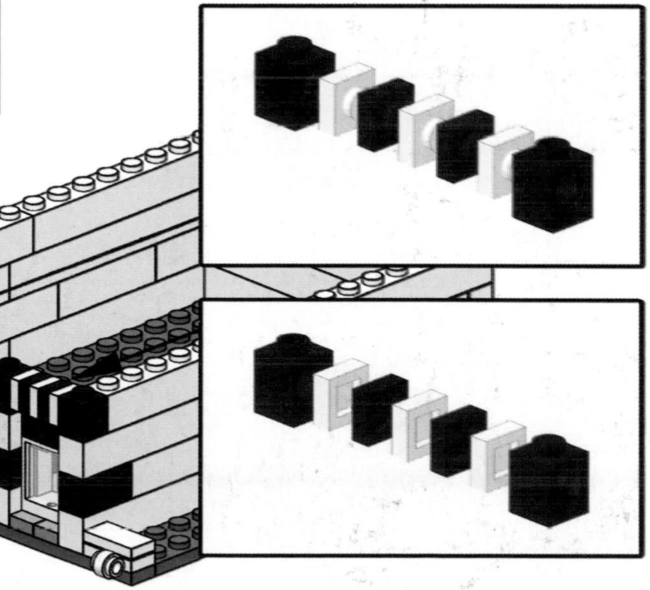

7

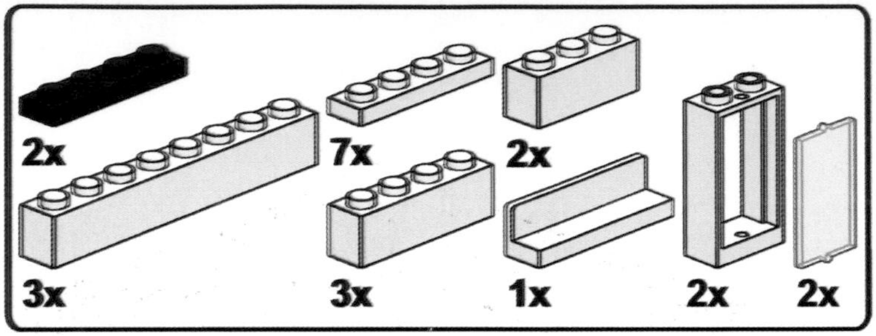
2x
7x
2x
3x
3x
1x
2x
2x

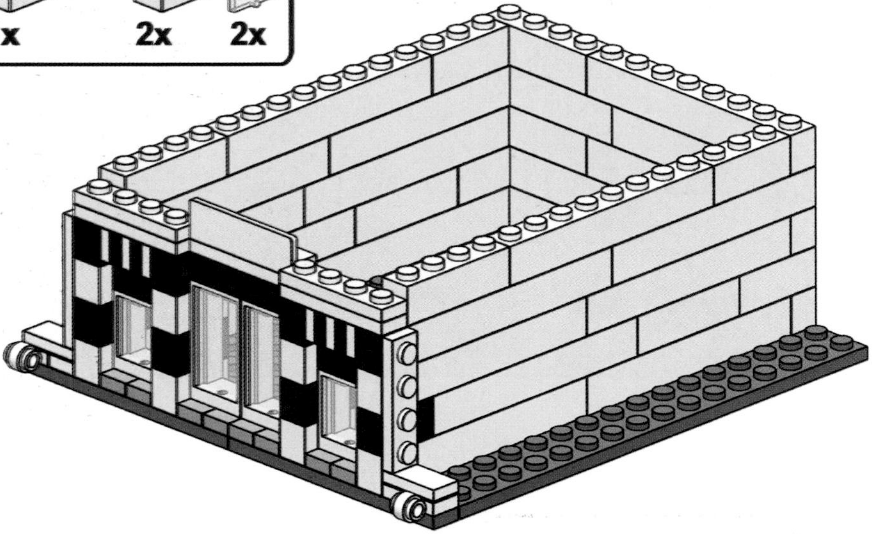

8

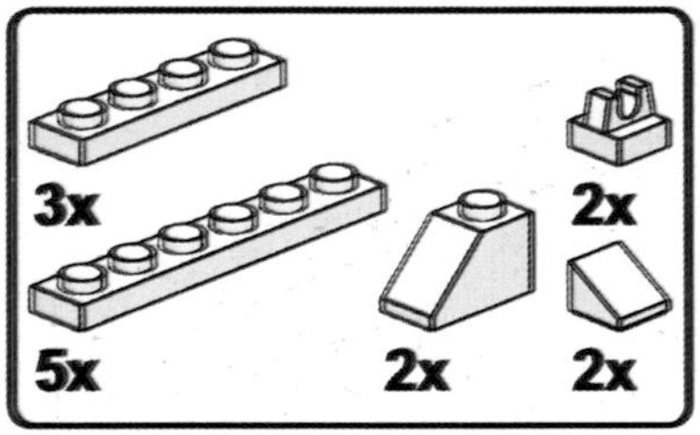
3x
2x
5x
2x
2x

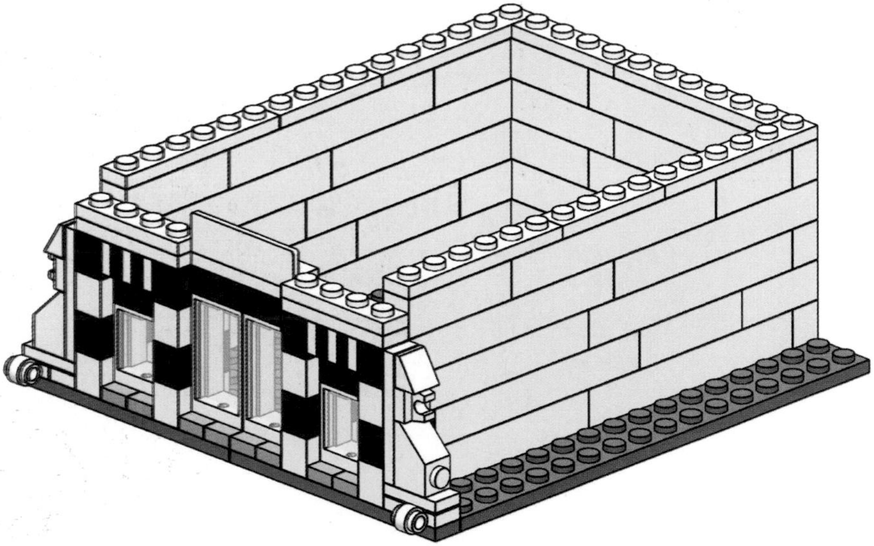

9

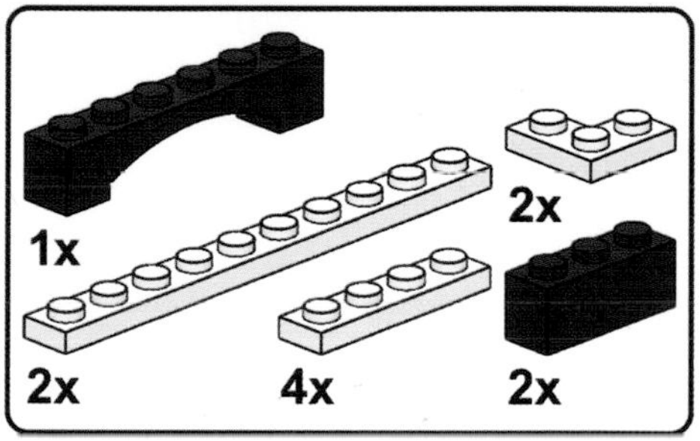
1x
2x
2x
4x
2x

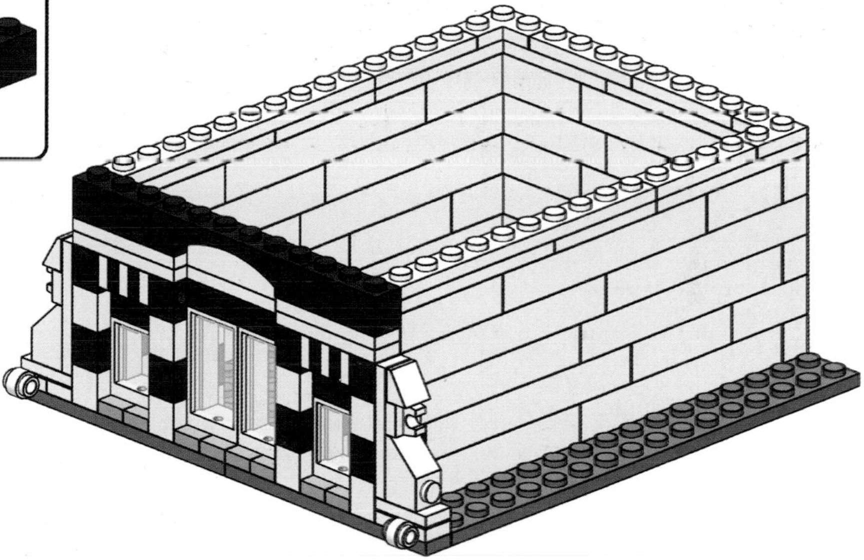

10

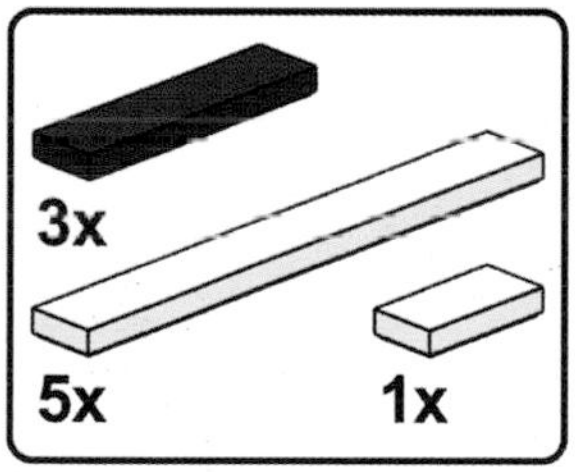
3x
5x
1x

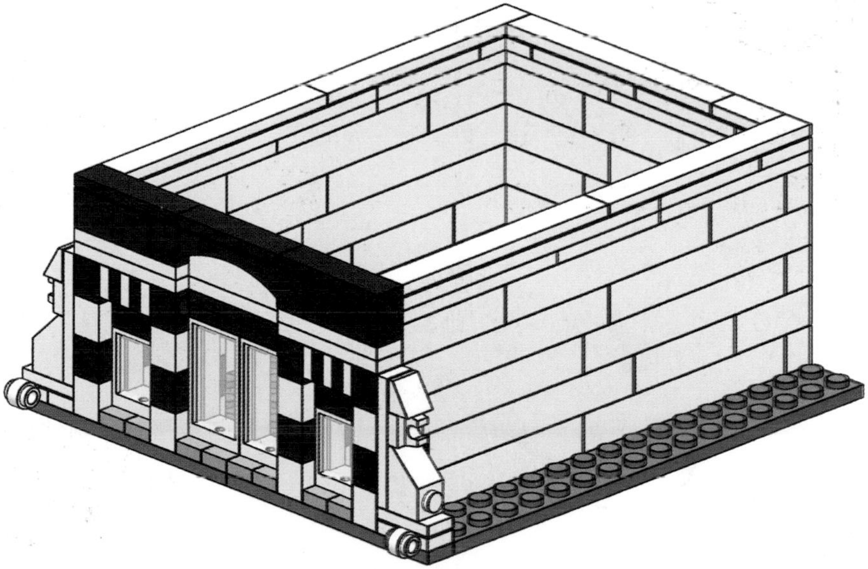

Roof

1

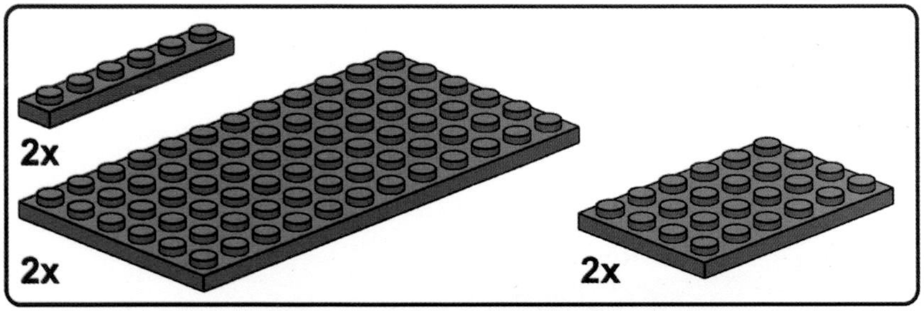

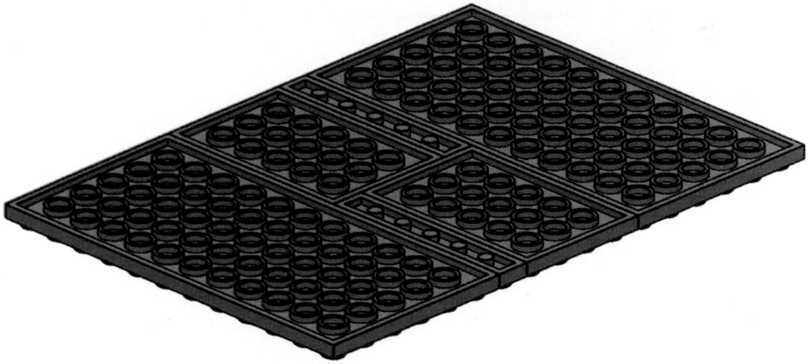

2

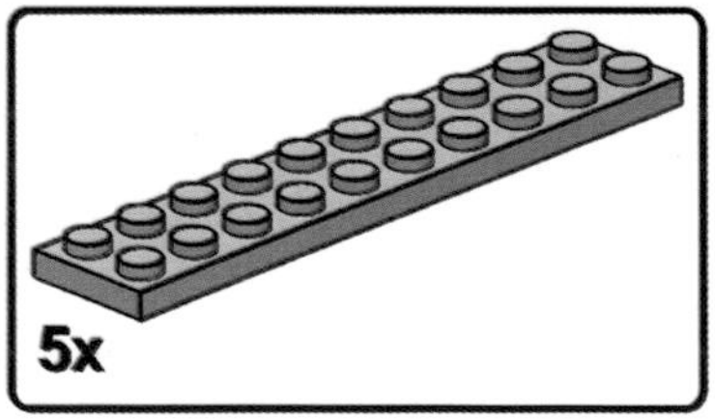

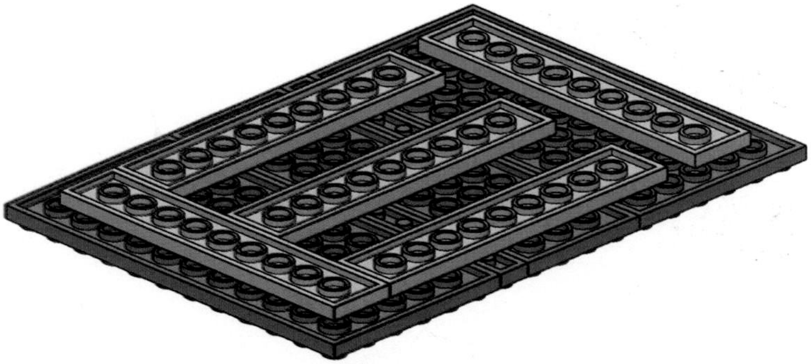

3

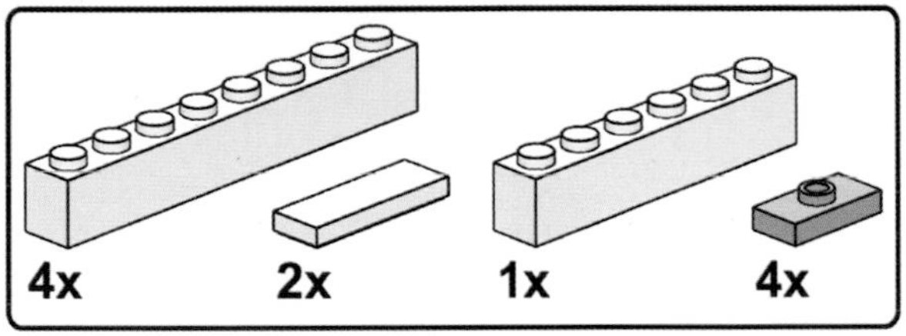
4x
2x
1x
4x

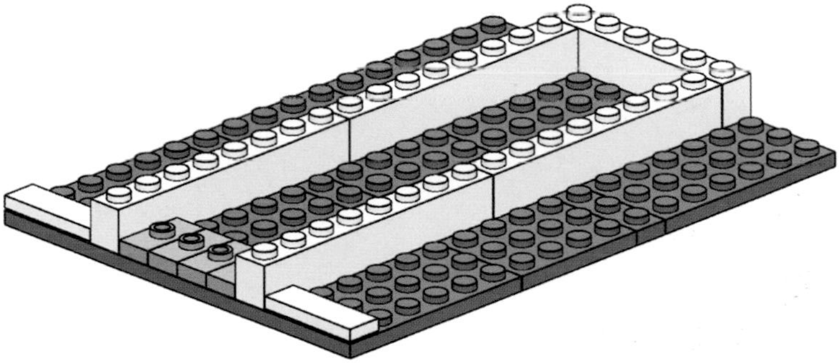

4

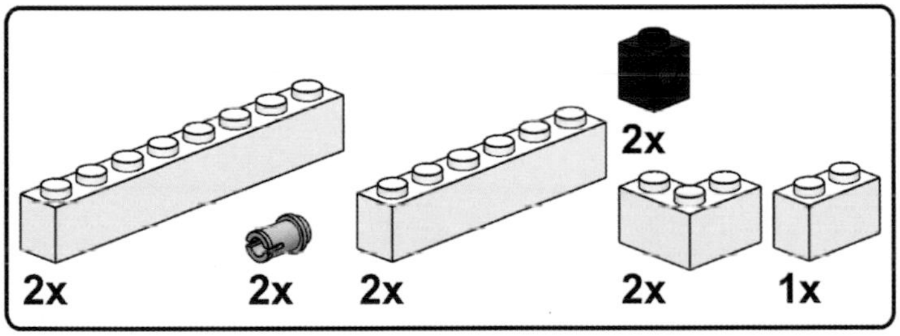
2x
2x
2x
2x
2x
1x

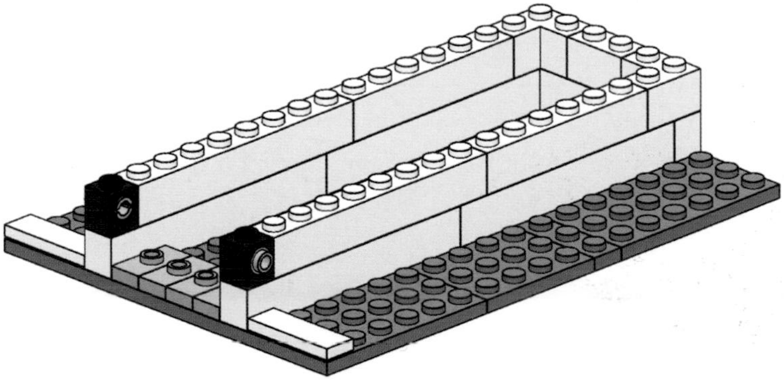

5

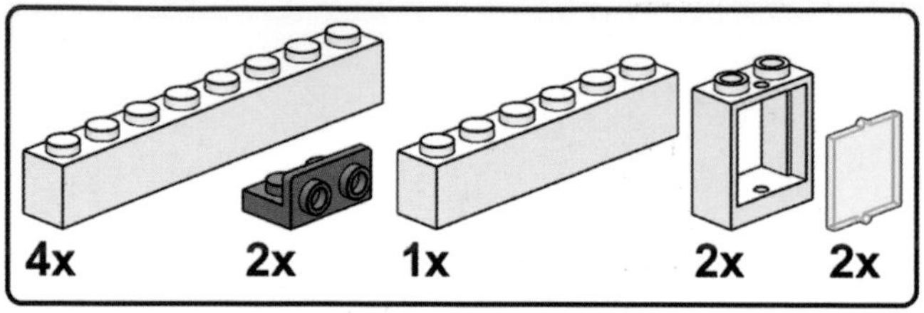
4x
2x
1x
2x
2x

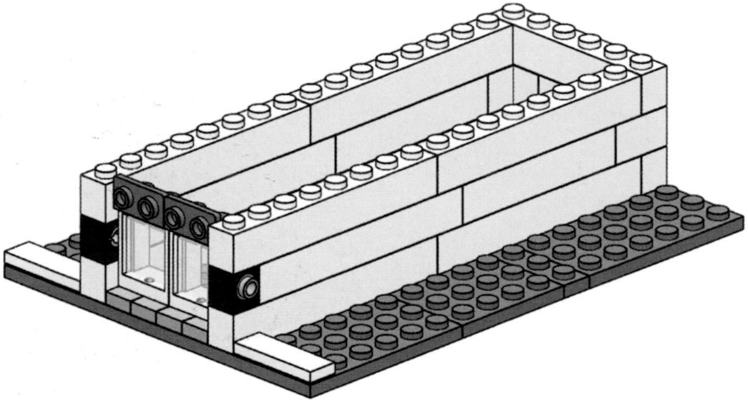

6

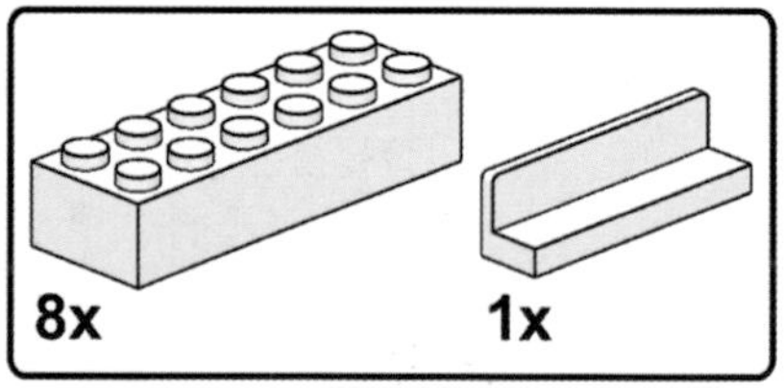
8x
1x

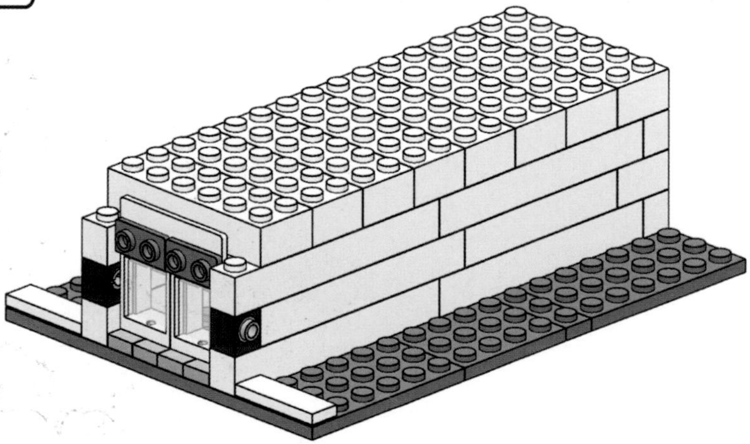

7

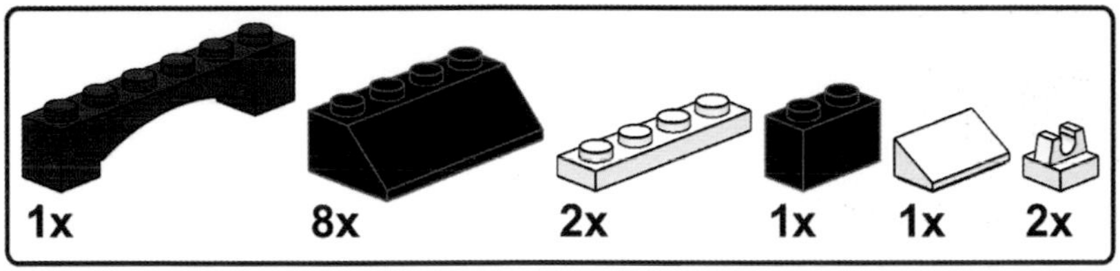
1x
8x
2x
1x
1x
2x

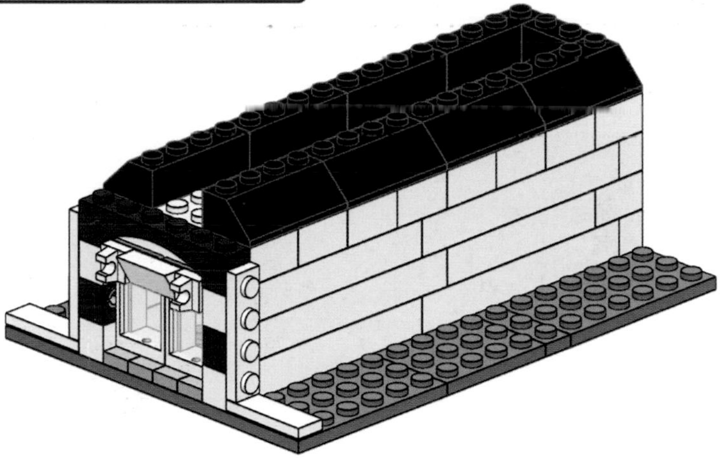

8

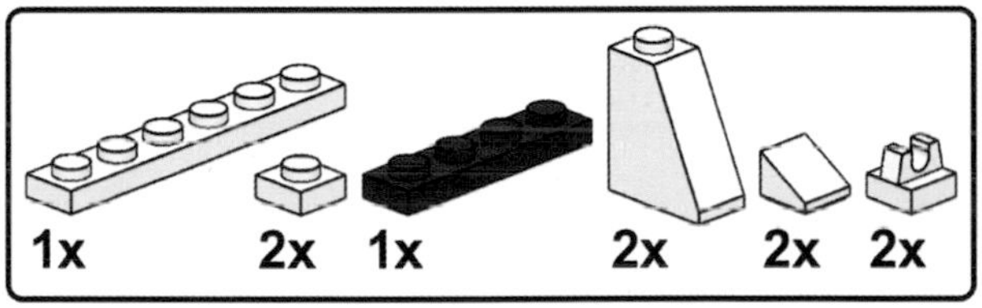
1x
2x
1x
2x
2x
2x

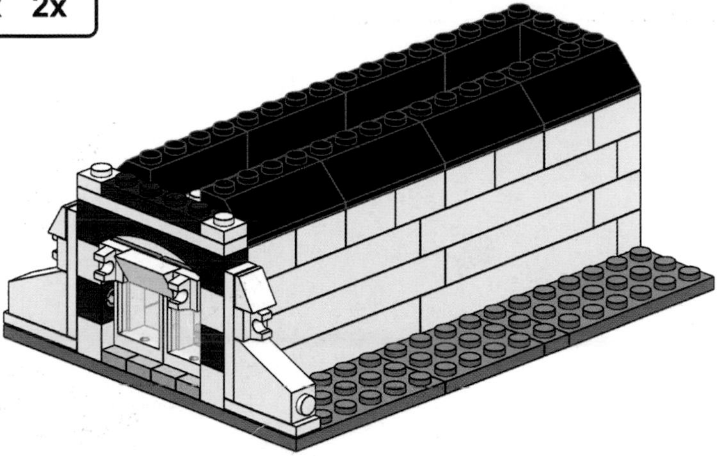

9

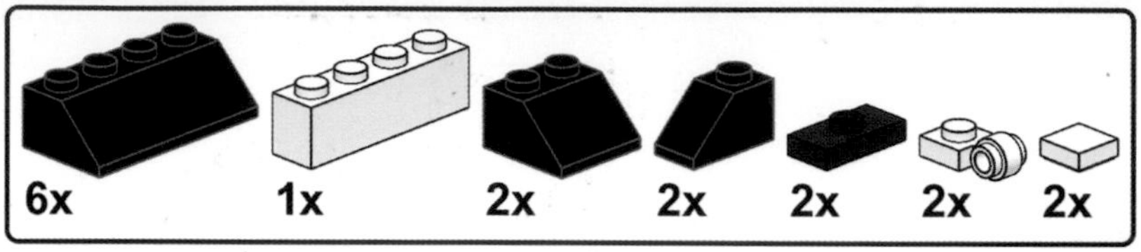
6x
1x
2x
2x
2x
2x
2x

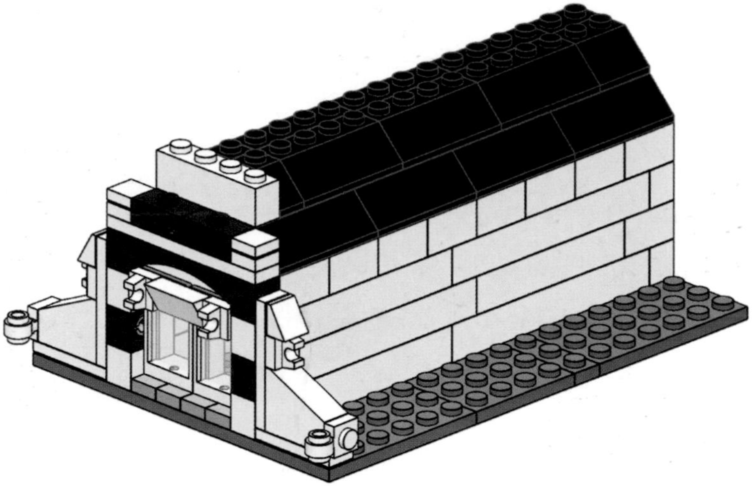

10

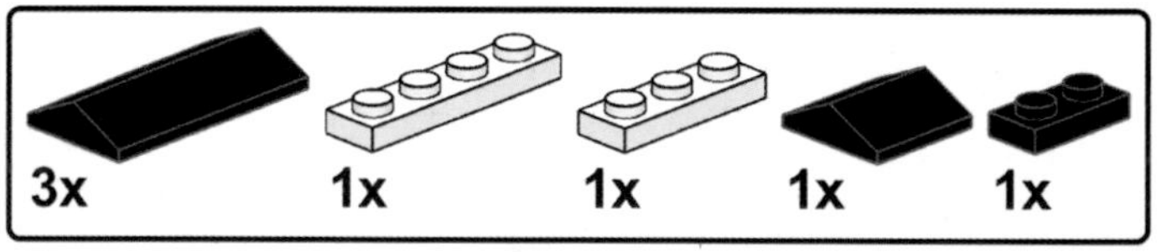
3x
1x
1x
1x
1x

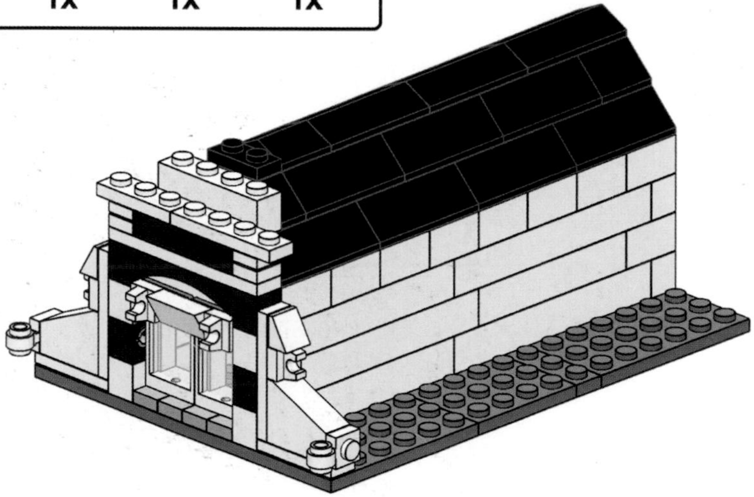

11

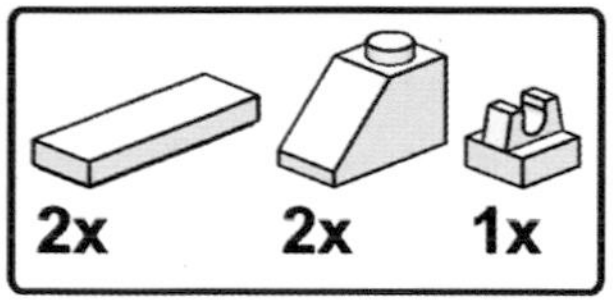
2x
2x
1x

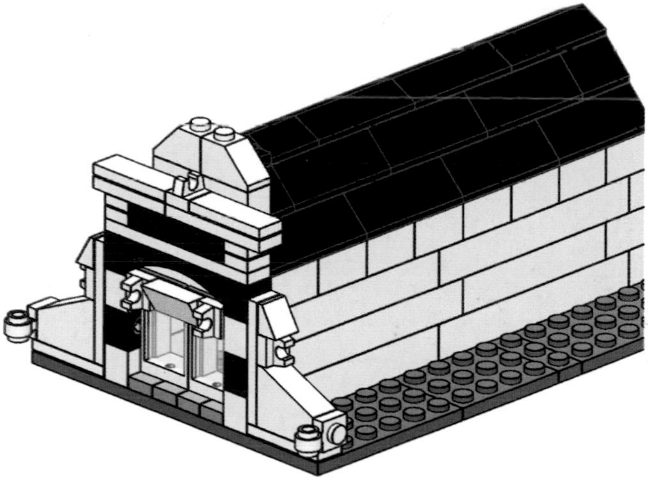

12

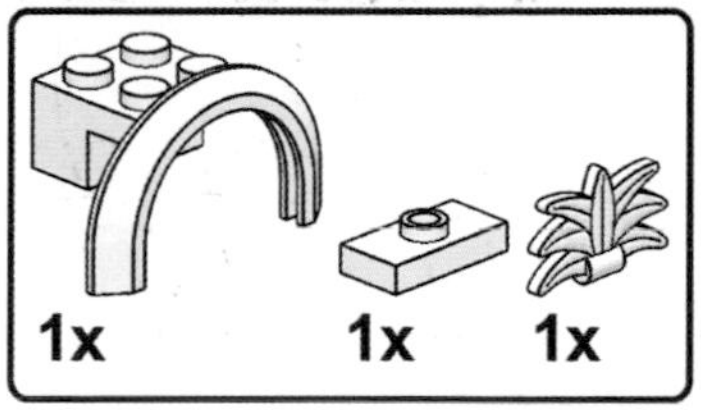
1x
1x
1x

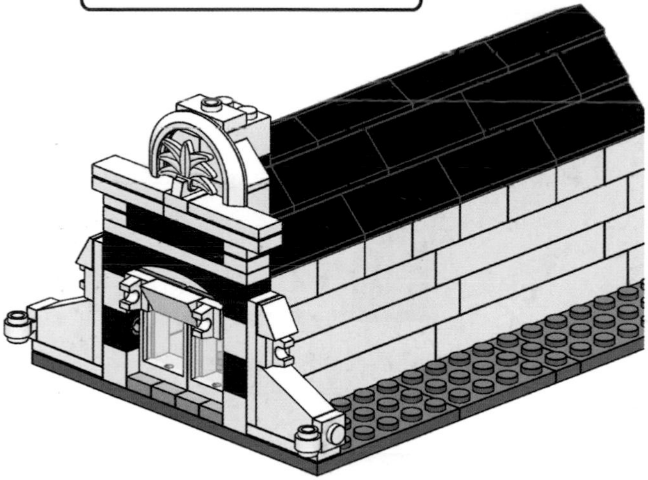

13

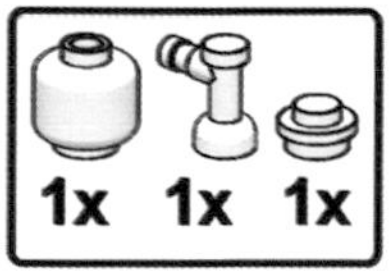
1x
1x
1x

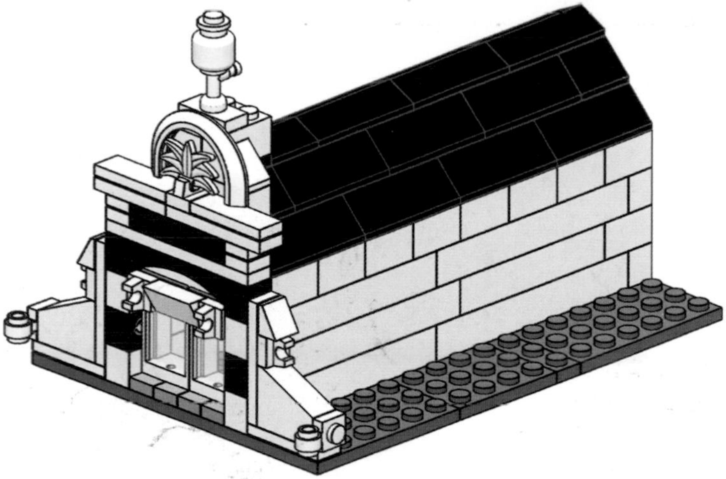

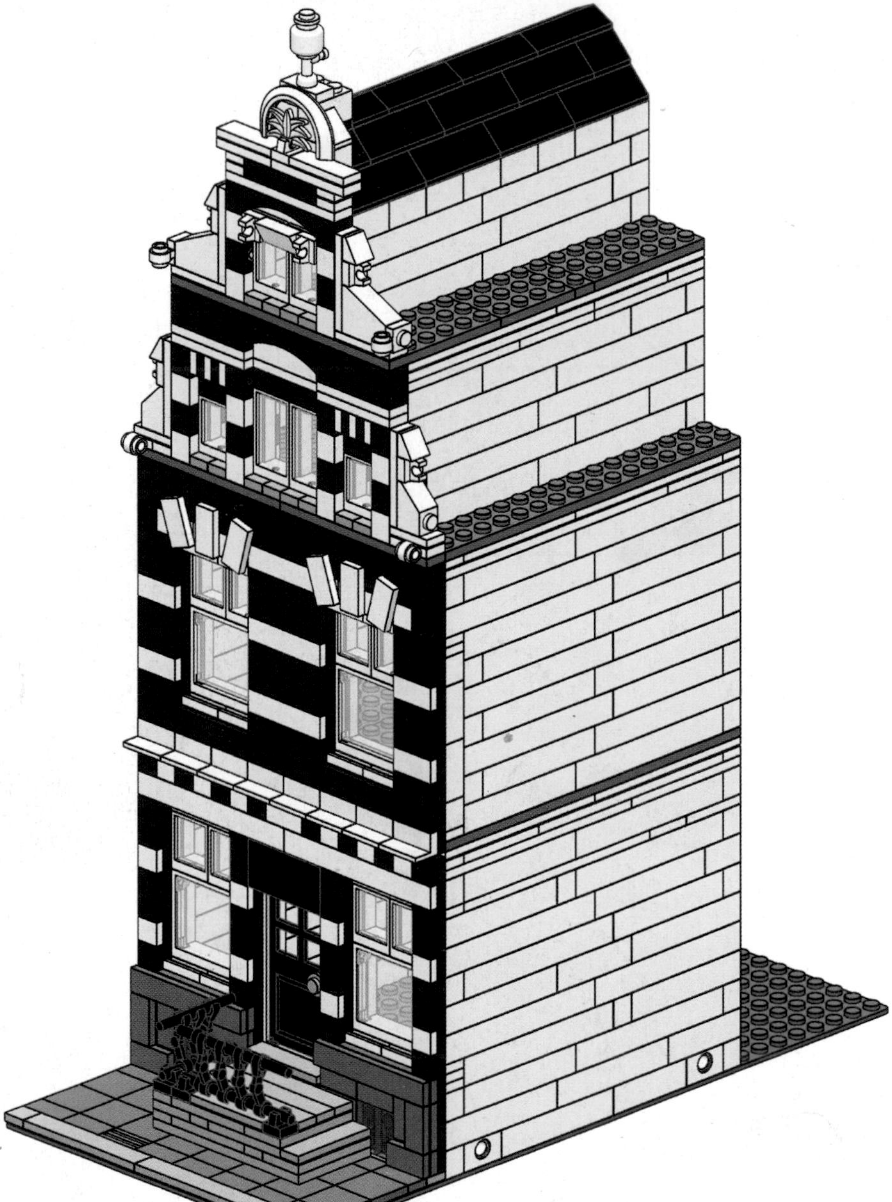

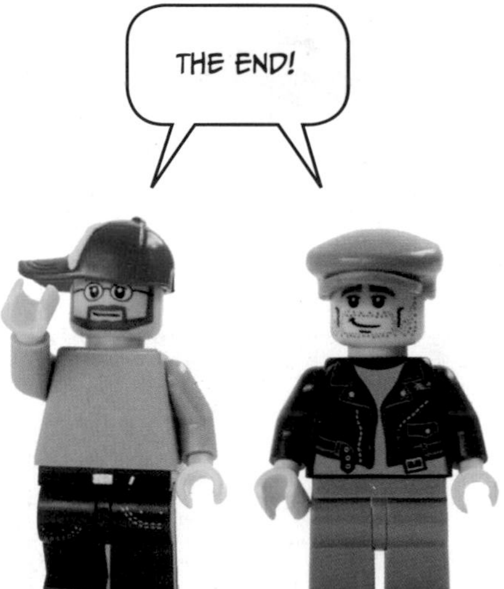
THE END!

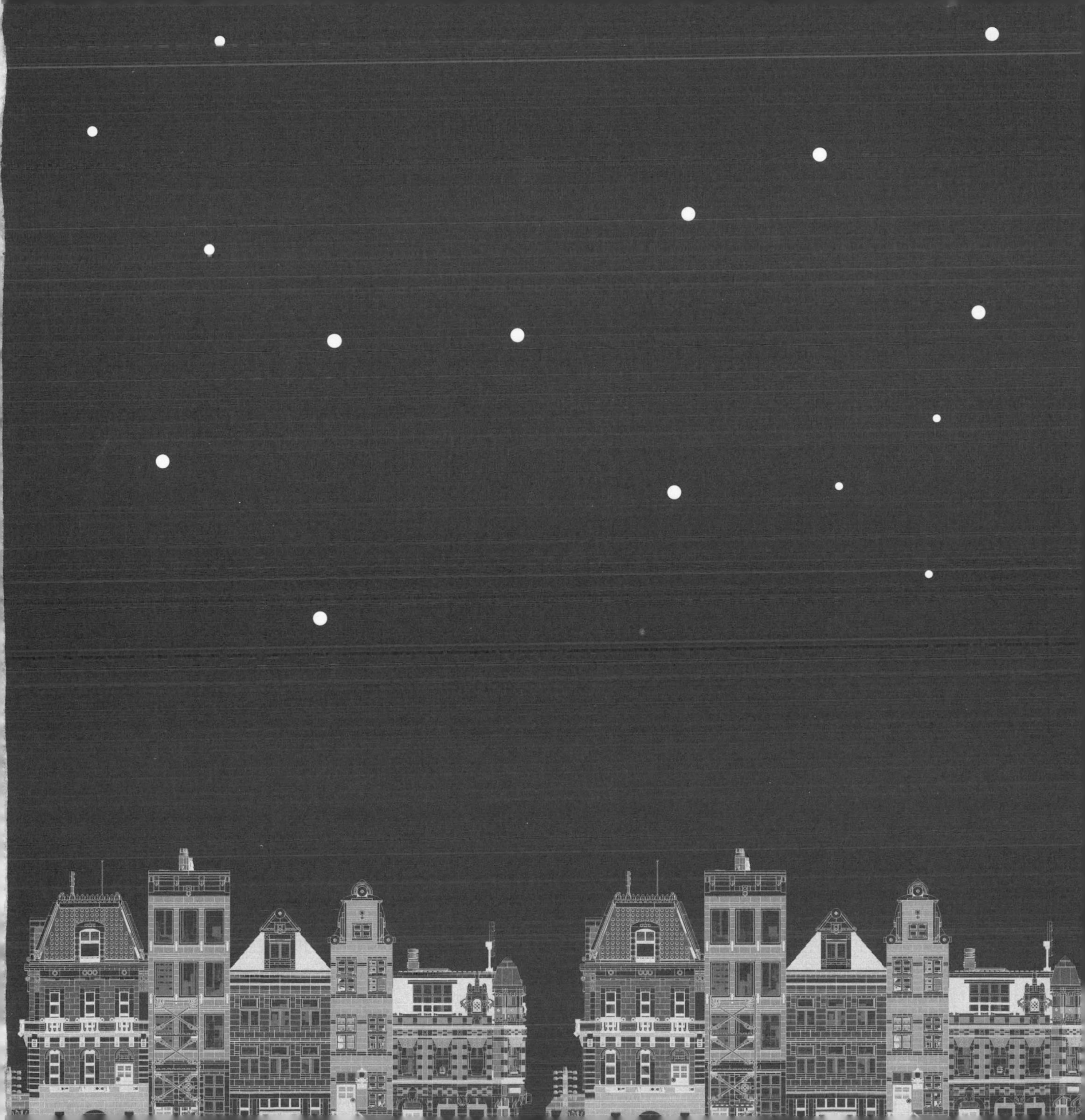

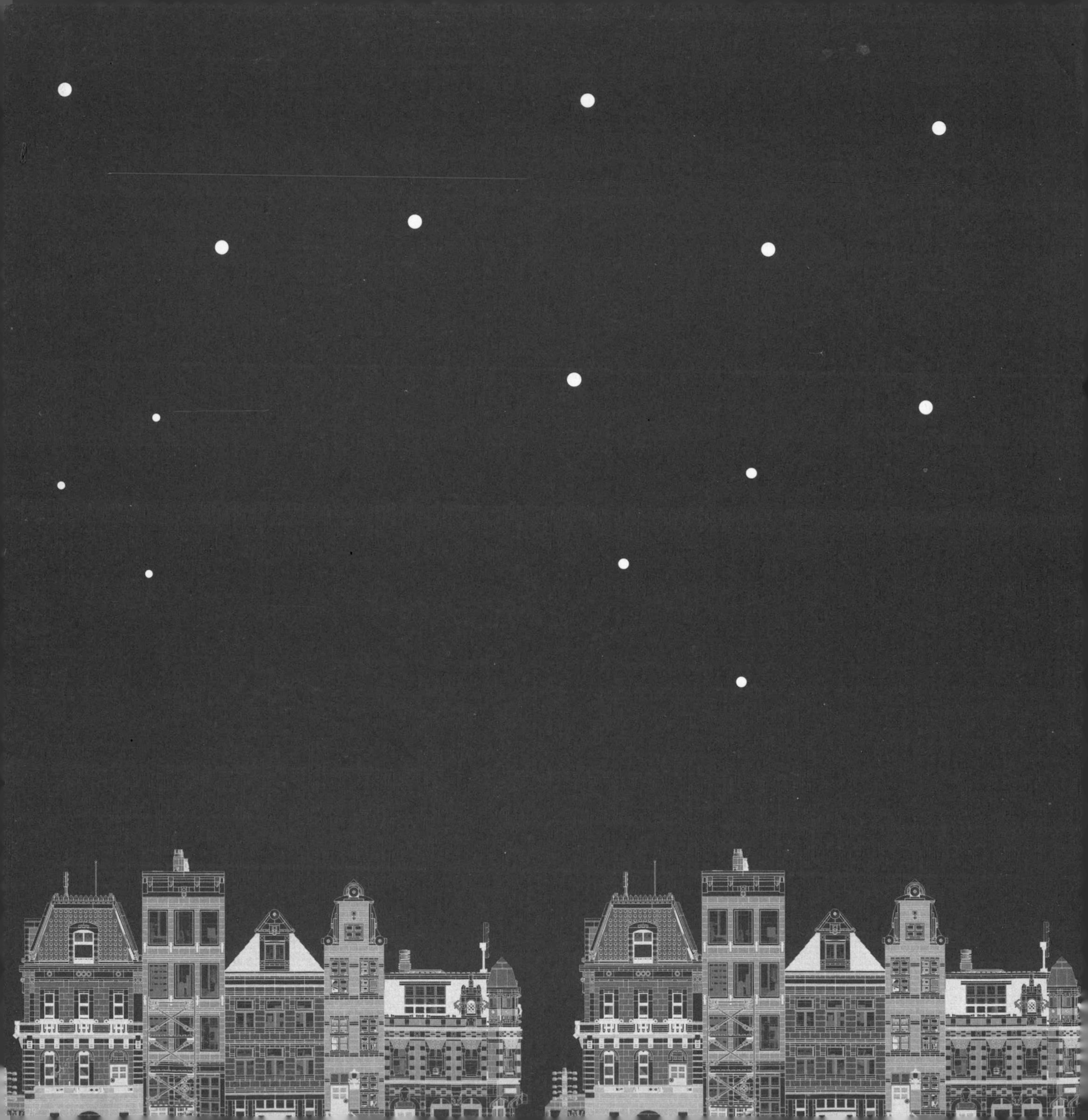